MW00831186

# SUPERNATURAL EN
# IN SHAKESPEARE'S ENGLAND

Bringing together recent scholarship on religion and the spatial imagination, Kristen Poole examines how changing religious beliefs and transforming conceptions of space were mutually informative in the decades around 1600. *Supernatural Environments in Shakespeare's England* explores a series of cultural spaces that focused attention on interactions between the human and the demonic or divine: the deathbed, purgatory, demonic contracts and their spatial surround, Reformation cosmologies, and a landscape newly subject to cartographic surveying. The book examines the seemingly incongruous coexistence of traditional religious beliefs and new mathematical, geometrical ways of perceiving the environment. Arguing that the late sixteenth- and early seventeenth-century stage dramatized the phenomenological tension that resulted from this uneasy confluence, Dr. Poole's groundbreaking study considers the complex nature of supernatural environments in Marlowe's *Doctor Faustus* and Shakespeare's *Othello, Hamlet, Macbeth,* and *The Tempest.*

KRISTEN POOLE is Associate Professor in the English Department at the University of Delaware. She specializes in the religious culture and literature of sixteenth- and seventeenth-century England. She is the author of *Radical Religion from Shakespeare to Milton: Figures of Nonconformity in Early Modern England* (Cambridge University Press, 2000), and has published articles in numerous scholarly journals.

# SUPERNATURAL ENVIRONMENTS IN SHAKESPEARE'S ENGLAND

*Spaces of Demonism, Divinity, and Drama*

KRISTEN POOLE
*University of Delaware*

CAMBRIDGE
UNIVERSITY PRESS

# CAMBRIDGE
## UNIVERSITY PRESS

University Printing House, Cambridge CB2 8BS, United Kingdom

Cambridge University Press is part of the University of Cambridge.

It furthers the University's mission by disseminating knowledge in the pursuit of education, learning and research at the highest international levels of excellence.

www.cambridge.org
Information on this title: www.cambridge.org/9781107463301

First published 2011
First paperback edition 2014

*A catalogue record for this publication is available from the British Library*

*Library of Congress Cataloguing in Publication data*

Poole, Kristen.
Supernatural environments in Shakespeare's England : spaces of demonism, divinity, and drama / Kristen Poole.
p.   cm.
ISBN 978-1-107-00835-9 (Hardback)
1. English drama–Early modern and Elizabethan, 1500-1600–History and criticism.
2. Supernatural in literature.   3. Space in literature.   4. Supernatural–History–16th century.
5. Supernatural–History–17th century.   6. Religion and literature–England–History–16th century.
7. Religion and literature–England–History–17th century.   I. Title.
PR658.S82P66 2011
822'.30937–dc22

2010045992

ISBN 978-1-107-00835-9 Hardback
ISBN 978-1-107-46330-1 Paperback

*To Martin*
*and*
*Corinna and Juliana*

# Contents

# *Figures*

# *Acknowledgments*

This book took over a decade to write, and thus my debts are legion. At many points the project was nudged, questioned, or sent reeling by the comments of others. Some of these people I know, and I have benefited from a chat over tea at the Folger, a hallway exchange at a conference, or a quick conversation with a colleague. Some of these people I don't know, and help came in the form of a comment at a conference panel, an email inquiry, or a random conversation on the train. It would take another chapter for me to detail these formative encounters here, so I should simply like to say thanks to all of those who have contributed, wittingly or not, to this book.

My interactions in the classroom have helped me to solidify my thinking on many of the topics in these pages, and I am thankful for my students through the years. The conversations that took place in a graduate seminar I taught on "Renaissance Space-time" at the University of Delaware, and a seminar I taught on the senses at the Folger Shakespeare Institute, were especially valuable. Two graduate students in particular, Joshua Calhoun and Hannah Eagleson, deserve a special hand; I'm sure I have learned as much from them as they have from me. Over the years I have benefited from the research assistance of Joshua Calhoun, Daniel Mason, Kelly Nutter, and Amy Sopko. I am grateful to the University of Delaware for General University Research Grants that enabled me to have this help.

The project was launched with two short-term fellowships, one at the Folger Shakespeare Library and one at the Huntington Library. I am grateful to the staff of both institutions, especially to those at the Folger who have generously offered assistance over the years.

Chapter 1 was previously published as "The Devil's in the Archive: *Doctor Faustus* and Ovidian Physics," *Renaissance Drama*, n.s. 35 (2006), 191–219. A very different iteration of Chapter 4 appeared as "Physics Divined: The Science of Calvin, Hooker, and Macbeth," *South Central*

*Quarterly*, 26 (2009), 127–52. And a much truncated version of Chapter 3 stands as "When Hell Freezes Over: Mount Hecla and *Hamlet's* Infernal Geography," *Shakespeare Studies*, 39 (2011), 152–87. For all of these, I benefited from the comments of the various editors – Mary Floyd-Wilson, Garrett Sullivan, and Carla Mazzio – and from some wonderful anonymous reader's reports. I am grateful to those journals for permission to include parts of those articles in this book.

While the contents of another small article ("Psychologizing Physics," *Shakespeare Studies*, 33 [2005], 95–100) do not directly appear in this book, writing that piece helped me to formulate and focus on my key ideas. The editor who asked me to write that submission was the late Cynthia Marshall, whose warm intellectual generosity, as manifest in an email correspondence that was longer than the article itself, continues to amaze and inspire me.

At Cambridge University Press, Reader A provided a detailed and crucial report that enabled me to better see my argument and to restructure the whole manuscript. Likewise, I profited from the final comments of Reader B (as in Bruce Smith, who graciously unmasked himself). Sarah Stanton was patient and supportive through a long process of revision. Rebecca Taylor smoothly ushered the manuscript into production. Andrew Dawes copy-edited the book with a keen eye and good humor, and Meg Davies (once again) swiftly produced an expert and artful index.

I am blessed with a most extraordinary writing group. This book simply would not exist without them. Through sharing drafts, camaraderie, and pretentious cheeses, the group provides me with a rich, sustaining, and fun intellectual life. The group has morphed as people have moved into and out of the Philadelphia area, and so through the years I have received invaluable feedback and support from Scott Black, Claire Busse, Edmund Campos, Alice Dailey, Jane Hedley, Matt Kozusko, Zachary Lesser, Laura McGrane, Nicole Miller, Scott Newman, Eric Song, Garrett Sullivan, Jamie Taylor, Evelyn Tribble, and Julian Yates. Most especially, Nora Johnson, Katherine Rowe, and Lauren Shohet have graciously read additional drafts and provided additional encouragement.

My neighbors and friends have preserved my sanity during the insane process of simultaneously writing a book and raising children. Michael Hanowitz and Tom Maciag, Shannon Coulter and Matthias and Lillian Ohr, Drury and Ellen Pifer (who doubles as a colleague), Steve Helmling (also a colleague), and, by long distance, Jennifer Carrell have sustained me with wine and laughter.

I tend to write with the aid of a computer and a cat. Thus at the risk of once again incurring the gentle (?) ridicule of my friends, I hereby acknowledge the feline contributions of both the old guard, Floh and my sorely missed companion Cleo, and the new guard, Katie and Pig.

My beloved daughters, Corinna and Juliana, have been growing up alongside this book. While they have often made it difficult for me to think about theology and physics (or, for that matter, to think at all), they dazzle with a spark of the divine and a sense of the real. Every day I am joyful just to see them, and I try to borrow from their unbounded energy, creativity, and enthusiasm for life.

When writing a book that in many ways is about early modern modes of mapping, it is convenient to be married to a cartographic historian, even if he is an Americanist. I met Martin Brückner in my first week of graduate school, and we soon began talking about our mutual interest in the conceptualization of space. The conversation has continued for the last two decades. In the BC era (i.e. Before Children), we even managed to co-author an article, "The Plot Thickens: Surveying Manuals, Drama, and the Materiality of Narrative Form in Early Modern England," *English Literary History*, 69 (2002), 617–48. This book (Chapter 5 in particular) is peppered with references to that piece. What I thought was a mere cul-de-sac of my intellectual life turned out to be the main road of the journey. I am happy, immensely grateful, and honored to have Martin traveling beside me.

# Note on the text

For sixteenth- and seventeenth-century sources, I have retained original spelling (with the exception of modernizing the long s), although I have standardized capitalization in book titles. The place of publication is London unless indicated otherwise. In my extended discussions of *Othello*, *Hamlet*, *Macbeth*, and *The Tempest* I have used Arden editions. Throughout the book, unless a different edition is specified, references to other Shakespearean plays are from Stephen Greenblatt *et al.* (eds.), *The Norton Shakespeare*, based on the Oxford Edition (New York and London: W. W. Norton and Co., 1997).

# Prologue: Setting – and unsettling – the stage

GUILDENSTERN: The scientific approach to the examination of
phenomena is a defence against the pure emotion of fear.

> Tom Stoppard, *Rosencrantz and Guildenstern are Dead*[1]

Rosencrantz and Guildenstern have come to visit. In a moment that is as
raw for the emotions expressed as for the witness of false friendship,
Hamlet attempts to describe his melancholy:

> ... indeed, it goes so heavily with my disposition that this goodly frame the earth
> seems to me a sterile promontory, this most excellent canopy the air, look you,
> this brave o'erhanging firmament, this majestical roof fretted with golden fire,
> why it appeareth nothing to me but a foul and pestilent congregation of vapours.
>
> (*Hamlet* 2.2.263–9[2])

The scene is familiar. It is not quite as iconic as the moment when Hamlet
gazes into the hollowed eyes of Yorick's skull, but the sentiment is the
same. That which is great and wondrous becomes, for the tortured prince,
base and decayed. Man, the paragon of animals, is also the "quintessence
of dust" (2.2.274). The majestic seems foul. It is a paradox that is
encapsulated in the play's insistent use of the word "rank" – that which
is noble; that which rots.[3]

As he tries to convey the source of his torment to his erstwhile friends,
Hamlet finds this juxtaposition of beauty and putrefaction in the very
space he occupies; heaven seems to him indistinguishable from the vapors
that rise from hell. He uses the theater as a visual aid: "[L]ook you," he
says, the imperative seemingly addressed to the audience as well as to his
immediate companions, "this brave o'erhanging firmament, this majesti-
cal roof fretted with golden fire." The gesture is towards the actual
heavens, the contemporary name given to the canopy which covered the
thrust Elizabethan stage. It is a rare Shakespearean instance of architectural self-consciousness (a dynamic almost, but not quite exactly,
metatheatrical), akin to the famous reference to the "wooden O" in the

prologue to *King Henry V*.[4] It is a moment in which the Globe seems to gloat. And yet, it appears "nothing ... but a foul and pestilent congregation of vapours." Heaven intermingles with hell; materiality is indistinguishable from the mist; the reality of solid architecture is compromised by the specter of a mysterious void. At this moment, the wooden O – the Globe itself – presents its own inherent paradox. Not only Hamlet's punning language, but the very setting in which he stands, becomes a site of interpretive and cognitive instability.

"Quintessence of dust": just as heaven merges with hell, so too this verbal oxymoron suggests a profound spatial disturbance. Audiences today are likely to understand "quintessence" as "[t]he most typical example of a category or class; the most perfect embodiment of a certain type of person or thing" (*Oxford English Dictionary* [www.oed.com.proxy.nss.udel.edu], def. 3.b), and take Hamlet's line to mean "man is the ultimate form of dirt." His original audience, however, probably would have comprehended "quintessence" as the "fifth essence existing in addition to the four elements, supposed to be the substance of which the celestial bodies were composed" (*OED*, def. 1.a), a definition popularized through alchemy. Man (to use Hamlet's word choice) is thus a mixture of the celestial and the terrestrial. The oxymoron here does not simply present the condition of humanity as an ontological paradox, but crashes a familiar Aristotelian cosmology. The spatial confusion that began on the stage spreads outwards to those in the Globe, encompassing the groundlings with their feet firmly planted in the dust.

We are perhaps attuned to the inflections of medieval philosophy and Christian humanism in Hamlet's speech.[5] It is more surprising to discover the resonance of cartography. As John Gillies has strikingly shown, this speech has strong verbal affinities with the text of Mercator's *Atlas*.[6] Then again, perhaps this should not be surprising, given the geographic context of Shakespeare's theater. To name a theater "The Globe" – or, more accurately, to re-name "The Theatre" the "Globe," as happened once the timbers of the original building were dismantled, floated across the river, and reassembled – is an act which deliberately locates the edifice within the sixteenth-century impulse to map.[7] This was the age of the great cartographers, of Ortelius and his *Theatrum Orbis Terrarum* (1570; translated into English in 1606) and of Mercator and his *Atlas* (1595; translated into English 1636). These are the foundational texts of modern cartography, although they contain still-vibrant residues of an older spatial consciousness. As Gillies states: "What has been called 'the Shakespearean moment' ... was also the moment of the new geography's most monumental statements. By the same token, it also represented the last flowering of the old 'cosmography', because both Ortelius and Mercator conceived of geography in cosmographic terms."[8] The Mercatorial over-tones of Hamlet's speech thus knit together the implications of his theatrical, global, and cosmic settings, and bring together residual and emergent spatial epistemologies.[9]

The cartographic and cosmographic significance of Hamlet's speech probably would not have been lost on his audience. Many of those gathered inside the Globe would have been aware of the maps that increasingly defined their space – not only the magnificent world atlases, but, closer to home, the English decorative county atlases commissioned by Queen Elizabeth and even the practical property maps increasingly necessary for calculating taxes. These are the maps which have provided such fertile ground for recent scholarship, as critics have unpacked their ideological function in the emergence of nationalism and "New World" exploration.

Hamlet's audience would also have been keenly aware of another of the Globe's geographies. This is a geography that is often lost on modern scholars, even though Hamlet points to it.[10] It is the geography of the supernatural and the afterlife, the geography of heaven and hell. Theater historians are, of course, aware that heaven and hell are part of the architectural structure of the Globe. William J. Lawrence discusses the theatrical use of the heavens – presumably painted with signs of the zodiac – as the place from which deities descend to the stage in a number of early modern plays.[11] The convergence of stage architecture and a cartographic sensibility is beautifully illustrated in a quote Lawrence takes from Heywood's *An Apology for Actors* (1612) describing the Roman theater: "The covering of the stage, which we call the heavens (where upon any occasion the gods descended) was geometrically supported by giant-like [A]tlas," the mythological figure whose name, in the wake of Mercator, became synonymous with a collection of maps.[12] Andrew Gurr directs our theatrical vision from above to below, writing that "[t]he painted heavens covering the stage in the amphitheatres provided an automatic visual signal for one stage locality, of course. The trap provided another, its position under the stage surface offering a hell for Marlowe's Barabbas and Faustus to sink into, for devils to spring from, and for the ghost of Hamlet's father to descend into before he speaks from his purgatorial grave under the earth of the stage floor."[13]

For scholars of the period, however, this architectural geography of the theater has remained largely a detail of performance studies, germane only to the comings and goings of characters on stage. The ramifications (ideological, theological, and theatrical) for an audience watching *Hamlet* – and many other early modern plays concerned with the supernatural – performed in a space mapping an eschatological cosmology have not been studied in depth ("eschatology" here referring to matters of the afterlife[14]). And yet, this might well have been the map that most concerned Shakespeare's audience. Surely emergent nationalism and curiosity about the New World affected the political and imaginative lives of Londoners in 1600, but that "undiscovered country" (3.1.78) of death and the afterlife was arguably a more immediate and pressing concern.

The wooden fixity of the Globe gives an illusion of geographical and eschatological certitude. But in fact during this period both natural and supernatural geographies were in a process of rapid transformation. The terrestrial globe itself was in the process of becoming unmoored. In 1600, very probably the date of the composition of *Hamlet*, Johannes Kepler signed a contract making him a junior partner of Tycho Brahe.[15] These mathematical geniuses, like others, were struggling to accommodate Copernicus's "discovery" of a heliocentric solar system with what they knew of the cosmos, of God, and of mathematics and the new instruments that gave them measurements of historically unprecedented accuracy. The new information sent heads and planets spinning. The changing cosmic landscape, and even the increasing precision used in surveying the fields beyond London's bounds, would profoundly transform not only terrestrial and planetary order, but eschatological geography as well. When earth was the center of the cosmos, heaven was up above the ether and hell and purgatory were below the ground. When the cosmos was rearranged, and mapping became a scientific undertaking, this spatial-theological organization was undermined as well. The present book is a study of such eschatological destabilization – of how a shifting supernatural geography was produced, experienced, and portrayed.

Hamlet's propensity for paradox, then, becomes a means of registering his own eschatological disorientation. Like lilies that fester – the paradoxical symbolic merger of bodily resurrection and corporeal decay – for Hamlet heaven and hell coexist in an impossible relationship. He clearly sees and describes the heavens, and yet they are clouded by foul vapors. His visual perception is in keeping with his muddled and contradictory attitudes towards the afterlife, his questions and doubts about heaven, hell, and purgatory. Indeed, Hamlet frets about fire for most of the play. He is caught between the medieval belief in purgatory and the Reformation denial of this space's existence.

The theater allows for the spatial representation and performance of this theological dilemma.[16] On stage, an actor stands below the heavens and above hell – the visual map is simple. But Hamlet's words disrupt the picture: what we see is not what he sees; what we thought was self-evident is not; what we thought we believed becomes clouded. This is not only a crisis of faith, or a contest of Catholic and Protestant theologies: it is, in very real ways, a crisis of cosmic geography.

# Introduction: The space of the supernatural

> By all means, they seem to say ... [l]et us not mix up heaven and earth, the global stage and the local scene, the human and the nonhuman. "But these imbroglios do the mixing," you'll say, "they weave our world together!" "Act as if they didn't exist," the analysts reply.
>
> Bruno Latour[1]

### MIXING UP HEAVEN AND EARTH

The turn of the seventeenth century was marked by a sense of cosmic disorientation. Transformations in religious belief brought about by the Protestant Reformation and transformations in modes of conceptualizing space brought about by the popularization of geometry profoundly affected understandings of the relationship between chthonic and super-natural geographies. As a centuries-old structure of cosmic and divine order pressed up against new cartographies and new theologies, the realities of earth, heaven, and hell warped. The confluence of multiple, often contradictory, spatial and theological epistemologies resulted in unsteady beliefs about the universe. This book sets out to explore some of the expressions of this destabilization. Specifically, it examines how the coexistence of often incompatible spatial understandings affected beliefs about, and the experience of, the supernatural.

In Western thought, conceptions about the nature of the supernatural have long been connected to ideas about the structure of space. Saint Augustine's *Confessions*, for instance, begins with a moment of spatial and spiritual vertigo. The text is addressed to God through an insistent and intimate second-person pronoun, but before Augustine can settle into a comfortable use of "you" he must find his divine audience. In his attempt to locate God in space, Augustine seems bewildered, perhaps even frantic·

6

Where *to* can I, already in you, call you to come? And where *from* would you be coming? Where *to* could I retire, outside heaven and earth, for God to come there to me, my God who has said, "I fill heaven and earth"? Since, then, you fill heaven and earth, do they contain you? Or do you fill them, with a surplus of you left over, beyond their containing? Then where, once heaven and earth are filled, does the overflow of you go? Do you, who contain all things, need no container because what you fill is filled by your containing *it*? Any receptacle containing you cannot confine you – were it broken, you would not spill out of it.[2]

Augustine's opening gambit acknowledges a desire to comprehend the world through containment – through shape and dimensions. A clear sense of a cosmic container would seem to ensure a clear sense of emplacement of the self, and thus would define that self's relationship to the divine. Such a sense of clarity, however, is revealed as contrary to God's nature. Augustine must move away from a quest to understand God's spatiality to a radical acceptance of his numinous existence: "Then what are you, God – what, I inquire, but simply God the Lord?" (p. 4). Once he is able to rest in this realization, Augustine can turn to a more inward and for the most part a calmer meditation.

The idea of a spatial God is, naturally, very old. In Acts 17:28, we read that "in [God] we live, and move, and have our being."[3] This notion – that the divine is spatial, and that humanity inhabits this god-space – itself reaches back to Plato. In the *Timaeus*, Plato established an ontological coherence of the universe through his claims that the demiurge had created a spherical cosmos in his own likeness. In explaining "the construction of the world," Plato describes how the creator decided "[a] suitable shape for a living being that was to contain within itself all living beings would be a figure that contains all possible figures within itself. Therefore he turned it into a rounded spherical shape, with the extremes equidistant in all directions from the centre, a figure that has the greatest degree of completeness and uniformity, as he judged uniformity to be incalculably superior to its opposite."[4] Geometry was thus both a sign and a function of divine perfection. This idea was to persist for millennia (and arguably still does, as recent rhapsodic claims of string theory's "elegance" carry neo-Platonic overtones[5]). When Augustine breaks the "receptacle" of God, when he refutes the notion of God and space as container, he thus also breaks away from a Platonic tradition of geometricizing space.

While the relationship of God and space is a topic with an ancient pedigree, the sixteenth century – a century in which both Augustine and Plato assumed intellectual pride of place – brought a new urgency to the conversation. The period is one of both religious and spatial upheavals.

It is marked by the convulsive shifts resulting from the Reformation and the exploration of the Americas. These two phenomena incited an imaginative and cartographic fervor that radically reconceived the place of the individual in earthly and eschatological geographies. In the mid sixteenth century, the cosmos was understood very much as it had been in medieval theology and ancient astronomy: humanity existed in a geocentric universe; hell and purgatory were in the center of the earth, heaven was beyond the outmost celestial sphere; earthly space was not yet widely perceived in terms of cartographic measurement; God and Satan interacted with mortals through the material conditions of their environment. By the mid seventeenth century, this vision of the cosmos had been radically altered: humanity was now spinning on a planet that orbited the sun; the location of hell, even its existence as a physical place, was in question, and purgatory had been largely abandoned; earthly space was deeply geometric and mathematical; the clockwork universe was leading into a conception of a distant clock-maker God, and a Satan who worked through witches and the physical world was becoming outmoded.

All of this required a transformation in how people conceptualized the cosmic "container." To an extent unprecedented in Western history, space was newly and widely imagined in geometric terms. From cheap surveying books designed to be taken into the field by small property owners to gorgeous ornamental atlases meant for display in the grand halls of the wealthy, from the geometric primers that popularized Euclid to the college lectures on mathematics delivered in the vernacular for a popular audience, geometric texts (including the mathematic, cartographic, cosmographic, and geodetic) proliferated. This phenomenon created a new geometric sensibility – a geometric epistemology – that influenced how people perceived and understood the world around them. In the mid sixteenth century, pioneering books of popular geometry needed to define the term "triangle" for an audience that was presumed to be geometrically illiterate; by the late seventeenth century, Isaac Newton was writing the *Principia* in a new language of formulae and geometric constructions. Newton's primary aim was to explain the laws of motion, and for this dynamic geometry he needed the inert backdrop of absolute space (a space itself conceptually organized through the three dimensions of the Cartesian coordinates). "Absolute space," as Newton defines it, "in its own nature, without regard to anything external, remains always similar and immovable."[6] Or, as Neil Smith and Cindi Katz have more recently put it, absolute space is the "conception of space as a field, container, a coordinate system of discrete and mutually exclusive locations."[7]

Absolute space is rigorously geometric. It is linear, quadratic, cubic. It does not bend or curve or allow for aberrations. It contains. It is therefore not the space of an earlier understanding of God and Satan, of angels and demons. Before the idea of the "supernatural" was extracted from the idea of the "natural," the hand of God and the footprint of devils could be seen in the space that people inhabited. Miracles and witchcraft were possible, even prevalent. Such events could involve a distortion of perceived space, and thus space itself must be labile, fluid, and plastic. Geometric, mathematical space, by contrast, would not so easily allow for such supernatural involvement. The fact that the "geometric turn" in early modern England (to borrow Henry Turner's phrase[8]) coincided with the craze for hunting witches is not, as it were, coincidental. The gradual geometricization of space corresponds with a flourishing interest in how that space – and natural laws more widely – can be violated by the demonic. In order to learn more about the construction of the material world, the operations of demonic creatures were subject to intense scrutiny. As Stuart Clark has argued, demonology was not an obscure or marginal field of inquiry, but a central part of early modern natural philosophy.[9] And early modern natural philosophy was in many ways concerned with understanding the container that is the cosmos.

Theology – and its less abstract realization in lived religious experience – was also in many ways environmental. Catholicism and Protestantism, to paint with an admittedly broad brush, required different understandings of the environment. The Catholic emphasis on intercession necessitated an environment that could accommodate ongoing interaction between the material world and the supernatural: long-dead saints could perform miracles, and be accessed through relics and special geographical sites such as holy wells; there were well-known portals to purgatory; angels participated in the mass; devils were present at the deathbed. But the Protestant emphasis on an unmediated relationship between God and the individual made such interactions unnecessary and even unbelievable. This is not to suggest that Protestantism was the religious equivalent of the Cartesian split between mind and environment, but that the Protestant sense of space was less dependent upon a network of material objects and places that signified mediation between the human and the divine.[10]

The often bitter parochial struggles over church interiors are indicative of the degree to which Reformation debates were in part about one's direct spatial environment; arguments, even the blows, which could attend the placement of the surface used to prepare the Eucharistic sacrament (known as the altar for Catholics, and the communion table for Protestants) give us a glimpse into how, on a very quotidian and local level, the spatial arrangement of the church indicated the congregants' relationship to God, and what was understood as "real" presence. The church building itself, a deeply and richly symbolic text, could signify the order of the universe. Traditionally, churches were oriented (that is, architecturally constructed so that priests and laity were facing east during the Mass); the very experience of the liturgy thus coordinated with earthly geography. But as Peter Harrison observes, citing and responding to Miri Rubin: "'in the Middle Ages the language of religion provided a language of social relation and of a cosmic order; it described and explained the interweaving of natural and supernatural with human action …' By the end of the sixteenth century this world was in chaos, and its once potent vision of the cosmic order, of the deeper meanings of the material realm, of the interpenetration of natural and supernatural, was in irrevocable decline."[11] In Harrison's view, this decline was a result of Protestant modes of biblical exegesis, as a new literalism replaced an allegorical hermeneutics dating back to Origen. "Protestant literalism … evacuated the spatial world of its symbolic significance"; "[i]n the new scheme of things, objects were related mathematically, mechanically, causally."[12]

The construction of space was thus of central import to early modern theology and religious belief. And yet we find within the period diametrically opposed notions of space: an understanding of space as mathematical and geometric, and an understanding of space as metamorphic and fluid. An environment that was understood as divinely constructed and ordered through geometry was not one that easily permitted the spatial fluctuations associated with supernatural actions. One of the great social paradoxes of the period was the simultaneity of a heightened geometrical awareness and a widespread fascination with supernatural, especially demonic, behavior that refuted a fixed sense of space. This simultaneity of what are in many ways oppositional epistemologies led to the anomalies and inconsistencies that are the subject of this book.

### THE HUMAN AND THE NON-HUMAN

The tension between more fluid and more geometric understandings of space finds a homology in early modern understandings of the body. At the turn of the seventeenth century, we find two dominant somatic paradigms.

On the one hand, there is the Galenic model of the humoral body; this model revolved around the understanding that health is determined by an economy of four humoral fluids: blood, phlegm, black bile, and choler. An imbalance in these humors would lead to illness. Thus much of the medical logic of the period depended upon regulating these fluids through diet and drainage (enemas, purgations, blood-lettings, etc.). The understanding of the body that was engendered by this theory is vividly described by Joseph Roach: the body "resembles a large bag containing juice-filled sponges of various shapes and sizes. Between sponges there is seepage, percolation, and general sloshing about, but not the regular cleansing action of continuous circulation. Equilibrium of these potentially stagnant juices defines health ... In sickness the body resembles a standing pool, clogged and befouled with diverse obstructions, excreta, putrifying humours, and soot from the fire of the heart."[13]

On the other hand, the period witnessed the rise of what Norbert Elias calls the *homo clausus*: the open and sloshy humoral body finds its antithesis in the body that is meticulously regulated and controlled.[14] As Elias's analysis in *The Civilizing Process* exhaustively indicates, attention to manners and the regulation of bodily functions – concealing most from the sight and hearing of others – created a body with boundaries that were imagined as mostly closed. Self-mastery of the body became a requisite skill for the genteel classes. This *homo clausus* existed in a world in which human and animal bodies were flayed and visually accessible to a degree barely imaginable today. From the vogue for still lifes of slaughtered animals to the ritual butchery of traitors to the prevalence of meat on display in the marketplace, bodies were opened for inspection.[15] Anatomy theaters were built so that an eager public could watch the dissection of cadavers for entertainment. While these opened bodies may seem to be antithetical to the idea of *homo clausus*, they are in fact part of a cultural project to better understand what lies beneath the skin. Renaissance anatomists like Leonardo da Vinci and Andreas Vesalius dissected bodies to reveal a series of mechanical systems; the anatomist's vision of the body in many ways opposes the idea of fluctuating humoral fluids. The viewing of the body was thus actually in the service of demonstrating how closed it truly is: early modern understandings of embodiment gradually shifted from a body conceptualized as largely open to the environment, to one that is perceived as sealed off from its surroundings. William Harvey's "discovery" of the circulatory system and the pumping heart proved a victory for the enclosed, mechanical, systemic body. We are the inheritors of this notion of the body, a body which exists, in the words of John

Sutton, "as a solid container, only rarely breached, in principle autonomous from culture and environment, tampered with only by diseases and experts."[16]

For the most part, scholarship on embodiment initially focused on better understanding the political, social, or psychological subject. It was driven by the desire to better comprehend the notion of "self." Thus while studies of the early modern self/body might acknowledge – as does Michael Schoenfeldt's – how Galenic theory "possesses a remarkable capacity to relate the body to its environment," the focus has been on the "inwardness of living, inhabited bodies."[17] More recently, scholars have turned to considering how early modern notions about the body influenced not just a sense of self, but also an understanding of the outward spatial environment. There is an increasing recognition of how profoundly strange the post-Cartesian notion that the body is "in principle autonomous from ... [the] environment" would have seemed to most people living in sixteenth- and seventeenth-century England. As Mary Floyd-Wilson and Garrett A. Sullivan, Jr. note, this newer scholarship "emphasize[s] the porousness of an early modern body that takes the environment into itself or spills out of its own bounds (or both). This criticism ... has also alerted us to the 'ecological' nature of early modern conceptions of embodiment – the way in which the body is understood as embedded in a larger world with which it transacts."[18]

A crucial mode of this transaction is that of microcosm and macrocosm. Within the period, we find an almost ubiquitous understanding that the universe is organized according to a homologous and interconnected relationship between body and world. Time and again, the researcher snuffling around in the archive, or even the student thumbing through an anthology of Renaissance literature, reads that the human body was a little cosmos that reflected and participated in the large cosmos that was the universe. This idea, emanating from Plato's *Timaeus*, would wend itself through the thought of patristic thinkers such as Origen and Ambrose ("the body of man is constructed like the world itself") and into the work of medieval writers like Aquinas and Hildegard of Bingen.[19] The stock patristic and medieval formulations of the idea of microcosm/ macrocosm appear in numerous sixteenth- and seventeenth-century texts. We could turn, for example, to Samuel Purchas's question in *Purchas His Pilgrim. Microcosmus, or The Historie of Man* (1619): "Is not the Haire as Grasse? the Flesh as Earth? the Bones as Mineralls? the Veines as Riuers? the Liuer, a Sea? Are not the Lungs and Heart correspondent to the ayrie and fierie Elements? the Braines, to the Clouds and Meteors ...? the Eyes, to Starres, or those two Eyes of Heauen, the *greater Lights?* and the circular forme of the Head, to the globositie of the Heauens?" (pp. 30–1). The human body was connected to the green under one's feet and to the outer reaches of a spherical universe. In a different iteration of this concept, the body becomes its own cosmic structure; for example, Thomas Adams writes in *Mystical Bedlam* (1615), "As man is a *Microcosmus*, an abridgement of the world, hee hath *heauen* resembling his *soule*; *earth* his *heart*, placed in the middest as a center: the *Liuer* is like the *sea*, whence flow the liuely springs of bloud: the *Braine*, like the *sunne*, giues the light of vnderstanding: and the *senses* are set round about, like the *starres*" (p. 9).

Given the epistemological prominence of microcosm/macrocosm in early modern England, the extensive recent scholarship on the body thus also gives us purchase on understandings of space. At their most basic, the two primary models of the body (as open and fluid, or as closed and mechanical) correspond to the two primary spatial models discussed above (labile and metamorphic, or rigid and geometric). That said, the concept of microcosm/macrocosm is multifaceted, and carries multiple implications. As Leonard Barkan notes:

Four approaches to cosmology arise from such speculation as Plato's and become the systems by which the bodies of greater and lesser worlds are united: the chemical geocosm, envisaging a world composed of the four elements; the astral geocosm, presupposing a heavenly cosmos that is both physical and spiritual; a numerical geocosm made up of abstract mathematical relations; and a natural geocosm comprised of the objects of this world as immediately beheld by the senses.[20]

The epistemological and cultural context of sixteenth- and seventeenth-century England allowed for diverse iterations of these four basic models.[21] Galenic and Paracelsan medical theories revolved around the first model, that of the chemical geocosm. Under this model (the one that has received the most attention from literary scholars), the ecology of the body is thus directly connected to the ecology of the environment. One's bodily health, and even what today we would term one's mental health (or even, on a more mundane level, one's "moods"), was organically related to the elements that compose the world and its climatic conditions, since the four humours (blood, bile, phlegm, and black bile) correspond to the four elements (air, fire, water, and earth).[22] As Aristotle would tell us, these elements themselves are in a state of motion and change. We encounter, in the words of Floyd-Wilson, "an ecology that undermines any conception [of] a solid, static, or contained self."[23]

A less observed phenomenon is the convergence of the second and third models – a meeting of the astral and the numerical geocosms. This was the work of cartography, and the meeting of innovative technology and ancient cosmography that John Gillies notes in Ortelius and Mercator.[24] Returning to Purchas, we find a chapter with the conventional title of "Man a little World, the correspondence betwixt him and the greater World" and this distinctly early modern, print- and cartography-inflected sentence: "This body is a Microcosme, & created after the rest, as an Epitome of the whole Vniverse, and truest Mappe of the World, a summarie and compendious other World" (pp. 25–6).

The paradigm of microcosm and macrocosm thus embraces the powerful convergence of the human body with the spatial configuration of the cosmos. These become united in geometry. When the body becomes a map, the cosmos becomes a map (and vice versa). And maps, of course, are constructed and read in the language of mathematics and geometry. Barkan writes that:

[n]either Plato nor Pythagoras specifically connects the numerical geocosm with the microcosm; yet the nature of their mathematical speculations is extremely influential for the microcosmic tradition. In the Pythagorean system, the whole cosmos is a series of entities standing in geometric proportion to one another. This proportion, or *analogia*, specifies a microcosmic relation among all the constituents of the cosmos. The human body as microcosm is the quintessential *analogia*: as the creator is to man's body, so is man's body to the world ... Chemistry provides the matter and geometry the form of the cosmos; the astral microcosm incorporates both systems in its own vision of wholeness.[25]

Body, space, and God are united through a divine geometry; medicine, cosmography, and theology are united in the new sciences and cartography. These are not abstract speculations. As Barkan argues, in the Renaissance the convergence of Platonic and Pauline Christianity and "anatomical empiricism" (p. 28) led to the microcosm being understood in both figurative and literal terms. Thus thinkers like Helkiah Crooke (author of *Mikrokosmographia, A Description of the Body of Man* [1615][26]) "believe in an extremely straightforward physical microcosm ... If God is in the world and the world is in man, then both man's body and the world's must be exhaustively read and analyzed if man is to grasp God. For these interpreters, the body may be a mere container of all the world's constituent parts" (p. 26).

Around the turn of the seventeenth century the various ways of conceptualizing the container of the human body therefore profoundly affected the ways of conceptualizing the container of the cosmos. As we have seen, the humoral body was understood to interpenetrate with the environment in a way suggesting that the cosmos is likewise porous, mutable, and fluid. The emergent model of the mechanical body seems to suggest a more stable macrocosm, however, and arguably contributed to the gradual demise of the microcosm/macrocosm paradigm. While the humoral body has excellent and ancient credentials connecting it to the environment, the emergent model of the mechanical body does not. Indeed, that is partly the point, as innovative thinkers sought to shuffle off the intellectual coil of Aristotle. It is tempting, for instance, to think of Vesalius's *De humani corporis fabrica* and Copernicus's *De revolutionibus orbium coelestium* – both of which were first published in 1543 – as having a micro/macro relationship to one another. However, both of these texts move away from the microcosm/macrocosm episteme: Vesalius's detailed dissections prioritize experiment over an adherence to Aristotelian authority and its underlying principle of correlating the human body with the four elements, while Copernicus's reliance on observation and recorded mathematical data rearranged the universe in such a way that man was no longer center and epitome.

Transformations in understandings of the body – as erratic and contradictory as those transformations may have been – implicitly necessitated a change in conceptions of the macrocosmic universe. And transformations in understandings of the structure of the universe – such as the radical remapping of the solar system propounded by Copernicus, Kepler, and Galileo – required a change in conceptions of the body. In the years on either side of 1600, then, people continued to rely on the model of macrocosm/microcosm to structure their physical and epistemological universe. But whereas this relationship had once been a means of stabilizing and cognitively organizing the relationship between human beings, spatial environment, and God, both the understanding of the macrocosm and the understanding of the microcosm were in a period of rapid if uneven transformation. Not only do cartographic pressures applied to the macrocosm influence the microcosm, but the shifting and contradictory understandings of the human body impact notions about the environment. And while in some ways these transformations could be seen as parallel – the new astronomy and the new anatomy both emphasize the mechanical – the development was hardly that neat. Contradictory, overlapping conceptions of the macro and the micro worlds could make their relationship discordant and confusing.[27] An age-old epistemological model for understanding the relationship of human beings and God's creation was morphing. Hamlet's sense of being entrapped by spatial and ontological paradoxes (as I discussed in my Prologue) is a symptom of this shift.

This epistemological fizzle could affect, in a very real and immediate way, how the individual perceived his or her relationship to the universe, and thus to God. Sixteenth- and seventeenth-century theologians (whose words were available to the public through publications and sermons) were themselves thinking of God through micro- and macrocosmic terms. Calvin, for instance, opens the *Institutes* by emphasizing that knowledge of God and knowledge of self are mutually constitutive. "Without knowledge of self there is no knowledge of God," reads the title to the first short section of the opening chapter; "Without knowledge of God there is no knowledge of self," reads the title to the second.[28] As I will discuss in Chapter 4, Calvin's God is intensely spatial. Calvin also positions the corporeal self as an integral, and exemplary, element of nature: "in regard to the structure of the human body one must have the greatest keenness in order to weigh, with Galen's skill, its articulation, symmetry, beauty, and use ... the human body shows itself to be a composition so ingenious that its Artificer is rightly judged a wonder-worker ... Certain philosophers, accordingly, long ago not ineptly called man a microcosm" (I: 53–4). The merging of the classical microcosm-macrocosm paradigm with Galen's somatic theory epitomizes Calvin's theology. Galen's humoral system, unlike the mechanistic view of the body that was to supersede it, was in a constant state of flux and movement, and was inherently unpredictable. If this body is the microcosm, the homologous macrocosm shares these qualities; the fluid economy of Galen's body is part of the fluid economy of Calvin's cosmos. Structure and symmetry are, to be sure, a part of this system, but that order is always qualified by fluctuation – humors in motion, God's providence in action. Calvin was caught up in this wider cultural tension as much as he was a producer of it: his emphasis on knowledge of the self as the path to knowing God contributed to the cultural importance of the sense of self; his emphasis on the instability and fluidity of God's creation rendered this self, in turn, volatile.

A century later the model of macrocosm-microcosm is frayed. In *ΑΓΓΕΛΟΚΡΑΤΙΑ ΘΕΟΎ. Or a Sermon Touching Gods Government of the World by Angels* (1650), Robert Gell decries "the wilfull ignorance of the present generation" who would deny the existence, or at least the agency, of Angels: "they heed not, that while they take away the operation of the Planets, Constellations, and Angels from the inferiour world, they divorce the heavens from the earth, and break *Homers* golden chain" (sig. D4$^r$). Those who disavow angels sever the links that connect micro-cosm and macrocosm. Yet the content of Gell's own sermon indicates the growing incompatibility of different understandings of the supernatural world. He fiercely argues for the presence of angels as the means of holding heaven and earth together, defending a traditional notion of beings who move freely through a space that allows for their amorphous existence. At the same time, his notion of truth is defined through "firmness and stability" (sig. B$^v$) and his cosmic space is geometric, since "the Empyrean heaven is foursquare ... signif[ying] the stability and settled estate of the blessed in the Kingdome of heaven" (sig. C4$^r$). We find the overlay of a macrocosmic-microcosmic notion of the world and the geometric sensibility which would privilege surety. The sermon, as we are told from the title page, was, appropriately enough, preached "before the learned Societie of Artists and Astrologers," whose knowledge hinged between ancient understandings of the stars and the new astronomy that contributed to the emergent paradigm of the mechanistic universe.

As this sermon indicates, different notions of the "container" of the universe affected understandings of how God and Satan live and move, how they interact (or don't) with human beings. Just as the early modern humoral body was conceptualized as an organism in a constant state of flux, with shifting consistencies and porous boundaries, so too the pre-geometric spatial universe had a certain mutability and porosity which allowed for traffic between heaven and hell, and angels and devils could enter into one's daily spatial environment. Space, not yet absolute, was fungible and permeable. The mechanical body rejected this fungibility and permeability, and the geometric space it came to inhabit was likewise more stable and constant. This changed the ways in which divine and demonic forces were manifest in the world. In the decades on either side of 1600, however, both of these bodies (the humoral and the mechanical) and both of their corresponding understandings of space (as fluid and as geometrical) were culturally present and viable.

## THE GLOBAL STAGE AND THE LOCAL SCENE

What, I wonder, would it feel like to inhabit this space, at once a metamorphic one that allowed for the regular incursions of the supernat-ural, and a geometric one that was stable and ordered? How would it feel to sit at the nexus of residual and emergent modes of spatial understand-ings which were transforming and being transformed by changing ideas about the divine and the demonic? "Sit" and "nexus" are actually too static – how would it feel to move through a world that was changing shape, both epistemologically and theologically?

These are historical questions, but they are not the questions of the historian. The methodologies of social historiography are of limited value in answering them. And while a sense of the self-in-relationship-to-God-in-relationship-to-space is Augustine's personal concern, these are not quite the questions of the theologian, either. How do we approach not a history of human thought or social movements, but of the actual *experience* of living inside a set of epistemologies and beliefs?

In trying to answer these questions, I turn to the literary historians and theorists who have done so much brilliant recent work on embodiment, on how people in the early modern period understood and experienced their somatic existence. The scholarship of Gail Kern Paster, Michael Schoenfeld, Mary Floyd-Wilson, Bruce R. Smith and many others has enabled us to speak about the experience of the body in earlier periods when social codes and medical understandings differed so much from our own.[29] Smith has dubbed this recovery effort "historical phenomenology."[30] Its body of scholarship provides a methodology and a vocabulary for understanding how people inhabited their bodies, and thus how they inhabited space. Like Smith, "[w]hat I am inviting you to negotiate in these pages is the difference between *ontology*, which assumes a detached, objective spectator who can see the whole, and *phenomenology*, which assumes a subject who is immersed in the experience she is trying to describe."[31] Or, to cast the project in the biblical terms that would have been more organic to the period, I am attempting to understand how people lived, moved, and had their being.[32] Since early modern space was hardly perceived as a neutral container, but rather as the habitat of God, angels, and demons, a sense of how people inhabited space gives us some purchase on how they experienced the supernatural.

That said, "people" rarely articulate their experience of the spatial surround. But poets and literary characters do.[33] Thus while I will be drawing from the work of religious historians, my archive is that of the theater. This is not the only place to look; the present book could well have been about Donne or Spenser, and one is always tempted by Milton.[34] Donne – Shakespeare's contemporary, and a figure who, like Hamlet, was caught between Catholicism and reformist religion – portrayed his own spiritual crises in geographic terms. Writing of his sickness, Donne proclaims: "As West and East/In all flatt Maps (and I am one) are one,/So death doth touch the Resurrection."[35] The map/body serves as a means of representing the paradoxical merging of death and resurrection and the insertion of the self into that spiritual paradox. This is similar to Hamlet's collapse of heaven and hell, and the way that his cartographically inflected portrayal of the theater's architecture positions his own person within that paradoxical eschatological space. A crucial difference between these two moments, however, is the emphatic "flatness" of Donne's map versus the three-dimensional space of the Globe. It is the latter I want to explore in this book. Specifically, I want to consider how theatrical characters *inhabit* space, and how different understandings of that space reflect different, often conflicting, understandings of the divine or the demonic.

To make an utterly obvious but crucial point: it is in the theater that we find physical, three-dimensional bodies moving in actual three-dimensional spaces. While the metaphysical conceits of Donne's poems or the metamorphic fictional space of Spenser's Faeryland work through many of the dynamics I have outlined above, the theater allows human bodies to enact some of the crises of faith which could result from contradictory spatial epistemologies. The theater enables and activates both metaphor and physical performance. As such, it is an ideal vehicle for expressing both the epistemological and phenomenological complexities of early modern space. Discussions of the cosmos could be highly abstract: Kepler thought that he had discovered the universe to be structured around internested Platonic solids (see Chapter 5). However, these discussions could also be highly visceral and sensory: the skeptic in Galileo's *Dialogue Concerning the Two Chief World Systems* argues against a Copernican model on the grounds that, if the earth is indeed hurtling around the sun, we would feel "a perpetual gale that drives with a velocity of more than 2,529 miles an hour," indicating that purported changes in cosmic geography led people to be self-consciously aware of their own physical experience of standing on the planet.[36] Demonologists could engage in esoteric debates about how demonic shape-shifting corresponded with the laws of physics; neighbors gathered around a friend's deathbed would be watching for real devils in a closed and fetid chamber. Neo-Platonists could contemplate divine geometry; surveyors handled instruments they felt resembled God. Theater engages this movement between the abstract and material, the epistemological and the phenomenological, ways of knowing and ways of experiencing.

Moreover, drama can stage the simultaneous interactions and intersections of multiple epistemologies and phenomenologies, of different ways of knowing, different types of experience. One consequence of the spatial and theological changes around the turn of the seventeenth century was that it was possible for those within the same community to have very different understandings (and experiences) of what we now call space-time.[37] Today neighbors might gather and express differences about politics or religion, but it is hard to imagine a heated debate, except in the most rarefied of circles, about the very laws of physics or the structure of the universe. In 1600, by contrast, the nature of the cosmos was itself controversial – and beliefs about this nature affected one's beliefs about religion or politics. And plays, as Wendy Wall succinctly puts it, "not only license strong expressions of affect but are particularly well suited for airing incompatible social discourses since they imagine a wide range of positions put in conversation with each other."[38] Thus in a play like *Macbeth* we witness the interaction of characters who seem to be inhabiting different, and fundamentally incompatible, spatial epistemologies.

If, in common with so much early new historicism, my literary focus is on drama, I thus hope my own methodology allows me to escape the tendency to consider these texts primarily as cultural artifacts. While asking historical questions, I hope to recuperate the particularity of imaginative literature. As Cynthia Marshall puts it:

the new historicist idea that texts do the work of culture and manifest power within it collapses textuality into culture, denying the imaginative space of writing. The force of textuality itself has gone largely unremarked, and the dialectical relation of texts to the culture within which they arise – the way writing arises from within a culture but exists at a self-conscious remove from it – has been neglected. What a culture in its official versions of itself is suturing together and publicly solidifying – such as the outlines of the individual subject in early modern England – texts designed for entertainment or meditation might be busily undoing.[39]

In addition to the individual subject towards whom Marshall gestures, we might also note that authorities in early modern England were deliberately trying to "publicly solidify" a national identity through a project of mapping and a Protestant identity through catechism – both of which could be represented, or undone, on the stage.

While both of these projects might have been successful (the populace became familiar with maps and children did indeed learn their catechism[40]), they created only surface uniformity. To draw an analogy from current physics, we find in early modern England (and probably in authoritarian cultures more broadly) something akin to the incompatibility of general relativity and quantum mechanics. "The notion of a smooth spatial geometry, the central principle of general relativity," writes

Brian Greene, "is destroyed by the violent fluctuations of the quantum world on short distance scales."[41] These fluctuations are known as "quantum foam."[42] While historians such as Christopher Haigh (see note 40) perform the invaluable work of combing local archives to document manifestations of religious belief and experience, literary scholars do well not simply to consider dramatic texts as yet another archive, or as documents that merely correspond with and reinforce other discursive fields. Rather, we might consider these plays the cultural equivalent of imaginative quantum foam – the chaotic, metamorphic, wonderful manifestation of the micro activity of individual beliefs, fears, desires, fantasies, sensations, words. The early modern theater may have been geometric, but audiences did not come to spend two hours with the "smooth spatial geometry" of a cultural absolute space; this makes for dull story. The spatiality of the theater offered the opportunity for enacted thought experiment, for the staging of foam. Plays performed around the turn of the seventeenth century thus offer a unique literary response to historical questions, questions that cannot be answered through other forms of archive (say, wills and church records).

The theater itself contributes to this imaginative ferment, as it models forms of space for spectators even as it incorporates the audience within a spatial dynamic. D. J. Hopkins notes that "[t]he word 'theater' in this period was not exclusively applied to purpose-built structures used for public performance; the word was used in a general way to describe any 'container' for things one might want to look at. Such a container could be a building, a single room, or a book."[43] The Globe was thus a container for examining the container of the cosmos. And yet the spatial order that was presented in the plays of the period was hardly consistent or epistemologically coherent. Hopkins notes that "the structures by which space itself had been perceived, used, and understood for centuries were changing, and nowhere in England were these changes more acute than in London, where, in the decades bracketing 1600, a range of social pressures brought about a radical change in representational practices," but he stresses that this was "a gradual, uneven, sporadic, and inconsistent transition that resulted in a period of spatial hybridity" (p. 23). London itself was a "post-medieval" city, as new cultural ideas were played out in a city with an architecture and infrastructure that still largely dated from an earlier time (p. 35), resulting in "a promiscuous intermingling of spatial practices at the historic juncture of medieval and early modern cultures, a period when performance coexisted with representational picturing" (p. 45).

The dynamic that Hopkins notes for the post-medieval city of London is similar to the one we find inside the theater (if I might indulge in my own moment of macrocosm-microcosm). Here, too, we find a "hybrid space of competing social and spatial practices" (p. 35). To return to the opening scene of this book's Prologue: Hamlet inhabits a theatrical space that translates medieval staging (the presence of heaven and hell) even as he seems to reference the new atlas of Mercator. These maps themselves are hybrids of medieval cosmography and the new mathematics. Hamlet's spatial paradox collapses ancient cosmic structures in a move that encompasses his audience, even as his soliloquy about inward emotional paradoxes sets him off as a visual icon of the discrete Renaissance "self."

As a space that is at once localized and an integral part of a wider cultural, representational, and performative network, the early modern stage thus allows for both focused and expansive imaginative engagement – both then and now – with these changes in spatial epistemology and practice. And a fundamental consequence of these changes was the inherent paradox of theater itself, at once a site of geometric stability and metamorphosis. Henry Turner, in the context of a chapter called "Theatre as a Spatial Art," observes that "[e]ach type of theatrical sign may be reduced to two primary iconic forms ... iconic signs originated from or pertaining to the *actor and his body,* and iconic signs originating from and pertaining to the *stage as an architectonic or spatial element.*"[44] An audience newly literate in geometric and cartographic constructions brings this sensibility to the theater, and early modern authors frequently play with these expectations (as I have argued elsewhere in the context of "plot"[45]). But even as the theater was associated with the regularity of the geometric, it was also feared – or desired – as a site of metamorphosis. David Hillman has written: "The basis of much of the anti-theatrical condemnation of early modern England was ... that plays affect bodies; that theatre destabilises corporeal (and other) boundaries – it can transform the very interiors of both actors' and audiences' bodies."[46] As Hillman reminds us, Jonas Barish noted that the theater was associated by its enemies with the shape-shifter Proteus.[47]

In the early modern theater, as in early modern theology and early modern science, the geometric and the protean thus coexist in uneasy ways. To return to the heuristic of microcosm-macrocosm, once the signs associated with the actor and his body become destabilized (in a world where a fluid, fungible somatic economy was a dominant paradigm) the stage as an architectonic or spatial element itself becomes destabilized. Or, to reverse the flow of argument: once geometric constructions of the cosmos are compromised by a residual but still lively sense of eschatological space, the body of the actor is potentially also compromised. The theater, then, offers a cultural locus for imaginatively exploring the epistemological friction between the containment afforded by absolute, mathematical space and the mutability of an older spatial model. And it offers a way of representing how that friction was lived and experienced, and how it affected religious belief.

*Supernatural Environments in Shakespeare's England*, then, explores the effects of overlapping spatial epistemologies and the consequence of this overlap for religious understandings in the decades surrounding 1600. The overarching organization of the book provides a spectrum of these different spatial epistemologies. The book opens with a chapter on what I call "Ovidian physics," the notion of an environment that is fluid and fungible. It closes with a chapter on geometric space, examining the fortunes of the triangle in early modern England. This shape assumed new prominence due to the rise of triangulated surveying practices and the triangle's increased use as a symbol of the Trinity; as the chapter demonstrates, the triangle comes to signify the confluence of geometry and divinity. Along this spectrum, the book is organized through a progressive series of spaces. Chapter 1 focuses on demonic contracts, considering how these documents can function as tracers to give a sense of environmental constructs. The chapter considers such contracts in an essay by Freud and in Christopher Marlowe's *Doctor Faustus*, and is foundational for establishing the book's methodology. From the spatial surround of a contract, Chapter 2 opens into the local space of the deathbed. The chapter considers the various understandings of supernatural activity as presented in the immensely popular *ars moriendi* literature of the sixteenth and early seventeenth centuries, and examines how *Othello* enacts the familiar deathbed scene to create a layered and multi-perspectival eschatological space. Chapter 3 widens the scope to the larger terrain of earthly locations for purgatory. The chapter positions *Hamlet* within contemporary debates about the actual geographical location of purgatory inside the earth, and especially the identification of the Icelandic volcano Mount Hecla as the northern purgatory; these discussions epitomize the early modern confluence of a new cartographic sensibility and older understandings about supernatural space. Chapter 4 turns to larger questions about cosmology, and from the demonic to the divine. Here I consider the prominence of cosmic space in the theology of John Calvin, who emphasizes a labile space that is utterly held together by God's providence. By contrast, Richard Hooker's sense of cosmic structure, which similarly anchors his theology, is one of natural laws and God's order. In *Macbeth* we find the impossible coexistence of both of these theo-spatial models. Chapter 5 examines the deep interdependence of geometry (and especially geodesy) and theology. In early modern England, the discourse, practice, and even the instruments of surveying were construed in theological terms. The specific environmental epistemology this engendered – an epistemology that is pointedly trinitarian – undergirds *The Tempest*. Finally, the book's Epilogue calls for the necessity of linking the "religious turn" and the "spatial turn" of recent scholarship, a linkage which brings into focus a notion of space that differs dramatically from the one presumed in much recent work on early modern cartography.

I begin now with one of the most significant obstacles in scholarly approaches to the supernatural, the problem of our disbelief.

# *The devil's in the archive: Ovidian physics and* Doctor Faustus

We may not staye heere within the limites of our owne reason, which is not able to reach vnto, or to comprehend what way Deuils should be able to haue such operations. We may not I say measure their nimblenes, & power, & subtilties in working, by our owne vnderstanding or capacitie.

George Gifford, *A Discourse of the Subtill Practises of Deuilles by Witches and Sorcerers* (1587), sig. Ci<sup>r</sup>

## MATTERS OF THE DEVIL

The problem is, how can we take the devil seriously?

That is to say, how can "we" – reasoning, skeptical, worldly individuals, skilled in analysis, prejudiced against superstition – approach Satan, reeking of brimstone, wreaking havoc with people's lives? How can we write a history of experiencing the devil without sterilizing or rationalizing the demonic? How can we look back through that period we have called The Enlightenment and study the devil's earlier dark participation in the world without bringing an innate mistrust of the tales we read and a latent condescension towards the people who tell them? How can we really study a devil we don't think is real?[1]

At one time, of course, the devil was as real as God – in a way, even more real, since he could be perceived directly as even the omnipresent deity could not. In the seventeenth century, John Rogers (the future Fifth Monarchist) saw devils everywhere. In his youth he was consumed by a "fear of Hell and the devils, whom I thought I saw every foot in several ugly shapes and forms, according to my fancies, and sometimes with great rolling flaming eyes like saucers, having sparkling firebrands in one of their hands, and with the other reaching at me to tear me away to torments. Oh the leaps that I have made, the frights that I have had, the fears that I was in." Rogers's environment was saturated with the demonic. Today, our response would be to diagnose him with a mental disorder; he would almost certainly be medicated and perhaps even institutionalized. But within his own period, Rogers's experience would not have been that atypical. While his ongoing perception of demons might have been extreme, the presence of devils in the world was a given, and something that the ordinary English man or woman would have experienced on a regular basis. From thunderstorms to erotic dreams, from the workings of the cosmos to the musings of the soul, the devil was an immediate, active presence in people's lives. He was ubiquitous and unavoidable.

I have taken Rogers's quote from Keith Thomas, who includes it in his seminal study *Religion and the Decline of Magic.*[2] Not that we should read it too closely: at the end of the previous paragraph, Thomas observes that "[t]he Devil who provoked high winds and thunderstorms, or who appeared dramatically to snatch a poor sinner at his cups and fly off with him through the window, is difficult for us today to take seriously" (p. 470). For all of the emotional intensity of Rogers's experience, Thomas primes us to take it lightly, or at least notes our propensity to do so.

Within the field of Renaissance studies, there are entrenched historical and cultural impediments to taking the devil seriously. In reading sixteenth- and seventeenth-century accounts of demonic activity it is, as Thomas suggests, sometimes hard to remain straight-faced. The devil provided a rational explanation for seemingly irrational events, such as medical conditions and weather systems. It is not so much that early modern people did not understand such things – they understood perfectly well that they were the work of the devil. But since our own understanding has shifted towards the invisible machinations of cells and atoms, their reason has become our irrationality.

Irrational beliefs are often associated with childhood, and there has long been a scholarly tradition of portraying the inhabitants of the sixteenth and early seventeenth centuries as immature versions of our more sophisticated selves.[3] The models of history that we inhabit invite us, perhaps even compel us, to conceptualize time as moving in terms of human development. Metanarratives of the Renaissance are especially prone to this developmental scheme, given how fundamentally the work of Jacob Burckhardt defined the field. The Renaissance, in Burckhardt's view, is a glorious story of coming-of-age; the entry into modernity is marked by the abandonment of (childish) superstition in favor of a more rational (adult) skepticism. Here is how he describes this process at the beginning of Part II of *The Civilization of the Renaissance in Italy*, the section entitled "The Development of the Individual":

In the Middle Ages both sides of human consciousness – that which was turned within as that which was turned without – lay dreaming or half awake beneath a common veil. The veil was woven of faith, illusion, and childish prepossession, through which the world and history were seen clad in strange hues ... In Italy this veil first melted into air; an *objective* treatment and consideration of the State and of all the things of this world became possible. The *subjective* side at the same time asserted itself with corresponding emphasis; man became a spiritual *individual*, and recognized himself as such.[4]

Following the italicized trail, the intellectual *Bildungsroman* that is Burckhardt's Renaissance becomes clear: an immature, illusory faith gives way to hard analysis; the medieval dreamer awakes into the assertive Renaissance Man; political individuation not only allows for analysis of the social system one inhabits but for a newly discovered sense of interiority, a sense of self that enables an appropriate (i.e. non-illusory) form of spirituality. While it has been nearly a century and a half since the book's first publication, the text is still relevant, even seminal, insofar as it established the normative paradigm for the emergence of modern individualism.

Today we are perhaps more sensitive to (or at least more self-conscious about) the ideological implications of these metanarratives, and the job of the scholar is to work through the complexities of medieval and early modern cultures, not to extol their simplicities. But the teleological, developmental paradigm is so ingrained in our critical tradition that it is hard to escape. Although this paradigm may have become more subtle as it moved its way through the influential work of authors ranging from Norbert Elias to Charles Taylor, it has nonetheless remained central for organizing discussions about early modernism.[5] Even more subtly, though more pervasively, the progressive teleology is implicit in our current label of choice, "early modern."[6] This historical orientation has led us to trace, rather single-mindedly, the etiology of modernity rather than the legacy of medievalism. An underlying obstacle to studying the devil of the sixteenth and seventeenth centuries is thus our predisposition, witting or not, to construe history as analogous to human growth and development, and the inherent tendency to patronize the youthfulness that attends this mode of thought.[7]

The arrival of this model of modern individualism also established the terms for scholarly inquiry. In Burckhardt's description, the assertion of the subject marks an appropriate distance from the object; the recognition of distinct subject-object relations turns men from pointless illusion to a valid and necessary "consideration of the State and of all the things of this world." We find here not only the seeds of future academic protocols – the analytical observer should be properly detached from the object of study – but also the creation of legitimate fields of study. "Things of this world" are germane; faith and illusion are not. The medieval propensity for theology is out; the Renaissance interest in science (both political and natural) is in.

This turn from faith to the world has been carried forward in most scholarship of the last century on religion. At the beginning of *The Sociology of Religion*, Max Weber makes the bald declaration: "The essence of religion is not even our concern, as we make it our task to study the conditions and effects of a particular type of social behavior."[8] Similarly, in the opening of *Religion and the Decline of Magic* Thomas presents his work as overtly anthropological: "In this task [i.e. 'to make sense of some of the systems of belief which were current in sixteenth- and seventeenth-century England'] I have been much helped by the studies made by modern social anthropologists of similar beliefs held in Africa and elsewhere" (p. ix). (In his comparison of medieval England with "primitive" societies, Thomas gives the familiar evolutionary narra-tive a twist; where Burckhardt maps the historical process onto human maturation, Thomas maps it onto global development.[9]) The shift from studying religion to analyzing historical *systems* of religion requires, ideally, "exact statistical data" (p. x). Writing in 1971, Thomas observes that "at present there seems to be no genuinely scientific method of measuring changes in the thinking of past generations," although he projects that "the records of the time will one day be systematically quantified," leading to "a more accurate version of the truth" (p. x). Thomas's faith lies in statistics – the "exact," "precise," "genuinely scientific," "systematically quantified," "accurate" means to reach the "truth" about early modern beliefs.

The new historicism that defined literary studies of the 1980s and 1990s was, from the point of view of many historiographers, notoriously inexact, imprecise, and unscientific. It did not seek to reveal "truths" so much as the cultural dynamics of representation. But here, too, the focus was on Burckhardt's "consideration of the State and of all the things of this world." Stephen Greenblatt powerfully argued that the theater, while perhaps still the realm of illusion, was a crucial vehicle in the (presumed) modern process of disenchantment, since the staging of religion emp-tied out its spiritual or sacramental element.[10] Greenblatt's work was influential in the resuscitation of a scholarly interest in religion,[11] which had fallen out of favor as a subject of intellectual inquiry in the wake of the Christian critics of the 1940s, 1950s and early 1960s (see Chapter 5). His approach set the tone for much subsequent scholarship, in that scholars "deal[ing] with religious issues, quickly translated them into social, economic, and political language."[12] The new historicist concern with power relations (bringing together the methodologies of Clifford Geertz and the politics of Michel Foucault) led to a consideration of the Church as one would consider the State. The study of religious beliefs was concerned with their participation in a political economy of oppression and subversion, of conformity and resistance.[13] This scholarship reinforces Weber's move away from the "essence of religion" to "type[s] of social behavior." More recently, responses to the "religious turn" in early modern studies have explored less sociologically based paths of analysis. There have been calls for a renewed commitment to theoretical approaches, and an interest in political theology.[14] These studies increasingly acknowledge that "[r]eligion remains strange, uncanny, even somewhat wild, in that it does not lend itself to cultural, materialist, or historicist modes of analysis that attempt to tame its enigmatic nature."[15]

Such familiar modes of worldly analysis leave us poorly equipped to really consider John Rogers's experience of devils, "whom [he] thought [he] saw every foot in several ugly shapes and forms, according to [his] fancies, and sometimes with great rolling flaming eyes like saucers, having sparkling firebrands in one of their hands, and with the other reaching at [him] to tear [him] away to torments." Such a statement largely slips through our available cultural, materialist methodologies. And psychoanalytic approaches impose anachronism: Rogers's contemporaries did not perceive him as delusional. We could choose to designate this moment as marginal to historical concerns, but that would also be to willfully deny the centrality of the demonic in sixteenth- and seventeenth-century England. At the very moment when Keith Thomas acknowledges that we don't take the devil seriously he also stresses how important it is to take the devil seriously. To extend my earlier quotation: "The Devil . . . is difficult for us today to take seriously. But in the sixteenth century, when all the forces of organised religion had been deployed for centuries in formulating the notion of a personal Satan, he had a reality and immediacy which could not fail to grip the strongest mind" (p. 470).

The problem posed by the demonic is not simply one of methodology; it rests on epistemology. How can we speak of the devil? The source of the dilemma is unwittingly suggested in Burckhardt's formulation of the developmental teleology. "In Italy this veil [of faith and illusion] first melted into air; an *objective* treatment and consideration of the State and of all the things of this world became possible." "Melted into air" can be understood as a little poetic flourish, or a flash of purple prose. The choice of metaphor is telling, however. What is being contrasted here is not just faith and reason, but different properties of the environment, different understandings of space and physics. In the medieval and Renaissance periods, in an age that allowed for and even privileged a demonic environmental economy, it was indeed possible for objects to "melt into air." (Whither have the witches vanished? asks Banquo. Responds Macbeth: "Into the air, and what seemed corporal/Melted as breath into the wind" [1.3.79–80].) The physical properties of early modern materiality and corporality differed from the properties of Burckhardt's modern vision of "all the things of this world." An early modern object could melt in a way that a modern one could not. Early modern physics – the dynamics of objects and the construction of space-time – differed from ours. That is to say – and this is all that really matters – the early modern perception and comprehension of physics differed from our own perception and comprehension of physics (which, in turn, already differ from that of Burckhardt's day). This difference is critical to understanding the environmental consciousness of people living in sixteenth- and seventeenth-century England.

This disjunction of the physical realities of different time periods thus leads us to replay a familiar scene from the Elizabethan stage. In Shakespeare's *A Midsummer Night's Dream*, the magical world of the woods is at odds with the rational world of Athens. As intellectuals, our response to tales of the supernatural and demonic encounters has been that of Duke Theseus, who assures his new bride that:

> ... I never may believe
> These antique fables, nor these fairy toys.
> Lovers and madmen have such seething brains,
> Such shaping fantasies, that apprehend
> More than cool reason ever comprehends.
> The lunatic, the lover, and the poet
> Are of imagination all compact.
> One sees more devils than vast hell can hold:
> That is the madman ...
> The poet's eye, in a fine frenzy rolling,
> Doth glance from heaven to earth, from earth to heaven,
> And as imagination bodies forth
> The forms of things unknown, the poet's pen
> Turns them to shapes, and gives to airy nothing
> A local habitation and a name.                    (5.1.2–17)

Perhaps in order to legitimate the study of English literature, a field which has had to defend itself for a century against the seemingly more practical, "hard" claims of science and business, we have become Theseus, a disbeliever in the midst of enchantment. While cool reason might allow for safer conversation with our Athenian colleagues (and administrators), it positions us, rather ironically, as adversarial to imagination, magic, and the supernatural. Witness Theseus's response to Hippolyta's recollection of a far-off time and mythic company:

> HIPPOLYTA: I was with Hercules and Cadmus once
> When in a wood of Crete they bayed the bear
> With hounds of Sparta. Never did I hear
> Such gallant chiding; for besides the groves,
> The skies, the fountains, every region near
> Seemed all one mutual cry. I never heard
> So musical a discord, such sweet thunder.
> THESEUS: My hounds are bred out of the Spartan kind,
> So flewed, so sanded; and their heads are hung
> With ears that sweep away the morning dew,
> Crooked-kneed, and dewlapped like Thessalian bulls,
> Slow in pursuit, but matched in mouth like bells,
> Each under each. (4.1.109–21)

To Hippolyta's poetic rendering of a memory from her fantastic past, Theseus responds with a physical description of his dogs. His speech is poetic, but it is, nonetheless, a factual, itemized, even thick description of his dogs. This exchange can serve as a synecdoche of the couple's relationship as a whole, as Theseus transports Hippolyta from a deep tradition of mythology and narrative into the Athenian milieu of reason and empiricism. This is the act of transportation that recurs in modern scholarship when we confront early modern fancies and "shaping fantasies" – Rogers's vision of devils becomes a fact in the service of post-Reformation history, just as Hippolyta is used as a means of discussing the social context of Elizabethan gender dynamics. Such moves sacrifice the work of "imagination bod[ying] forth" to sociological analysis, and leave little room or direction for studying the *experience* of magic and belief.

## ANTIQUE FABLES

One consequence of this historical orientation has been an undue focus on historical skeptics and disbelievers, those whom we perceive as emerging modern voices. In particular, we have appreciated those who exhibit a healthy skepticism toward the devil; we are more at home, for example, with Reginald Scot's *Discoverie of Witchcraft* than with King James's *Daemonology* (since, as Katharine Eisaman Maus observes, "to us the skeptics look obviously right and the witch-hunters are hard to take seriously"[16]). Our propensity to gravitate towards the disbelieving Scot as a spokesman for sixteenth-century attitudes on witchcraft is symptomatic of our desire to find kindred spirits within the period. This desire has caused us to overlook the fact that in his own day Scot's views would have been considered more radical than rational; as Stuart Clark has discussed, the vast majority of sixteenth- and seventeenth-century writing on witchcraft eschewed extravagant positions of excessive belief or disbelief, espousing a middle ground between these positions.[17]

The predilection to view Scot as a voice of reason finds a counterpart in our tendency to locate fellow skeptics among early modern playwrights. One critic confidently proclaims (with no supporting evidence whatsoever) that: "We can surmise with almost complete certainty that Marlowe's attitude towards witchcraft would have been much the same as Scot's."[18] Like Marlowe, Shakespeare has also been perceived as reassuringly modern on account of his apparent disinterest in the devil. John D. Cox has considered the evolution of our understanding of Shakespeare as a skeptic, arguing that the historical narrative put forth by E. K. Chambers in *The Medieval Stage* (1903) continues to shape the critical approach to stage devils. In Cox's analysis, Chambers constructed a "scheme that interpreted stage devils in a narrative of teleological secularization."[19] According to this scheme, stage devils were a feature of "the religious superstructure that drama eventually outgrew" as it made its "gradual evolution toward its brilliant secular flowering in the work of Shakespeare" (p. 2). Shakespeare's canon contains only two stage devils, both in the early *Henry VI* plays, but as Cox shows devils appeared in no less than forty-one plays staged between *Faustus* and 1642 (pp. 210–11). Shakespeare, in other words, was not the death of the devil.

Cox's account of Chambers's continuing influence might be overstated,[20] but in some ways Chambers's scholarly response to devils is not so different from ours a century later. In *The Elizabethan Stage*, Chambers sets out to create a comprehensive archive of documents pertaining to the Elizabethan theater.[21] His efforts mark a rejection of Romantic approaches to literary study, largely reliant upon subjective character analysis, in favor of a more historical approach. But inevitably, given the time in which the documents were produced, the archive contains traces of the supernatural that, for Chambers, sit uncomfortably with other forms of historical records. While Chambers dutifully includes these documents, he cordons them off, segregating them from texts that he considers to have more legitimacy. He notes, for example, how Marlowe's *Doctor Faustus* "became the centre of a curious *mythos*, which was used to point a moral against the stage."[22] This *mythos*, as students of the period well know, is that during the performance of *Doctor Faustus* actual devils were wont to appear on stage.[23]

Chambers cites as an example of this phenomenon:

N.D. "J.G.R." from manuscript note on "the last page of a book in my possession, printed by Vautrollier" (1850, 2 *Gent. Mag.* xxxiv. 234), "Certaine Players at Exeter, acting upon the stage the tragical storie of Dr. Faustus the Conjurer; as a certaine nomber of Devels kept everie one his circle there, and as Faustus was busie in his magicall invocations, on a sudden they were all dasht, every one harkning other in the eare, for they were all perswaded, there was one devell too many amongst them; and so after a little pause desired the people to pardon them, they could go no further with this matter; the people also understanding the thing as it was, every man hastened to be first out of dores." (3: 424)

Exeter was not the only place that experienced theatrical demons. Chambers also notes William Prynne's account in the anti-theatrical compendium *Histriomastix* of:

The visible apparition of the Devill on the stage at the Belsavage Play-house, in Queen Elizabeths dayes (to the great amazement both of the actors and spectators) while they were there prophanely playing the History of Faustus (the truth of which I have heard from many now alive, who well remember it) there being some distracted with that feareful sight (f. 556). (3: 423–4)

Chambers's framing of these accounts as a "curious *mythos*" categorically relegates them to the world of fantasy, the quaint relics of an immature age. "Curious" not only gestures towards the bizarre, but towards the curioso, or the curiosity; "*mythos*" designates them as antiquated and untrue. Appearing after the serious, scholarly matter of dating all of the extant editions of the play, these accounts are presented as merely an amusing little something for the collector to put in his *Wunderkammer* of theatrical oddities. These are not, Chambers would have us believe, documents that have a practical function or that deserve serious analytical scrutiny.

In labeling the on-stage appearance of *Faustus*'s demons a myth "used to point a moral against the stage," Chambers offers his own pragmatic explanation for the accounts, suggesting that they were circulated as anti-theatrical propaganda. No doubt William Prynne took a certain amount of glee in deploying a story which provided proof of the theater's status as the devil's playground. Maybe Prynne even made the story up: although he claims to be able to produce witnesses that remember the event from Elizabethan days, he offers no supporting evidence. Or maybe the old people who claim to remember seeing the devils are themselves spinning old wives' tales, or have memories fogged with time. But what Prynne's account does indicate is that the possibility of devils on the stage was a real one for him, and a real one for his audience; even if the account is a form of propaganda, it would only work as such if it were believed to be true. This was a matter in which "the people ... [understood] the thing as it was": the real incursion of demonic agents into the daily space and time of their lives. We could, of course, offer theories of mass hallucination to justify the tales of *Faustus*'s devils, but such explanations would need to willfully, perhaps condescendingly, explain away contemporary claims of the "truth" of this experience. Prynne's account, whatever its motivation, is signaled as a real event, with witnesses still testifying to its veracity.

Literary scholars have followed Chambers's lead in relegating these stories to the realm of anecdote rather than archive, even though they appear in the same type of document that we trust for other types of theater history. While the "myth" of *Faustus*'s on-stage devils is widely known, it seems only to be deployed for the purposes of seasoning an undergraduate lecture or adding a little zest to a scholarly essay.[24] It has not, to the best of my knowledge, been the subject of any sustained, pointed inquiry. But the degree to which our own culture is dismissive of the possibility of devils on stage is countered by the degree to which early modern people took such events seriously. Although the accounts are brief, they indicate an acceptance of real demonic presence that spanned the divide between actor and audience, theater-goer and anti-theatrical polemicist, Elizabethan and Carolinian.

If our own position of disbelief (at least vis-à-vis the devil) can be an intellectual asset, allowing for greater objectivity, it can thus also be a liability, leading us to dismiss as a valid field of inquiry that which we consider "illusion" (in Burckhardt's term). Not that the devil has been entirely off limits, but we have tended to view him only anamorphically, most often through studies of witchcraft. As the subject of sociological investigation, witches are used as a means of analyzing complex communal structures and relationships.[25] As a locus of feminist analysis, the testimonies of early modern women claiming allegiance with the devil are read – however sympathetically – through a diagnostic lens that reveals responses to the strictures of patriarchy.[26] In the interest of cultural critique, the devil is generally explained away, rationalized, sanitized.

Even if we do want to confront the devil directly, to "understand the thing as it was," it is difficult to analyze the supernatural in a manner that adheres to familiar evidentiary protocols. The devil's archive slides between the mundane and the fantastic. Take, for instance, a type of document that appears regularly in witchcraft trials: the demonic contract. This paper or parchment, containing a signed agreement between an individual and Satan, was frequently used as legal evidence, its terms, both then and now, subject to scrutiny by legal scholars.[27] But analysis of the bond's content can lose sight of the extraordinary nature of the object itself, which could move freely between hell and earth, and which sometimes had to be retrieved from the beyond. These types of documents are the closest thing we have to a text written in the devil's hand, and their material properties are a constitutive element of their reception. This materiality offers us a mode of analyzing sixteenth- and seventeenth-century demonic belief that circumvents illusion and fantasy. It gives us something to hold on to as we engage a world in which the supernatural was not the irrational. These contracts also serve as tracers which allow us to follow their movement, and which thus enable us to reconstruct, however provisionally and locally, the contours of an environment in which metamorphosis, rather than "laws," defined the properties of matter and the space in which it moved.

## THAT IS THE MADMAN

Today we pathologize the devil. Thus Duke Theseus's definition of "One sees more devils than vast hell can hold: That is the madman" might easily apply to John Rogers. In this view, the devil is not merely an illusion, but a delusion, a phantom that appears only to the mentally ill. Sigmund Freud provides an explanation for the devils seen in earlier centuries: "the demons are bad and reprehensible wishes, derivatives of instinctual impulses that have been repudiated and repressed."[28] The demons that today are internalized, so the reasoning goes, were once projected into the external world. More generally, as Freud would have it, religion itself is a neurosis, a cultural response to a primordial guilt over killing the father. Freudian psychoanalytical thought, based upon an empiricism and a reality-principle that for Freud was inherently atheistic, leaves little room for the discussion of religious belief other than in a diagnostic mode. (And it is worth noting that Freud, too, positions belief in the devil as part of a larger teleological and historical paradigm of human development; in a discussion about the devil, Freud likens "neurotic illnesses in earlier centuries" to the "neuroses of childhood."[29]) It is thus with no small degree of surprise that we meet Freud immersing himself in the study of archival demonic contracts. In his essay "A Seventeenth-Century Demonological Neurosis," he offers us an unexpected methodological model for analyzing the devil as a real presence.

The essay opens, as usual, with a case history. The patient is Christoph Haizmann, a seventeenth-century Bavarian painter. Haizmann, it appears, had the rather ill-advised habit of entering into pacts with the devil. This tendency first came to light in 1677, when Haizmann experienced convulsions while visiting a church. Suspicious local officials began to inquire if he had by any chance held intercourse with Satan, and a repentant Haizmann soon confessed that he had, alas, signed a pact with the devil, a bond which was due in just a few short weeks. Through the benevolence of a village priest, Haizmann was taken to the shrine at Mariazell, where it was hoped that the Blessed Virgin would intervene and recover the bond, a document which happened to be written in blood. At Mariazell, Haizmann underwent an intense period of penance and soon encountered the devil himself, who, in the shape of a dragon, returned the bond. The attending clerics themselves did not see the demon; Haizmann simply ran from the priests to a corner where he perceived the devil and then returned, miraculously, with the fateful document in hand. After this encounter a happy and healthy Haizmann departed to live with his sister in Vienna, but was soon beset by more demonic seizures. He suddenly recalled that there had in fact been a *second* devilish bond, this one written in ink; he returned to Mariazell where another undisclosed miracle retrieved this paper as well. Free at last, Haizmann entered the Order of the Brothers Hospitallers, resisted the devil's subsequent bargaining attempts (which took place only after Haizmann had indulged in too much wine), and died uneventfully in 1700.

To the student of early modern history, Haizmann's narrative will appear ordinary enough: these things happen. In Freud's own account of this incident, however, we find an extraordinary departure from his usual mode of analysis. Freud is brought on the case by the director of the former imperial Viennese record office who discovered the manuscript in his library's holdings (and who was intrigued by the similarities with the story of Faust).[30] Given Haizmann's frequent seizures and convulsions, Freud is asked simply to provide his medical opinion. The title of this curious essay, "A Seventeenth-Century Demonological Neurosis," indicates Freud's ultimate diagnostic resolution. But the final diagnosis doesn't begin to contain, or even really address, the evidentiary issues the essay raises. Within the essay, Freud almost immediately casts aside his role as medical consultant and assumes the pose of textual scholar. He is clearly basking in the opportunity to delve into such historical documents, and begins with a lengthy and detailed description of the manuscript, "an exact copy of which lies before [him]" as we are told from the onset (p. 73). Unlike his other case notes, this report is full of bibliographic and paleographic detail.

Freud rather quickly analyzes Haizmann's case and arrives at the pedestrian diagnosis that the devil is a father figure. His obvious fascination with the case does not revolve around the workings of neuroses, but rather the evidentiary questions raised by this archive. He enters into an extended and intricate attempt to date the two bonds, the one written in blood (let's say the A-text) and the other in ink (the B-text). As we slowly learn, these incredible documents – alleged to have been to hell and back – were no longer contained with the manuscript, so Freud could only work with transcriptions. He detects chronological inconsistencies in the supposed relationship of the A-text to the B-text, and spends nearly a chapter trying to reconcile them: like the original compiler, whom he describes as "between two fires" (p. 97n), Freud enters into an editorial hell. Finally (after five full pages of such analysis in the Standard Edition), he emerges to conclude that the B-text (the bond written in ink) was invented by Haizmann at a later date; he does not question the date of the A-text (the bond written in blood). Freud's conclusion that the bonds were fraudulent – that they were written by Haizmann in an effort to deceive the clerics – is a startling one, not because we are shocked to discover that the documents were of mundane origin, but because it becomes apparent in retrospect that an alternative outcome to Freud's line of inquiry might have been to confirm an infernal origin (for why else would he spend so much time disproving a demonic occurrence?). Given the seriousness with which Freud analyzes Haizmann's documents – bonds which have allegedly been in traffic with Satan, after all – we might for an instant forget that we are dealing with an author who is an avowed atheist.

Freud is particularly impressed by the factual – one might even say clinical – nature of the documents. We are surprised to find him treating these documents as the historical record of real, actual events. After Haizmann's first encounter with the dragon-devil, Freud interjects an editorial paragraph on the reliability of the evidence. "At this point a doubt as to the credibility of the clerical reporters may well arise in our minds and warn us not to waste our labours on a product of monastic superstition ... But the Abbot Franciscus's testimony dispels this doubt. Far from asserting that the assisting clerics saw the Devil too, he only states in straightforward and sober words" that Haizmann rushed to the corner alone (p. 77). Throughout, the priestly scribes and witnesses are praised for their candor in disclosing the facts of the case. Where they might have produced a medieval hagiography, the priests are frank even about such uncomfortable details as Haizmann's post-miracle relapse. Freud's admiration is reiterated: "It is once more to the credit of the clergy that they have not concealed this" (p. 77), he writes, and "[w]e have occasion yet again to acknowledge that in spite of the obvious purpose of his efforts, the compiler has not been tempted into departing from the veracity required of a case history" (p. 78). Freud's emphasis here on the "sober" reporters resisting "temptation" counterbalances Haizmann's own drunkenness and problematic susceptibility to the Tempter. Moreover, the compiler's "veracity" is not just a sign of moral integrity, but a token of professional ethics. Defending himself (and psychoanalytic practice more generally) from popular objections that a case might be distorted by the importation of connections which "do not in fact exist," but are merely a product of "uncalled-for ingenuity" (p. 84), Freud writes: "I will not preface my reply with the words, 'to be honest' or 'to be candid', for one must always be able to be these things without any special preliminaries" (p. 84). Analyst and cleric alike thus adhere to a similar code of evidentiary protocol. The document, in Freud's hands, is neither a piece of clerical propaganda nor religious fantasy, but a credible account suitable for further scientific analysis: "We can see that what we are dealing with really is a case history" (p. 80). Freud and the priests thus become unlikely colleagues.

We soon encounter another character: the hypothesized intelligent skeptic. Throughout his writings, especially in early works like the *Introductory Lectures to Psychoanalysis*, Freud frequently ventriloquizes a member of his audience who raises legitimate and sensible objections to psychoanalytic methods and assertions. This time, however, Freud's skeptic is one of the converted, we might even say one of us: "Now I am writing for readers who, although they believe in psycho-analysis, do not believe in the Devil" (p. 98). This skeptic protests that it is "absurd for [Freud] to bring such an accusation against the poor wretch ... For ... the bond in blood was just as much a product of [Haizmann's] phantasy as the allegedly earlier one in ink. In reality, no Devil appeared to him at all, and the whole business of pacts with the Devil only existed in his imagination" (p. 98). Efforts to date the manuscripts, in this view, are immaterial, since the documents are merely the manifestation of Haizmann's pathology. The skeptic suggests that to pursue this inquiry further, and with the strange fervor Freud brings to the task, is at best strangely misguided, at worst further persecution of a suffering neurotic.

Freud's own voice quickly returns to admit: "I quite realize this" (p. 65). His next sentence, however, begins with a significant "but":

But here, too, the matter goes further. After all, the two bonds were not phantasies like the visions of the Devil. They were documents, preserved, according to the assurances of the copyist and the deposition of the later Abbot Kilian, in the archives of Mariazell, for all to see and touch. We are therefore in a dilemma. Either we must assume that both the papers which were supposed to have been given back to the painter through divine Grace were written by him at the time when he needed them; or else, despite all the solemn assurances, the confirmatory evidence of witnesses, signed and sealed, and so on, we shall be obliged to deny the credibility of the reverend Fathers of Mariazell and St. Lambert. I must admit that I am unwilling to cast doubts on the Fathers ... [who] have established a good claim to our confidence. (pp. 98–9)

In other words, the textual discrepancies and corruptions of the two bonds force us to choose: either we must believe that Haizmann concocted and exploited sham demonic documentation, or else we must suspect the clerics of producing a fraudulent archival narrative. Contrary to the views of his hypothesized reader, Freud is not immediately willing to synthesize the "fact" of the bonds' existence with the "fact" of Haizmann's neurosis; he resists the obvious possibility that Haizmann suffered from a neurosis and, as a product of this neurosis, fabricated his own demonic documentation. Instead, Freud refuses to view the evidence as symptomatic, and insists on a dichotomous construction of truth, a "dilemma" that must be logically resolved: either Haizmann is a sort of confidence man, or we must lose confidence in our fellow scholars. Freud opts for the former, accusing Haizmann of willful forgery. While this move preserves the professional integrity of a band of clerics with whom Freud has allied himself, it threatens to undermine the neurotic motivations for Haizmann's physical ailments. Perhaps the impoverished Haizmann did not suffer from a neurosis at all, but was merely some sort of picaresque trickster (producing fraudulent documents in order to receive free room and board at Mariazell).

As Freud constructs the case, then, the accusations of fraud seem to negate the operation of neurosis. After discrediting the authenticity of the bonds, Freud can only recoup a neurosis by turning his attention to another piece of the archive, Haizmann's diary, and here again the essay seems to present Satan as a plausible character. While the demonic bonds were fabricated, the diary, Freud assures us, "bears the stamp of veracity" (p. 100). Here, then, is Haizmann's veritable experience as expressed in the diary: "He saw himself in bright flames and sank down in a swoon. Attempts were made to rouse him but he rolled about in the room till blood flowed from his mouth and nose. He felt that he was surrounded by heat and noisome smells, and he heard a voice say that he had been condemned to this state as a punishment for his vain and idle thoughts. Later he was scourged with ropes by Evil Spirits . . ." (p. 102). Insisting on the document's "veracity" – a charged term throughout the essay – Freud considers this text within the evidentiary protocols he had previously discussed, "the veracity required of a case history" (p. 78).

But what is the truth that Haizmann records? Is the diary truthful in its depiction of neurotic hallucinations? Or is it truthful in its relation of Haizmann's physical experience? It is clear that Haizmann and those around him believed in the reality of the devil. But the distinction between Haizmann's truth and Freud's truth is strangely blurred. The vexed status of "veracity" in this essay emanates from Freud's peculiar treatment of the evidence. In part, it is the material presence and form of these texts – the compiler's manuscript of testimonials, Haizmann's own diary – that present a crucial component of the analytical procedure. Even the bonds with the devil, which Freud considers with surprising earnestness, are significant because they exist, or at one time presumably existed, in a material form: "After all, the two bonds were not phantasies like the visions of the Devil. They were documents, preserved . . . in the archives of Mariazell, for all to see and touch." So convinced is Freud of the one-time existence of these documents that he does not even comment on the fact that the demonic bonds alone have disappeared from the otherwise intact archive he holds before him, so that he can only work with an "exact copy" (and how can one verify the accuracy?).

Despite their ghostly absence, the bonds have an emphatic material presence. This materiality raises intriguing procedural questions for the postmodern historian reading early modern documentation. In Freud's account it is not merely the materiality of the bonds which is at stake, but the materiality of the devil himself. Interestingly, Freud, who elsewhere distances himself from a belief in the supernatural, here never questions, mocks, or devalues the clerics' belief in the devil as a real and present agent in human affairs; to the contrary, Freud repeatedly expresses his greatest esteem for the priestly reporters and praises their accuracy in recording their experience. Likewise, Freud applauds the veracity of Haizmann's diary even after he has declared the bonds fraudulent. That the devil is an experiential part of life for the people of late seventeenth-century Vienna appears to stand as fact. While Haizmann's particular demonic experiences are provided neurotic origins in the final paragraphs of the essay, the devil's prominence in the social experience remains unrefuted.

This case complicates what Peter Gay has referred to as Freud's "stark vista of a historic confrontation in which educated atheists were pitted against unlettered believers."[31] Here the confrontation is presented in terms of two groups of educated believers: the honest clerical scribes and the savvy Viennese intelligentsia. Freud's willingness to defend the former before the almost scoffing dismissal of the latter does not, of course, indicate a latent belief in the devil. Rather, Freud is playing, as it were, devil's advocate. Freud's mode of archival analysis confronts these documents on their own material terms, and in the process accepts an episteme in which eschatological figures interact with worldly individuals. In other words, Freud appears sensitive to the complex dynamic of applying, shall we say, Freudian modes of thought to a society in which it was normal to meet the supernatural. For the priests of Mariazell, as for most sixteenth- and seventeenth-century Europeans, encounters with the devil, if not frequent, were real enough: these things *happened*. What I think Freud wishes to accomplish in this bizarre case is the recognition of the historical truth that at one time, and for a long time, the devil was perceived as a material presence, one who even participated in the cultural production of text. This reality must be seriously acknowledged and confronted by the modern (or postmodern) thinker whose own reality is primarily informed by a post-Enlightenment rationalistic and scientific skepticism, and whose perception of the supernatural has been transposed into an understanding of the psychological.

By privileging the fact that the documents *exist*, that they are there in the archive "for all to see and touch," Freud seems to be feeling his way towards the precepts of historical phenomenology. In such a methodology, as Bruce Smith states, "[t]exts not only represent bodily experience; they imply it in the ways they ask to be touched, seen, heard, even smelled and tasted."[32] The material artifacts of human experience are not only its record, but its constitutive elements. They provide a means of reconstructing subjective experience – of tracing the subject's movement through, perception of, and engagement with the world. The demonic contract is a particularly salient text for this purpose, since it not only serves to document an abstract agreement, but is in and of itself the mediator between Satan and the self, the material trace of the interaction between devil and human, the form through which this encounter takes place.

And yet the demonic contract also takes us to the edges of phenomenology. The demonic contract might reek, for example, of brimstone; it was a document that could be stored on earth or archived in hell. It might melt into – or out of – air. Our own experience of the everyday doesn't prepare us for analyzing a document that has an infernal provenance. Our experience with material texts hasn't led us to question the laws of physics. But the demonic contract, in its material form, raises the question: how do we historicize matter itself? Or, to ask it otherwise: how do we study the historical experience of phenomena when past ontological understandings differ so significantly from our own? How do we overcome our Newtonian sensibility, which favors the assumption that matter adheres to immutable laws within a mathematical space, an understanding that is so innate we don't even recognize it as a prejudice?

### TURNING SHAPES

Both as a play and as a character, Faustus revolves around the vicissitudes of material text. *Doctor Faustus*, or, more properly speaking, the *Doctor Fausti*, have bedeviled scholars for years, as the A- and B-texts have romped through the centuries, wrestling for supremacy, alternately finding themselves crowned with legitimacy and spurned as bastards. The debate over the authenticity of these playtexts remains ongoing, as it is often more about changing scholarly attitudes towards the theater, authorship, and materiality than it is about the texts themselves. But these are not, per se, the two texts I have in mind. For within *Doctor Faustus* we find a sort of embedded demonic archive in the form of the two bonds Faustus writes up committing himself to the devil. (Shall we say the $A^1$-text and the $B^1$-text?)

As in the case with Christoph Haizmann, the contracts (especially the first) are emphatically, even hyperbolically material. Faustus initially seems to think that an oral gentleman's agreement will suffice to sell his soul to the devil, but Mephistopheles is determined to procure a written bond for his master.

| FAUSTUS: | . . . Now tell me what saith Lucifer thy lord? |
|---|---|
| MEPHISTOPHELES: | That I shall wait on Faustus whilst he lives, |
| | So he will buy my service with his soul. |
| FAUSTUS: | Already Faustus hath hazarded that for thee. |
| MEPHISTOPHELES: | But now thou must bequeath it solemnly |
| | And write a deed of gift with thine own blood, |
| | For that security craves Lucifer. |
| | . . . |
| | Then, Faustus, stab thy arm courageously, |
| | And bind thy soul that at some certain day |
| | Great Lucifer may claim it as his own, |
| | And then be thou as great as Lucifer. |
| FAUSTUS [*cutting his arm*]: | Lo, Mephistopheles, for love of thee |
| | Faustus hath cut his arm, and with his proper blood |
| | Assures his soul to be great Lucifer's, |
| | Chief lord and regent of perpetual night. |
| | View here this blood that trickles from mine arm, |
| | And let it be propitious for my wish. |
| MEPHISTOPHELES: | But Faustus, |
| | Write it in a manner of a deed of gift. |
| FAUSTUS: | Ay, so I do. [*He writes.*] But Mephistopheles, |
| | My blood congeals, and I can write no more. |
| MEPHISTOPHELES: | I'll fetch thee fire to dissolve it straight. |
| | . . . |
| | See, Faustus, here is fire. Set it on. |
| FAUSTUS: | So. Now the blood begins to clear again. |
| | Now will I make an end immediately. |
| | [*He writes.*] |
| | . . . |
| | *Consummatum est.* The bill is ended, |
| | And Faustus hath bequeathed his soul to Lucifer.[33] |

I include this passage at length to demonstrate the overdetermined materiality of the demonic bond. From Faustus's perspective, the act of cutting his arm, and the blood which trickles from his wound, is testament enough of his oath, as if he is engaging in a ritual of blood brotherhood. But for Mephistopheles, the blood is ink; he adamantly requires a written document, claiming that the piece of paper is necessary for Lucifer to have the "assurance" and "security" he needs to trust in the arrangement.

The mechanics of writing are highlighted throughout this scene, and it becomes artificially protracted, emphasizing the production of the text and its material form. Faustus's declaration of "*Consummatum est.*

The bill is ended,/And Faustus hath bequeathed his soul to Lucifer"
would seem to draw the moment to a close, and indeed we soon find
ourselves watching a dumb show of devils, giving clothes and crowns to
Faustus and then performing a little dance. After this interlude we
might expect the dramatic action to move on, but we discover that this
was only a break in the contract-signing scene, and we return to the
issue of the bond:

| | |
|---|---|
| FAUSTUS: | Then Mephistopheles, receive this scroll, |
| | A deed of gift of body and of soul – |
| | But yet conditionally that thou perform |
| | All covenants and articles between us both. |
| MEPHISTOPHELES: | Faustus, I swear by hell and Lucifer |
| | To effect all promises between us both. |
| FAUSTUS: | Then hear me read it, Mephistopheles. |
| | "On these conditions following: |
| | First, that Faustus may be a spirit in form and substance. |
| | Secondly, that Mephistopheles shall be his servant, and be by him commanded. |
| | Thirdly, that Mephistopheles shall do for him and bring him whatsoever. |
| | Fourthly, that he shall be in his chamber or house invisible. |
| | Lastly, that he shall appear to the said John Faustus at all times what shape and form soever he please. |
| | I, John Faustus of Wittenberg, Doctor, by these presents, do give both body and soul to Lucifer, Prince of the East, and his minister Mephistopheles; and furthermore grant unto them that four-and-twenty years being expired, and these articles above written being inviolate, full power to fetch or carry the said John Faustus, body and soul, flesh, blood, into their habitation wheresoever. By me, John Faustus." |
| MEPHISTOPHELES: | Speak, Faustus. Do you deliver this as your deed? |
| FAUSTUS [*giving the deed*]: | Ay. Take it, and the devil give thee good of it. |

(2.1.88–113)

Once again we seem to arrive at a moment of closure when Faustus
proclaims "receive this scroll," and yet he still goes on to read the
document in its entirety. The bond contains little, if anything, that the
audience doesn't already know; the purpose of reading the contract
(probably with a large scroll as a stage prop) is to underscore its material
presence. The document functions, of course, both as the inscription of an

abstract contract and as the material record of a transaction between Faustus and the devil, but at this moment the bond's evidentiary qualities take precedence. Here, form trumps content, as the play insistently draws our attention to the document's materiality.

The scroll creates a disconcerting juxtaposition of the mundane and the supernatural, but perhaps even more powerfully it creates a paper trail – not as a record of past events, but as something that we can trace (or not) moving through different cosmic spheres. As a familiar object moving between earth and hell, the scroll invites all sorts of speculation: How will it get there? Will it have the same appearance in hell? Where will it go once it gets there? Does Satan have a secretary?

Some of these issues seem to be on Faustus's mind, too, for his first question after delivering up the contract is: "Tell me, where is the place that men call hell?" (2.1.116). The subsequent discussion about infernal geographies is not incidental or a non sequitur to the lengthy bond-writing, but an extension of the scene, describing the space into which the bond will be transported. Mephistopheles's answer for the location of hell at first seems evasive, as he responds that hell lies:

> Within the bowels of these elements,
> Where we are tortured and remain for ever.
> Hell hath no limits, nor is circumscribed
> In one self place, but where we are is hell,
> And where hell is there must we ever be.
> And, to be short, when all the world dissolves,
> And every creature shall be purified,
> All places shall be hell that is not heaven. (2.1.119–26)

Mephistopheles's description wanders from identifying a specific location, to paradoxically proclaiming that hell is limitless, to asserting that it is more of a state of mind, to positioning it within a language of essential elements and alchemical purification. The answer presents not so much a list of options as an interconnected set of conditions, in which space and mind and physics are mutually constitutive and dependent. It vascillates between the multiplicitous logic of analogy and the rigors of binarism. It layers forms of belief.

Faustus himself embodies this layering. To Mephistopheles's account of hell, Faustus bluntly proclaims: "I think hell's a fable" (2.1.127). The comment, in a conversation with Mephistopheles, carries obvious ironies. Faustus's smirking denial of hell's existence continues even in a dialogue with hell's ambassador:

| | |
|---|---|
| MEPHISTOPHELES: | Ay, think so still, till experience change thy mind. |
| FAUSTUS: | Why, dost thou think that Faustus shall be damned? |
| MEPHISTOPHELES: | Ay, of necessity, for here's the scroll |
| | In which thou hast given thy soul to Lucifer. |
| FAUSTUS: | Ay, and body too. But what of that? |
| | Think'st thou that Faustus is so fond to imagine |
| | That after this life there is any pain? |
| | No, these are trifles and mere old wives' tales.[34] |

(2.1.128–35)

Taken off the stage, Faustus's skepticism may seem (to us) a familiar, comforting rationalism. But within the context of the play, his refutation of hell is clearly irrational. What is so strange about this moment is that Faustus becomes Freud and Haizmann at once. Faustus maintains a detached cynicism about the existence of hell even as he has personally signed a demonic contract and conversed with devils. Like many modern historians, he fictionalizes evidence of the demonic;[35] proof of hell, he contends, comes only from narrative, and the lowest kind at that – "fables," "trifles," "old wives' tales." But Mephistopheles counters this accusation by brandishing the bond that Faustus himself has just written (and which we, the audience, witnessed). Mephistopheles's argument might border on the tautological, except that it is not so much the content of the bond as its form which matters. Mephistopheles emphasizes the material text ("for here's the scroll") as its own form of evidence; it has already become archive.

When he declares hell a fiction, Faustus finds himself in company with the reformer William Tyndale, who, as Stephen Greenblatt has discussed, declared purgatory to be "a poet's fable."[36] In his study of purgatory, Greenblatt opens up avenues for exploring how an early modern poetic sensibility directed perceptions of eschatology. Greenblatt asks, "what if we take seriously the charge that Purgatory was a vast piece of poetry?"[37] In other words, what if we push on the metaphors that pervade sixteenth-century eschatological discourse until we arrive at the extreme position that the entire purgatorial ideology was itself a poetic construction? This is the path that Faustus seems to have taken in his own contemplation of hell (at least at this point in the play – he later has a desperate change of heart, prompting the composition of the second bond). Faustus's skepticism is part of what makes him familiar – part of what identifies him as a Renaissance man in a play so indebted to medieval dramatic forms. But if his disbelief locates him closer to us (Freud's idealized audience of those who "do not believe in the devil"), it estranges him from many, probably even most, of his contemporaries. As Smith notes, inhabitants of six-teenth- and seventeenth-century England would have been more likely "to see material reality where our own preconceptions prompt us to see only metaphor."[38]

We have been prompted to see only metaphor, for example, in studies of early modern appropriations of Ovid. Jonathan Bate contends that the Elizabethan understanding of Ovidian metamorphosis was "psycho-logical and metaphorical instead of physical and literal"; it is a conten-tion with which Lynn Enterline seems to agree.[39] At first glance, *Doctor Faustus* hardly seems to be an Ovidian play. But references to the classical poet are threaded through *Doctor Faustus*: in the performance of the Seven Deadly Sins, Pride is "like to Ovid's flea" (2.3.108–9);[40] the opening Chorus likens Faustus to Icarus (20–1) and Faustus woos Helen by comparing her to the nymph Arethusa (5.1.111), both characters in *The Metamorphoses*;[41] Faustus "play[s] Diana" and puts horns on Benvolio, who had just declared that "[he'll] be Actaeon and turn [himself] into a stag" (4.1.101; 99–100). The reference to Acteon and Diana seems to bring us into the realm of Petrarchan poetics, where Ovid's tale does indeed establish a complex constellation of metaphoric relations. In *Faustus*, however, the emphasis is not on the fragmentation (literal and figurative) of the subject, but on the possibility of transformation, of metamorphosis.

The play transforms the metamorphic metaphor into a mode of phys-ical reality. In his musings on the advantage of demonic servants, Valdes assures his friends that:

> Like lions shall they guard us when we please,
> Like Almaine rutters with their horsemen's staves,
> Or Lapland giants, trotting by our sides;
> Sometimes like women, or unwedded maids ... (1.1.118–21)

We might at first hear similes, but as the play progresses it becomes clear that this "like" is not performing a metaphoric operation but a literal one. The last and seemingly most important item in Faustus's demonic contract is the ability to dictate Mephistopheles's form: "Lastly, that he shall appear to the said John Faustus at all times what shape and form soever he please." (Lucifer, in turn, promises Faustus that "thou shalt turn thyself into what shape thou wilt" [2.3.160].) The "pliant" (1.3.29) Mephistopheles soon transforms himself from a dragon to a friar at Faustus's command ("I charge thee to return and change thy shape" [1.3.23]), setting off a chain of transformations. The play becomes one of shape-shifting: Mephistopheles says to Dick, "Be thou turnèd to this ugly shape,/For apish deeds transformèd to an ape"; and to Robin, "Be thou transformed to a dog" (3.3.41–2, 45); Robin later recounts that "one of [Faustus's] devils turned me into the likeness of an ape's face" (4.5.50); Faustus and Mephistopheles take on the shapes of the cardinals (3.1.116–7); Benvolio proclaims, "an I be not revenged for this, would I might be turned to a gaping oyster and drink nothing but salt water" (4.1.163–4); a "horse is turned to a bottle of hay" (4.4.33); Wagner threatens the unfortunate Robin, "I'll turn all the lice about thee into familiars" (1.4.20) and promises "I'll teach thee to turn thyself to a god, or a cat, or a mouse, or a rat, or anything" (1.4.41–2).

Since the days of Eden, shape-changing has of course been one of the devil's greatest tricks, a central element of his modus operandi. But in *Faustus* this idea of metamorphosis, like the demonic contract, becomes overdetermined. (The heightened emphasis on bodily transformation is all the more striking given its performative limitations.) The idea of metamorphosis, I would argue, appears not in the service of poetics, but of physics; the endless allusions to transformation indicate a material world that is eminently plastic, one which is accepting of devils and the physics which allow them to travel through a flexible system of time and space. The play itself transforms the metamorphic metaphor into a mode of physical reality. Indeed, Faustus's initial fantasies of power are about changing the world – literally. He wants the ability to modify the cosmos ("Be it to make the moon drop from her sphere") and to reconfigure the planet ("Or the ocean to overwhelm the world") (1.3.35–6). He wants to reconfigure geopolitical spaces: "And make a bridge through the moving air/To pass the ocean; with a band of men/ I'll join the hills that bind the Afric shore/And make that country continent to Spain" (1.3.103–6). His quest for knowledge, perhaps in pursuit of these geographic ambitions, leads him "to prove cosmography" (Chorus, Act Three, 20). Thus "He views the clouds, the planets, and the stars,/The tropics, zones, and quarters of the sky,/From the bright circle of the hornèd moon/Even to the height of *Primum Mobile*" (Chorus, Act Three, 7–10).

Ultimately the universe is not, as Faustus would have it, pliant to his will, but absolute and unwavering. This realization comes crashing upon him as he meets his final hour. He commands, "Stand still, you ever-moving spheres of heaven" (5.2.135) only to admit, "The stars move still" (5.2.142). Again he makes demands and faces defeat.

> Mountains and hills, come, come and fall on me,
> And hide me from the heavy wrath of heaven!
> No? Then will I headlong run into the earth.
> Gape, earth! O, no, it will not harbour me.
> You stars that reigned at my nativity,
> Whose influence hath allotted death and hell,
> Now draw up Faustus like a foggy mist
> Into the entrails of yon labouring cloud,
> That when you vomit forth into the air,
> My limbs may issue from your smoky mouths.  (5.2.150–9)

His string of imperatives demand a plastic, molten environment, one in which mountains can move, the earth can open, and Faustus himself can be, as it were, melted into air and absorbed into a cloud. But all in vain. Having exhausted environmental options for transformation, he turns to himself: "Now, body, turn to air ... O soul, be changed into small waterdrops" (5.2.178, 180); but these commands are no more effective. Faustus's will has run headlong into "the secrets of astronomy," which, as the Chorus of Act Three tells us, are "Graven in the book of Jove's high firmament" (line 3).

We have, then, two visions of the universe. In one view, the world is mutable and metamorphic; in the other, it is immutable and static. It is both/either slippery and/or concrete. The tension between these two perspectives runs through the play. As we have seen, the abstract concept underlying a contract and the ancient metaphors of transformation both become emphatically real. The emphasis placed upon the two has a diametrically opposed effect, however. In highlighting the importance of the material form of the bond, we are presented with a physical absolute, or a physical object that confers truth because of its physical existence. The paper bears and constructs its own veracity, demanding that we treat it as real form (just as Freud approached the documents from Mariazell). This material constant is juxtaposed against a metamorphic environment. It is not just the devil who changes shape, and is therefore so cunning and devious. It is potentially anyone or anything surrounding Faustus. The bond seems to anchor time, space, and selves while the world of Faustus (until the very end) is shifting, transient, and physically instable.

Just before his death, Faustus seems to voice this tension between the mutable and immutable worlds when he frantically calls out, "O, Pythagoras' *metempsychosis*, were that true,/This soul should fly from me and I be changed/Into some brutish beast" (5.2.169–71). In this exclamation, physics meets metaphysics, geometry meets poetry. The specter of being changed into a brutish beast brings us back to Ovid and his Acteon. Once again, the myth is realized as Faustus is ripped limb from limb by the demons, his body scattered across the stage. Pythagoras's philosophy of metempsychosis, what we might call reincarnation, presents the entirety of human existence as a continual process of transformation, and eschatology as metamorphosis. Pythagoras himself claimed to have lived several lives in different forms, and was reputed to have recognized the soul of an old friend in the body of a dog.[42] (We are reminded of Wagner's promise of knowing how "to turn thyself to a god, or a cat, or a mouse, or a rat, or anything.") And yet, of course, Pythagoras was also a pre-eminent mathematician, providing theorems without which the world could not be measured. Or made: through its influence on Plato's *Timaeus*, which in turn influenced Christian humanism, Pythagorean geometry was at the heart of the Renaissance understanding of God. In his preface to Peter Ramus's *The Way of Geometry* (1636), William Bedwell wrote, "Plato saith, That God doth alwayes worke by Geometry."[43] A geometric God is one that works through reason and principles, creating order out of chaos. A geometric God is on his way to becoming an Enlightened God.

The invocation of Pythagoras is a culmination not only of tensions within the play, but of tensions within Marlowe's England. Pythagoras is a figure in whom God and the devil meet. He evokes a sense of divine reason and ordered beauty even as he evoked irrational thoughts of metempsychosis and an amorphous world. He serves as shorthand for a God working by geometry and a devil working by plasticity. In this, he perhaps serves as the forerunner of that other great icon of early modern ambivalence, Sir Isaac Newton, at once a founding father of our mathematical universe and a practitioner of alchemy, where belief in Ovidian physics was put into practice.

Today we are comfortable in a geometric universe, one in which space is measured and rational.[44] Inherent to this concept is a stability of objects, and thus a relative stability of bodily forms. People don't turn into stags; meat doesn't turn into maggots. Such was not entirely the case in early modern England. Recent studies of the early modern experience of the body have revealed a corporeality that is radically alien to our conception of physicality. In contrast to the modern tendency to distinguish between physical and mental states, the early modern reliance on humoral theory created a direct relationship between state of body and state of mind.[45] In contrast to our tendency to imagine a discrete entity of the body that moves through, but is not directly related to, its environment, humoral theory again allowed for, and even necessitated, a fluid relationship of body and world.[46] Even racial difference, that which to us seems most obviously genetically determined, was perceived as an environmental, humoral consequence.[47] To generalize, whereas our own understanding of the body – and by extension, of the self – is predicated on determined, static, and discrete boundaries, the early modern body as a self was understood to be constructed by a system, or an interconnected set of systems, that was fluid, dynamic, and fungible.

To take the devil seriously is to take this corporeality seriously – indeed, to acknowledge how even at a fundamental environmental level perceptions of the world are deeply historically contingent. We don't have the devil barging into our daily lives (or at least, many of us don't) because he does not fit into a world conceived in cubic, stable terms. But for those in the sixteenth and seventeenth centuries, the world had not yet congealed into its current shape. Thus demonic incursions, whether appearing through rocks, trees, as dragons, or as other people, were possible within the laws of physics – or rather, in a physical world that did not follow human laws. Perhaps the devil's demise (which Keith Thomas cannot link to technological innovation [pp. 657, 661]) was caused, like most modern extinctions, by a loss of habitat, as the world beyond systemic ways of knowing was gradually encroached upon and transformed by "development."

## TO AIRY NOTHING, A LOCAL HABITATION AND A NAME

While Ovid's poems certainly had a profound impact on the psychological and metaphoric life of many inhabitants of sixteenth- and seventeenth-century England, his writings may also have influenced an understanding of the physical and the literal. The fundamental trope of *The Metamorphoses* is one that reinforced – and arguably conditioned – cultural understandings about the acts of the devil and his minions. (It is important to note that early modern commentators often cite Ovid as a classical expert on witchcraft.[48]) Far from being incongruous with the concerns of *Doctor Faustus*, Ovid and the notion of metamorphosis enhance the play's portrayal of the devil and his world. Just as the devil's contract is emphatically material, so too the notion of transformation is decidedly physical: in *Doctor Faustus*, metamorphosis is not working in the service of poetics, but of physics. Indeed, *Doctor Faustus* operates according to what I call Ovidian physics, an understanding of the world in which matter and space are perceived as fluid and plastic.

Such a conception may seem to be the stuff of fantasy or antique "illusion." Stevie Simkin describes *Doctor Faustus* as "the most archaic of Marlowe's works, predicated as it seems to be on an understanding of the world that takes for granted the existence of the supernatural realm. Indeed, physical reality and the spiritual cohabit the stage in a way that roots the play in the medieval tradition of mystery and morality drama."[49] Such a reading, however, is based upon a fundamental misunderstanding of early modern notions about the supernatural. As Clark reminds us, our own use of the label "supernatural" for the demonic is itself anachronistic; within the period, debates about the devil emphatically claim him as part of the natural world.[50] In fact, studying the acts of the devil was seen as a key to understanding God's universe. Far from being a retrograde medieval holdover, demonology was a primary field of exploration for the natural philosophers. Clark states that "we would do better to associate demonology with development and, indeed, 'advancement', in natural knowledge than with stagnation or decay. If the devil was a part of early modern nature, then demonology was, of necessity, a part of early modern science."[51] Clark's own magisterial study demonstrates how inquiries into the demonic played a crucial role in natural philosophy, including speculation on physics.[52]

The actual physics of demonic metamorphosis were a topic of debate; at stake were the properties of matter and the devil's power over the material world. The case for the devil's ability to transform people into animals had some powerful advocates, including the influential Jean Bodin, who believed that the devil could transform witches into dogs, cats or werewolves.[53] On the whole, however, experts were inclined to disbelieve the phenomenon. Clark writes: "Witchcraft narratives and confessions often depended on the changing of witches or their victims into animals, and the case of lycanthropy was especially well discussed. Yet ... [experts could not] accept the phenomenon itself as real. It was philosophically and morally distasteful to suppose that the human *anima* could function in an animal body (and vice versa), and impossible for the devil to either effect the transfer or transmute substantial forms."[54]

The conflicted beliefs surrounding demonic metamorphosis are illustrated in John Cotta's *The Triall of Witch-craft, Shewing the Trve and Right Methode of the Discouery* (1616), a text that frames its discussion of witchcraft in terms of natural philosophy.[55] Cotta discusses metamorphosis at great length, first in the context of "the workes of the Diuell by himselfe, solely wrought without the association of man" (p. 27). Working solo, "the Diuell doth shew himselfe by voices and sounds in trees, canes, statues, and the like: so doth he in diuers other outward shapes and formes of other creatures. Thus he appeared vnto *Eua*, and spake vnto her in the shape of a Serpent ... Of his appearance in diuers other formes likewise are many testimonies" (pp. 28–9). Thus the devil can – and regularly does – morph his own being. Assuring his audience that his sources on the subject are far from superstitious old wives' tales, Cotta contends that he will only discuss authors:

as by the common consent of times, and generall voice of all Writers, exact credit and esteeme. In this kinde what a multitude of Examples doth the whole current and streame of all Writers of all ages afford? Who almost that readeth any ancient classical Author, can auoide the common mention of fained gods, and goddesses ... offering themselues vnto men and people, sometimes in one shape, sometimes in another ... All Christians, who know God, his word, and truth, and thereby beleeue one onely true God, must needs assure themselues that all these were, euill Spirits, and Diuels. That such were, all times, ages, histories, and records of times with one vniuersall consent confirme. (pp. 29–30)

To these classical authors, Cotta adds biblical authority, citing, among other examples, that "*Pharaoh* [did] see & view with his eyes those great and mighty Sorceries, water turned into blood, rods into Serpents, Frogges caused to issue out vpon the face of the earth" (p. 31). But while Cotta's devil can transform himself and other matter, he is constrained by the laws of nature when it comes to putting human souls into animals:

It is written by some Authors, that the diuel hath perswaded some foolish Sorcerers and Witches, that hee hath changed their bodies and substances, into Catts, Asses, Birds, and other creatures, which really and indeed without illusion ... is impossible vnto him to doe. For there can be no reall or true transmutation of one substance or nature into another, but either by creation or generation ... hee cannot be able to commaund or compasse any generation aboue the power of Nature, whose power is more vniuersall and greater then his. (pp. 33–4)

The reader of Cotta's account thus emerges with a sense of both the possibilities and the limits of demonic metamorphosis; it is at once a fundamental part of the devil's existence, and yet irreconcilable with the human constitution.

If the actual metamorphosis of humans into animals was deemed unlikely, scholars nonetheless acknowledged the reality of the *perception* of such change, and attempted to account for it in ways that conformed to their understanding of the natural order. The devil had many tricks up his sleeve, many ways to play a sleight of hand with physics. He had speed on his side: he could replace a human being with a wolf so quickly that it would appear that the man had been transformed. He had the skill of deception:

he could wrap men in the shape of a wolf and thus deceive the senses. He could manipulate the elements: he could condense the air between viewer and object to create an illusory "aerial effigy." And, in an explanation that lies a hair's breadth away from true metamorphosis, he "could achieve ... 'transfigurations', changing not the substance but the accidents of things to give them the appearance of more drastic alteration."[56]

These esoteric explanations for the appearance of metamorphosis did not trickle down into popular understandings of the demonic, however. Even if they had, demonologists admitted that the devil was so skilled at illusion that it would take an expert to distinguish between real and illusory physical effects.[57] And even if people did understand that metamorphosis was an illusion, this understanding would provide small consolation for the devil's victims. As Maus writes, "'Imaginary' effects are no less threatening, to many witchcraft believers, than 'real' or material ones ... That a young girl may not 'actually' have become a filly, but only seemed to become a filly to herself and others, is almost a distinction without a difference in a system in which mental convictions play such a crucial role."[58] Thus for most people in early modern Europe metamorphosis remained firmly entrenched as one of the devil's talents. Witchcraft narratives and confessions – again, documents that fully qualified as legal evidence – frequently depended upon claims of metamorphosis, and witchcraft pamphlets of the period commonly assert that the devil changed people into animals.[59]

Metamorphosis, then, was commonly perceived as an integral part of the reality of Marlowe's world. Demonic transformations were part of an epistemology which accepted the belief that meat turns into maggots, the idea that devils take to the stage, the logic of alchemy, and the notion that documents are transported between earth and hell.[60] This was an epistemology that was not yet subject to the seventeenth-century mechanistic philosophy (most potently articulated by Descartes) that "declar[ed] matter to be totally inert, completely devoid of any interesting property."[61] At the end of the sixteenth century, the possibilities of natural magic, occult phenomena, and demonic intervention were all still very real. My interest here is not simply in tracing how *Doctor Faustus* maps onto contemporary debates in natural philosophy, but in contemplating how the play presents a model of inhabiting this metamorphic environment – how it creates a sense of the lived experience of Ovidian physics.

Metamorphosis is the space between binaries; it is the moment of both/and rather than either/or. It is about process and movement rather than static ontological conditions. The distinction between the psychological and the physical, or between the physical and the spiritual, or between the metaphorical and the literal, ceases to hold. Ovidian physics is at once poetic, a product of the imagination, and material, a way of experiencing the world. It is, in the dual meanings of the word, literal – that which is written and that which resists metaphor, that which is produced by text and that which pertains to the physical world.

We find an analogy for this relationship in another Ovidian trope, that of dismemberment (a phenomenon also present in *Faustus*, as the play ends with a discussion of the doctor's severed limbs). This notion of fragmentation affected both the abstract construction of self (a shattered one, according to Cynthia Marshall) and the material practices of early modern Europe (the "culture of dissection" described by Jonathan Sawday).[62] The idea of bodily fragmentation spanned the poetic and the physical, rendering them not only interconnected, but intertwined and mutually constitutive. So too the metamorphic sensibility I am describing weaves together, or between, the intangible and the tangible. Smith writes that historical phenomenology "accepts the ontological premises of deconstruction but directs attention to the sentient body caught up in that situation, positioned among the cultural variables set in place by new historicism and cultural materialism."[63] Ovidian physics is just such a deconstructive ontology taken into the material world; the same sliding, morphing properties we now recognize in text were once, and for many, properties of the very space in which they lived.

To take the devil seriously, then, is to accept the reality of Ovidian physics, to acknowledge an environmental, material consciousness and comprehension that differed radically from our own. Just as scholars have examined the theory of the four humors not as an arcane and abstract medical system, but as a belief about embodiment that shaped lived experience, so too I should like to think about Ovidian physics as a mode of inhabiting a material and spatial environment. Indeed, the analogue between humoral theory and Ovidian physics is an integral one. Both notions are governed by a logic of fungibility and mutability. That the world could be malleable is a logical conclusion if the environment plays macrocosm to the microcosm of the humoral body. (And vice versa – the humoral body reflects the plasticity of the environment.[64]) Leonard Barkan describes how "Ovid has created what will stand for centuries as the translation of Platonic cosmology, with its lore of the elements and parallels between microcosm and macrocosm, into a poetic form whose dynamic, owing precisely to the flux among the elements and to the relation between microcosm and macrocosm, is metamorphosis."[65] Ovidian physics might be perceived as humoral logic writ large in the universe – "cosmologic," as Gail Kern Paster puts it.[66] Just as fluids in the humoral body morph into one another, so too, in the world of Ovid – or of the demonic – matter is eminently transformable. Men can be transformed into stags, girls into birds, nymphs into water. Contracts with the devil can melt into air. "Too, too solid flesh [can] melt, thaw, and resolve itself into a dew" (*Hamlet,* 1.2.129–30). (Shakespearean verse abounds with such changes of physical states.[67]) Ovidian physics is the lived experience of a poetic mode that itself interpolates cosmology.

For those living in the sixteenth and early seventeenth centuries, belief in a devil who could transform himself into a bush, or in fluid eschatological spaces with their inherent distortion of matter – belief in a universe that was molten – was a given. John Rogers, whom I quoted at the beginning of this chapter, further articulates his experience of the demonic: "I thought trees sometimes good Angels, sometimes bad, and looked upon bushes as the Dens of Devils."[68] Rogers perceived a world of shape-shifting and unstable matter. We should note that Rogers's comments appear in the context of a spiritual autobiography, and that these experiences of the devil took place between 1639 and 1642, when Rogers was twelve to fifteen years old. The commentary carries its own degree of irony, as the mature author (the narrative ends in 1665, when Rogers was thirty-eight) reflects on the imaginative excess of his youth, when the world was perceived "according to [his] fancies." Rogers's mapping of his own development vis-à-vis the devil corresponds with that of his time: a metamorphic understanding of the universe was becoming archaic by the end of the seventeenth century. As Lorraine Daston has discussed, Robert Boyle attacked natural philosophers who endowed nature with "plastic powers and capricious deviations."[69] A developmental paradigm was emerging that would cast the beliefs of even someone like Prynne as the follies of youth. The narrative arc of Rogers's autobiography is thus the story that would be told of modernism outgrowing superstition. Rogers anticipates, scripts, and self-consciously embraces the trajectory that Burckhardt and his followers would impose upon an epoch.

Central to the creation of this paradigm was the divorce of empirical science and the fictional imagination. Thomas Sprat writes in *The History of the Royal-Society of London* (1667) that the aim of the Society was "to make faithful *Records,* of all the Works of *Nature,*" and that "to accomplish this, they have indeavor'd, to separate the knowledge of *Nature,* from ... the devices of *Fancy,* or the delightful deceit of *Fables.*"[70] (It was "the *Poets* [who] began of old to impose the deceit" [p. 340].) Ovidian physics, as the duality of the term suggests, is a mode of thought and perception that does not recognize a division of imagin-ation and reality; it admits that our knowledge of nature is intercon-nected with the devices of fancy. It acknowledges that reality is an imaginative construct, and that phenomenology requires the work of fantasy as much as epistemology.

To study the devil is to study beliefs about nature and the nature of belief. I would like to suggest that Ovidian physics does not simply describe the local dynamics of *Doctor Faustus*, or the wider complexities of religious belief in late sixteenth- and early seventeenth-century Eng-land. Rather, Ovidian physics models the very concept of belief itself. Much recent scholarship has been invested in parsing the distinctions between Catholic and Protestant, medieval and modern. While these studies provide an important corrective to earlier work that might have overlooked the significance of such differences, we should remember that the history of belief is not a sedimentary formation, a calcified accretion of historical layers that provides a clear record of progressive change. Rather, it is, to borrow another geological metaphor, metamorphic: these layers are subject to cultural pressures which render them molten, mobile, and interpenetrating. In this sense, the world of *Faustus*, with its shifting shapes and labile coexistence of skepticism and the diabolical, offers a better model for belief than the developmental progression mapped by Rogers. Ovidian physics offers an alternative to teleology, and provides an analytical mode that is not driven by etiology or genealogy. It is the study of flux, not stasis, transformations rather than formations.

Since our own world generally makes a clear distinction between fact and fiction, reality and metaphor, it is difficult to imagine a category that bridges this fundamental binary, a division that organizes not only our daily lives but our scholarly research. The devil resides somewhere betwixt, akin, within and adjacent to metaphor and reality, metaphysics and empiricism, literature and history. But however ill-equipped we might be to seriously approach that which moves between, above, and outside of the binary of the material and the immaterial, the sixteenth- and seventeenth-century English were comfortable in the place of fancy. Or at least, it was a place they liked to explore and inhabit and think about. It was a place they were comfortable feeling uncomfortable about. It was a place that was subjected to serious intellectual inquiry, and served as the source of story. It was the place not so much of fact and experience as of belief.

Such was the world of the devil.

CHAPTER 2

# *Scene at the deathbed:* Ars moriendi, Othello, *and envisioning the supernatural*

OTHELLO: This honest creature doubtless
Sees and knows more – much more – than he unfolds.
William Shakespeare, *Othello, the Moor of Venice* (3.3.246–7)

Throughout its whole career Shakespearian criticism has been governed, and limited, by its heritage of naturalism ... The result has been that we are content not to understand, nor even to see, a perspective in his plays for which naturalism does not provide a focus.
Bernard Spivack, *Shakespeare and the Allegory of Evil*[1]

## SIGHTLINES

The previous chapter considered the spatial and material dynamics of a demonic environment. Doctor Faustus's engagement with devils reveals a physical world that is plastic and metamorphic. While Marlowe's play realizes contemporary understandings about demonic activity, the doctor's experiences were fairly unique. Not everyone signed contracts with the devil. Everyone did, however, face the devil at their deathbed. We now look to the supernatural environment that was culturally the most prominent: the space of the deathbed. But "looking" is not so simple, as the deathbed entailed its own complex modes of vision and knowledge.

You don't know what you don't know. The popular adage has ramifications not only for realms of knowledge, but for ways of knowing. You don't know what you can't know because it is beyond your ways of knowing. In his influential book of a half-century ago, from which I have drawn my epigraph, Bernard Spivack presented a modulation of this idea: you don't see what you don't know. You can't perceive that which is beyond your modes of perception. In Spivack's account, a critical tradition of understanding the Shakespearean stage through the lens of naturalism had rendered certain elements of the plays invisible to the scholarly eye. In particular, critics were blind to the drama's affiliations with elements of supernaturalism carried forward from earlier religious drama, such as the Vice figure which, Spivack argues, underlies the character of Iago. Spivack writes, "it is because our only habituation for three centuries has been to a stage and a literature that imitate [the] familiar motives of human life that we confront in Iago, and not only in him alone on the Elizabethan stage, a partially concealed order of motivation we no longer recognize, the logic and energy of which elude us" (p. 23). How, to borrow a turn of phrase from Othello, might we see and know more – much more – about this partially concealed supernatural order?

At the time that Spivack was writing, the scholarly project of dating the plays had largely come to a close, allowing critics to escape the Victorian emphasis on character study and turn instead to situating the plays within a biographical context, as "the sheer stride and turn of poetry and vision reveal the playwright's pilgrimage" (p. 451). Bucking the dominant tendency of the day to "concentrate our view on Shakespeare's private development" (p. 451), Spivack sets out instead to historicize the practices and idioms of the theater itself:

One phenomenon, as fundamental as it is elusive, exists, however, to complicate such a [biographical] survey: the conventions of [Shakespeare's] stage are on a pilgrimage of their own – toward naturalism. The moving finger of the dramatist writes, as it were, on the moving surface of his dramaturgy. It is a truism that the Renaissance meant, among other things, the redirection of human energies toward the possibilities of mortal life on the plane of the natural world. And we are generally aware of the parallel redirection of Renaissance art when we speak of *quattrocento* painting and sculpture. But it is not yet a truism – in fact, it is scarcely a datum of our knowledge – that the dramatic art in which Shakespeare and his fellows worked was undergoing a similar revision of values and, consequently, of technique. The metaphoric dramaturgy that had preached the timeless crisis of the soul and enacted its impalpable world gave way, in his time, to the dramatic imitation of literal human life and historical event, marking the beginning of the great cycle of the naturalistic stage which ... shows, in our own time, unmistakable symptoms of decay. To say that the drama imitates life or an action is to raise the question as to what we mean by either. It is probably more useful to say that technique imitates subject, and in the sixteenth century the English theater was in process of change from one great subject to another. Although by the time the drama reaches Shakespeare it ostensibly imitates natural forms, its dramaturgy still retains features, its stage properties, and its playwrights' habits that belong to "the artifice of eternity." (*Shakespeare and the Allegory of Evil*, pp. 451–2)

Embedded in this quote, almost in passing, is the utterly germane reference to the *quattrocento* visual arts. The allusion holds together a series of parallels: as the subjects of Renaissance intellectual inquiry become more humanistic, more about the natural world than the supernatural, so too the visual arts become more focused on depictions of human beings in their earthly habitat. And just as the visual arts of Renaissance Italy became more concerned with human affairs in a natural world, so did the dramatic arts of Renaissance England. Implicit to these interlocking parallels is the fundamental artistic and scientific achievement of *quattrocento* arts: the Renaissance rediscovery of linear perspective, to borrow the title of an influential book on the subject.[2] Linear perspective was essential in the redirected focus from the "impalpable world" to the environment of "literal human life" (as Spivack puts it in the quote above). For the Renaissance artist, "linear perspective fixed their eyes more intensely on the natural world,"[3] a phenomenon that presumably contributed to the focus on naturalism Spivack detects in the history of literary criticism.

The decades since the publication of Spivack's book have witnessed a profusion of scholarly writing on the techniques and history of the sixteenth- and seventeenth-century stage, so that this field is no longer "scarcely a datum of our knowledge." We know, for instance, that over the course of the seventeenth century theatrical architecture would increasingly enable the deployment of linear perspective in performance, as "unified and framed scenes came to dominate other spatial arrangements."[4] (In early seventeenth-century England, this phenomenon was perhaps most present in the court masque.[5]) In reproducing linear perspective on the stage, the theater was catching up with an increasingly dominant habit of perceiving space; as Edgerton notes, as "perspective pictures proliferated, especially through the medium of printed books, more and more people from all walks of life began to be aware of the underlying mathematical harmonies of nature which perspective articulates."[6]

But while our understanding of early modern dramaturgy has deepened, we still have a blind spot vis-à-vis the theater of this period, one that is the product of a devotion to naturalism: we still lack a sustained theoretical framework for analyzing the supernaturalism of the early modern stage. While Spivack was prescient in turning away from biographical criticism before postmodernism of the 1960s would declare the author to be dead, his move towards the edge of the supernatural did not lead to sustained inquiry in that field. Rather, a different type of naturalism came to dominate literary studies: an interest in considering how texts represented different manifestations of the (racial, gendered, class) Other. Such studies are surely of value in making visible identities and dynamics obscured by structures of social oppression, but, to return to the quote from Spivack that serves as my epigraph, "The result has been that we are content not to understand, nor even to see, a perspective in his plays for which naturalism does not provide a focus." Our purchase on the sixteenth- and early seventeenth-century experience and portrayal of the supernatural is arguably no greater now than when Spivack wrote his book. Indeed, we are perhaps even further removed from a perspective on the supernatural, as more recent historicism has argued for theater's role as an agent of disenchantment. Stephen Greenblatt, himself discussing references to the Vice figure in an early seventeenth-century anti-exorcism tract, writes: "For Harsnett, the attempt to demonize the theater merely exposes the theatricality of the demonic; once we acknowledge this theatricality, he suggests, we can correctly perceive the actual genre of the performance: not tragedy, but farce."[7] More broadly, Greenblatt contends that: "Performance kills belief; or rather acknowledging theatricality kills the credibility of the supernatural" (p. 109). While this statement is problematic as a summary of the relationship between performance and belief in early modern England – as I will discuss below, the *ars moriendi* texts, perfectly respectable even with most of the Protestant establishment, were self-consciously theatrical, employing techniques of drama as a way to give shape and order to the demonic trials of the deathbed – it is probably fair enough to say that for most twenty-first century scholars the supernatural does not present itself as a credible subject, and earlier representations and discussions of the supernatural, with their quirky devils, do indeed appear farcical (see my discussion of this at the beginning of the previous chapter). But to back-read modern incredulity (and an attendant modern ridicule) onto early modern beliefs about the supernatural closes off to rigorous scholarly consideration a central concern of sixteenth- and seventeenth-century men and women.

In this chapter, I propose that one approach to analyzing the supernatural is to consider its visual dynamics, and the attending spatial environment that these dynamics construct or imply. If linear perspective was a key element in the development of naturalism and naturalist modes of perception, then perhaps stepping away from this perspective allows for a vision of the supernatural. Linear perspective is a technique for creating verisimilitude, a visual reproduction of our spatial surround. Ways of representing and ways of seeing in perspectival artwork frequently depend on the understanding that human subjects inhabit human bodies which have discrete relational locations in geometric space. Linear perspective is based on "the assumption that visual space is ordered a priori by an abstract, uniform system of linear coordinates,"[8] and that bodies can be located within these coordinates. It presupposes the metaphysical position – one which tacitly persists even in our own culture – that space is organized according to what Edgerton deemed innate "underlying mathematical harmonies" (p. 164). While art historians study the epistemological and phenomenological complexities of Renaissance theories of perception,[9] linear perspective, as a way of shaping the visual imagination, requires picturing discrete material bodies occupying particular locations in a geometrically structured space.

Such an understanding of what it means to inhabit this space – or to see others within it – does not hold, however, for inhuman supernatural beings. To exploit Spivack's own choice of spatial metaphors, the nebulous "artifice of eternity"[10] does not sit easily within the "mortal life on the plane of the natural world." Supernatural beings, who do not necessarily have material bodies, do not always conform to worldly geometry. Moreover, they were not always, or even often, universally visible. Perspectival art and perception presuppose a normative visual accessibility; while points of view might be contested, and while artists might play with different subject positions, there is a general assumption that the objects and persons depicted are visible to all. Linear perspective presupposes that artist, viewer, and subjects share a common metaphysical field. The vagaries of the supernatural, however, work against this assumption: two viewers inhabiting the same space might well have completely different visual experiences. And as angels and demons were largely invisible in the early modern period, frequently reported to be seen by a single individual, they have become un-visible for dominant scholarly modes of perception and analysis, as they do not participate in what has become our normative visual field.

*Othello* might seem like unpromising proving ground for exploring the constructions of space, both natural and supernatural. Indeed, in his own study Spivack dismisses the relevance of the play's environment. Writing of the so-called great tragedies, Spivack remarks:

And in each of them, with one exception, it achieves its cosmic meaning through the language of a moral astronomy and is dyed into high relief by the iterated imagery and visionary atmosphere of the play. The apparent exception, in spite of the giant evil in it, is *Othello*. From it seems to be absent that quality of transcendental vision that creates in *Hamlet*, in *Lear*, in *Macbeth* . . . a level of meaning above the merely dramatic level of action, conflict, and passion. Also absent from it is that characteristic thematic imagery which in the other great tragedies elucidates the evil into symbol and metaphor and weaves out of them the imaginative texture of the play. The pervasive motif of disease and death in *Hamlet*; the elemental, weather-beaten, bestial world of *Lear*; the blood and darkness, the fear of sleeplessness of *Macbeth* – these great unitary atmospheres do not appear to have a counterpart in *Othello* . . . This is not to say that *Othello* is without its cosmic reference[s], or devoid of thematic iterations both imagistic and verbal. But these are somehow irrelevant to the enormous evil in the play or lack the clairvoyant power to interpret it into a statement or an atmosphere that could be perspicuous to the imagination of the reader. (*Shakespeare and the Allegory of Evil*, pp. 50–1)

Again, while Spivack's book now qualifies as an antique, the point he makes continues to ring true for current scholarship on these plays: the environment of *Othello*, by contrast with those of the other tragedies of this period, hardly seems malign, its imagery ostensibly less mysterious and less efficacious in creating an imagined atmosphere of evil.

In this chapter I will argue the opposite case, maintaining that the intensely domestic setting of *Othello* is also one of the most supernatural and, specifically, most demonic of the Shakespearean canon. Just as Spivack contends that Iago's character becomes more fully comprehensible when we understand the presence of the medieval figure of the Vice, so too I will contend that the environment of *Othello* as a site of supernatural activity comes into focus when we recognize the degree to which the visual and dramatic tradition of *ars moriendi* literature subtends the play. *Ars moriendi* – literally, "the art of death" – was a vastly popular genre of the sixteenth century, originally focusing on the invisible battle between the dying person and demons. Over the course of the century, as *ars moriendi* literature absorbed a number of cultural influences (especially those associated with responses to the Reformation), it acquired a generic density that rendered it a complex and contradictory form.

A similar generic complexity is at the heart of Spivack's book. Spivack was motivated by what seemed to be a scholarly impasse: the mismatch between Iago's stated motives for his treachery and his own jovial verbal patterns renders him unreadable to modern eyes. For Spivack, the "partially concealed order" that we can't quite see is the persistence of the Vice figure from late-medieval moral drama, that notoriously crafty deceiver descended from earlier stage devils.[11] Iago, in Spivack's argument, is a "hybrid" formation, "a transitional figure, hovering between profoundly different modes of drama, upon whom a conventional human nature has been superimposed; and the double image is opaque to every effort to view it as a coherent personality or to give it psychological formulation" (*Shakespeare and the Allegory of Evil,* p. 33). A similar hybridity, a similar type of double image, is inherent to the very setting of the play when the play's emphasis on the bedchamber introduces the visual connotations of *ars moriendi* literature. Spivack's Iago is thus the characterological analogue to D. J. Hopkin's recent description of post-medieval London's "spatial hybridity," as emergent modern forms of markets and identities took place within an extant physical infrastructure that dated from previous centuries.[12]

*Othello* presents its own spatial hybridity, as the interior space of the bedchamber is at once the scene of early modern domesticity and the traditional site of engagement with the supernatural, since the deathbed was perceived as a moment of combat between the dying person's soul and the devil (or, devils, as the demonic presence could be either singular or plural). The result is not only double vision in the sense of seeing both a familiar domestic interior and a site of infernal conflict, but a form of double vision that is itself a mode of perceiving the demonic.

Fundamental to the visual and textual traditions of *ars moriendi* literature are the acknowledged distinctions of seeing: the dying person sees demonic personages, the attendants at the deathbed do not. Within the same spatial field, there are two different visual realities. This form of double vision, of simultaneously seeing and not seeing, becomes a culturally inscribed way of perceiving a space inhabited by the demonic. Over the course of the sixteenth century, as the *ars moriendi* tradition increasingly recorded this type of perception through dramatic stagings of deathbed dialogues, such final encounters with Satan accentuated the dual visions present when a person was dying. This mode of registering the presence of the demonic comes to inform the final scenes of *Othello,* a play already revolving around the problematic status of "ocular proof" and devilish duplicity. Ultimately, the double vision of the deathbed is itself rendered complex and contorted by the multilayered historicity of the *ars moriendi.*

## SITES OF DEATH

"The tragic loading of this bed" (5.2.361):[13] the bed of *Othello*'s final act does indeed become loaded, weighted not only with human bodies but laden with iconographical significance. As Bettie Anne Doebler demonstrated several decades ago, the scene of Desdemona's deathbed is practically ripped from the pages of an *ars moriendi.* Doebler contends that "the visual dominance of the bed in Act V was for Shakespeare's audience pervasively suggestive of the deathbed scene in the *ars [moriendi]*," and she further points to the crowd that accumulates around the bed following Desdemona's murder (including Othello, Emilia, Montano, Gratiano, Iago, Lodovico, Cassio, and Officers) as visually recreating the congested scene depicted in the *ars moriendi* woodcuts.[14] To an early modern audience, well versed in the art of death, the recreation of this tableau most likely would have been unmistakable.

The *ars moriendi* tradition may be said to begin with Jean Charlier de Gerson's *De arte moriendi* (c. 1408), something of a do-it-yourself guide to the rituals and protocols of dying.[15] The text was designed to be used when a priest was unavailable, a not-unlikely scenario during the plague years. While following the official liturgy, the book allows for a lay companion to guide *Moriens* (a dying person, in the convenient terminology of the *ars moriendi* tradition) through the spiritual progress of death. Central to the genre is the idea that at the deathbed devils besiege *Moriens* with five last, powerful temptations: to give up faith, to fall into despair, to give up patience, to have a false sense of spiritual pride, and to be overly attached to worldly things (including loved ones).[16] These temptations were frequently illustrated in continental *ars moriendi* texts, including fifteenth-century "block books," or picture books for the illiterate. These texts depict a bedridden *Moriens* battling the grotesque demons that swarm around him. In the *ars moriendi* tradition, the deathbed temporarily transforms the mundane and the quotidian – the house, the chamber, the bed – into a site of eschatological battle, as the everyday, material realities of this world come into contact with supernatural agents. It was widely understood to be the scene of an intense, knock-down spiritual brawl between a dying person and the devil with his minions. Recognizing that *Moriens* was in a diminished physical state, and aware that this was the last chance for a spiritual victory, the devil rallied his forces for a full assault on the soul. In all his monstrous forms, Satan would take advantage of his weapons: *Moriens*'s own painful, guilty memories and secret, illicit doubts about God, his fondness for this physical world, even his affection for family and friends. Throughout the assault, *Moriens* could see the devil, hear his voice, and sense the pain he inflicted. This was a conflict that awaited nearly everyone (except for those unfortunate enough to meet a sudden, unshriven death), and the stakes of the outcome were high: according to Catholic belief, one's success or failure in this contest determined the fate of one's soul in the afterlife.

The genre entered English with an anonymous manuscript called the *Book of the Craft of Dying*, which was published by Caxton as the *Art and Crafte to Know Well to Dye* (1490; reprinted by Pynson 1495). In the sixteenth century the *ars moriendi* became a dominant literary form. The genre proved a resilient and elastic one, moving across linguistic and technological boundaries, affording women as well as men an authorized voice, and epitomizing the historical moment even as it migrated across three centuries.[17] At the turn of the seventeenth century, the *ars moriendi* tradition contained overlapping Protestant and Catholic theologies and overlapping emphases on damnation and domesticity (as I will discuss below). Within the field of these multiple vectors, however, the deathbed encounter with demons remained a constant element of the genre, probably due to the vivid illustrations of demonic combat in sixteenth-century *ars moriendi* texts.

The *ars moriendi* was deeply dependent upon a visual and mental picture. To take an early sixteenth-century example, we can look at *The Dyenge Creature* (1514), which contains an Everyman-esque drama of *Moriens* desperately seeking succor from a cast of characters that includes reason, conscience, faith, hope, and charity (title page of 1506 imprint reproduced as Figure 1). Although the presence of demons is only mentioned once towards the beginning of the text, it is the threat of demonic punishment that spurs *Moriens* to call for aid: "[H]ere is my bad aungell redy and is one of my chefe accusers with legions of f[i]ends with hym," he cries (sig. A2ᵛ). The bedside demons are the motivation for the subsequent text, and the images which accompany the written book powerfully establish the demons' presence. Such images become a hallmark of the genre in the early sixteenth century.[18] (For examples, see Figures 2 and 3.)

The *ars moriendi* images, emblazoned on the minds of a reading and viewing audience, are intriguing because they present a vision of a reality that observers at the deathbed could not see. While nearly all authors of *ars moriendi* texts presume the actual presence of the devil at the deathbed,[19] it was also nearly universally assumed that the devil and his minions were only visible to *Moriens*. The scene of demonic conflict – the heart of the narrative structure – is at once utterly invisible to the onlookers, and vividly present to *Moriens*. To put it even more broadly, the demons are at once insensible to the audience, and sensible (not only through vision, but through bodily sensation) to the dying person. For those who experienced these demons, they were perceived as horrifyingly real. This is exemplified in the diary of the Elizabethan Jesuit priest William Weston. In 1588, Weston visited a dying man who was besieged by demons. This *Moriens* relates his agony (here translated from Weston's original Latin):

Figure 1 Anon., *The Dyenge Creature*. London, 1506. Title page.

Figure 2 Anon., *Ars moriendi*. London, 1506. Sig. A1ᵛ.

"Can't you see," he said, "the room is full of devils? Yes, here where we are. They're in every nook and cranny. In the ceiling, in the walls. A thousand. More. Terrible black devils, with fearful faces. They mutter and terrify me. They go on and on. They never stop. They're savagely cruel. They say they'll drag me down to the bottom of hell. I have the cursed creatures inside me. In my bowels. I am full of them. They claw me to pieces. They tear me in all directions – torture me, body and soul, with a thousand torments. It's not as if I were going to be snatched away instantly and smothered in pain. I seem to be hurled into hellfire already."[20]

The difficulty in representing this experience in a woodcut is that what is so vivid and sensual to the dying remains invisible and insensate to the spectators. The *ars moriendi* illustrations thus must present a perspectival amalgam: viewers see *Moriens* from the perspective of a deathbed observer, and yet also see the demonic swarm that could only be seen by *Moriens*. Aron Gurevich describes this visual dynamic of the *ars moriendi* illustrations:

A favourite theme of medieval art is the death-bed scene. In addition to the relatives and priest surrounding the dying man, and the saints, God the Father, Christ and the Virgin standing around the bed, loathsome demons bustle here as

Figure 3 Anon., *The Doctrynall of Dethe*. London, 1532. Title page.

well. There are two planes in the picture. Mortal people are visible to everybody, but the heavenly powers and demons only to the artist. This is the secret of the meeting of the two worlds ... The apparently empty bedroom is in actuality tightly crowded – here paradise, hell and the world are brought closely together.[21]

Gurevich describes the mode of seeing required for this image as "double vision" (p. 187), but this is not quite as simple as representing two different scenes. A striking feature of the *ars moriendi* tradition is that the reader is expected to imagine the deathbed battle from two radically different points of view. Human spectators at the deathbed focus on a lone *Moriens*; *Moriens* himself looks out at angels and demons. The artist combines these two perspectives in depicting both *Moriens* and the supernatural creatures which only the dying can see, overlaying multiple and logically inconsistent points of view. The point of view of the artist – and thus of the viewer – merges incongruous angles of sight, seeing *Moriens* from the position of a spectator, seeing the demons from the position of *Moriens*. The viewer is thus required simultaneously to see from different spatial points and to perceive mutually incompatible metaphysical realities.

By the mid sixteenth century, the *ars moriendi* images, in their traditional form, had fallen out of fashion. Visual elements of the genre continued to appear – a figure of the dying man in bed appears in Christopher Sutton's *Disce mori. Learne to Die* (1601; sig. B12ᵛ) and on the title page of William Perkins's *Deaths Knell: Or, The Sicke Mans Passing-Bell* (1628 edition), and an angel transports the soul of a dying man on the title page of Robert Hill's *The Path-vvay to Pietie* (1629 edition) – but the classic deathbed illustration largely drops from the pages of death literature. While the woodcuts themselves may have become outmoded, the scene they depict paradoxically becomes even more animated, as the *ars moriendi* texts become longer and more dramatic. The once-static and even marginal image of the deathbed becomes colorfully enacted within the pages of the ongoing genre. Ralph Houlbrooke writes of the original *ars moriendi* that "[c]oncrete images convey a sense of diabolical presence much more emphatically and vividly than the text of the book itself."[22] While this may be true for the early block books, as the genre became more elaborate and more textual over the course of the sixteenth century lengthy dialogues came to dramatize the familiar tableaux of the *ars moriendi*.

Such dialogues serve as the textual equivalent of the visual mode for representing multiple points of view. With the increasing inclusion of deathbed dialogues, the *ars moriendi* became an emphatically and self-consciously performative genre. Since the devil remained invisible and inaudible to all but *Moriens*, the witnesses of the deathbed thus could only perceive one half of this encounter, much like hearing only one end of a telephone conversation or watching a boxing match with the Invisible Man. It was therefore the responsibility of the dying person to make the course of the demonic struggle accessible to the onlookers. *Moriens* thus faced a dual challenge: not only to fend off the devil with his dying breath, but to be conscious of rendering the progress of the fight perceptible and interpretively accessible to those watching him die. The onus on the dying person was to make evident, through whatever gestures and articulations were possible, the progress of the death struggle, and the onus on the living spectator was to evaluate these signs and to discern the ultimate outcome, the fate of the soul in the afterlife.

Demonic dialogues increasingly served as the vehicle for making *Moriens*'s battle sensible to the deathbed attendants. Erasmus's *Preparation to Deathe* (1538), for instance, takes us deep inside the moment of demonic strife. Like most of the texts in the *ars* tradition, this one assumes the reality of devils, and is geared towards arming *Moriens* for the deathbed encounter.[23] Crucially, *Moriens* needs to be able to anticipate the devil's verbal strategies, and be able to counter them. This exchange is modeled when, in a striking move, a long third-person excursus on how to address the devil spontaneously transforms into a heated second-person dialogue. While the exchange between the devil and *Moriens* is in prose, with designated speech tags, here is what an excerpt would look like on the page if printed in more conventional dramatic form:

DYUELL:   Thou shalt be haled downe to hell.
MAN:   My heed is in heuen.
DYUELL:   Thou shalt be damned.
MAN:   Thou art a barratour, and a fals harlot, no iudge, a damned fende, no damnour.
DYUELL:   Many legions of dyuels wayte for thy soule.
MAN:   I shoulde despaire, yf I had not a protectour, which hath ouercom your tyranny.

(*Preparation*, sig. F6$^{r-v}$)

And so on. Erasmus provides us with the soundtrack for the familiar *ars moriendi* woodcuts, as we can suddenly hear the dialogue that would otherwise remain inaudible.

We can glimpse the evolution of this genre by considering a text published half a century later, Philip Stubbes's *A Christal Glasse for Christian*

*VVomen containing, a Most Excellent Discourse, of the Godly Life and Christian Death of Mistresse Katherine Stubs* (1592). Here, Philip records the death of his wife Katherine; rather than the general "Man" of Erasmus's book, we find something of a purported transcript of an actual dying woman trying to render public her final momentous battle with Satan. Philip describes how a visible transformation in Katherine's appearance and demeanor signals to the gathered company that Satan has arrived on the scene. Whereas the pious Katherine had delivered her creed

with a sweete, louely and amiable countenaunce, red as the Rose, and most beautifull to beholde, nowe vpon the sudden, she bent the browes, shee frowned, and looking (as it were) with an angry, sterne, and fierce counte-naunce, as though shee sawe some filthy, vgglesome and displeasant thing: shee burst foorth into these speeches following, pronouncing her wordes (as it were) scornefully, and disdainfully, in contempt of him to whom shee spake. (sig. C2ᵛ)

The ensuing "wonderfull conflict" is presented as being "betwixt Sathan and her soule" (sig. C2ᵛ), but it is a contest that was outwardly articulated. The pamphlet's title page positions the text as a form of transcript, claiming that the author has "[s]et downe [her confession and the satanic combat] word for word, as she spake it, as neere as could be gathered."

   While this battle is presented as a monologue, throughout the speech we are able to reconstruct Satan's lines, since there are numerous instances when Katherine responds to an invisible interlocutor. Here is just part of the speech, with my own reconstruction of Satan's missing lines in boldface:

How now Satan? what makest thou here? Art thou come to tempt the Lords seruant? I tell thee, thou hell-hound, thou hast no part nor portion in me: nor by the grace of God neuer shalt haue. I was, now am, and shall be the Lords for euer. **Oh? You can't seriously think that a sinner like you can get into heaven.** Yea Satan, I was chosen & elected in Christ to euerlasting saluation before the foundations of the world were laid: and therefore thou maist get thee packing; thou damned Dog, and goe shake thine eares, for in me thou hast nought. **You are a sinner and therefore shall be damned.** But what doest thou say to my charge, thou foule fiend? **YOU ARE A SINNER AND THEREFORE SHALL BE DAMNED.** Oh that I am a sinner, and therefore shall be damned: I confesse in deed that I am a sinner, and a grievous sinner, both by originall sinne, and actuall sinne, and that I may thanke thee for. (sig. C2ᵛ)

As the discourse continues, Katherine becomes even more helpful to her audience in relaying the dialogue, resorting to the use of indirect quotation: "But what sayest thou more, Satan? Doest thou aske me how I dare come to him for mercy, hee being a righteous God, and I a miserable sinner?" (sig. C3$^r$). And again: "What more, Satan? Doest thou say, it is written, that God will rewarde euery one according to his workes, or according to his desertes?" (sig. C3$^r$). In one particularly fascinating sentence, we find a series of parentheses in which Katherine insistently reminds her listening audience that she is speaking to Satan, and Philip relates Katherine's own body language for his own reading audience. "Christes armes were spread wide open (Satan) vpon the Crosse (with that she spread her owne armes) to embrace [me], and all penitent sinners: and therefore (Satan) I will not feare to present my selfe before his footestoole, in full assurance of his mercy for Christ his sake" (sig. C3$^r$). The first and third set of parentheses are in Katherine's voice; the second is in Philip's. We find here an encapsulated version of the double vision, and the double act of translation: Katherine sees Satan, and needs to manifest that vision to her audience; Philip sees an emphatically Christ-like Katherine seeing Satan, and relates that vision with a detail of her physical action (one that reads very much like an embedded stage direction).

In the end, having prevailed, the valiant Katherine calls with "sweete smiling laughter" on her audience to actually see the fiend in his shameful retreat: "[D]oe ye not see him flie like a coward, and runne away like a beaten cocke?" (sig. C3$^v$). Not only does she point out the fleeing Satan, but she also urges her audience to see the legions of angels who have defended her: "For do you not see infinite millions of most glorious Angels stand about me?" (sig. C3$^v$). While these angelic hosts might continue to elude the actual sight of the deathbed attendants, the angels could well become visible in the mind's eye, as Katherine Stubbes's words describe the familiar tableau of the *ars moriendi* woodcuts. Indeed, the whole of the deathbed dialogue seems designed to enable the spectators to witness a supernatural encounter that they cannot actually see.[24]

The complicated visual dynamics of the *ars moriendi*, negotiating between different experiences of a visual (and metaphysical) reality, become even more complex in light of the theological developments accompanying the Protestant Reformation. In its origin, the *ars moriendi* epitomizes a medieval Catholicism that granted the individual a significant degree of personal eschatological agency. Good works could mitigate a purgatorial sentence. So too a good death was essential to establishing a speedy passage to heaven. In the medieval Catholic tradition, the final moments of life could make you or break you. On the one hand, a lifetime of virtue could be thrown away in a moment of deathbed despair, ensuring either eternal damnation or an extended sentence in purgatory; on the other hand, a lifetime of debauchery could be wiped clean with a genuine deathbed confession and appeal to God. As Houlbrooke puts it, "[a]s the tree fell, so would it lie."[25] Thus, the final encounter with Satan and his minions was the key moment in determining one's salvation or damnation. Erasmus succinctly expressed this idea: "For this is of mans lyfe the last parte (as it were) of the playe wherof hangeth eyther euerlastynge blysse of man, or euerlastynge damnation. This is the laste fyghte with the enemy, wherby the souldiour of Christe loketh for eternall triumphe, yf he ouercome: and euerlastynge shame, if he be ouercome" (sig. A2r).

Predicated on a final wrestling match with the devil, the *ars moriendi* literature that enters into the sixteenth century might seem to have little to offer the Reformation, when, as Peter Marshall puts it, "the theology of death underwent its Protestant makeover."[26] Over the course of the sixteenth century, the ascendancy of Calvinist theology and an emphasis on double predestination "rendered nonsensical the idea of the deathbed as a place of final ordeal where salvation could be won or lost."[27] For Calvinist Protestants, soteriology was the domain of the divine, and was not subject to human agency. A centuries-old understanding of the experience of the deathbed was thus in the process of becoming intellectually obsolete: the idea of a final demonic combat would not sit easily with reformist theologies dependent upon ideas of predestination, as neither the devil nor the dying individual had any agency in determining a person's salvation.

Such a transformation would appear to take the theological and dramatic wind out of the sails of the *ars moriendi*, but in the hands of reformed authors the genre not only adapted but flourished. Thomas Becon, the chaplain to Thomas Cranmer during the reign of Edward VI, would give the genre a Protestant spin in *The Sicke Mannes Salue*; first published in 1561, the text would go through eighteen subsequent editions by 1632.[28] (As Beaty notes, this was not only the most popular text of a prolific author, "but it was one of the top best sellers among Elizabethan devotional books in general" [*The Craft of Dying*, p. 110].) The text is overtly hostile to Catholic practices surrounding death. The characters in the text discuss the practice of prayers for the dead, which the "papistes" claim are for the forgiveness of sins. This prompts Epaphroditus, the *Moriens* of the text, to pipe up from his deathbed, "I haue nothing to doe with papistes, nor with their doctrine … I b[e]leue that a man, euen in this world, hath perfect and full remission of al hys sinnes, or else he shall neuer haue it. God in thys world doth eyther forgeue all the faultes, and the payne due for the same, or els he forgeueth none at all. I feare nothing at all the popes boyling fornace (I meane purgatory). Christes bloud is a sufficient purgatory for my sinnes."[29]

Such a declaration might seem to make a deathbed struggle with Satan theologically superfluous, but this element of the genre is rather oddly and incongruously preserved even in a description of the elect:

EPAPHRODITUS: Sathan now in this my sickenesse doth so molest and trouble me that me thincke I feele a very hell wythin my brest.

PHILEMON: The manner of Sathan, which is the common aduersary of all men, is, when any man is greuously sicke & like to dye, straightwayes to come vppon him at the begynning very fiercely, & to shew hymself terrible vnto him, & to caste before hys eyes such a myste that, except he taketh heede, he shall see nothing but the fierce wrath and terrible iudgemente of God agaynst sinners, agaynst sinne, desperation, death, & hell, and whatsoeuer maketh vnto the better confusion of the sicke mans conscience.

EPAPHRODITUS: So is it now with me.

PHILEMON: Feare not. It is his olde propertie. If you had lead as holy and as perfect a life as euer did man in this world, yet woulde he deale on this maner with you. He knoweth right well that the time of your departure is at hand, and that God will shortly call you from this sorrowefull & mortal life vnto a blessed and immortall life. Therfore laboureth he vnto the vttermost of his power to plucke you from so ioyfull a state, & to make you his pray. But be you not afraide, for whom of Gods elect hath he let passe vnassailed, vntempted, or vnproued? ...

EPAPHRODITUS: Yea, but how shall I resist the deuyll.
...

PHILEMON: With fayth, with prayer, & wyth the word of God.     (p. 116)

This final advice does not quite comfort Epaphroditus, and for several more pages he worries about his lack of good works while his friends assure him that he is indeed among the elect. The extended discussion against the backdrop of an invisible battle with inner and outer demons is the narrative climax of the text, and shortly before his death a calm Epaphroditus finally declares: "God be thanked. I am now well quieted in my conscience and feare Sathan nothing at all. I thinke my selfe at this present so strong and so throughly enarmed against the deuill and all his wicked army that I am nothing afrayde to enter battell with him, but am fully perswaded that by the helpe and power of my graund captain Jesu Christ, I shal ouerthrow him ..." (p. 123). Thus, while *The Sicke Mannes Salue* ultimately does exemplify Protestant soteriology, the demonic ordeal itself does not disappear from the drama of Protestant death.

The notion of an ultimate demonic combat, then, would continue to play a central imaginative and narrative function in reformed iterations of the genre. Epaphroditus's final victorious declaration heralds one of the ways in which the genre would morph from an emphatically Catholic one into a privileged Protestant one. While the Protestant deathbed stripped *Moriens* of eschatological agency, it provided an opportunity to reveal one's true state of election to the attending witnesses. The function of the gaggle of onlookers shifts: once a form of afterlife support group, they now become an audience to a final performance. A good death provided, to oneself and to one's neighbors, proof of salvation. This understanding spawned the popular literary genre of the good death, as the hotter sort of Protestants set down the feats of "spiritual athletes" (to borrow once more from Houlbrooke[30]) who managed to pull off amazing deaths. In Philip Stubbes's report of his wife's death, for example, the febrile, post-partum Katherine is portrayed as mounting an eloquent death speech in which she asserts her creed; the length of a sermon, her reported final words read more like a précis of reformist theology ("The Sacraments ... are Seales and signes of holie things, and therefore cannot be the things themselues" [sig. B4ᵛ]) than a personal farewell to friends and family, or even a personal address to God.[31] It is important to note the fact that "[a]ccounts of death-bed experiences were produced in large numbers, with the edifying words of dying saints avidly recorded,"[32] indicating a reciprocity of literary form and actual human experiences: *ars moriendi* literature provided a template for dying, while artful deaths provided additional material for more *ars moriendi* literature.

Historians enjoy pointing out the theatrical qualities of *ars moriendi* literature. Nathan Johnstone writes, "Philip Stubbes' account of his wife Katherine's dying combat with the Devil is suggestive of the theatre which could surround such public expressions of the dialogue" (*The Devil and Demonism*, p. 131). Johnstone's use of "theatre" here seems to signify something like "histrionics." In a related vein, Philippe Ariès writes of medieval death: "The drama no longer took place in the vast reaches of the beyond. It had come down to earth and was now enacted right in the bedroom of the sick person, around his bed." Eamon Duffy, describing the block book *artes moriendi*, notes that "[t]he temptation to despair was pictured as a theatrical troop of demons enacting in the sickroom a pageant of all the deadly sins." Ralph Houlbrooke observes, "Godly Protestants were usually described as playing an active role in the drama of their own deathbeds," that "[t]he dying man holds centre stage for much of the time," and that "[t]he achievement of a 'good' death transformed the process of dying from tragedy into triumph. Both the individual at the centre of the drama and the members of the audience might be reassured and sustained." Donald Duclow writes, "the *Ars moriendi* constitutes the script for a dramatic performance: *Moriens'* bedroom becomes a stage; the interrogations and prayers supply texts to be recited; and there are ample stage directions for the dying and those attending them."[33]

But the deathbed dialogue is not simply related to drama by a metaphoric filament; the form resonates, in very powerful ways, with the actual theater. The theatrical idiom is not a twenty-first century imposition onto a sixteenth- and seventeenth-century genre, but is part of the fiber of the *ars moriendi* texts. Sixteenth-century *ars moriendi* literature frequently relies upon, is framed by, exploits and extols a theatrical vocabulary. Christopher Sutton, for example, writes in *Disce mori*:

If nothing else ... the daily insta[n]ces of death before vs, do evidently shew, what shall in like manner shortly betide our selues. The enterlude is the same, wee are but new actors vpon the stage of this world ... All are actors of seueral partes: they which are gone, haue played their partes, & we which remaine, are yet acting ours: only our Epilogue is yet for to end. (p. 18)

Death had the necessary elements of theater: players, a script, an audience, and the performance space of the bedchamber. *Ars moriendi* literature provided a script for death, including the lines for the dying person, the deathbed attendant, and even the devil. Deaths were often, and ideally, a public event: "Indeed, a private death was regarded as something of a misfortune; to choose it might be regarded as a perverse refusal of social and religious duties."[34] For instance, when Oliver Heywood's son seemed to be dying, the neighbors were invited to watch his death.[35] The spectators at a death signaled communal solidarity, but they were also there to judge the death and to rehearse their own. Death was an art, to be fashioned and mannered, the final and in many ways the ultimate proof of one's civility.[36] Given the profound social, personal, and eschatological consequences of the deathbed, individuals were exhorted to rehearse their deaths in advance. Richard Whitford, for example, suggests that practice makes perfect in his book *Of the Dayly Exercyce and Experience of Deathe* (1537).

In a society that was deeply ceremonial and performative, in which all the world was a stage, death was often a final public opportunity to shape one's own public persona. But we fundamentally misread the early modern scene of death if we overlook the reality of deathbed demons, if we fail to acknowledge the widespread acceptance of the reality of these devils for

both *Moriens* and the audience. We miss the point if we consider Katherine
Stubbes as just a deathbed drama queen, or explain away the sighting of
demons as the medical consequence of fever-induced hallucinations.[37]
Deathbed accounts of seeing demons, and the theatrical modes of these
accounts (especially the deathbed dialogues), were not purely about self-
fashioning or delusion. Rather, they were a form of translation across
metaphysical states, "provid[ing] theatrical conventions whereby the dying
could present themselves as interpretively accessible to the living."[38] While
the drama of death borrowed forms and techniques from the rising professional theaters of the latter sixteenth century, it was not presumed to traffic
in illusion, representation, or what later generations would come to know
as the willing suspension of disbelief. The deathbed exchanges – between
*Moriens* and attendants, between *Moriens* and the devil – were about the
very real belief in and experience of the demonic. They served to mediate
between different ontological and experiential realities occurring in the
same space – a doubleness that an emergent understanding of space would
increasingly disallow, as linear perspective developed into Cartesian mathematics and ultimately Newtonian physics.

Indeed, doubt concerning demonic deathbed temptations was slowly
growing over the course of the sixteenth century.[39] One early Lutheran
text, *A treatyse to teche a ma[n] to dye* (1537), directly disavows the deathbed
demons, asserting: "the feare of the deuell and howe he shall assayle vs at
the houre of deth" is simply a teaching that clerics use for "the multitude
of simple people" in order to prompt better behavior (sig. E2$^v$–E3$^r$); the
appearance of the devil at the deathbed is but a "phantasie [that shall]
vanyshe awaye by and by," as it is merely the consequence of the dying
man's sickness (sig. E7$^r$). Such outright instances of skepticism, however,
are rare. More typically, Protestant *ars moriendi* temper claims of the
devil's presence by medicalizing or domesticating the deathbed.
Christopher Sutton's *Disce mori. Learne to Dye* (a phenomenally popular
text that went through subsequent editions and printings in 1600, 1601,
1602, 1604, 1607, 1609, 1610, 1612, 1613, 1616, 1618, and 1626) sets out to
cool the scene of the deathbed.[40] Instead of battling writhing demons,
Sutton puts forth a comfortable recipe for redemption: "First therefore
take a good quantity of repentence, two handfuls of faith in the passio[n]
of Christ, put both together with a purpose, by the helpe of God for to
walke vpon it in holinesse of life, and apply this good receit, for thy sickely
Soule, which hath taken a dangerous surfet in sinne" (pp. 186–7). (Sutton
continues: "The lump of dried figges . . . haue also their conuenient vse.")
As the seventeenth century moved forward, less emphasis was placed on

the deathbed as a site of final judgment.[41] *The Doctrine of Dying-Well* (1628) emphasizes that death could come at any moment, and thus the Christian should be in a continual state of readiness; in a departure from some of the fire and brimstone that laps the edges of previous *artes moriendi*, in this text "death to the godly is nothing else but a bridge ouer this tempestuous sea of this troublesome world to paradise" (sig. B3ᵛ). Jeremy Taylor's *The Rule and Exercises of Holy Dying* (1651) might be said to round off the genre, and moves away from the earlier tradition of placing heavy emphasis on death as a public, social spectacle.[42]

While Catholic and Calvinist theologies of the deathbed were incongruous, this does not mean that the one neatly supplanted the other. On the contrary, competing understandings of the soteriology of the deathbed, with their attendant differences in understandings of the demonic, could be held strangely together. While some Protestant authors try to overwrite the scene of the deathbed, domesticating the space and thus expelling the physicality of the demonic, the devils from the older *ars moriendi* texts continue to appear as a palimpsest. The most striking instance of such a conflation of oppositional beliefs is exemplified in the writing of William Perkins, London's late sixteenth-century superstar preacher and prolific author, widely understood to be translating Calvin for an English audience. In his *A Salue for a Sicke Man: Or, A Treatise Containing the Nature, Differences, and Kindes of Death; as also the Right Maner of Dying Wel* (1595), Perkins deliberately sets out to reconfigure the familiar deathbed scene. Rather than imagining the traditional scene of an invisible eschatological drama unfolding around the bed, Perkins repeatedly naturalizes the scene; the only demons are the bodily humors. The state of the man's soul remains inscrutable, and Perkins urges his audience to read what previously had been perceived as signs of mortal combat with the devil as the purely physiological consequences of somatic failure. As such, it would seem that there is no invisible battle for *Moriens* to make visible to onlookers:

As for other straunge events which fall out in death, they are the effects of diseases. Ravings and blasphemings arise of the disease of melancholy and of frensies, which often happen at the end of burning feavers, the choller shooting vp to the braine. The writhing of the lippes, the turning of the necke, the buckling of the ioynts and the whole bodie, proceede of cramps and convulsions, which follow after much evacuation ... Now these and the like diseases with their symptomes & stra[n]ge effects, though they shall deprive man of his health, and the right vse of the parts of his body ... yet they can not depriue his soule of eternall life. (15–16)

Perkins asks his readers for compassion towards the dying person, and to desist from the widespread practice of observing the process of death in order to discern a person's state of salvation. He writes that "we must learn to reforme our iudgements of such as lie at the point of death … And by the outward condition of any man, either in life or death, we are not to iudge of his estate before God" (p. 17).

And yet, even Perkins ultimately accepts as a matter of course the presence of demons at the deathbed. Perkins's emphasis on a rational medical explanation for the torments of death is abruptly compromised in the final pages of his book. On page 109 we arrive at "FINIS," but this closure is disrupted by a brief, appended section entitled "An addition, of things that came to my minde afterward." Here Perkins returns, stunningly, to the image from the *ars moriendi* tradition he has so adamantly opposed: "The last combate with the devill in the pang of death, is oftentimes most dangerous of all" (p. 109). While Perkins proposes that the dying man remain passively committed to God, *Moriens* clearly participates in deciding his fate at this critical moment.[43] Not only does this postscript seem to reveal the tensions and fissures in Perkins's own theology, but it also seems to undermine his earlier claim that the dying man cannot be judged. In the end, Perkins envisions a final tug-of-war for the soul, one that appears utterly incompatible with Calvinist eschatology. The *ars moriendi* framing of the deathbed appears to be so internalized and so culturally pervasive that it seeps back even into those texts that deliberately try to eschew it.

### PERSPECTIVES ON 'OTHELLO'

The *ars moriendi* tradition – with its interplay of the visual and the textual, the meditative and the dramatic, traditional belief and emergent skepticism – positioned it as a rich genre for the theatrical consideration of the supernatural. As a genre that had morphed from a primarily visual one (the medieval block books for the illiterate) into a heavily dramatic one (increasingly oriented around providing scripts for the traditional *ars moriendi* images), the *ars moriendi* literature offered a productive model for the enactment of a pictorial tradition that was itself reflecting, constructing, and structuring notions about human-supernatural interactions. In short, at the turn of the seventeenth century, the *ars moriendi* blended the imagistic and the dramatic. This integration positioned the genre as ripe for appropriation by the theater. As Doebler suggests, the motivation to reach for the *ars moriendi* over the other types of religious literature available at the turn of the seventeenth century "no doubt had something to do with the visual or iconic qualities which make it especially appealing for the stage."[44] Recent scholarship on early modern drama has largely emphasized the auricular nature of performance, rather than the visual, leading to what has become a truism that audiences of, say, the Globe theater went to hear a play, not see one – a critical commonplace that, as Gabriel Egan has demonstrated, is patently untrue.[45] Marguerite A. Tassi has compellingly argued for the prominence of the visual experience in early modern drama: "playgoers experienced drama as a sensuous, mixed media; not only did they hear poetry and grand oratory in the theater, but they also witnessed impressive visual phenomena like the Dance of Death, dumb show tableaux, and statues coming to life."[46] *Othello*'s portrayal of the *ars moriendi* deathbed scene is more than a display of theatrical virtuosity, or the flash of an intertextual visual quote. Rather, the iconography of the *ars moriendi* which comes to structure *Othello* is part of a larger genetic connection between this genre and the play. *Othello*'s engagement with the *ars moriendi* is not simply on the level of visual homology; the connection inflects the drama's visual dynamics, and the larger sense of environment created by that sense of vision. Let us turn now to that stage, in order to consider how the *ars moriendi* created the visual conditions for the supernatural environment of *Othello*.

*Ars moriendi* illustrations focus on the dying man in his bed, and it is striking to recognize how prominently beds feature throughout *Othello*. Michael Neill has written that the bed in *Othello* is "the imaginative center of the play."[47] Indeed, perhaps even more than Venice or Cyprus (the story's geographical settings), beds provide a recurrent visual site for the play, and the atmosphere of the drama is shaped by that of the bedchamber. It is virtually certain that the original production of *Othello* included a bed on stage.[48] The use of a bed was not entirely unusual for Shakespeare's company; according to Richard Hosley's survey, of the 153 plays written for the troupe as it made its way through the Theater, the Curtain, the First Globe, the Blackfriars, and the Second Globe, 21 called for the staging of a bed.[49] But the rarity of the bed becomes more pronounced when we consider the history of the original Globe, where *Othello* would have first been produced. Of the 34 plays performed at the Globe between 1599 and 1613, only 2 require a bed on stage: *Othello* and Barnaby Barnes's *The Devil's Charter* (1607).[50] The emphatic presence of the bed in the final act thus would have been more pronounced, given how seldom an audience saw one on stage.

And it is not only the physical presence of the stage prop that signals the importance of the bed: the playtext has been priming us for its arrival.

"Bed" appears in *Othello* far more than in any other play (with the exception, not surprisingly, of *Romeo and Juliet*).[51] Beds provide a recurring off-stage location from which various characters are continuously coming or going. Early in the play Brabantio laments to the Duke that his grief over Desdemona's marriage "[h]ath raised [him] from [his] bed" (1.3.54). When Roderigo, suffering from his love-sickness, cries out to Iago, "What will I do, think'st thou?", he is given the quite practical advice, "Why, go to bed and sleep" (1.3.304–5). After Cassio's drunken ruckus wakes Desdemona and Othello, they finally return to bed; Othello reassures Desdemona, "Come away to bed ... 'tis the soldier's life/To have their balmy slumbers waked with strife" (2.3.249; 2.3.253–4). Later, when their marital relations have deteriorated, Othello will change his tone, ordering Desdemona, "Get you to bed/On th' instant" (4.3.5–6), which Desdemona will relate to Emilia when she says that Othello "hath commanded me to bed" (4.3.11).

Perhaps not surprisingly, considering his association with the devil and the culturally pervasive visual iconography placing the devil at the deathbed, Iago is especially obsessed with beds. While he clearly possesses an active sexual imagination (as exemplified in the infamous line "an old black ram/Is tupping your white ewe" [1.1.87–8]), many of his sexual comments and innuendos specifically involve the materiality of the bed. He suspects both Othello and Cassio of having had sexual relations with his wife, and in declaring these suspicions he focuses on details of the bed: of Othello he declares, "it is thought abroad that 'twixt my sheets/He's done my office" (1.3.386–7), and he "fear[s] Cassio with [his] night-cap too" (2.1.305). Arden editor E. A. J. Honigmann's gloss on this line points out that nightcaps are not typically the romantic attire of lovers, and thus "Iago's sense of humour runs away with him" (p. 182n). This line might be read as a comic moment, but more powerfully it signals Iago's obsession not just with a fear of being cuckolded, but of someone actually taking his place in his own bed – of being not just with his wife, but 'twixt his sheets and in his nightwear.

This focus on the space of the bed pervades Iago's speech. While bantering with Desdemona, he gratuitously comments that women are "Players in your housewifery, and housewives in ... /Your beds!" (2.1.112–3). When informing an alarmed gathering that the commotion caused by Cassio's drunkenness has been calmed, he invokes the image of a couple undressing before going to bed: the company are "friends all, but now, even now,/In quarter and in terms like bride and groom/Divesting them for bed" (2.3.175–7). His imagined bed-scenes crescendo as he stokes

Othello's jealousy. He suggests, feigning innocence, that there could be no harm for Desdemona "to be naked with her friend [Cassio] in bed/An hour or more, not meaning any harm?", to which an incredulous Othello responds, "Naked in bed, Iago, and not mean harm?" (4.1.3–5). Where Desdemona had once declared that Othello's "bed shall seem a school" (3.3.24), Iago subverts the emotional security of the general's marriage bed by covering it with suspicion: "There's millions now alive/That nightly lie in those unproper beds/Which they dare swear peculiar: your case is better./O, 'tis the spite of hell, the fiend's arch-mock,/To lip a wanton in a secure couch/And to suppose her chaste" (4.1.67–72). (The use of "couch" links this passage to Othello's earlier comment, "The tyrant custom, most grave senators,/Hath made the flinty and steel couch of war/My thrice-driven bed of down" [1.3.230–2], showing that Othello is not only inexperienced in the ways of love, but in the ways of beds.) Iago's concentration on the bed reaches its chilling climax when he recommends Othello's method of uxoricide: "Do it not with poison, strangle her in her bed –/even the bed she hath contaminated" (4.1.204–5). Sensing that her end is near, Desdemona, for her part, emphasizes the purity of her marriage bed by asking Emilia to "[l]ay on my bed my wedding sheets" (4.2.107).[52] (Emilia would later confirm – unprompted, and as something of a non sequitur to Desdemona's request to be unpinned – that she has "laid those sheets you bade me on the bed" [4.3.20].) Othello, in the end, is also fixating on the bed: "Thy bed, lust-stained, shall with lust's blood be spotted" (5.1.36).

Neill's own account of the visual and imaginative potency of the bed pertains to *Othello*'s miscegenation. In a survey of theater history, Neill notes that the extreme audience response to the on-stage bed "suggests that [it] was ... intensely identified with the anxieties about race and sex stirred up by the play" ("Unproper Beds," 390). Within the period of the play's composition, the bed also signaled cultural anxieties. "Not only in its obvious challenge to patriarchal authority and in the subversion of gender roles implicit in its assertion of female desire, but in its flagrant transgression of the alleged boundaries of kind itself, the love of Desdemona and Othello can be presented as a radical assault on the whole system of differences from which the Jacobean world was constructed. The shocking iconic power of the bed in the play has everything to do with its being the site of that assault" ("Unproper Beds," 410–11).

Neill's analysis of the function of the bed within the play's exploration of early modern attitudes towards race is thoroughly convincing – but not exhaustive. I would contend that the bed also activates, and registers, another set of cultural anxieties. In addition to signifying as a site of sex and marriage, the bed indicated the space in which human beings were virtually guaranteed an encounter with the supernatural. (And while negotiating interactions with a racial "Other" might be one of the most prominent anxieties in our own culture, and thus part of the scholarly motivation to trace genealogies of racial constructions, within the early modern period anxieties about the supernatural were arguably more pressing.) As mentioned above, the scene of Desdemona's death establishes a visual tableau that reproduces an illustration from the *ars moriendi* woodcuts. The clustering of characters around Desdemona's body "suggests the visually crowded woodcuts, in which the *Moriens* is surrounded by friends and foes of a supernatural or symbolic nature as well as by members of his family."[53] The visual consonance with the *ars moriendi* texts is further enhanced by what Doebler considers "the most explicit allusion to the tradition," Gratiano's reference to the "better angel" at the side of a dying Brabantio (see 5.2.206–7).[54]

As Othello considers the murderous action he is about to take, he approaches the sleeping Desdemona and kisses her. She rouses and asks the utterly domestic question, "Will you come to bed, my lord?" (5.2.24). Othello, however, launches into the line of questioning prescribed in the *ars moriendi*, and the transformation of the bedchamber into the site of eschatological battle and judgment is sealed with his declaration, "Thou art on thy death-bed" (5.2.51). In addition to the visual components, the scene thus also imitates – or rather, mimics – the traditional verbal script of the *ars moriendi*.

Desdemona's death presents a skewed enactment of the deathbed ritual as prescribed by the *ars moriendi*, with Othello, perversely, guiding her through the rituals of a good death, those intended to aid *Moriens* against the devil's assault. The learned and civil Desdemona and the self-fashioned Othello clearly know the right way to die, and the scene follows form as they stick to many of the formalities urged by the *ars moriendi* texts. Othello plays the role of the deathbed attendant, guiding *Moriens* through prayer and the process of death: "Have you prayed tonight, Desdemon?"; "If you bethink yourself of any crime/Unreconciled as yet to heaven and grace,/Solicit for it straight"; "Think on thy sins"; "Peace, and be still"; "Sweet soul, take heed/Take heed of perjury"; "Therefore confess thee freely of thy sin"; "Thou art to die"; "I say amen" (5.2.24, 26–8, 40, 46, 50–1, 53, 56, 57). Desdemona goes through the motions of a good *Moriens*, although in her panic and fear she plays the part less well. She offers the standard deathbed prayers to God ("Then heaven/Have mercy on me"

[5.2.33–4]), but as she begs for her death to be postponed she also exhibits that she is suffering from some of the traditional deathbed temptations, such as fear of death, impatience, and a desire to stay in this world. For an audience attuned to the resonance of the *ars moriendi* in this scene, Othello's dual role as deathbed attendant – inhabiting the position of the compassionate caregiver who was to aid *Moriens* through a torturous demonic trial – and brutal murderer-judge creates a moment of cognitive and generic dissonance that would render these lines chillingly horrific.

Even as Desdemona attempts to conform to the protocols of the genre, she also breaks out of the form, twisting the notion of "mercy" from a religious to a marital context:

OTHELLO:      Therefore confess thee freely of thy sin . . .
DESDEMONA:    Then Lord have mercy on me.
OTHELLO:      I say amen.
DESDEMONA:    And have you mercy too. I never did
              Offend you in my life, never loved Cassio
              But with such general warranty of heaven
              As I might love: I never gave him token.
OTHELLO:      By heaven, I saw my handkerchief in's hand!

                                                    (5.2.53–62)

This is one of the most tumultuous moments in the play. Othello finally reveals what has been haunting him, and thus Desdemona finally comprehends the mistaken cause of her husband's rage. More significantly, the moment lurches violently from one generic mode to another. In a quick pivot, the scene reverts from the reassurances of traditional *ars moriendi* dialogue ("Lord have mercy on me."/"I say amen.") back into tragedy, as a victim pleads with her murderer for mercy. Othello's invocation of the handkerchief at this point also directly connects this scene with the earlier one that Othello took for definitive "ocular proof," when he thought he saw Cassio laugh about Desdemona's advances and presumed that Cassio had given the sacred handkerchief to a whore (4.1.75–166). As the audience knows, that scene was an object lesson in gross misreading. Or, more accurately, it was a scene of grotesque misinterpretation. Iago sets up a dialogue that Othello can only partially hear and poorly see, given that Iago speaks partly *sotto voce* and that Othello witnesses the scene from a concealed and distant position, enough so that he cannot clearly see the handkerchief. ("Iago: And did you see the handkerchief?/Othello: Was that mine?" [4.1.170–1]). As Iago intends, Othello's "unbookish jealousy must construe/Poor Cassio's smiles, gestures, and light behavior/Quite in the wrong" (4.1.102–4).

This observation scene, seemingly worlds removed from the supernatural encounters of the deathbed, has structural affinities with the scene of demonic temptation from the *ars moriendi*. (Interestingly, it is one of the scenes most frequently cut in production.[55]) Iago sets up the scene to create another moment of double vision: Othello, watching from afar, sees and hears one version of Cassio and Iago's encounter; Cassio and Iago experience a different version of the dialogue. In the *ars moriendi* tradition, the *Moriens* has a responsibility to faithfully translate the demonic encounter to the onlookers. Here, Iago sets up a mocking inverse of that dynamic, deliberately setting out to mislead the "unbookish" Othello with a series of equivoques.

Othello's invocation of that earlier scene during his murder of Desdemona not only calls attention to the conventions of the *ars moriendi* in the breaking of them, but also highlights the audience's own position as voyeurs. As Othello had once observed Iago and Cassio from a distance, the audience now watches Othello and Desdemona. Critics have remarked upon the voyeuristic quality of *Othello*, but have associated this voyeurism primarily with sexual dynamics.[56] While sexual voyeurism may well be at play in the rape-like murder scene, audiences of the deathbed were also traditionally positioned as voyeurs of a private demonic temptation, albeit one that they couldn't see. But just as Othello was set up to "construe/Poor Cassio's smiles, gestures, and light behaviour/Quite in the wrong," so too the play confounds the conventional pattern of witnessing a death, as the identification of demons becomes a complex and contradictory interpretive exercise. The identity confusion surrounding the elements of the demonic that flicker in and out of sight renders the deathbed scene frustratingly inaccessible to interpretation.

Othello's certainty about the "ocular proof" he has seen rubs against the grain of a supernatural visual culture that allows for multiple perspectives, visual incoherence, and skepticism. And indeed, *Othello* is deeply located within this supernatural context. References to "heaven," for instance, appear in this play far more than in any other Shakespearean text,[57] and the play is peppered by recurrent invocations of hell and its inhabitants. Martin Elliott takes issue with Helen Gardner's view that "'Devil' is a cliché in this play, a tired metaphor for 'very bad,' as 'angel' is for 'very good'" and that "[t]heological conceptions help us ... little," arguing that this reading "omits the landscapes of heaven and hell – and of heaven on earth and of hell on earth – by which Othello's imagination has been dominated with particular vividness through the play."[58]

Of course, many of the play's references to devils are, like many of the references to heaven, more idiomatic than actual.[59] But beyond metaphor and invective, the characters see – or think they see, or almost see – the devil in one another. As Othello undergoes his change of heart, he begins to associate Desdemona with the demonic. He strikes her and calls her "Devil!" (4.1.239), and in response to Lodovico's chastisement cries "O devil, devil!" (4.1.243), seemingly referring to Desdemona. He contemplates "some swift means of death/For the fair devil" (3.3.480–1). A passage that begins as a humoral diagnosis gradually insinuates an affinity with the devil. Othello takes Desdemona's hand, and observes:

> Hot, hot, and moist. This hand of yours requires
> A sequester from liberty, fasting and prayer,
> Much castigation, exercise devout,
> For here's a young and sweating devil, here,
> That commonly rebels.          (3.4.39–43)

And, in a moment that reads like a blazon through a blender, Othello swirls together his wife's body, sins, belongings, and demonic identity: "Pish! Noses, ears, and lips. Is't possible? Confess! handkerchief! O devil!" (4.1.42–3).

Othello is probably alone in perceiving Desdemona as a devil (in spite of the "demon" embedded in her name). In fact, an audience was much more likely to associate Othello himself with the devil. From the very beginning of the play, Iago links Othello with the devil in the minds of his auditory. He warns Brabantio, "the devil will make a grandsire of you" (1.1.90) and reassures Roderigo that Desdemona can be won with, "Her eye must be fed, and what delight shall she have to look on the devil?" (2.1.223–4). When Othello proclaims, "Arise, black vengeance, from the hollow hell" (3.3.450), he "call[s] down on himself the spiritual blackness of his theatrical forebears ... identif[ying] himself finally with the devil."[60]

Most importantly, Othello's skin color locates him firmly within the familiar visual iconography of the demonic. (The Jacobean actor's skin was even darkened with the "oil of hell."[61]) Virginia Mason Vaughan writes, "Black/white oppositions permeate *Othello*. Throughout the play, Shakespeare exploits a discourse of racial difference that by 1604 had become ingrained in the English psyche."[62] The immediate positioning here of black/white discourse in the context of race typifies most of the recent scholarship on *Othello*. The critical focus on race (and gender) perhaps makes the play more relevant to our own social concerns (as

Vaughan observes, the play addresses "larger issues of cultural exchange and conflict that still plague us"[63]), but this is not the only, or even the primary, way in which conceptions of black/white "had become ingrained in the English psyche" at the turn of the seventeenth century.[64] The opposition had deep and real eschatological significance, as the devil was commonly depicted as a black man.[65] The tradition dated back to medieval mystery plays,[66] and "the identification of the black man with the devil developed fully in the drama of the English Renaissance."[67] Even more specifically, the devil was associated with the Moor. ("Moor after Moor paraded on stage, and . . . so many were self-proclaimed as well as alleged agents of hell that their image as devils must be considered to have been a fairly fixed one"; the connection "between the Moor and the devil . . . was probably the most facile and the most frequently used of all the associations."[68]) To cite just one contemporary instance from the *ars moriendi*, Roberto Bellarmino wrote that "the Divel appeared . . . in the forme of a blacke-More."[69] Moors were also associated with death, partly by virtue of skin color and partly by phonetic alliance: "Moor" was associated with "Mors," the Latinized term for death (or, according to Erasmus, "the grekes call dethe in theyr langage moros"[70]). In addition, "Moriens" not only signified the dying person but was an English word for blackamoor.[71]

Othello's darkness cues an early modern audience to read him as satanic, but part of the cognitive disconnect of the early part of the play is that his self-presentation and interaction with other characters – Iago's racial epithets aside – belie that identification. At the deathbed, however, the demonic associations are brought to the fore. Emilia directly accuses Othello of being the devil immediately after Desdemona's death. Traditionally a moment in which the living might assess *Moriens*'s state of salvation, here the speculation takes us past Desdemona's fate, as she and Othello are positioned as the warring angelic and demonic forces that surround the deathbed:

OTHELLO:  She's like a liar gone to burning hell:
         'Twas I that killed her.
EMILIA:  O, the more angel she,
         And you the blacker devil!
OTHELLO:  She turned to folly, and she was a whore.
EMILIA:  Thou dost belie her, and thou art a devil.
         . . .
OTHELLO:  O, I were damned beneath all depth in hell
         But that I did proceed upon just grounds
         To this extremity.          (5.2.127–37)

Othello becomes both man and devil. His humanity is undermined by a visual tradition that associates his color with Satan, by Emilia's insistent accusations, and perhaps even by his own self-incriminating comment of damnation.

The deathbed identifications turn yet again when Othello himself is repositioned as the *Moriens*. Having declared "Here is my journey's end" (5.2.265), he looks to Desdemona and envisions their encounter in the afterlife. "When we shall meet at compt [i.e. Judgment Day]/This look of thine will hurl my soul from heaven/And fiends will snatch at it" (5.2.271–3). But that distant day seems to become a present reality as Othello exclaims:

> Whip me, ye devils,
> From the possession of this heavenly sight!
> Blow me about in winds, roast me in sulphur,
> Wash me in steep-down gulfs of liquid fire!    (5.2.275–8)

Located in the context of the *ars moriendi* tradition, this speech signals not an abstract moment of self-loathing, but quite possibly *Moriens*'s obligatory relation of the demonic tortures he is experiencing. Like Katherine Stubbes or the Jesuit William Weston's *Moriens*, Othello makes manifest to his onlookers the pre-mortem suffering of the dying at the hands of the devils. (Does some of the sulphur seep out? Emilia says of villainy, "I think I smell't" [5.2.188].)

And yet, if Othello is a *Moriens* seeing devils, he cannot quite see Iago. The ensign has been dropping hints throughout the play that he associates with the demonic. He boasts, "If sanctimony, and a frail vow betwixt an erring Barbarian and a super-subtle Venetian, be not too hard for my wits and all the tribe of hell, thou shalt enjoy her" (1.3.355–8). Elsewhere, he chuckles at his own hypocrisy: "Divinity of hell!/When devils will the blackest sins put on/They do suggest at first with heavenly shows/As I do now" (2.3.345–8). However, Othello searches in vain for definitive ocular proof of a demonic identity: "I look down towards his feet, but that's a fable./If that thou be'st a devil, I cannot kill thee" (5.2.283–4). The cloven hooves, the visible signs of the devil, elude Othello, and thus he can only see Iago as a "demi-devil" (5.2.298) – although Othello's inability to slay Iago suggests that he may, after all, be the devil. At the close of a play in which the label of "devil" was hurled freely, we thus encounter both Othello's graphic descriptions of demonic torment, and the flatness of skepticism. *Othello* mashes a rich literary tradition for shaping supernatural interactions with an emergent skepticism that subverts that tradition.[72]

The aggregate effect of these demonic identifications is an uneasy sense that devils might well lurk in the midst of the company. Different characters might perceive demonic influence differently, and those perceptions might differ from those of the audience, but taken together the play shimmers with suspicions and the possibility of a devilish presence.

The sense of the devil's ubiquity, and yet elusiveness and unreality, contravenes the interpretive protocols of *ars moriendi* literature. *Othello's* integration of the *ars moriendi* signals to its seventeenth-century audience that they should engage in the heightened mode of reading and interpretation required by the genre. They are to assume the multifaceted task of critiquing the death, studying the roles of deathbed attendant and *Moriens*, and searching for traces of Satan. But even as it provides a clear invocation of this genre, the play contorts the elements of the *ars moriendi*, presenting a deathbed scene that, like the body of a loved one disfigured by disease, is at once wholly known and grotesquely strange. If the *ars moriendi* provided the comfort of genre, arranging the unknown and frightening experience of death into a patterned and predictable form (giving death a textual and hence cognitive home, as it were), *Othello* preys upon that sense of comfort and destroys it, presenting a death that adheres to the *ars* protocols enough to make it recognizable and yet deviating from the genre enough to make it monstrous. Just as the on-stage bed provides a false emblem of domestic security, so too the invocation of the *ars moriendi* provides a false gesture of generic safety.

This signifying indeterminacy translates into visual complexity. Diverse literary critics have commented on types of visual duality in *Othello*. Paul Yachnin writes that "Desdemona is transformed into a *spectacle of duplicity* within Othello's theatre of the gaze." Bernard Spivack writes of the play's "*double image*," and notes that, "if we require a paradigm of the endless bewilderment with which honest Iago afflicts us, we have only to try to see Othello through his ancient's *bifocal vision* – both as the 'lusty Moor' and as the middle-aged man of 'weak function.'" Virginia Mason Vaughan writes of Desdemona, "Instead of looking for psychological consistency in her characterization ... we must see her refracted through patriarchy's *bifurcated lens*." Lois Potter observes, "Uneasiness about Othello's physical contact with Desdemona was based on a *double vision*." Jack D'Amico writes, "Working with the *dual image* of the noble, tawny Moor and the dark-complexioned devil, Shakespeare revealed how a man could be destroyed when he accepts a perspective that deprives him of his humanity." More broadly, but still invoking a sense of seeing double, in his edition of the play E. A. J. Honnigmann positions a metaphysical battle in the visual field just behind the main dramatic action: "Critics . . . have found it necessary to comment on the fierce dispute of Good and Evil in *Othello* – justifiably, since this *less visible* conflict is somehow connected with the human drama that we *observe in the foreground.*"[73] (Italics mine throughout.)

To an extent, double vision is an inherent element of theater: we watch actors playing characters, and are aware of the duplicity. In the early modern theater, audiences watched boys play the parts of women and artisans play the parts of kings. But the scholarly tendency to comment on various forms of double vision in *Othello* suggests a dynamic that is unique, or at least accentuated, in this play. Indeed, throughout the play we find characters (most typically Iago) alerting us to that which is seen and that which is concealed. In frustration, Othello accuses Iago of acting "As if there were some monster in [his] thought/Too hideous to be shown" (3.3.110–1).

This double vision is where *Othello* converges and diverges with the *ars moriendi* tradition. For while the deathbed scene presents a visual reconstruction from the *ars moriendi*, that scene teasingly suggests its own hermeneutics, only to subvert them. The fundamental dynamic of *ars moriendi* literature, in both its visual and dialogic forms, is relatively straightforward. A dying person lies in bed and is accosted by demons. The dying person makes the physical reality of these demons legible to the attendants – he provides mediated ocular proof of their presence, as it were. The *Moriens* sees demons; the attendants see *Moriens* seeing demons. As the *ars moriendi* scene in *Othello* becomes twisted and gnarled, however, these sightlines become contorted. The number of those perceiving the devil creates a swirling vision of half-seen demons. And the number of characters associated with the devil (Iago, Othello, even Desdemona) overruns the scene of the deathbed, as identifications with attendants, *Moriens*, and demonic agents become clouded and collapse. The traditional iconography of the *ars moriendi* – *Moriens*, attendants, devils – converge in *Othello* such that vision, and interpretation, become difficult. Greenblatt has written of another play: "For all the invocation of the gods in *King Lear*, it is clear that there are no devils" and that "it is impossible, in [*King Lear*], to witness the eruption of the denizens of hell into the human world."[74] But in *Othello*, it seems clear that there *are* devils, or should be, given the dramatic form provided by the *ars moriendi*, a genre whose raison d'être is largely to enable an audience a mediated means "to witness the eruption of the denizens of hell into the human world." The problem in *Othello* is that while an audience (and the characters within the play) might assume that there are devils present, the spectators cannot clearly map out who they are, as demonic identifications shift in and out of focus and become overlaid with one another.

*Othello* presents a scene that an audience versed in *ars moriendi* literature should be able to read, and yet makes that scene unreadable. The flickering of demons is perhaps a consequence of demonic manipulation of the visual field: while the devil could not occupy more than one space at a time, according to some sixteenth-century experts "he could ... present illusory objects to the senses by influencing the air or wrapping fantastic shapes around real bodies."[75] Such activity, giving the illusion, if not quite the reality, of bodies occupying multiple points in space, cannot be easily accommodated, or adapted at all, within a space conceptualized in geometric terms. The effect of instable demonic identities is the destabilization of the visual scene, and by extension the play's larger environment. Here we find a moment in which "technique imitates subject," as Spivack puts it: the contortion of the visual reflects the experience of the demonic.

From this demonic encounter we find a dynamic that should feel familiar, given our own critical moment and interest in identity formation. Let's return to a passage quoted above:

> Whip me, ye devils,
> From the possession of this heavenly sight!
> Blow me about in winds, roast me in sulphur,
> Wash me in steep-down gulfs of liquid fire!    (5.2.275–8)

These lines are read by Barthelemy as a collapse of human self and supernatural Other: "The Moor now condemns himself with the language commonly used to damn black fiends, as though he has assumed not only the role of the tormented but also of the tormentor, the damned and the damning" (*Black Face Maligned Race*, p. 158). Similarly, he writes of "the basic duality of Othello's character, a duality that is constantly at work in the play. In the end, however, the separate parts become one in Othello, and the good becomes inseparable from the evil, Justice from the Moor, the playwright from the dissembler" (p. 161). This moment of identity compression participates in, and perhaps even proceeds, the play's collapse of racial and geographic identities. The play's very title – *Othello, the Moor of Venice*  presents a Gordian knot that has intrigued the minds of a recent generation of scholars, who profit from a deepened and more nuanced understanding of early modern notions of national, racial, and religious identities.[76] The fraught nature of Othello's own self-identification is epitomized in the moment of his suicide, when, famously, the "turbaned Turk" (5.2.351) and the "Venetian" (5.2.352) impossibly and incongruously compress into a self-annihilating "he that was Othello" (5.2.281).

Othello's wrenching collapse epitomizes a larger quality of the play: the disorientation caused by a skewed visual and spatial environment. Edward Pechter notes that, "Despite all the critical attention understandably devoted to 'ocular proof' and 'the gaze,' the play's language ... works by multiplying and condensing incompatible images and contradictory significances to produce an effect not of mastery – a privileged vantage from which to fix meanings, as in a stable visual field – but of giddiness verging on nausea."[77] Of the conflict between Turk and Venetian, Pechter writes:

Where is the center? Where is the margin? It is not that we cannot answer these questions (really one question with two parts), but as we are propelled by Iago through the violently shifting emotional landscape at the beginning of the play's action, each answer lasts only long enough for suggestions to emerge requiring us to change places: *here* becomes a strange and unfamiliar place, *there* turns into the position from which we find ourselves engaging with the action ... In *Othello* ... our guide is Iago, and from his anxiety-driven and anxiety-producing perspective, the erosion of the distinction between here and everywhere transports us violently into nowhere, an amorphously engulfing space where the constituting differences of individual identity, as between black and white, self and other, seem to be collapsing ... into a monstrous undifferentiation. (*Othello*, pp. 37–8)

The eschatological space of the bedchamber suffers from the same collapse of identity defined by more earthly boundaries. The visual dynamics of that space, as constructed in the *ars moriendi* texts, clearly define the here of the spectators from the there of the dying – at least, the idea that these two positions entail two different points of view is a prominent feature of the genre.

*Othello* takes that double vision and lets it run amok. The traditionally demarcated boundaries of the deathbed offered spatial and eschatological protection: while *Moriens* was subject to demonic torture, the nearby attendants were safely insulated. The *ars moriendi* illustrations and their dramatization through textual dialogue, while exemplifying a type of multiple vision and perspective that does not conform to the increasingly normative linear perspective, do at least put the devil in his place. *Othello* borrows the form, but only to undo it. In this play, the plurality of visual perspectives destabilizes the relationship of earthly and eschatological spaces, resulting in boundaries that are terrifyingly undifferentiated, and a devil loose in the world.

# CHAPTER 3

# When hell freezes over: The fabulous Mount Hecla and Hamlet's infernal geography

PROSPERO [to Ariel]: I'll chain thee in the north for thy neglect,
Within the burning bowels of Mount Hecla;
I'll singe thy airy wings with sulphurous flames,
And choke thy tender nostrils with blue smoke.
John Dryden's adaptation of *The Tempest*[1]

Their Question was of purgatory, where,
And whether 'tis at all, if so, 'tis here.
David Lloyd, *The Legend of Captaine Iones*
*relating his Adventure to Sea* (1631), p. 14

## MAPPING PURGATORY

Desdemona's deathbed, as I discussed in the previous chapter, stages a form of double vision, as an audience is drawn to perceive the bed as both an earthly and an eschatological space.[2] I turn now from the enclosed, domestic location of the bed to consider a similar dynamic on a much wider geographic scale. This chapter will explore the "undiscovered country" of the afterlife (to borrow Hamlet's familiar phrase), examining how beliefs about the supernatural interacted with a cartographic epistemology. Specifically, I turn to the status of purgatory in *Hamlet*. For many in the field of early modern studies, this might seem to be well-worn terrain, the site of contests over religious beliefs, theologies, and ideologies within the period itself, and the site of scholarly struggles to interpret these contests within our own time.[3] While purgatory certainly became a flashpoint for competing politico-theologies from the earliest days of the Reformation, it was not only the source of abstract beliefs or the impetus for religious practices.[4] It was also a point of geographical speculation. An integral part of the debates, discussions, and general curiosity about purgatory was its actual location. This focus on geographical specificity has gone virtually unexamined, and it is what

I will consider here. One of the places most frequently identified as the site of purgatory was the Icelandic volcano Mount Hecla. As I will argue, while this volcano is never mentioned by name, it is Mount Hecla that shimmers throughout *Hamlet* as the geographical locus of purgatory, the prison of Hamlet's father's ghost.

The early modern fervor to map the environment was not restricted to the surface of the globe. The undiscovered country of death was also folded into a discourse of exploration and discovery.[5] This phenomenon has been discussed by Philip Almond, who quotes, for instance, from Joseph Glanvill: "*Indeed*, as things are for the present, the LAND OF ESPIRITS is a kind of *America*, and not well discover'd *Region*; yea, it stands in the *Map* of *humane Science* like *unknown Tracts*, fill'd up with *Mountains, Seas, and Monsters*."[6] Glanvill's emphasis on the unknown perhaps does not do justice to those in the sixteenth and seventeenth centuries who applied the newfound geometric and cartographic knowledge in an effort to better comprehend the spatial details of the netherworld. Robert Burton, in his *Anatomy of Melancholy* (1621), collates some examples of how various authors were calculating the space of hell:

Franciscus Ribera, in cap. 14. *Apocalyps.* will have hell a material and local fire in the centre of the earth, 200 Italian miles in diameter, as he defines it out of those words, *Exivit sanguis de terra – per stadia mille sexcenta, & c.* But Lessius *lib.*13. *de moribus divinis, cap.* 24. will have this local hell far less, one Dutch mile in diameter, all filled with fire and brimstone: because, as he there demonstrates, that space, cubically multipled, will make a sphere able to hold eight hundred thousand millions of damned bodies (allowing each body six foot square) which will abundantly suffice.[7]

This mathematical approach to understanding the reality of hell – the idea that it is "material and local," and thus has a diameter and cubic space – persisted throughout the early modern period. In 1714 Tobias Swinden, in *An Enquiry into the Nature and Place of Hell*, ridicules Drexelius's calculation that there would be 100,000,000,000 of the damned in a hell that was only one square German mile. Swinden does not attack the mathematical approach, but its inaccuracy: the interior of the earth is clearly insufficiently large to house all of the souls of the damned, and therefore Swinden argues that, based on mathematical calculations, hell must instead be located inside the center of the sun.[8]

This intensely materialist approach to the space of the dead is paired, however, with an oppositional movement towards fictionalizing hell and purgatory altogether. Burton's authorial voice, Democritus Junior, meditates on this controversy:

What is the centre of the earth? is it pure element only, as Aristotle decrees, inhabited (as Paracelsus thinks) with creatures, whose chaos is the earth: or with fairies, as the woods and waters (according to him) are with nymphs, or as the air with spirits? . . . Or is it the place of hell, as Virgil in his Æneides, Plato, Lucian, Dante, and others poetically describe it, and as many of our divines think? In good earnest, Anthony Rusca, one of the society of that Ambrosian College, in Milan, in his great volume *de Inferno, lib.1.cap.47.* is stiff in this tenet, 'tis a corporeal fire tow, *cap.* 5, *l.2.* as he there disputes. "Whatsoever philosophers write (saith Surius), there be certain mouths of hell, and places appointed for the punishment of men's souls, as at Hecla in Iceland, where the ghosts of dead men are familiarly seen, and sometimes talk with the living: God would have such visible places, that mortal men might be certainly informed, that there be such punishments after death, and learn hence to fear God." (pp. 317–18)

Democritus Junior then proceeds to include the counter-argument to Rusca's assertion of the reality of geographical hellmouths. Those who disbelieved the actuality of hell or purgatory considered it purely fictional:

But these and such like testimonies others reject, as fables, illusions or spirits, and they will have no such local known place, more than Styx or Phlegethon, Pluto's court, or that poetical *Infernus,* where Homer's soul was seen hanging on a tree, & c., to which they ferried over in Charon's boat, or went down at Hermione in Greece, *compendiaria ad inferos via,* which is the shortest cut, *quia nullum à mortuis naulum eo loci exposcunt* (saith Gerbelius), and besides there were no fees to be paid. Well then, is it hell, or purgatory, as Bellarmine: or *Limbus patrum,* as Gallucius will, and as Rusca will (for they have made maps of it), or Ignatius parlour? (p. 318)

He closes off the debate with this comment that perhaps epitomizes the stance of many people in the period, torn between the theological debates about the existence of purgatory and their own beliefs about death: "I will end the controversy in Austin's words, 'Better doubt of things concealed, than to contend about uncertainties, where Abraham's bosom is, and hell fire'" (p. 319).

Early modern discussions about the place of purgatory swung between these poles of materialism and fiction. Perhaps following suit, recent scholarship on purgatory in *Hamlet* has also been polarized. On the one hand, Margreta de Grazia, in Hamlet *without Hamlet,* has shown how the modern emphasis on Hamlet's psychological interiority has obfuscated the play's materiality and concerns about the land, its engagement with the actual mud and loam of the earth.[9] Thus in her reading "the graveyard scene conjoins concern about Last Things with issues of entitlement"

(p. 142), since "in 1600 the eschatological setting might have brought to mind more immediate issues of [land] allocation" (p. 140) – "Doomsday" suggesting both divine judgment and land ownership (pp. 140–2), of both the hereafter and the very earthy here. On the other hand, Stephen Greenblatt, in *Hamlet in Purgatory*, notes that sixteenth-century religious reformers who wished to discredit belief in purgatory frequently resorted to labeling it a "fable," a charge which positions the idea as antithetical to material reality.[10] Greenblatt contends that Protestants considered "not only the fraudulence of Purgatory, its lack of scriptural basis, and its corrupt institutional uses but its special relation to dream, fantasy, and imagination."[11]

Both of these arguments, in their different ways, are right. When we look past a modern, introspective Hamlet, we recognize the earthiness of *Hamlet*, an earthiness that surrounds the play's questions of the afterlife, from the issue of where to bury its many dead bodies to the location of purgatory. At the same time, anyone rooting about in the archive of early modern polemical religious literature will regularly encounter accusations that purgatory is a "fable." Contemporary accusations of purgatory's fictionality do indeed inform the play, as Greenblatt has extensively demonstrated. As the afterlife appears in *Hamlet*, then, it is both a material, loamy, rotten affair and the subject of abstract, philosophical, fantastical musings.

In its association with a specific geographical location and fable, Mount Hecla, too, is a site that swirls together the materially real and the fabulous. It is a space that was charted on maps and the source of legend; it is a place that collapses the distinction between the empirically carto-graphic and the fantastic. Icelandic natural historians writing in Latin for a European audience at the end of the sixteenth century (a period in which Iceland was popularly in vogue) had to confront this rather idio-syncratic "Icelandic environment [that] was popularly conceived of as having its own life," one in which "the natural and the supernatural merged."[12] Identifying the specific location of Denmark's purgatory in Mount Hecla, then, provides more than just a topical allusion for a detail of the play; it provides a referent that comes attached to an epistemo-logical understanding of the environment that does not segregate the natural from the supernatural, or earth from purgatory. Within a variety of early modern texts – madrigals, maps, exploration narratives, *Hamlet* – Mount Hecla sits at the nexus of a cultural investment in mapping the environment and beliefs about the supernatural. In better understanding the dynamic interplay of these modes as they pertain to sixteenth- and seventeenth-century conceptualizations of Mount Hecla, we can better understand the supernatural environment of *Hamlet* itself.

In *Purchas His Pilgrimage, or Relations of the VVorld and the Religions Obserued in al Ages and Places Discouered, from the Creation vnto this Present* (1617), we read of the northern adventures of the explorer Henry Hudson:

Henry Hudson, 1607. discouerd further North toward the Pole, then perhaps any before him. He found himself in 80. deg. 23. minutes, where they felt it hot, and dranke vvater to coole their thirst. They saw land (as they thought) to 82. and further: on the shore they had Snow, Morses teeth, Deeres hornes, Whalebones, and footing of the other beasts, vvith a streame of fresh water. The next yeere 1608. he set forth on a Discouerie to the North-east, at vvhich time they met, as both himself and *Iuet* haue testified, a Mermaid in the Sea, seene by *Thomas Hils* and *Robert Rainer*. Another voyage he made 1609. and coasted New-found-land, and thence along to Cap Cod. His last and fatall voyage was 1610. vvhich I mentioned in my former edition, relating the same as *Hesselius Gerardus* had guided me, by his card and reports, who affirmeth that he followed the way which Captaine *Winwood* had before searched by *Lumleys inlet*, in 61. deg. so passing thorow the strait to 50. & c. But hauing since met with better instructions, both by the help of my painfull friend Mr. *Hakluyt* ... and specially from Him, who was a speciall setter forth of the voyage, that learned and industrious Gentleman Sir *Dudley Digges* ... hauing receiued full relations, I have been bold with the Reader to insert this Voyage more largely.

In the yeere 1610. Sir *Thomas Smith*, Sir *Dudley Digges*, and Master *Iohn Wostenholme*, with other their friends, furnished out the said *Henry Hudson*, to trie if through any of those Inlets, which *Dauis* saw, but durst not enter, on the Westerne side of *Fretum Dauis*, any passage might bee found to the other Ocean called the South Sea. There [sic] Barke vvas named the Discouerie. They passed by Island [i.e. Iceland], and saw Mount *He[c]la* cast out fire (a noted signe of foule weather towards; others conceiue themselues and deceiue others with I know not vvhat Purgatorie fables hereof confuted by *Arngrin Ionas* an Islander, who reproueth this and many other dreames related by Authors, saying, that from the yeere 1558. to 1592. it neuer cast forth any flames) they left the name to one harbor in Island, *Lousy bay*: they had there a Bath hot enough to scald a fowle.[13]

This passage is a mine rich in the details of exploration. We are told of the travelers' experience of heat, and of the water that cooled it. We see – like the gemstones scattered on the snow in a famous blazon in Petrarch's sonnets – "Snow, Morses [i.e. walrus] teeth, Deeres hornes, Whalebones."

The account is careful to document its sources: "as *Hesselius Gerardus* had guided me, by his card [i.e. map] and reports." The identities of explorers are specific: "Sir *Thomas Smith*, Sir *Dudley Digges*, and Master *Iohn Wostenholme*." There is a careful recording of time (1607, 1608, 1609), and a precise orientation in space (80. deg. 23. minutes, etc.).

In the course of their voyage, the explorers encounter a mermaid: "at vvhich time they met, as both himself and *Iuet* haue testified, a Mermaid in the Sea, seene by *Thomas Hils* and *Robert Rainer*." The veracity of this encounter is assured by the double frame of witnesses, by the testimony of Hudson and Iuet on one side, and the eyewitness report of Hils and Rainer on the other. While the sighting of the mermaid is granted the status of fact, another view is dismissed as a fiction: they "saw Mount *He[c]la* cast out fire (a noted signe of foule weather towards; others conceiue themselues and deceiue others with I know not vvhat Purgatorie fables hereof confuted by *Arngrin Ionas* an Islander, who reproueth this and many other dreames related by Authors, saying, that from the yeere 1558. to 1592. it neuer cast forth any flames)." The popular association of Mount Hecla with purgatory is explained away in this lengthy parenthetical digression. In contrast to the "reports" that verified previous aspects of the experience, here the "Authors" who claim a connection of the volcano with purgatory are refuted by a native observer who has documented the years in which it was inactive; the fires of purgatory, presumably, burn continuously, so a hiatus dispels the notion that this is a portal to the netherworld.

This parenthetical moment in Purchas may be seen as participating in the strategy of considering purgatory a "fable," the literary "dreame" of "Authors." But the fictionalizing of purgatory here is hardly simple or complete. We find in this moment the declared fiction being disproved by recorded fact; we find authorial dreams being argued against with the habits of recorded measurement associated with what today we call science. And the very necessity of Purchas's parenthetical disclaimer about Mount Hecla stems from a robust tradition of identifying this volcano as a locus of post-mortem purgatorial punishment. What we find here, in short, is the idea of purgatory located within the discursive cross-currents of both the fabulous and the materially real, of story and discovery, of skepticism and belief. It is, like the volcano Mount Hecla that Henry Hudson's men saw from the side of their ship, a space that invites at once the rigors of empiricism and the elusive qualities of fantasy.

While sixteenth- and seventeenth-century debates about purgatory frequently revolved around theological positions and biblical exegesis, they also revolved around the question of whether or not purgatory was a physical, geographical space. I have already touched upon this idea in reference to Burton's *Anatomy of Melancholy*, but I will now explore it more fully. Certainly we encounter arguments against purgatory like those of the early sixteenth-century reformer John Frith – for purgatory, "we haue no infallible evidence, but only phantasicall imaginacio[n]s"[14] – but these positions find a counterweight in those who argued about purgatory's actual location. Those who sought to discredit belief in purgatory did so not only with a wave of the hand and the derogatory epithet of "fable," but also through the pressures of empirical and cartographical evidence. In sixteenth- and seventeenth-century discourse, "purgatory" was located not only on the fault line of theological difference, but also on the fissure of poetry and proof.

A definition of purgatory from 1659 sums up a dominant understanding of the idea of purgatory: it is "a subterraneous *caue*, fill'd with *flames* and horrid *instruments* of torture, which his there confined and imprison'd soul must, till expiated endure."[15] Purgatory, like hell, was largely presumed to be located within the earth. This vague sense of underwordly geography opened the idea up to critique. Andrew Willet, for example, makes an emphatically Protestant attack on the Catholic map of the netherworld in his *Synopsis papismi, that is, A generall viewe of papistry wherein the whole mysterie of iniquitie, and summe of antichristian doctrine is set downe, which is maintained this day by the Synagogue of Rome, against the Church of Christ, together with an antithesis of the true Christian faith, and an antidotum or counterpoyson out of the Scriptures, against the whore of Babylons filthy cuppe of abominations* (1592). In "An Appendix, concerning the place of Hell," he sets out the Papist position: "The place where damned spirites are tormented, they say, is about the center of the earth, the lowest of all places, and nothing lower then it" (p. 607). He then parses the concept more finely:

Their *Limbus Patrum*, the place of darkenes, where the Fathers were before Christ, is, say they, in the highest parte, and as it were the brimme of hel ... Betweene these two places there is a great gulfe or space, and there is Purgatory ... Wherefore they conclude, *veros inferos esse loca subterranea*: That the subterrestrial and infernall places doe properly make hell ... And so hell should be properly a place of punishme[n]t: because of the farre distance from heauen. (p. 607)

The Aristotelian epistemology that structures this geography (that which is ontologically lowest should be at the midst of the earth) is combated with lengthy close reading and application of Scripture. If, in the harrowing of hell, Christ descended to the "very hart and midst of the earth, which is the center" (p. 608), then, according to this Catholic geography, wouldn't he have liberated the damned, instead of "the Fathers [who] were before Christ" residing not in the middle, but on the "brimme"? This mismatch of geometry and religious tradition creates an illogical aberration of divine justice and Christ's mercy.

While repeatedly affirming the existence of a place of punishment, Willet argues about centers, margins, and semantics: "We deny not but that God hath prepared, and that there is a place of vnspeakable torments ordeined for the deuill and his angels, and all damned soules: but that this place should be in the center of the earth, the places alleadged proue not: for the word *Aybssus* translated, the deepe, is sometime taken figuratiuely in a metaphore, as *Rom. 11.33* ... Neither must this word *abyssus*, of necessitie be referred to the earth, for there are *abyssi maris*, the depths of the Sea, *Exod. 15.8.* as well as of the earth" (p. 608). Willet sums up the Protestant position (specifically labeled as such within the text) in this way:

That there is a locall place of torment prepared for the deuill and his angels, we doubt not, being so taught in the Scripture, *Math. 25.41.* A place of darknes, *2. Pet. 2.4.* Farre distant from the heauenly mansions of the blessed, *Luke 16.26.* Neither doe we deny but that it may be in the earth, or wheresoeuer els it pleaseth God: but wheresoeuer hel is, there is but one: that deuision of hell into three or foure regions, we vtterly condemne, as a mere deuise of man without Scripture: and this we say, that the place of hell causeth not the torment, but the wrath and curse of God. (p. 609)

"[W]heresoeuer hel is, there is but one": the location of hell is numinous, unknowable; its division into discrete territories unfounded and ridiculous.

Willlet's arguments are similar to those of John Veron. In *The Hvntynge of Purgatorye to Death* (1561), Veron articulates the prevalent anti-Catholic arguments against the existence of purgatory. The popish mass, perceived as a corrupt money-making enterprise, is predicated on the existence of purgatory – "this faigned purgatory, and vaine opinion of praying for the deade, which be onely grounded vpon the foolishe imaginations and dreames of a sorte of superstitious and coueteous persons" (sig. A4ᵛ). To lose the physical, spatial reality of purgatory would result in a profound loss of ecclesiastical income. Clergy thus have a vested interest in maintaining belief in purgatory as a particular location. In a section of his text labeled "the cosmographi [sic] of hel or the limbe & of purgaorye" (153ᵛ), four interlocutors discuss a sermon they heard "aboute a fifteen or syxtene daies agoo in the chiefe paryshe churche of this town" (154ʳ). The sense of verisimilitude created by the specificity of time and place will prove a stark contrast with the absurdity of the priest's claims to know the geographical location of purgatory. A seemingly extraneous marginal note appears to be a summary of the sermon: "Center is the point yt is in ye veri mids of ye earth & there about they say that hel with ye limbe & purgatorye is" (154ᵛ). One of the Protestant interlocutors in the dialogue freely acknowledges the reality of hell, given its undisputed status in the Bible, but maintains that "We haue no neede to enquyre of the place. For, I thinke that there is no man, that is desirouse to goe thither" (155ᵛ). When pressed for a particular location for hell, he answers thus: "But if thou doest aske of the situation and of [sic] the place, I wil au[n]swere and saye, that it is situated or appointed to be withoute thys materiall and earthely worlde" (155ᵛ). With hell understood as a place outside of material, earthly space, geographical questioning is pointless: "We ought not then to enquyre in what place it is situated, but how it maye be exchewed & escaped" (155ᵛ–156ʳ). In a discussion of the book of Job, a central feature of hell is determined to be its immeasurability. There is no time, "For, there the Su[n]ne & the Moone haue not their course for to compasse and measur it" (158ʳ). And there is no calculable space: "There be then no maner of bou[n]des or lymites for to measure and limite places or landes" (158ʳ).

In contrast to this Protestant notion of a dematerialized, immeasurable hell, the priest's understanding of purgatory is mocked as being subject to geographic and even geodetic precision. One character comments, "We do much esteem Ptolomee, & many other great & excellent Geographes, as well emong the Grekes, as emong the Latynes: yet I thinke, yt now can be fou[n]d emong them al, that did so konningly describe & paynte out in all his Geographie, the hole earth with al the partes, contreyes and regio[n]s therof, as this maister doctor, did set & paynte out before our eyes those infernal and lowe parties" (160ᵛ). (A marginal note defines "A geographe" and "Geogra.[phie]," indicating the novelty of these terms.) The priest is ridiculed as a potential tour guide of "those infernall regions and countreys" (161ᵛ). Most interestingly, the priest's interest in knowing the exact situation of purgatory is compared to that of a money-grubbing landlord. The emergence of land surveying (which I will discuss in the final chapter) was driven in large part by the desire of landlords to have a more accurate way to assess revenue from rents and leases. The priest is purportedly motivated by similar desires, since income from purgatory has already been established as its raison d'être:

DIDIMUS:     Notaries do take very muche payn and are verye diligente too expresse in their deedes and writtings the situation and bou[n]des of the houses, landes, and tenementes, that they do writt of, but none could I euer fynde in all my lyfe so experte and kunninge, that was able too sette out so perfectly the situation and butting of euery house and lande, that he doth writte of, as our master doctour was to measure and limite hell, the lymbe and purgatorie. As farre as I can perceyue, he can tell in what Climate they be all, what eleuation of the Pole they haue, how many degrees thei sta[n]de one from an other, on what syds they be situated or lye, whether it be in the East or in ye West in the Northe or in the South.

EUTRAPE:     Ye do not take it a mysse, But ye oughte not too meruayll that bothe he, and all his felowes be so diligente, & take so greate payn to measure & limite those places, and specially purgatorye. For, they haue no better possession than that, in all the hole worlde, nor that yeldeth vnto the[m] greater reuenues, rentes and profit.

There is neyther kyngdome, lordshippe, lande nor heritage, that is more fruytefull vnto their lordes and owners, than purgatorie is vnto them. Therefore, my fre[n]de, it is no wonder if they be so afraid to lose it, or that some bodye shuld remoue the boundes and markes of it.

. . .

DIDIMUS:     We maye knowe by that, or at lest we maye surmyse, that he doeth not onelye speake by heare saye, but that eyther he hym selfe hathe ben there in personne, or that he hath hadde a master very kunninge and experte in that kinde of Geographie. For, we doo see that the best Geographes, and mooste experte Cosmographes, are shamefullye deceyued in the description of the earthe, and of manye contryes and regions, whiche are farre better knowen of vs, and of whiche, wee maye haue more certayne experience than of those infernall contryes.

Therefore, I do not doubte, but that this master doctour could verye well make and compasse a Mappe or Carte of those low and infernall regions, and sette theym oute muche better vntoo vs, than the paynters haue paynted them in the Churches, or Prynters in the Shepeheardes Kalender.

(159ᵛ–161ʳ)

The friction between the geographic and even geodetic discourse – of an interest in measures and degrees, metes and bounds – and the presumed imaginary nature of the location being surveyed produces an effect of the absurd. Veron's text participates in what Peter Marshall has identified as "a central component of the Protestant strategy for demolishing

Purgatory," the emphasis on the "spurious geographic locations and spatial relationships [of netherworld spaces] to each other, to demonstrate the unreality of these places through an ironic evocation of their very concreteness."[16] While I have focused on only two exemplary texts here, this interrogation of infernal geography was widespread. Marshall writes: the "intense hostility to the Roman teaching on the next life remained a staple of anti-papal polemic throughout the period. While this polemic attacked Purgatory on a number of fronts – its association with clerical abuses, its inculcation of unchristian fear, its alleged disparagement of Christ's Passion – a persistent theme was the absurdity of the Catholic geography of the afterlife, its tendency to particularize and localize imaginary realms, to map out the confines and borders of the hereafter."[17]

Early modern debates about the existence of purgatory, then, were not merely abstract exercises in theology. Nor were they primarily focused on purgatory's status as a fable. The force of thinking about purgatory as fantasy came from the equal and opposite reaction of thinking about purgatory as a physical space. Discussions of purgatory therefore brought together a constellation of contemporary concerns: the role of the imagination and varying perspectives on how to read Scripture and different theological positions on the nature of divine justice, to be sure, but also an emergent geographic sensibility, one which encompassed issues pertaining to mapping, land ownership, discovery, mathematics, etc. Within the period, purgatory is a topic of interest not only because of the controversy over whether or not it exists, but because it presents the challenge of comprehending the supernatural in a newly cartographic world. Encounters with purgatory – as a reader, as a voyager, and, as in Hamlet's case, as a witness of the supernatural – sparked questions not just of purgatory's validity, but of its possible location, and how that location might or might not be accommodated into a geographic consciousness.

*Hamlet* itself is caught not only in early modern theological cross-currents, but in the geographical ferment that coincided with cultures of religious belief.[18] Part of the emotional uncertainty of how to relate to the dead emanates from a geographic uncertainty about where the dead reside. In *Hamlet*, we encounter a space similar to that in Henry Hudson's brush with the supernatural: in the midst of a landscape imagined through early modern territorial and cartographic protocols (the nation state and the geodetic map), purgatory maintains a disconcerting presence, its fabulous, discredited flames still burning within an empirical geography.

DENMARK, NORWAY, ENGLAND, HELL

*Hamlet* is a play about interiority, a study of inwardness that epitomizes the function of literature and the exploration of psychology more generally. Such is the traditional reading. However, this understanding of the play, as de Grazia has compellingly argued, back-reads the text through the lens of modernity. The critical focus on Hamlet's "deep and complex inwardness" (Hamlet *without Hamlet*, p. 1) ignores the play's key premise, that of the prince's dispossession. And "[a]s Hamlet's dispossession has been ignored, so, too, has *Hamlet's* investment in land" (p. 3). "In a world in which men fight and kill for land . . . the importance of the realm to Hamlet might well be a given. It does more than give substance to his state of dejection at the play's start: it knits him into the fabric of the play. The play opens with threatened invasion and ends in military occupation. Framed by territorial conflict, it stages one contest over land after another" (pp. 2–3). In addition to staging disputes over earthly territory, I argue that the play struggles to reconcile chthonic and eschatological spaces.

The action of the play is presented against a backdrop of frenetic activity and international political tensions. *Hamlet* is a family drama, and a personal drama, happening in the midst of military action worthy of *Henry V.* In the opening scene, Marcellus seeks to know the reason for the general burst of activity: "[w]hy this same strict and most observant watch/So nightly toils the subject of the land," why "such daily cost of brazen cannon/And foreign mart for implements of war," "[w]hy such impress of shipwrights, whose sore task/ Does not divide the Sunday from the week" (1.1.70–5).[19] What, in short, is the reason "that this sweaty haste/Doth make the night joint labourer with day"? (1.1.76–7) Why the toil, the sweat, the haste, the labor through the sabbath and the night? Why the cannons, why the ships? Marcellus seems exasperated by the lack of information. "Good now, sit down, and tell me he that knows," he implores (1.1.69). "Who is't that can inform me?" he demands (1.1.78). What is going on? Somebody tell me!

Horatio can answer: "That can I./At least the whisper goes so . . ." (1.1.78–9). His direct offering of explanation qualified by the acknowledgment that he knows only rumors, Horatio launches into a complicated and detailed account of political affairs:

> . . . Our last King,
> Whose image even but now appeared to us,
> Was as you know by Fortinbras of Norway
> Thereto pricked on by a most emulate pride
> Dared to the combat, in which our valiant Hamlet
> . . .

Did slay this Fortinbras, who by a sealed compact
Well ratified by law and heraldry
Did forfeit with his life all these his lands
Which he stood seized of to the conqueror;
Against the which a moiety competent
Was gaged by our King, which had return
To the inheritance of Fortinbras,
Had he been vanquisher, as by the same co-mart,
And carriage of the article design
His fell to Hamlet. Now, sir, young Fortinbras,
Of unimproved mettle, hot and full,
Hath in the skirts of Norway here and there
Sharked up a list of lawless resolutes
For food and diet to some enterprise
That hath a stomach in't, which is no other,
As it doth well appear unto our state,
But to recover of us by strong hand
And terms compulsatory those foresaid lands
So by his father lost. And this, I take it,
Is the main motive of our preparations,
The source of this our watch, and the chief head
Of this post-haste and rummage in the land.   (1.1.79–106)

If this were *Henry V*, we would be in France, awaiting the invasion of a hot-headed prince with a disregard for laws of inheritance and land transfer. Fortinbras the younger appears as a sort of amalgam of Hotspur and Hal, attended by the type of rag-tag force assembled by Falstaff, trying to take by force lands which passed hands through a just and highly codified structure (one of "sealed compact," "article[s]," all "well ratified by law").

If we take Marcellus's "sit down" as a cue for an embedded stage direction, the action of the scene shifts from the hasty comings and goings of numerous characters (Barnardo, Francisco, Horatio, Marcellus) and the rapid-fire of one-line dialogue exchanges to a more visually static stage and a slower, complex narrative history an early modern audience was presumably meant to take in. What is striking about this lengthy political account is its explanatory function. The description of the conflict between Fortinbras and Hamlet (or, perhaps more properly speaking, between the Fortinbrases and the Hamlets, as the conflicts of the fathers descend to their heirs) is given in the immediate wake of the ghost's departure. It provides an explanation not only for the wider preparations for martial conflict, but for the ghost itself.[20]

The speech seems to be the continuation of a moment forty lines earlier, in which Barnardo tried to explain about the ghost to the newly arrived Horatio and Marcellus:

BARNARDO:                    Sit down awhile,
               And let us once again assail your ears
               That are so fortified against our story
               What we have two nights seen.
HORATIO:                         Well, sit we down,
               And let us hear Barnardo speak of this.
BARNARDO:     Last night of all,
               When yond same star that's westward from the pole,
               Had made his course t'illume that part of heaven
               Where now it burns, Marcellus and myself,
               The bell then beating one—
                                         *Enter Ghost.*
MARCELLUS:    Peace, break thee off, look where it comes again.
                                         (1.1.29–39)

The exchange – one for which, this time, the participants are unquestionably seated – seeks to offer a measured, reasonable account of the sighting of the ghost, a figure that "harrows [its observers] with fear and wonder" (1.1.43). Barnardo begins his speech in the spirit of a deposition, clearly stating the time of the event (as measured both by the stars and the clock) and the witnesses. The report is interrupted by the ghost's return. Horatio's subsequent description of political events (quoted earlier) resumes the conversation, and Barnardo jumps back in to connect the dots: "Well may it sort that this portentous figure/Comes armed through our watch so like the King/That was and is the question of these wars" (1.1.108–10).

The appearance of the ghost is thus folded into an account of earthly territorial conflicts. The war over land provides a logical explanation for the ghost's appearance; the underworld and the earthly world appear to be part of one political continuum.[21] Horatio says as much when he follows Barnardo's explanatory comment with his own offering of a supernatural/ political precedent: "In the most high and palmy state of Rome,/A little ere the mightiest Julius fell,/The graves stood tenantless and the sheeted dead/Did squeak and gibber in the Roman streets" (1.1.112–15). He further observes that these and other acts were "prologue to the omen coming on/ Have heaven and earth together demonstrated" (1.1.122–3). That heaven and earth work in conjunction – or, in the case of the ghost, that purgatory and earth do so – seems to Horatio an acceptable explanation for the ghost. Horatio had, after all, been brought onto the scene precisely because of his initial skepticism about the ghost. Marcellus presents Horatio to the other watchmen (and to the theater audience) by announcing that:

> Horatio says 'tis but our fantasy
> And will not let belief take hold of him,
> Touching this dreaded sight twice seen of us.
> Therefore I have entreated him along
> With us to watch the minutes of this night
> That if again this apparition come,
> He may approve our eyes and speak to it.    (1.1.22–28)

Later, after the first encounter with the ghost, Barnardo triumphantly turns to Horatio, asking where his skepticism now lies:

BARNARDO:    How now, Horatio, you tremble and look pale.
             Is not this something more than fantasy?
             What think you on't?
HORATIO:     Before my God, I might not this believe
             Without the sensible and true avouch
             Of mine own eyes.
MARCELLUS:   Is it not like the King?
HORATIO:     As thou art to thyself.
             Such was the very armour he had on
             When he the ambitious Norway combated.
             So frowned he once, when in an angry parle
             He smote the sledded Polacks on the ice.    (1.1.52–62)

Horatio's skepticism is initially pitted against the prospect of ocular proof; he is brought to the site of the ghost's appearance that he may "approve our eyes," as Marcellus puts it. The proof offered by the "true avouch/Of [Horatio's] own eyes," however, pales in comparison to the political logic that explains the ghost's appearance. Appareled in his familiar armor, King Hamlet, even as a ghost, continues to participate in geo-political affairs. The region of the netherworld thus becomes one more political space of the play, integrated into the vague geography in which Denmark, Norway, Poland, and England are close neighbors.

This cluster of countries was probably familiar to an early modern English audience. Over the course of the sixteenth and seventeenth centuries, it became normative to view the earth from the side, to gaze at a form belted by the equator. But of course there is no determined "side" to a sphere, and other perspectives are equally legitimate, although they might now be disorienting to modern eyes. Thus, it is rather startling

Figure 4 Gerard Mercator, *Atlas novus, sive, descriptio geographica totius orbis terrarum.*
Amsterdam, 1638. Vol. I, Fol. C2–3.

to find that Mercator's *Atlas* begins its discussion of the earth's regions by staring down on the world from above, looking directly at the top of the earth's imaginary axis (see Figure 4). As John Gillies has demonstrated, *Hamlet* is a play that is informed by, and perhaps even directly conversant with, Mercator's *Atlas*.[22] Looking at this opening map, the one that corresponds with the textual descriptions of the depicted countries, the affairs of Denmark, Poland, Norway, and England would appear to be of the utmost worldly importance. It is again a bit startling to our own geopolitical sensibilities to realize that, within the organization of Mercator's *Atlas*, England is grouped with these northern areas, rather than with continental Europe. (Within the text, the countries are presented in this order: Iceland, England, Scotland, Ireland, Norway, Denmark, Russia, Poland . . .)

Yet another country becomes more visible when the earth is seen from this perspective: Iceland. When, as became customary in early modern cartography, the planet was cleaved in two along its axis and the hemispheres flayed for a comprehensive viewing of the earth, Iceland did not suffer a happy fate. While Iceland is comfortably whole (albeit folded in a page crease) in Mercator's vision of the north, in his dual hemisphere world map the county is shorn in two – one half clings to the western edge of the eastern hemisphere, while the other half clings to the eastern edge of the western hemisphere. In viewing the world in its entirety, Iceland appears so insignificant as to not invite concern about its undignified division. But in its home map, Iceland appears as more of a geo-political player, as much a neighbor of Norway and England as, say, Poland (see Figure 5).

Iceland featured prominently in the region's medieval history of territorial contests, its saga of waxing and waning political powers. As Gunnar Karlsson observes, in the early modern period Iceland underwent a political development that was the inverse of that of most European countries. Whereas other countries became open to ever-burgeoning networks of trade and communication, Iceland, which in medieval times had been "the battlefield of great powers, competing for its country's products" (mainly fish[23]), in the seventeenth century "remained outside the mainstreams of trade and became for centuries a remote satellite of a minor trading power."[24] Prior to receding from the European political stage, Iceland was an important part of the territory that was controlled by the merging and diverging crowns of Norway, Sweden, and Denmark, with the latter being the most enduring and influential.[25] In terms of trade with Iceland, around 1400 the English superseded the Norwegians; around 1500 the English were superseded by the Germans; and around 1550 the Germans were superseded by the Danes, who held an Icelandic trade monopoly until 1787.[26] Writing about Iceland in 1559, William Cuningham notes, "It is now much trauailed to of english me[n], & Danes."[27] In the fifteenth century the English, interested in the wealth of fish, came to dominate the country to such an extent that this period has been dubbed "the English century" in Icelandic historiography.[28] The relationship between the English, the Danes, and the native population was not exactly pacific; amongst other dubious exploits, the English captured the Danish governor and hauled him back to England, and also kidnapped Icelandic children.[29] The English do not seem to have made a lasting impression on Iceland in terms of fishing practices or language, but, as Karlsson writes, "[i]t may be that the English Iceland traffic had a more profound and lasting effect in England than in Iceland. It was the first regular long-distance ocean sailing that was undertaken by the English. Thus it served as a rehearsal for sailing to North America in the 16th century" (*Iceland's 1100 Years*, pp. 121–2). Iceland, then, was part

Figure 5 Detail from Gerard Mercator, *Atlas novus, sive, descriptio geographica totius orbis terrarum*. Amsterdam, 1638. Vol. I, Fol. C2–3.

of the English experience of exploration. Interest in Iceland was fuelled by an increasing number of travel reports and "other foreign comments upon the Icelandic condition" which appeared at the end of the sixteenth century; Iceland also began appearing on European maps at this time, such as those by Ortelius (1590), Mercator (1595), and Hondius (1611).[30]

One feature of Iceland's topographical landscape was of particular interest to the English public. We return to Mount Hecla, the volcano observed by the sailors on Henry Hudson's ship. This volcano was such an identifying topographical feature that it is visible even on the tiny bifurcated Iceland that appears on the dual-hemispheric opening map of the world in Mercator's *Atlas*. It becomes more visible in the Iceland that appears on the map of the polar region (see Figure 5). And in the map of Iceland proper we clearly see Mount Hecla, "vel mons perpetuo ardens": the mountain of perpetual burning, spewing fire and brimstone (Figure 6). The scene encompassing the volcano and the ship in the foreground could easily be used to illustrate the encounter of Henry Hudson's men with Mount Hecla. We can almost imagine the port side view from the ship, hidden from us, where slack-jawed sailors marvel at seeing an entrance to purgatory, intermingled with those who scoff at their belief, and with those who were not sure what to believe. (It is worth noting that the ship might not be engaged in exploration. With its guns a-blazing, it might be one of the insufficient number of Danish ships sent to protect the island from the North African pirates then roaming the North Atlantic.[31]) Indeed, this image of the ship and Mount Hecla serves well as an emblem of the argument I want to make about the description of Henry Hudson's voyage in *Purchas*, the status of purgatory in *Hamlet*, and, more broadly, about the ontological and epistemological position of purgatory for an English audience around 1600.

Mercator's map of Iceland epitomizes the coexistence of purgatory and empirical cartography. The inscription on Mount Hecla, "*mons perpetuo ardens*," seems to imply more than a geological fact, especially since the volcano was not perpetually burning. The perpetuity of the fire suggests an eschatological significance. Indeed, the prose commentary accompanying the map reports the volcano's association with the dead, its reputation for "mak[ing] a great noise, which the inhabitants say is the howling and lamentation of soules."[32] This vivid and detailed pictorial depiction of a legendary entrance to purgatory or hell is found in close proximity to the map's scale, set off to the side. This is a modern map, one that flags its mathematical and geodetic precision, one that, in contradistinction to its medieval predecessors, has scored lines upon the face of the earth and sea.

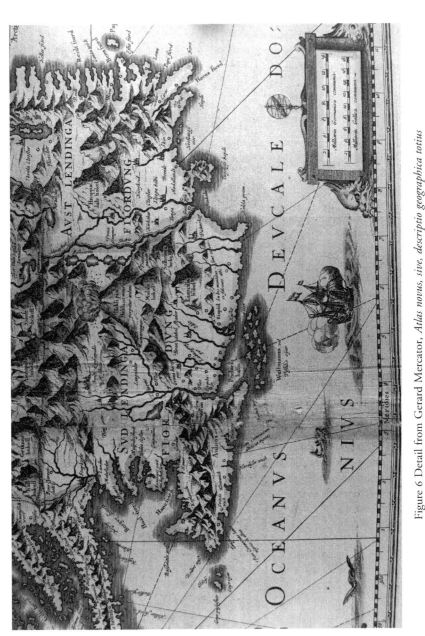

Figure 6 Detail from Gerard Mercator, *Atlas novus, sive, descriptio geographica totius orbis terrarum.* Amsterdam, 1638. Vol. I, Fol. D2–3.

The ship and its population are thus floating between signs of cartographic accuracy and a picture of a renowned eschatological space.[33]

Mount Hecla was a flashpoint in the discussions about the reality of purgatory and its purported geographical existence. Under Danish rule, Iceland had officially become Protestant in 1538. For subsequent Protestant bishops, the prominent existence of a volcano that was a reputed portal to purgatory or hell was an embarrassment. Thus Bishop Guðbrandur (who was also a geographer and the first Icelandic cartographer, whose map of Iceland was included in Ortelius's atlas[34]) commissioned Arngrímur Jónsson to write a corrective about the Icelandic geography. Arngrímur was a continentally trained humanist who published his writings about Iceland in Latin and clearly directed them towards an international audience; his "work was much admired in Denmark, and he was largely responsible for the growing antiquarian interest in old Icelandic literature, and for bringing Icelandic studies into the international scholarly arena."[35] His *Brevis Commentarius de Islandia* (Copenhagen, 1593) is the text cited in *Purchas His Pilgrim* as evidence that Mount Hecla cannot be an infernal nether region of torment, based on the fact that the volcano did not throw forth any flames between 1558 and 1592.[36] Similarly urged by the bishop, Arngrímur's contemporary Oddur Einarsson "was anxious to correct what he felt to be an unfavourable external impression of Iceland"[37] and took up the issue of Mount Hecla's association with the afterlife in his natural history of Iceland, *Íslandslýsing. Qualiscunque descriptio Islandiae* (1589). "In spite of Oddur Einarsson's attempt to rehabilitate Hekla, however, it remained associated with Hell-fire for centuries. In Icelandic cartography of the period and well into the eighteenth century, Hekla looms large on both Icelandic and foreign maps, often appearing as the central feature of the island."[38]

An excerpt of Arngrímur Jónsson's text was translated into English in Richard Hakluyt's *The Principal Nauigations, Voyages, Traffiques and Discoueries of the English Nation*, vol. I (1599). Dismissing as poppycock the association of volcanoes with the supernatural, Arngrímur-via-Hakluyt writes:

is it possible therefore that [fierie mountaines] should seeme strange, or monstrous, whenas they proceed from naturall causes? What? Doe they any whit preuaile to establish that opinion concerning the hell of *Island* . . . ? For my part, I thinke it no way tolerable, that men should abuse these, and the like miracles of nature, to auouch absurdities, or, that they should with a kinde of impietie woonder at them, as matters impossible. As though in these kindes of inflammations, there did not concurre causes of sufficient force for the same purpose.

There is in the rootes of these mountaines a matter most apt to be set on fire, comming so neere as it doeth to the nature of brimstone and pitch. There is ayer also, which insinuating it selfe by passages, and holes, into the very bowels of the earth, doeth puffe vp the nourishment of so huge a fire, together with Salt-peter, by which puffing (as it were with certeine bellowes) a most ardent flame is kindled. For, all these thus concurring, fire hath those three things, which necessarily make it burne, that is to say, matter, motion, and force of making passage: matter which is fattie and moyst, and therefore nourisheth lasting flames: motion which the ayer doeth performe, being admitted into the caues of the earth: force of making passage, and that the inuincible might of fire itselfe ... doeth bring to passe. (p. 556)

Thus the phenomenon of the volcano is not a "matter impossible," but a "miracle of nature." Brimstone and pitch are not the materials of demonic torment, but natural agents in a geological process, likened to the man-made tortuous instruments of contemporary warfare.

Such natural explanations for the flames of Mount Hecla must confront, however, a deep legacy of the place's association with purgatorial suffering. The fifth book of William Cuningham's *The Cosmographical Glasse Conteinyng the Pleasant Principles of Cosmographie, Geographie, Hydrographie, or Nauigation* (1559), "in whiche the partes of th' Earthe, perticulerlye (according to the late obseruations of Cosmographers in oure age) are exactlye described. With the Longitudes and Latitudes of Regions," provides an analysis of Iceland in these scientific terms, and then notes: "Rou[n]de about this Ila[n]d, for the space of 6. or 7. mo[n]thes, th' Ise swimmeth, making a miserable sound, & noise, so that th' inhabitauntes suppose that in the mount Hecla, & in this Ise, the soules of men & women, are tormented" (p. 176). Purchas quotes Olaus Magnus who "obserued, that this ice was violently cast against the Rockes by force of the winds, and so made a mournfull sound afarre off, as if miserable howlings were heard there. Hereupon the *Islanders* thinke the soules of the damned are tormented in this Ice" (p. 649). Arngrímur, translated in Hakluyt, similarly writes, "But round about the Iland, for the space of 7. or 8. monethes in a yere there floateth ise, making a miserable kind of mone, and not vnlike to mans voice, by reason of the clashing together. The inhabitants are of opinion that in mount *Hecla* and in the ise, there are places wherein the soules of their countreymen are tormented" (p. 562). Arngrímur takes on the Icelandic "historiographers" who "say that, both in the Isle, and in mount Hecla we appoint certain places, wherein the soules of our countrimen are tormented" (p. 563). He argues that the sounds of the shifting ice do not resemble men's voices, and falls back upon standard Protestant arguments against purgatory.[39] After having reported accounts of the tormented souls of Hecla appearing to their friends, however, the dismissal of the topic feels weak and pro forma. The effect of rational explanations for Mount Hecla's howling souls was often, perhaps, merely the perpetuation and further dissemination of the tales of infernal activity.

It could be that the tales of Hecla's moaning and wailing souls were just too inherently fascinating to be countered with reason. In a popular late seventeenth-century dictionary, these sounds have become part of the pithy definition of the place: "*Hecla*, a Mountain in *Iseland* sending forth a noise like the cries of to[r]mented persons."[40] The underground cries, while often explained away as the noise of shifting ice, and the sightings of ghosts, are afforded the status of fact in some cases. Gabriel Richardson, in *Of the State of Europe* (1627), describes "*Hecla*, feareful with apparitions of dead men, nourishing the opinion of Popish Purgatory" (p. 39). The factuality of the apparitions themselves does not seem to be questioned; the author merely disapproves of them being used to further the notion of purgatory.

Another clear source of contemporary fascination was the fact that Mount Hecla could remain perpetually covered in snow while inwardly full of fire.[41] The simultaneous presence of snow and fire was, for many, a sign of the place's purgatorial status; others attempted to explain this as a natural phenomenon. We return to Arngrímur-via-Hakluyt, who includes a poem by Pontanus describing a volcanic eruption (in which the air seeks "to ridde it selfe from vncouth dungeon") with the disclaimer, "I thought good to adde these things, not that I suppose any man to be ignorant thereof: but least other men should thinke that we are ignorant, and therefore that we will runne after their fable, which they do from hence establish." He continues:

But yet there is somewhat more in these three fained mountaines of *Island*, which causeth the sayd writers not a little to woonder, namely whereas they say that their foundations are always burning, and yet for all that, their toppes be neuer destitute of snowe. Howbeit, it be seemeth not the authority and learning of such great clearks to marueile at this, who can not but well know the flames of mount *Aetna*, which (according to *Plinie*) being full of snowe all Winter, notwithstanding (as the same man witnesseth) it does always burne. Wherefore, if we will giue credit vnto them, euen this mountaine also, sithens it is couered with snowe, and yet burneth, must be a prison of vncleane soules: which thing they haue not doubted to ascribe vnto *Hecla*, in regard of the frozen top, and the firie bottom. And it is no marueile that fire lurking so deepe in the roots of the mountaine, and neuer breaking forth except it be very seldom, should not be able continually to melt the snow couering the toppe of the sayd mountaine. (p. 557)

The argumentative twists and turns here are intriguing. The author's ostensible goal is to disassociate Mount Hecla from the popular assumption that it is an "vncouth dungeon." And yet, in turning to the authorities of Mount Aetna, he inadvertently seems to reassert precisely that point. The rational disproving of the "marueile" of the coexistence of fire and ice is again overwhelmed by the fact that the authorities to whom Arngrímur turned for geological-climatological proof are the very ones who also assert that Mount Aetna is "a prison of vncleane soules."

Mount Hecla, unlike St. Patrick's purgatory, was taken seriously. While St. Patrick's purgatory became a common synecdoche for all that was risible in Catholic theology, Mount Hecla appears to have been more the subject of scholarly inquiry and a point at which religious and scientific conversations intersected. We might consider, for instance, the description of Hecla in Mercator's *Atlas*, which intermingles the geological, the economic, and the supernatural:

Not far distant from *Hecla*, are mines of brimstone, the onely merchandise almost and custome of the Iland, for the merchants lade their ships therewith, and carry it away: when this mountain is in his fury, it soundeth like horrible thunder, casteth out huge stones, vomiteth brimstone, doth fill all far and near with ashes, that a man cannot till the ground within 10 miles of it. They that of curiosity approach near unto the mountain to contemplate the nature and causes of this burning, are easily swallowed up quick within one gulfe or other, for there are many, and covered over with ashes, that no man can take heed to himselfe: this place therefore they call the prison of cursed souls. And withal it hapneth when the ice thaweth, for 3 whole moneths, that great stakes dashing against the shoare, make a great noise, which the inhabitants say is the howling and lamentation of soules ... But these things are either fabulous, or, without doubt, delusions of devils. Jonas himselfe thinketh them fabulous. (p. 46)

"This place therefore they call the prison of cursed souls": the phrase is ambiguous. It connects the curious investigators who "contemplate[d] the nature and causes of this burning" and thereby perished in the volcano with the howling souls that the local inhabitants believed to be in purgatory. It brings together the known dead and the fabled dead. The final explanation for the howling souls is presented as a choice between the fabulous and the demonic; the assertion that Jonas (Arngrímur) considered them fables, coupled with the phrase "without doubt" applying to the devils, suggests that the author of this passage leans towards a (rational) demonic explanation. What we find, then, is the intermeshed discourses of cartography (this is, after all, Mercator's *Atlas*), natural philosophy, demonology, and fantasy. The text does not parse the distinctions amongst these for us.

Another instance of Mount Hecla sitting at the intersection of fiction and science can be found in the writings of Johannes Kepler, an ardent Lutheran. Kepler chose to open his allegorical lunar geography, *Somnium, sive Astronomia Lunaris* (1634; written 1609), in Iceland. The frame narrator falls asleep, and dreams he is reading a book which begins: "My name is Duracotus. My home is Iceland, which the ancients called Thule."[42] Kepler wrote the extensive notes for the text himself, and they reveal a sense of geography that reflects Mercator's depiction of the northern world, with Iceland, Scotland, England, Norway, and Denmark huddled together in a tight region.[43] Kepler also states in his notes that he chose Iceland as the setting because he "saw in this truly remote island a place where I might sleep and dream and thus imitate the philosophers in this kind of writing" (Lear, *Kepler's Dream*, p. 87), but "[i]t was not, however, because of the islands that Plutarch named in the Icelandic Ocean that I chose Iceland for the hypothesis of my *Dream*. One reason, among others, was that at that time there was on sale, in Prague, Lucian's book about the trip to the moon ... along with stories of St. Brendan and St. Patrick's purgatory in the subterranean regions of Iceland's volcanic Mount Hekla" (Lear, *Kepler's Dream*, p. 88). (The locating of St. Patrick's purgatory – which is actually in Ireland – within Mount Hecla suggests that the volcano was becoming the pre-eminent northern purgatorial site; a Dutch tract makes a similar association of the two places.[44]) More generally, Kepler sources his information thus: "The history of Mount Hekla, the volcano, is known from maps and geography books" (Lear, *Kepler's Dream*, p. 91). The editor of the text's modern English translation, John Lear, offers his own explanation of why Kepler would open his fictionalized scientific treatise in a place identified as purgatory. "Whereas Plutarch's *The Face of the Moon* began with physics and ended with metaphysics, Kepler reversed the pattern in anticipation of his critics at Tübingen. He appealed to the Aristotelian need for an answer to the question of final cause by implying that the moon was habitable at least by the disembodied souls of men if not by living men. Souls in those days were far more important than warm bodies, a fact Kepler recognized by summoning a representative spirit from the moon to Iceland, the site of St. Patrick's earthly purgatory" (Lear, *Kepler's Dream*, p. 46; Lear follows Kepler's mislocation of St. Patrick's purgatory). In addition to such metaphysical motivations, however, Iceland was also the hub of much geographical exploration for those trying to discover a northern passage. (Iceland not only gave the English practice at colonization, but also served as the destination of Columbus's trial run before he braved the voyage west to the Americas [Lear, *Kepler's Dream*, p. 47].) Lear notes, "Altogether, it would have been difficult to choose a more logical place than Iceland from which to launch a scientific expedition to explore beyond the earth" (p. 48). To this we might add that many of Kepler's notes suggest that he associated Iceland with his colleague Tycho Brahe.[45] Iceland, then, is the scene of heavy traffic, both of the living and the dead. It is a site that lends itself to philosophy and to scientific exploration.

A similar instance of the scientific encountering the philosophical at Mount Hecla is found in Burton's *The Anatomy of Melancholy*. In his section "Digression of Air" in the second part of the book, "Cure of Melancholy," the authorial voice of Democritus Junior imagines himself as a long-winged hawk, floating and swooping above the earth, providing an overview of the geography of the entire planet, and wondering about its many natural features. He wonders about the earth's topography, and about what lies beneath its surface. "If it be solid earth, 'tis the fountain of metals, waters, which by his innate temper turns air into water, which springs up in several chinks, to moisten the earth's *superficies* ... Or else it may be full of wind, or a sulphureous innate fire, as our meteorologists inform us, which sometimes breaking out, causeth those horrible earthquakes ..."[46] In order to find out for himself, "I would have a convenient place to go down with Orpheus, Ulysses, Hercules, Lucian's Menippus, at St. Patrick's purgatory, at Trophonius' den, Hecla in Iceland, Ætna in Sicily, to descend and see what is done in the bowels of the earth: do stones and metals grow there still?"[47] This sentence brilliantly synthesizes the convergence of the mythological, the theological, and the scientific. Democritus Junior's desire is that of modern scientific inquiry – to understand the geological composition of the earth and to examine its stones and metals. The imagined means of achieving this knowledge, however, is to become a figure of classical mythology who can descend into one of the known portals of the Christian afterlife.

Mount Hecla, then, was a prominent site on early modern cartographic representations of the northern world, and was also an important location on the popular geography of the imagination. The arrival of Iceland on European maps in the 1590s, the dissemination of Icelandic natural histories, and the island's exotic and vivid volcanic features made it a point of interest for natural philosophers.[48] Mount Hecla's ancient association with hell and purgatory made it a subject of interest for theologians and poets in a period when the reality of purgatory was still a matter of heated dispute. Mount Hecla's fame was probably not only the result of theological tracts and scientific curiosity, but the consequence of heavy sea traffic between England and Iceland (a country supplying the English not only with fish, but with the sulfur necessary for making gunpowder). The sailors and fishermen surely told travelers' tales upon their return. In London, these stories would have not only provided entertainment in the alehouse, but fodder for study in the extended urban amateur scientific community Deborah E. Harkness has portrayed in her fascinating book.[49] As a space, then, Mount Hecla encompassed fantasy and empiricism, and engaged the imaginations of the popular and the elite.

### 'HAMLET' IN HECLA

The question about the netherworld in *Hamlet* is not simply, "is it, or is it not?" The question is also, "if so, where?" *Hamlet*, famously, is obsessed with the geography of death, with the burial of the body, with the thinness of the line between the ontological states of the living and the dead. Concerns about the place of Ophelia's burial, for instance, are not just questions about real estate, or about the morality of suicide, or about the ability of wealth and privilege to override canon law. The scenes at Ophelia's grave, with their insistent earthiness, interrogate in immediate sensory ways the relationship of the material body to death.[50] And the more emphatic the sense of bodily decay (Ophelia's, Yorick's, Alexander the Great's) the more the play questions not just the whereabouts of flesh-turned-clay, but also the whereabouts of the soul. Where is Ophelia now? Where is Yorick? Where is Hamlet's father?

While these questions are the subject of abstract philosophical meditations, they are also subjected to the pressures of literalism. Greenblatt writes that "[t]he desperate impatience that Hamlet expresses is to know why the Ghost has returned, not whence it has returned" (*Hamlet in Purgatory*, p. 238). But the "whence" – and the "where" – of the Ghost are issues of both performative and conceptual import for the play. As de Grazia points out, the play insistently identifies the floor of the stage as "here," the "here" of Denmark (Hamlet *without Hamlet*, p. 37). The spatial interplay of the Danish here and a purgatorial hereafter are dramatically represented in the swearing scene. Writes de Grazia, "When underground, occupying the region theatrical tradition continued to reserve for devils, the Ghost falls into the ranks of the damned and diabolic" (p. 41). Yet, as would be visible in performance, the actors running around on the top of the stage trying to locate the "old mole," and the actor presumably running around under the stage – with only thin panels separating him from the groundlings (p. 42) – are in close physical proximity. The scene stages a dizzying set of spatial relations: the bodies of human actors above and below a stage; the armored, material body of a dead father under the earth his son stands upon; a spirit imprisoned in a distant eschatological space.

Where is this eschatological space? If the Ghost is returning from an actual, geographical purgatorial space, there would have been three dominant popular alternatives for this location: St. Patrick's purgatory in Ireland, Mount Aetna in Sicily, and Mount Hecla in Iceland, all renowned entrances to the afterworld. Hamlet does, in fact, specifically mention St. Patrick. After his private encounter with the ghost, in which he learns of his father's murder, Hamlet is joined again by Horatio and Marcellus. They beseech him to say what he has learned, but Hamlet is reluctant to repeat the ghost's message for fear that his friends will reveal it. After securing a promise of discretion, Hamlet begins to tell the tale: "There's never a villain dwelling in all Denmark/But he's an arrant knave" (1.5.122–3). As Harold Jenkins glosses the line, "The disclosure which Hamlet was apparently about to make he suddenly turns into a jest."[51] Actually, the statement both is and is not a jest; thinking of Claudius, it is truth to Hamlet, but in its generality it becomes a witticism. The line marks a pivot from the chilling seriousness of the conversation with the Ghost to the double entendres that mark Hamlet's "antic disposition" which he "puts on" a bit later in the scene (1.5.170):

HORATIO:    These are but wild and whirling words, my lord.
HAMLET:     I am sorry they offend you – heartily,
            Yes, faith, heartily.
HORATIO:    There's no offence, my lord.
HAMLET:     Yes, by Saint Patrick, but there is, Horatio,
            And much offence too. Touching this vision here,
            It is an honest ghost – that let me tell you.    (1.5.132–7)

The invocation of St. Patrick partakes in the verbal dualism of the scene. Horatio's casual "There's no offence" (an early modern variety of "no problem, don't worry about it") is met by Hamlet's assertion that there is indeed an offence – namely, the unrevealed fratricidal murder of his father. "By Saint Patrick" contributes to the double registers at work here, serving at once as a formulaic idiom and as a deeply significant local reference.[52] It is just shortly after this exchange that the ghost once again makes his presence known from below, with his imperative "Swear" (1.5.149). Hamlet responds in a jocund way: "Art thou there, true-penny?/Come on, you hear this fellow in the cellarage?" (1.5.150–1); "Well said, old mole, canst work i'th' earth so fast?" (1.5.161). The scene's repeated sense of "dwelling" (in the cellarage; in a mole tunnel) positions St. Patrick's purgatory as a possible home for the ghost. The "by" in "by Saint Patrick," in a play so concerned about the precise whereabouts of the dead, could also function as a spatial preposition. And yet, the reference, as with so much of the language in this scene, simultaneously suggests truth and jest, since, as Greenblatt notes, "For later Elizabethan and Jacobean writers, the pilgrimage site in Ulster had become part of a repertory of Irish jokes"; St. Patrick's purgatory was "a standing joke for Protestants."[53] We seem to be informed of the ghost's whereabouts in purgatory even as we are reminded that there is no such thing.[54]

If the Ghost is not in St. Patrick's purgatory, might we look to Mount Aetna? We note Hamlet's line, "my imaginations are as foul/As Vulcan's stithy" (3.2.79–80). While there are scattered references to Vulcan in Shakespeare's plays, this is the one instance in which the god is associated with his underground workplace ("stithy": a forge, smithy. *Oxford English Dictionary*, 3; Hamlet's line is the first example the *OED* cites for this word). Thompson and Taylor gloss the line thus: "The workshop or forge of Vulcan, the blacksmith-god; it was reputedly situated underneath Mount Etna and hence associated with the notion of hell" (p. 302n). The reference to Vulcan's underground workshop carries through a visual image from the players' speech about Pyrrhus in Act 2. There, "the hellish Pyrrhus" (2.2.401) appears almost as a devil, with "sable arms," "Black as his purpose," with a "dread and black complexion," "Roasted in wrath and fire" (2.2.390–1, 393, 399). Pyrrhus finds himself in an Ilium with a "flaming top" (2.2.413), in which "vengeance sets him new a-work" as did "the Cyclops' hammers fall/On Mars's armour" (2.2.426, 427–8) – the Cyclops being Vulcan's laborers. (In Peter Heylyn's *Mikrokosmos* [1625], we read that people "suppose [Mount Aetna] to be the shoppe of *Vulcan*, and the *Cyclops*; the grosse Papists hold therein to be purgatory" [p. 444].) The invocation of Vulcan here might be specific to Mount Aetna, but it could also be tied more generally to the neologism "Volcano." The *Oxford English Dictionary* cites the first English usage as being from Purchas ("**1613** PURCHAS *Pilgr.* VIII. xiv. 686 A Vulcano or flaming hill, the fire whereof may be seene ... aboue 100 miles"), but the word also appears in John Florio's Italian-English dictionary of 1598 ("a hill that continually

burneth and casteth out flame and smoke"[55]). A volcano very much in
evidence in Shakespeare's part of the world in the late 1590s was not
Mount Aetna so much as Mount Hecla, which erupted for six straight
months in 1597.[56] By the mid seventeenth century, Robert Boyle is writing
simply of "the famous *Volcan-Hecla,* in *Island.*"[57]

Contemporaries repeatedly equate Mount Aetna and Mount Hecla.[58]
The cultural popularity of Mount Hecla as a northern alternative to
Mount Aetna is illustrated in a song by Thomas Weelkes, one of
England's most famed composers of madrigals. In 1600, Weelkes pub-
lished a collection that included "Thule, the Period of Cosmographie,"
the first part of which goes as follows:

> Thule, the period of cosmographie,[59]
> Doth vaunt of Hecla whose sulphureous fire
> Doth melt the frozen clime and thaw the sky;
> Trinacrian Etna's flames ascend not higher.
> These things seem wondrous, yet more wondrous I,
> Whose heart with fear doth freeze, with love doth fry.

(The author of the text of "Thule" is unknown, but "[s]o many texts
Weelkes set echo Shakespeare that some people suggest the two men
collaborated."[60]) The volcano here marks a convergence of geographic
and Petrarchan discourses, providing a northern orientation for the "I"
caught in the purgatory of love. While the Petrarchism is hardly unique,
what is of interest here is the way in which Hecla is positioned as a
northern counterpart to the famed Sicilian landmark ("Trinacrian": Of
Sicily; Sicilian. *OED*). While the two volcanoes are typically identified as
being parallel, in the madrigal they are positioned almost as rivals; Thule
"vaunts" of Hecla, and positions it in a comparative context ("Etna's
flames ascend not higher"). The madrigal implies that the Sicilians could
keep their purgatory, thank you very much; the north had its own. As
Mary Floyd-Wilson has discussed, the English sense of self-identity was
very much dependent upon their "frozen clime." "England's northern
climate and the English people's northern status colored their perspective
on everything from fashion to medicine to politics."[61] *Hamlet* is definitively a northern play, taking place in a space that is "very cold" (1.4.1),
even "bitter cold" (1.1.6). It is thus fitting for the northern purgatory to be
located in the frozen country of Iceland, rather than the Mediterranean
climes of Sicily.

The ghost of Hamlet *père* appears dressed for the weather of a northern
purgatory, wearing "the very armour he had on/When ... He smote the

sledded Polacks on the ice" (1.1.59–60, 62).[62] His appearance in armor also invokes another association of Mount Hecla. In a sixteenth-century tract, we read that there "are particular Purgatories, assigned vnto them for some special cause."[63] Mount Hecla's special assignation appears to be military deaths. We read in Purchas: "The common people thinke the soules of the damned to be tormented here: it is certayne that diuers and horrible spirits are obserued in this Mountayne and about it; for if a Battaile be fought in any place, the *Islanders*, especially they that sayle and fish in the Sea neere to *Hecla*, know the day of the Battaile fought, although they know not where it be done: for they see (as they report) wicked spirits going forth, and returning, and bringing soules with them" (p. 648).[64] While Hamlet's father did not die in battle, the repeated references to armor, and what we know of the other characters' memories of him, identify him as a martial leader.

In Veron's *The Huntinge of Purgatorye*, we read again that different purported entrances to purgatory were associated with different types of deaths and manifestations of spirits. Here, though, Mount Hecla is the purgatory for those who were murdered:

[O]f the pyt of Islond, that is to saie: how that there be spirites that offer the[m] selues visible vnto men, for to do the[m] seruice: In that place, they see visions of those, that haue ben drouned, or slayne by some other violent death, which shew them selues before men of their acquayntaunce, in so much that they, that know nothinge of their death, do thinke verely, that they be ye very persones their selues, and ye[t] they see them before their eies: wherby it cometh to passe, that some times they go about to take them by the hande, perceyuinge not that they be visions, tyll they see them too vanishe awaye before their owne faces. (sig. Z1$^{r-v}$)

The phrase "that know nothinge of their death" here is ambiguous; do these spirits reveal themselves to men who do not know that they are dead, or, more intriguingly, does the phrase apply to "slayne by some other violent death," meaning that people do not know of the murder? In either case, the homicidal conditions of Old Hamlet's death make this Icelandic volcano his appropriate post-mortem abode.

Throughout the play, there are phrases which could be taken as geographical gestures towards the snow-covered peak of Mount Hecla. Claudius's comment to Gertrude in the wake of Polonius's murder is strange: "The sun no sooner shall the mountains touch/But we will ship him hence" (4.1.29–30). As there are no mountains in Denmark, the statement does not seem to apply to the immediate environment of the play; linked with Claudius's intention to have Hamlet killed, and that "hence" could mean "from this world, from this life" or "elsewhere (than in this world); in the next world. *Obs.*" (*OED*, "hence," *adv.* def. 3 and 3b), the lines associate distant mountains and the afterlife. Ophelia, in her mad sorrow for Polonius's death, sings "White his shroud as the mountain snow" (4.5.36) – another possible visual image of a famous white-capped mountain associated with the afterlife. And, in a play that repeatedly invokes geographical direction (the "star that's westward from the pole" [1.1.35], "yon high eastward hill" [1.1.166], "this heavy-headed revel east and west" [1.4.17]), Hamlet's exclamation that he is "but mad north-north-west" (2.2.315) employs the directions of a compass (such as those commonly depicted on maps and in navigational treatises). This reference has seemed to baffle editors of the play,[65] but we might pose a simple question of geography: what is north-north-west of where Hamlet stands in Denmark? Iceland. And what is in Iceland that would make him mad? Mount Hecla, the site of purgatory for murder victims, including those who were secretly murdered by brothers who then proceed to wallow in "a couch for luxury and damned incest" (1.5.83) with the dead man's wife – the site, presumably, where Hamlet's father is being sub-jected to tortures so horrible they cannot even be told (1.5.14–20). Cause for madness (and anger), indeed.

The Ghost's lament, "My hour is almost come/When I to sulphurous and tormenting flames/Must render up myself" (1.5.2–4), may seem generic enough, except that contemporary commentaries on Mount Hecla repeatedly emphasize that the volcano is an important regional source of sulfur (also known as brimstone, a substance of biblical as well as worldly import, as it was a key ingredient in gunpowder).[66] More generally, contemporary descriptions of Iceland nearly always identify it as a pro-tectorate of Denmark. To an English audience with even a vague sense of their place on the map, there might well have been a sense of being sandwiched between Danish territory, with Denmark to the northeast and Iceland to the northwest. And a Danish Iceland was home to one of the most studied and debated possible entrances to the afterlife. If a Danish king is sent to purgatory – the nearness of which is dramatically indicated by the ghostly voice emanating from underground – to which other purgatory would he go, if not Mount Hecla? After all, he owns it. (From contemporary sources: "Island called of Ptollo. Thyle, is an Ilan[n]de suiecte to the king of Denmarke"; "This Island being subject to the *Danish* Crown, is govern'd by a particular Vice-Roy, sent thither by the King of *Denmark*"[67])

The coexistence of purgatory and the court at Denmark is suggested throughout the play. The Folio's line of "Denmark's a prison"[68] powerfully aligns the space of Denmark with the space of purgatory, given that the Ghost lives in a "prison-house" (1.5.14). The imagined and real soundscape of the play also perhaps holds purgatorial allusions. For a play that has no actual battles, *Hamlet* is full of cannons; they are being made or purchased (1.1.72), shot off as part of the king's drinking sprees (1.2.126), used as a metaphor for rumor (4.1.42), and used as part of wordplay (5.2.141). (Additionally, there is the homophone of "canon" [1.2.132; 1.4.47].) The play calls attention to this soundscape when, after Q2's stage direction "A flourish of trumpets and two pieces goes off," Horatio questions, "What does this mean, my lord?" (1.4.6), and learns that it signifies that the king "[k]eeps wassail" (1.4.9). Details like the cannon fire that accompanies Claudius's drinking binges have been ascribed to a bit of Danish local color, but perhaps the locale they evoke lies elsewhere.[69]

The Icelandic volcanoes are repeatedly associated with cannons and gunfire. Arngrímur-via-Hakluyt (Hakluyt, perhaps not incidentally, being an author with whom Shakespeare appears to have been familiar[70]) describes an eruption of Mount Hecla: "and so (euen as in vndermining trenches, and engines or great warrelike ordinance, huge yron bullets are cast foorth with monstrous roaring, and cracking, by the force of kindled Brimstone, and Salt-peeter, whereof Gunne-powder is compounded) chingle and great stones being skorched in that fiery gulfe, as it were in a furnace, together with abundance of sande and ashes, are vomited vp and discharged" (pp. 556–7). Mercator describes an eruption of Hecla's sister volcano Mount Helga: "with so great noise and thunder did cast up fire and stones, that fourscore miles off, they beleeved great canons to be shot off" (p. 46); in Purchas we read of an eruption by Hecla in which "after the Earthquake followed a horrible cracke, that if all warlike Ordnance had beene discharged, it had beene nothing to this terrour" (p. 648); in Mercator's *Historia Mundi* (1635) an eruption of Hecla's neighbor Mount Helga leads people to think "some great pieces of Ordnance had beene shot off" (p. 36). Similarly, Jo[h]annes Jonstonus in *An History of the Wonderful Things of Nature Set Forth in Ten Severall Classes* (1657), notes, "Hecla, that lightned the whole Island. An hour after, the Island shaked, then there followed a terrible noise, that if all the Guns for Warr were shot off, they were nothing to this terrible noise … *An.* 1580, it vomited out fire with such a noise, that for 80 miles men thought the great Guns were discharged. The common people think the souls of the damned, are there tormented" (p. 72). Thus, while one would like

Horatio's line "This bodes some strange eruption to our state" (1.1.68) to
signify volcanic activity, within the early modern period the newly named
volcanoes were identified with earthquakes and cannon fire, not "erup-
tions." The sound of cannons in *Hamlet* creates an auditory allusion to
volcanoes.[71] The effect is that purgatory is at once over there and right
here, a phantasm and physically real.

Most importantly, the specter of Mount Hecla haunts the graveyard
scene. In a notoriously complex and powerful theatrical moment, Laertes
and Hamlet confront each other at the grave of the dead Ophelia. In a
move that breaks a series of taboos – of decorum, of respect for the dead,
of expressing incestuous desire – Laertes leaps into Ophelia's grave. In the
original staging, he seems to have jumped into a depression created by the
lowering of the trapdoor.

> LAERTES:   O, treble woe
> Fall ten times double on that cursed head
> Whose wicked deed thy most ingenious sense
> Deprived thee of. Hold off the earth awhile,
> *Leaps in the grave.*
>
> Till I have caught her once more in mine arms.
> Now pile your dust upon the quick and dead,
> Till of this flat a mountain you have made
> T'o'ertop old Pelion or the skyish head
> Of blue Olympus.                    (5.1.235–43)

The imperative to the graveside attendants ("Now pile your dust upon the
quick and dead") is a suicidal death wish in a play where young people
contemplate, threaten, or commit suicide (Hamlet, Horatio, Ophelia).
Laertes fantasizes about being buried alive, and his choice of referents (the
mountains Pelion and Olympus) transposes the pathetic scene of yet
another hugger-mugger, imperfect funeral rite into mythic terms and
proportions. (In Greek mythology, in the war with the gods the giants
piled Pelion on top of the mountain Ossa in order to reach the home of
the gods, Mount Olympus [Jenkins, *Hamlet*, p. 390n].) In the stage
direction for the first quarto, "Hamlet leapes in after Laertes." While this
action might be contested,[72] Hamlet undoubtedly verbally leaps in after
Laertes, following his metaphoric lead only to surpass him:

> HAMLET:   'Swounds, show me what thou'lt do.
> Woul't weep, woul't fight, woul't fast, woul't tear thyself,
> Woul't drink up eisel, eat a crocodile?
> I'll do't. Dost come here to whine,

To outface me with leaping in her grave?
Be buried quick with her, and so will I.
And if thou prate of mountains, let them throw
Millions of acres on us till our ground,
Singeing his pate against the burning zone,
Make Ossa like a wart.                    (5.1.263–72)

Hamlet counters Laertes's "pile your dust upon the quick and dead" with the assertion that they shall both be "buried quick" with the dead Ophelia. And Laertes's mountains shall be outdone by Hamlet's "millions of acres," an accumulation that leads to the top of the mountain touching the "burning zone." Jenkins has glossed this reference thus: "that part of the celestial sphere within which the sun supposedly moves, corresponding to the tropical zone on earth" (*Hamlet*, p. 392n).

The cosmological resonance might well be there, but it is overpowered by the emphatic earthiness of the scene as a whole. De Grazia writes, "In the graveyard scene, everything – props, dialogue, gesture – combines to convert the floorboards to elemental earth . . . Everything in 5.1. is focused on that little patch of recessed ground that at the Globe would have been indicated by the open trap, the $5' \times 2'$ rectangle at the center rear of the stage floor" (Hamlet *without Hamlet*, pp. 37, 129). Throughout the play, the stage floor has been referenced as Danish soil (pp. 36–7), and discussions of land ownership seem to become concentrated at Ophelia's grave. The banter between Hamlet and the gravedigger not only signifies the materiality of the earth through the action of digging with a shovel and chucking around human remains found in the dirt, but also in the constant references to the legal mechanisms of land ownership, down to the tanner's hide, associated both with the parchment upon which contracts were written and units in which land was measured (the Anglo-Saxon "hide").[73] Even in his frenzied mountain-building fantasy, Hamlet is thinking in specifically geodetic terms, "millions of acres," although the hugeness of the number is one that admittedly would challenge an early modern surveyor's skills.

The imagery here is particularly intense, perhaps because the images do not serve an analogical purpose, as they typically do in Shakespearean plays. Instead, Laertes and Hamlet co-create an imagined environment that they inhabit from within. They imagine themselves – with their feet quite possibly still within the lowered region of the stage that was earlier inhabited by a spirit in purgatory – inside the base of a massive mountain, one with a burning top. They imagine themselves into the space of

Vulcan's stithy, a space alluded to earlier in the play. They imagine themselves, it would seem, into Mount Hecla – "the hel of *Island*, shut vp within the botome of one mountaine."[74]

This scene, in many ways the emotionally climactic one of the play, is part of a broader spatial dynamic. *Hamlet* begins with inward move-ment, as people move towards Elsinore. Hamlet has come home from Wittenberg; Fortinbras's army is about to invade; the Ghost returns from purgatory; Rosencrantz and Guildenstern arrive from Wittenberg; the players come to the castle. But then the play turns to an outward movement, as people move away. Laertes goes to Paris; Fortinbras is only passing through on his way to Poland; the Ghost recedes; the players leave; Rosencrantz and Guildenstern depart for England. As does Hamlet. Hamlet's ostensible errand to England, to collect tribute money (3.1.169; 5.2.39), puts him in the position of Hamlet the Dane, heir to the Danish throne, traveling through his empire, an empire in which Iceland would have been in the same political category as England, part of the Danish territory of conquest. For the rest of the play, the geographic horizons seem to expand. Hamlet's encounter with pirates is part of traveling in the North Atlantic (even if anachronistic-ally). His inky cloak is traded for his seafaring clothes. Instead of messengers arriving with news, sailors do the job. As part of this expansion, the Ghost, once so spatially near, drifts off. But in imagining himself inside of a mountain for the dead that bears an uncanny resemblance to Mount Hecla, Hamlet seems to have followed him after all.

As Greenblatt notes, representing purgatory on the Elizabethan stage would have been politically dangerous, given that Protestant reformers were trying to shut down the doctrine and the locale, and given that officials were wary of perceived Catholic sympathizers. Purgatory could be referenced in jest, "[b]ut it could not be represented as a frightening reality. *Hamlet* comes closer to doing so than any other play of this period." It does this through "a network of allusions: 'for a certain term,' 'burned and purged away,' 'Yes, by Saint Patrick,' '*hic et ubique*'" (*Hamlet in Purgatory*, p. 237). We can refine this position even further by con-sidering *which* variety of purgatory *Hamlet* seems to represent. As we have seen, purgatory was not just an abstract theological concept, but a space associated with particular geographic locations. It was a feature not only of the psychological landscape, but of the actual landscape – even if it was subjected to the oppositional pressures of skepticism and empiricism. So, is *Hamlet's* purgatory that of Mount Hecla? In a definitive sense, no. The place is never named.[75] But in a suggestive sense that integrates with the general geography of the play, I would say yes.

## "IS NOT THIS SOMETHING MORE THAN FANTASY?"
### ('HAMLET', 1.1.53)

What are the consequences – for reading *Hamlet*, for appreciating the dynamics of theater, for understanding the place of purgatory in early modern England – of identifying Mount Hecla as the locus of *Hamlet*'s purgatory? Most basically, this identification provides another layer for comprehending the historicity of the play's spatial dynamics. *Hamlet*, perhaps more than any other Shakespearean drama, carries a deep and rich legacy of Freudian, or more generally psychoanalytic, readings (that Freud was influenced by this play in constructing his own theory of the Oedipal complex is a critical commonplace). These readings, while certainly offering valuable insights, have tended to obscure the play's original historical situation. Recognizing the cultural significance of Mount Hecla and Iceland at the turn of the seventeenth century helps us to better understand the play's northern geography and the implications of that setting.

*Hamlet* itself seems to tease the audience about the location of purgatory. The play repeatedly constructs the afterlife in the binary terms of heaven and hell, but points towards the missing third place of purgatory. As Anthony Low notes of the play: "if there is no mention of Purgatory, in several places there are significant absences, where the word would seem to be appropriate ... The best evidence of omission ... may be Hamlet's outcry immediately after the ghost vanishes: 'O all you host of heaven! O earth! *What else?/*And shall I couple Hell? O fie! Hold, hold my heart'" (1.5.92–3; italics added).[76] I agree with Low that there is consistently something troubling about these expressions, although I disagree with his explanation, that they signaled a character and a population that had forgotten purgatory. (While Low's was an important article in reintroducing the idea of purgatory in a critical climate of new historicism, its fundamental premise – "As was the case in England, so in Hamlet's Denmark. Purgatory is not just abolished but effectively forgotten, as if it never were" (p. 459) – has been debunked by revisionist historians.) Far from being forgotten in either Shakespeare's England or Hamlet's Denmark, purgatory was very much on people's minds, whether as a source of pamphlet humor or as part of an ongoing theological debate.[77] But what Low brings to the fore is the eschatological lacuna deliberately introduced in the play. The lacuna is not there because an audience could not remember what the third place had been, but because purgatory was such a heated topic of speculation and its representation on stage potentially scandalous.

The presence of purgatory, even if this presence is manifest only through allusion and visual illusion, compromises the ostensible eschatological binary of heaven and hell. *Hamlet* is a play which in many ways sets forth binaries and the dominance of twos. People come in pairs (Hamlet and Hamlet, Fortinbras and Fortinbras, Rosencrantz and Guildenstern); and Hamlet speaks in a pattern of doubling (e.g. "too too sallied flesh" [1.2.129]). The most prominent example of such binary thinking is presented in what is probably the most famous question of Anglophone literature: "To be, or not to be" (3.1.55). Yet the crystalline clarity of the formulation of this question belies the fact that it is never answered, nor can it be, given how the ontological distinction of living and dead is muddied throughout the play. Purgatory in *Hamlet* is not simply a geographic location, but serves the function of compromising normative ontologies and epistemologies. In her own reading of *Hamlet's* telling of the fall of Troy (a narrative which, as I discussed above, resonates with allusions to volcanoes), Gail Kern Paster writes that "[t]he imagery invokes not only the landscape of hell but also the inner body-scape of early modern physiology" – one that is deeply humoral.[78] For Paster, this is part of her larger interest in thinking about how Shakespeare's characters' "passions are embodied and what embodiment means in a pre-Cartesian physical world" (p. 246). A "pre-Cartesian" world here signifies one that is not yet dualistic, with the familiar mind-body split. But the staging of purgatory also makes visible, if it doesn't quite bring into focus, a pre-Cartesian world which also did not yet have a modern immaterial-material split.

In the previous chapter, I explored how the textual and pictorial tradition of *ars moriendi* literature trained an audience to read the deathbed as a site that entailed multiple points of view, with individuals at the same event experiencing different realities and different interactions with the eschatological. *Othello*, I argued, dramatized this mode of perception. *Hamlet*, a play that in so many ways is about playing and the very nature of theater, performs a similar dynamic but in a more specifically theatrical vein. If the site of purgatory that lurks behind the play is Mount Hecla, we find multiple geographic relationships. Mount Hecla is a distant volcano in Iceland, and yet very present: the locus of the Ghost under the stage, and the imagined space of Ophelia's grave. This play on shifting and overlapping geographic referents is itself a hallmark of the early modern theater.

Theatrical double vision was an important part of the spatial dynamics of the early modern stage. The Jacobean theater, as Russell West observes, was "an ostentatiously spatial art-form."[79] Thus, "The material existence of the theatre – not only the much discussed question of stage design, but the more fundamental one of the inherently spatial character of theatre as an art-form – mediated between the larger space of social reality in its most concrete aspects, and the plays with their thematic treatment of issues of spatiality" (*Spatial Representations*, p. 3). Drama of this period frequently called attention to the engagement of multiple, simultaneous spatial frames. West considers dramatic moments in which Jacobean plays invoked the theaters' urban setting of contemporary London. The reference to a real-life tavern near the Globe in *Twelfth Night* creates a situation in which "the fictional place of the tale and the real context of performance are superimposed upon each other, to the point where the boundary between the two threatens to dissolve" (*Spatial Representations*, p. 43). Similarly, a line in *The Alchemist* about a house in Blackfriars produces "a blurring of the demarcation between reference to the fictional place performed on the stage, that of a house in the Blackfriars quarter, and reference to the real place of performance, Blackfriars theatre. Fictional and real locality are condensed so as to refer simultaneously to two ostensibly mutually exclusive levels of spatial localization" (*Spatial Representations*, p. 43). And in *Bartholomew Fair*, "Jonson plays even more consciously with this oscillation of incongruence and congruence of performance space and fictional space ... though the Hope theatre is not Smithfield, it none the less smells exactly like it, thus wafting the spectators directly to the fictional location of the action" (*Spatial Representations*, p. 43). In sum, West argues that "[t]he Jacobean stage thus produces an overlapping of two modes of spatial reference, a sort of 'double consciousness' encompassing normally mutually exclusive modes of representation (referential and fictional). The spectators are obliged to participate in a form of double vision, being simultaneously conscious of the fictional world as an intact entity convincing enough to displace the real, and of the stage as a manifestly limited performance space which butts up against other spaces, those of the audience, and of the position of the theatre in a real quarter of London" (*Spatial Representations*, pp. 43–4).

The theater's self-referential invocation of the space of London is one form of double vision. Within Shakespearean drama we often find

another spatial doubling, one in which actual locations are coupled with
fantasy spaces. François Laroque studies this dynamic in an essay that
employs a dizzying range of visual analogies:

> So, real geography in Shakespeare often seems to be paired with a kind of
> imaginary twin or double place: the city of Verona and the forest in *The Two
> Gentlemen of Verona*, Athens and the wood in *A Midsummer Night's Dream*, the
> court and the forest of Arden in *As You Like It* or Venice and Belmont in *The
> Merchant of Venice* ... [The geographical couplings] work as a kind of *trompe
> l'œil* ... provid[ing] the spectator with a perspective effect, or anamorphosis,
> when the place changes or dissolves into another as in a masque ... This
> palimpsest-like geography, which superimposes stratum upon stratum, meaning
> upon meaning, with further associations provided by puns, echoes and corres-
> pondences, combines the classical, the medieval and the early modern in a
> constellation of routes leading to no particular place or centre ... In this way,
> Shakespeare's European maps take us into the heartland of fantasy. They lead
> us to a number of vague territories or forests where fairies, witches, hungry
> bears, rich heiresses with a golden fleece or magic handkerchiefs are just so
> many signs that history is always interspersed with *fabula* and real topography
> with fantasy.[80]

From *trompe l'œil* to anamorphosis to palimpsest: these all provide various
ways for using the language of the two-dimensional visual arts to express
an art that not only represents space, but is itself spatial.

   *Hamlet* dramatizes a supernatural environment which doesn't consider
eschatological spaces as carefully distinct and bounded from chthonic
ones: in the graveyard scene, Hamlet and Laertes are fleetingly in purgatory just as much as they are in Denmark. Depending upon one's beliefs,
this duality can be seen either in West's terms or Laroque's. If one held a
belief in the physical reality of purgatory, then "fictional and real locality
are condensed so as to refer simultaneously to two ostensibly mutually
exclusive levels of spatial location." If, however, one held purgatory to be a
fable, then we find the interspersion of "real topography with fantasy."
Either of these dualities participates in the representational dynamics of
Mount Hecla's purgatory. As it was associated with Mount Hecla, purgatory held an ontological status that was at once insistently material and
emphatically immaterial. Mount Hecla was composed of rock and brimstone, but was also associated with fable. It was a point on the map and
part of an ecclesiastical fiction. It was a mountain and the home of
ethereal souls.

   Recognizing the geographic specificity attached to discussions of
purgatory enables us to further reconsider its role on the stage, and indeed

the theater's representation of supernatural geographies more broadly. If we see purgatory as a "fable" (*pace* Greenblatt *pace* Tyndale), then the theater, in its traffic in fantasy and illusion, itself becomes a vehicle for conveying a doctrine that has been evacuated and fictionalized. If, however, we see purgatory as both fabulous and real, as both the stuff of story and a site of hard materiality – seeing purgatory as Mount Hecla appears on maps of Iceland, with hellfires burning next to a navigator's compass – then the staging of purgatorial space becomes something altogether different. The stage is not a site for pointing up defunct religious beliefs, but a site in which the complexities of supernatural space can be better portrayed than in any other artistic medium. The inherent nature of the theater, with its constant invitation to see and not see, to see actors' bodies and great kings, to see a wooden O as well as bloody battles, lends itself to the depiction of an early modern supernatural geography. This depiction is not purely representative, but suggests how a supernatural environment might have been experienced and inhabited off stage as well.

# CHAPTER 4

# Metamorphic cosmologies: The world according to Calvin, Hooker, and Macbeth

With what clear manifestations [God's] might draws us to contemplate him! Unless perchance it be unknown to us in whose power it lies to sustain this infinite mass of heaven and earth by his Word: by his nod alone sometimes to shake heaven with thunderbolts, to burn everything with lightnings, to kindle the air with flashes; sometimes to disturb it with various sorts of storms, and then at his pleasure to clear them away in a moment.

John Calvin, *Institutes of the Christian Religion*[1]

## OPENINGS

Around the turn of the seventeenth century, English depictions of the supernatural often entailed a duality, a simultaneous presence of the stable and the labile, the seen and the unseen, the material and the fantastic. These dualities, I have been arguing, are a consequence of conflicting latent spatial epistemologies. The various spaces I have been examining – the space of a contract, the deathbed, and purgatory – have been terrestrial. I turn now to the cosmological, to spatial structures of the universe. Cosmological structures are integral to two of the period's important theologians, John Calvin and Richard Hooker. In the former, we find an understanding of creation as having a spatial order that is subordinate to the fluctuations of God's providence; this leads to a world that is full of the possibility of unanticipated mutability. In the latter, we find a model of creation that is more rigid in adhering to immutable divine laws; this leads to a world that privileges the predictable and the absolute. *Macbeth*, I will argue, stages an impossible simultaneity of these incompatible, even irreconcilable understandings of divine cosmic structure.

*Macbeth* opens with a bang. "Thunder and Lightning," reads the famous stage direction of the First Folio. Very very frightening. On the tip of their toes or the edge of their seats, those in the audience at the Globe might have thrilled at the sounds and the lights and the smells of a pyrotechnic opening, as the special effects of the early modern theater – these (somewhat) controlled explosions of gunpowder – transported the audience in an instant to a stormy encounter of demonic agents:

1 WITCH:    When shall we three meet again?
            In thunder, lightning, or in rain?
2 WITCH:    When the hurlyburly's done,
            When the battle's lost and won.
3 WITCH:    That will be ere the set of sun.
1 WITCH:    Where the place?
2 WITCH:    Upon the heath.
3 WITCH:    There to meet with Macbeth.
1 WITCH:    I come, Graymalkin!
2 WITCH:    Paddock calls.
3 WITCH:    Anon!
ALL:        Fair is foul, and foul is fair:
            Hover through the fog and filthy air. [*Exeunt.*][2]

The brevity of this terse opening scene (here quoted in its entirety) belies its dramatic effect in the theater, as we enter the play through an eerie exchange of – and with – the witches.

The sensory experience of *Macbeth*'s opening, and the implications of this experience within a Protestant England, have recently been discussed by both Bruce Smith and Jonathan Gil Harris. For Smith, the charged opening is one of Shakespeare's "quite obvious devices for establishing the auditory field of the play within the first few moments."[3] The auditory experience was, according to Smith, what made the early modern theatrical experience exciting; the theater "lies at the intersection of . . . oratory, conversation, and liturgy" (p. 270), although in bringing the three together it supersedes them all. This auditory theatrical experience is, in Smith's account, a highly spatialized one. We read – in a single paragraph – of "the acoustic field," a "field of sound," the "acoustic space," the "field of hearing," and the "auditory field." This is a field with "horizons" and a circumference (p. 271).

Smith's work on the phenomenology of the early modern theatrical experience is deeply impressive. Jonathan Gil Harris offers an important modulation to this groundbreaking approach, however. He comments, "As satisfyingly total as historical phenomenology's panoptic mappings of moments and sensory fields may seem to be, we might also do well to embrace [a] more speculative, provisional, and temporally unfixed mode of polychronic reading."[4] This polychronicity is "a palimpsesting of diverse moments in time, as a result of which past and present coincide with each other" (467). Whereas Smith studies the soundscape of early modern England, Harris turns to the smellscape, and in particular the explosive squibs (which contained a stinky combination of sulfurous brimstone, coal, and saltpeter) used to create the thunder and lightning at the beginning of *Macbeth*. ("[T]he play most likely began not just with a bang, but with a stink."[5]) The sensory experience of smelling gunpowder and sulfur in the theater evokes a range of olfactory connotations – the recent Gunpowder Plot, the devils from older modes of medieval drama – which leads to a multilayered temporality. Harris writes, "[I]n order to explode the empty homogeneous time of the present, Shakespeare and the King's Men used their smelly squibs as temporal explosives ... shatter[ing] the olfactory coordinates of Protestant time" (485).

Harris is right to question the stable space-time presumed in much scholarship on historical phenomenology. But we must also exercise caution in assuming a hegemonic "Protestant" time or space. Protestantism was itself polychronic and polyvocal. At the turn of the seventeenth century, it was securely ensconced as the English state religion, and was, in various forms and degrees, largely the popular religion as well. But this Protestantism was far from being theologically or politically consistent, encompassing elements from Luther, Zwingli, Calvin, Beza, and a host of other reformers, both foreign and domestic. While incipient nationalism often demanded an emphatically Protestant identity to distinguish England from its rival Catholic states, the Elizabethan settlement also allowed the church to retain elements of medieval Catholicism that would have been abhorrent to continental reformers. In sum, as the historian Philip Benedict has written, "while the Church of England remained predominantly Reformed – indeed, Calvinist – in its theological orientation as the sixteenth century drew to a close, its mingle-mangle of austere doctrines ... and half-reformed rituals at once placed it in a distinctive position in relation to Europe's other Reformed churches and made it singularly unstable."[6]

This unstable and inconsistent Protestantism contributed to similarly unstable and inconsistent understandings and sensory experiences of the very structure of space. In the next chapter, I will establish the interconnection of surveying and theology in early modern England, mapping out ways in which geometry was divine and the divine was geometric. Here, though, I will demonstrate that a spatial understanding of God was hardly uniform or uncontested. Whereas Harris writes of shattered "coordinates" of time (itself a post-Newtonian, mathematical way of conceptualizing space-time), I would like to explore the complicated constructions of the spatial "field." Protestant theologies were built upon fundamentally different cosmologies, upon different understandings of the cosmic order of things. There were, within the range of Protestant thought, diverse spatial epistemologies that, when brought to the theater, rendered the phenomenological field anything but consistent. The experience of inhabiting contradictory spatial epistemologies was itself dramatized in *Macbeth*.

The double helix of the Reformation and the Renaissance transformed an age-old model of the universe, a cosmic order that was perfect and unchanging. As classical astronomy cracked before the new astronomical discoveries of the sixteenth and seventeenth centuries, the structure of space itself became uncertain. The emergence of various new models for the structure of the universe (as put forth by Copernicus, Brahe, Kepler, Galileo and others), as well as a heightened emphasis on spatial constructs in mechanical discussions of motion, was not disconnected from various strands of early modern theology. Theology was interwoven with the new astronomy and natural philosophy more generally. The different ways in which the universe was conceived – as labile or stable, mutable or static – reflected, in turn, diverse understandings of God. Moreover, these various understandings of the spatial environment affected how the individual self, moving through these spaces, was expected to comprehend and experience the divine.

While theologically inflected conceptions of the cosmic order were not clearly or discretely defined, at the turn of the seventeenth century we might locate two primary models: that of a cosmos dependent upon an unknowable and unpredictable divine will, and that of a cosmos predictably ordered by divinely established natural law. The first of these, while beautifully structured, is at heart a cosmos with potential for motion, modulation, transformation. The second, while allowing for the occasional miracle, is a cosmos structured by a solid and immutable frame. These two models are exemplified in the writings of John Calvin and Richard Hooker. Where Calvin would trust in a Providence that could manipulate the precise movements of the universe, Hooker would place his faith in a God who established and adhered to natural law. Where Calvin's theology depends upon a universe that is unpredictable in its transformations, Hooker's theological vision requires a reliable cosmic order.[7]

*Macbeth* stages these competing theological cosmologies. John Stachniewski has written, "Of all Shakespeare's plays, *Macbeth* contains the most insistent religious language."[8] *Macbeth* is arguably also one of the most spatially oriented plays, as the shifting geographies of the supernatural often bring the characters to an intense self-awareness of their placement in both local and cosmic spatial settings. The central character, in particular, finds himself in a disorienting nexus of competing and contradictory cosmic environments. The play does not allow for a unified spatial field and thus a normative sense of proprioception, the sensation of the body-in-space. But if we do not find here the stable field of space-time assumed in work on historical phenomenology, we also do not find Harris's notion of palimpsest, a text that is itself the product of chronology. Rather, we discover two cosmic structures – one of radical contingency, one of determined laws – impossibly coexisting within the same space of the play. The result is a world which, theologically and physically, ceases to make sense. The overdetermined sensory experience of the play's opening creates a heightened awareness of the physical experience of the body, but the environment of that body creates cognitive and theological dissonance.

The opening of the play sets the stage for a disordered space-time. Time, space, atmospheric conditions and planetary motions become jumbled together. The answer to the witches' question of "when?" is posited not so much in temporal as atmospheric terms ("in thunder, lightning, or in rain"). The "hurly-burly" is timed by "the set of sun." While the answer to "Where the place?" seems straightforward ("Upon the heath"), that sense of definitive emplacement becomes undermined as the witches seem to "hover through the fog and filthy air" (and, as Harris points out, this is the same air the Globe's audience inhabits, thanks to the smoky squibs). Where are we? When are we? The coordinates of both time and space are shattered, and the effect on the audience – with ears perhaps still ringing from the theatrical thunder, and nostrils stinging from the gunpowder – is one of disorientation. Through much of the rest of the play the audience will witness Macbeth himself trying to recover a sense of solid space, trying to make sense of his environment, trying to force spatial fixity upon a world in which daggers hover and woods move.

We find in *Macbeth* a spatial manifestation of what in the first chapter I deemed "Ovidian physics," a sense of the world as labile and fluid. It is easy to see how such physics hold in moments of demonic interactions. What is perhaps less obvious is that demonic physics are not far removed from Calvin's understanding of divine control of the universe. It is not just local circumstances that are subject to Ovidian physics: in Calvin's *Institutes of the Christian Religion* we find a theo-cosmology of radical physical contingency. It is tempting to consider the spatial aberrations in *Macbeth* as part and parcel of a demonic environment, but these spatial contortions, and the irregularity of celestial motion, are the types of cosmic activity that Calvin uses as proof of an omnipotent God. Within this shifting, unpredictable world, Macbeth seems to cling to an idea of space that we find expressed by Richard Hooker, the notion that God's presence is manifest in cosmic order and natural law. We find within *Macbeth* the clash of competing theological cosmologies, and the impossibility of existing within irreconcilable space-times.

## PROVIDENTIAL SPACE-TIME

Calvin's theological understanding of the cosmos was a radical departure from earlier models, which depended upon an Aristotelian comprehension of the universe. As late as the end of the seventeenth century we find Richard Allestree writing, "There is a Place, where the *Woman* is *clothed with the Sun, and the Moon under her Feet, Rev. 12*. Where the Church, and every Member of it, is robed with Glory, and far above the reach of any Mutability."[9] The vision of this heavenly perfection is contrasted with the conditions of earth, which "is the *Moon's* chief Region, her very Exchange as it were, to vent all her Varieties, and nothing, save alteration, continues here" (p. 90). This portrayal of the cosmos merges the mysticism of Revelation with Aristotelian physics, according to which the universe is divided between sublunar regions of ongoing change and supra-lunar regions of immutability. Allestree's contrast between earthly "alteration" and heavenly immutability reflects a prejudice against the idea of change that is a central element of the Aristotelian cosmos. For millennia, change was a feature of the imperfect terrestrial realm, while a lack of change characterized celestial perfection. Although the celestial element (ether) could move, it did not change, unlike the four earthly elements (earth, fire, air and water) which morph into one another. The woman with the moon at her feet is clearly in that ethereal realm, and the deceased members of the church who have joined her are in a paradise of immutability, above the changes that mark our fallen world. Heaven, in this Christian appropriation of the Aristotelian cosmic geography of internesting spheres, has a particular location, in the ether that comprises the supralunary sphere.

In his exposition of the Lord's Prayer in the *Institutes of the Christian Religion*, Calvin also maintains that "Our Father who art in heaven" signals that God is "lifted above all chance of either corruption or change" (II: 902–3). But this unchanging God does not abide in a particular place: "From this we are not immediately to reason that he is bound, shut up, and surrounded, by the circumference of heaven, as by a barred enclosure . . . [God] is not confined to any particular region but is diffused through all things" (II: 902). Calvin's emphasis on this universal divinity would affect his notion of physics, a subject which seems to have greatly interested the reformer.[10]

One of the myths about Calvin is that he rejected the science of his day, and was laughably retrograde in his refusal to accept a heliocentric vision of the universe. As Alister McGrath has shown, Calvin's alleged rejection of Copernicus's heliocentric theory of the solar system – an "assertion [that] is slavishly repeated by virtually every subsequent writer on the themes of 'religion and science'" – is based upon an unsubstantiated claim first made by the nineteenth-century dean of Canterbury, Frederick William Farrar.[11] Farrar's claim blossomed into a fully fabricated quote in Andrew Dickson White's *History of the Warfare of Science with Theology* (1896), and, as McGrath notes, "[m]odern treatments of the theme 'Calvin and Science' have . . . been dominated by this fiction."[12] Far from being inimical to scientific developments, Calvin appears to have been deeply intrigued by sixteenth-century astronomical inquiries; his magnum opus, the *Institutes of the Christian Religion*, is steeped in cosmological language. Astronomical concepts, and a broader exploration of God's participation in cosmological physics, provide the starting point for Calvin's *Institutes* and become integral to the way in which he positions his reader vis-à-vis God. Fundamental to Calvin's rhetorical strategy and theological mission is an attempt to reorient his readers in their perception of their place in the universe; a human relationship with the divine, Calvin contends, is only possible once the individual has an acute self-awareness of his place within God's creation – which is ultimately equated with God himself. We are asked to become aware of the motion of the universe, for instance, so that we might become aware of ourselves. For Calvin, this cosmic proprioception is part of a recognition that knowledge of God and knowledge of self are mutually constitutive.

From the very opening of Calvin's *Institutes*, we enter into a spatial mode of understanding God. God is that in which man "'lives and moves'," Calvin writes, citing Acts 17:28 (I: 35). God is not only the creator of the universe, here he *is* the universe. The first book of the *Institutes* contains soaring and jubilant prose extolling the reader to consider the world around him. Calvin writes, "You cannot in one glance survey this most vast and beautiful system of the universe, in its wide expanse, without being completely overwhelmed by the boundless force of its brightness" (I: 52). Exploring and mapping the order of the physical universe is a means to come to the beauty of the invisible God. "To be sure," Calvin continues, "there is need of art and of more exacting toil in order to investigate the motion of the stars, to determine their assigned stations, to measure their intervals, to note their properties" (I: 53). Astronomy is even used as an example of a human activity that is purely for the soul. "Of what concern is it to the body that you measure the heavens, gather the number of the stars, determine the magnitude of each, know what space lies between them, with what swiftness or slowness they complete their courses, how many degrees this way or that they decline?" (I: 57).

Calvin's language of measurement – of "magnitude," "distance," "degrees" – creates an impression of an ordered universe, and thus a God, that is accessible through reason and calculation. Calvin speaks of "the most beautiful structure and order of the universe" (I: 63). The aesthetic beauties of this order also lead to the marvel of temporal regularity. God "stationed, arranged, and fitted together the starry host of heaven in such wonderful order that nothing more beautiful in appearance can be imagined; and who so set and fixed some in their stations that they cannot move; who granted to others a freer course, but so as not to wander outside their appointed course; who so adjusted the motion of all that days and nights, months, years, and seasons of the year are measured off; who so proportioned the inequality of days, which we daily observe, that no confusion occurs" (I: 181). This is a universe, and thus a God, whose beauty lies in its order and rationality. Calvin's God, it appears, is a structuralist.

But the vision of this ordered world that Calvin has constructed turns out to be partly an illusion, and the idea that we can fully know the order of the universe through scientific study and calculation is revealed as little more than human arrogance. (If Calvin were Milton, we would be surprised by our sin.) God is inscrutable, his ways unknowable. The movement of the cosmos, although often appearing ordered, is not steadfast, but subject to the gestures of a numinous deity. Calvin describes how God "sustain[s] this infinite mass of heaven and earth by his Word: by his nod alone ... to compel the sea, which by its height seems to threaten the earth with continual destruction, to hang as if in mid air" (I: 59). This last aspect is particularly intriguing. According to the properties and weight of water, Calvin believed, the sea should be overtaking the heavier landmass, but God keeps it artificially depressed.[13] Life on land is thus incredibly precarious, and human beings are continuously at the mercy of God.

Calvin scoffs at the idea that the universe is maintained by some energy force. He derides man's "carnal sense" and emphasizes its limitations in comprehending the universe: "[Carnal sense] contemplates ... some general preserving and governing activity, from which the force of motion derives. In short, carnal sense thinks there is an energy divinely bestowed from the beginning, sufficient to sustain all things" (I: 197). (We might call this force gravity.) For Calvin, the universe is not sustained by energy and motion, but simply by God's providence. As a reminder of this, God has periodically altered cosmic motions. Calvin notes that God once held the sun still in one degree for two days (I: 199, citing Josh. 10:13), and on another occasion he adjusted its shadow by ten degrees for the benefit of King Hezekiah – a story that is told both in II Kings (20:11) and Isaiah (38:8) (I: 199). In these cases, Providence trumps System. Indeed, God's "omnipotence ... is [not] only a general principle of confused motion ... but one that is directed toward individual and particular motions" (I: 200). Calvin, then, perceives environmental phenomena that we would consider as aberrations of the laws of physics – the artificial depression of sea-level, or changing the degrees of the sun – not as alarming disturbances of the natural order, but as proof of God's ongoing intervention in the macro- and micro-events of the world.

Calvin was hardly the first person to contemplate God's relation to the natural world. Francis Oakley sketches two distinct strands of thought that ran from classical philosophers to the early modern scientists, and notes "a sharp dichotomy between Stoic and related views of the natural law as immanent in the world, and the view, characteristic of the seventeenth century *virtuosi*, that the laws of nature were imposed upon the world from the outside by the decree of the omnipotent God who created it."[14] After the thirteenth century, Oakley argues, the Hellenistic concept of God's immanence in the world was superseded by the Semitic notion of an external lawgiver, and this position was given its fullest articulation by William of Ockham. Ockham's emphasis upon the omnipotence and freedom of God has led some "to suppose that Ockham conceived of God as a wholly capricious Being" (442–3), but this is not the case; Ockham "believed that although God's absolute power can suffer no limitation, it normally expresses itself in accordance with the order which has actually been ordained" (443). Thus, "it is true that God will normally act in accordance with the supernatural or natural order which he has ordained but it must not be forgotten that, of his absolute power, he could always abrogate the present moral and natural economy, or momentarily transcend it, as he does in the case of miracles" (443). This, essentially, is the understanding of God's relation to nature that would wend its way through to Boyle and Newton.

While Calvin is indebted to this medieval inheritance, his God is not about cosmic laws. Emphasizing God's creative force, Calvin presents a deity that is still very much engaged with his creation – the universe of the *Institutes* feels like one that is perpetually being created, one that is malleable and contingent, and always deeply dependent upon an ever-present Creator. This dependence, although revealed in incidental moments, is pervasive, an ongoing condition of the environment. In this emphasis on radical contingency, Calvin differs from the likes of Ockham and Boyle. Interestingly, both of these thinkers, centuries apart, turn to a story from the Book of Daniel to illustrate God's ability to overrule a prescribed natural order: when King Nebuchadnezzar threw Daniel's three companions into a fiery furnace, they emerged unscathed with their clothes unsinged (Daniel 3:15–27).[15] The moment is local, dramatic, and contained, an isolated incident of God intervening in human affairs, a moment of breaking a set of physical laws. Calvin's aquatic example of God's providence – the suppressed sea – is, by contrast, expansive, mundane, and continuous, revealing the ongoing state of God's control over human existence and his dynamic presence within creation.

For Calvin, God's providence – his unpredictable and unknowable will – supersedes any sense of natural "laws," and this is what makes God worthy of reverence. Calvin writes that he "does not repudiate what is said concerning universal providence [i.e. the notion of divinely established cosmic order], provided they in turn grant [him] that the universe is ruled by God, not only because he watches over the order of nature set by himself, but because he exercises especial care over each of his works" (I: 203). Calvin presents belief in an unerring, immutable and universal law of nature – which, as we have seen, he repeatedly conceptualizes in terms of motion, energy, and physical bodies – as a form of fraud verging on blasphemy. Belief in a universal law strips God of his power, it "take[s] from him the chief thing: that he directs everything by his incomprehensible wisdom and disposes it to his own end" (I: 202).

God's awesome power, to Calvin's mind, is thus not that he is able to construct an intricate system to govern the flow of the universe, but exactly the reverse: that he is able to direct every interaction on an individual basis. "Nothing," Calvin writes, "takes place by chance" (I: 203); "nothing at all in the world is undertaken without his determination" (I: 205). Such a belief extends God's role in the universe from the macro-events of the sea to the smallest micro-division of water: "if we accept these things, it is certain that not one drop of rain fall without God's sure command" (I: 204).

By debunking man's misguided faith in the laws of physics, Calvin restores God's free will, or providence. The restoration of God's free will in turn eliminates our own. Once we humbly accept God's providence and control over the universe, we cannot fail to see that God controls us as well. Indeed, Calvin enters into a discussion of God's control over man's actions by using the same language of motion he used for the universe: "Let them now say that man is moved by God according to the inclination of his nature, but that he himself [i.e. man] turns that motion whither he pleases. Nay, if that were truly said, the free choice of his ways would be in man's control" (I: 204). For Calvin, human motion is the result not of man's self-direction, but of God's "choice and determination" (I: 205). Man is part of the same theological ecosystem as planets and raindrops; *all* physical motion is directed by God, and to think that human beings alone have self-determination is folly. The utter surrender of human autonomy and direction, the utter renouncing of human will and the acceptance of a universe that is thoroughly controlled by God, is the essence of Calvin's theology. As Charles Trinkaus sums it up: "the major emphasis of [Calvin's] theology was not merely upon the benevolence, the omniscience, and the omnipotence of God, but also upon his omnioperative character, his constant supervision and control of all events, natural and historical and spiritual, and his wise and rational utilization of all men as instruments of his purpose."[16]

Calvin himself identifies this as his radical break with the past: "[God] does not move the will in such a manner as has been taught and believed for many ages – that it is afterward in our choice either to obey or resist the motion" (I: 303). As we can see here, Calvin now employs the language of "motion" to describe the will. The unfolding of Calvin's reasoning thus goes something like this: we are directed to look to the universe, and wonder at its magnificence. We then discover our error in perceiving (what I will anachronistically call) a clockwork universe, a system with its own steady machinations and laws of movement. We become aware that God directs the movements of the heavens, and the sea, and the raindrops. It then follows logically that, as physical bodies, God directs us as well ("not even one hair can fall from our head without his will" [I: 219]). Having been brought to that point, it is not much of a step to the realization that God also controls the motion of our will ("whatever we conceive of in our minds is directed to his own end by God's secret inspiration" [I: 231; citing Prov. 21:1]).

Calvin's Christian subject, then, at once inhabits and is inhabited by God. "[I]n him we live, move, and have our being" (Acts 17:28): Calvin returns to this verse six times in Book I of the *Institutes*.[17] It functions at once as a touchstone and as an indicator of shifting frames of reference, since what it means to "live, move, and have our being" in God changes over the course of the book. Initially, the verse refers to the spatial emplacement of the individual. The first book of the *Institutes* denaturalizes space – it forces readers to become self-conscious of their place in the universe, a universe which is at once systemic and arbitrary, at once a source of awe and comfort. In its focus on cosmology, the *Institutes* participates in the sixteenth-century cartographic impulse, the drive to map out the cosmos, the planet, the nation, the county, the estate. Calvin's theological cartography, though, becomes three-dimensional – his cosmos, and thus his God, is one of motion. His spiritual cartographer – the individual in a relationship with God – is caught up in, and a part of, divine movement. In this way, reading Book I of the *Institutes* is an exercise in phenomenology. Calvin's opening gambit in the *Institutes* is to locate his reader in very physical ways within the dynamics of a very physical universe. Book I emphasizes motion not as an abstract concept, but as something that can be physically manipulated by God; from the waves in the sea to the motion of raindrops, from the bodies of sparrows to the hairs on the reader's head, God utterly manipulates the material world.

Having led us into a contemplation of the physical environment we occupy, the verse from Acts 17:28 assumes a different (and for Calvin, a deeper) significance as it becomes an expression of the overwhelming and pervasive power of God in our lives. Calvin uses physical facts to lead his audience to a particular psychological self-awareness. For Calvin, experiencing this physical world becomes part of a mindset that makes the reader receptive to God's grace. While later books of the *Institutes* would encourage disengagement with the material world, Calvin's opening strategy is to place his reader firmly within the cosmos of a numinous God.[18]

Thus, as the historian W. J. Torrance Kirby observes, "Calvin asserts ... that human reason is naturally able to discern eternal power and divinity through a contemplation of the splendor of the natural order with the rational creature as its principle glory. The proper image of the divine glory is displayed in the rational human soul. Calvin quotes Ovid's *Metamorphoses* ..."[19] This is true, and yet the passage from Ovid that Calvin chooses to cite as a reference point for discussing the splendor of the natural order and human rationality is, I would contend, a sly, perhaps even winking rhetorical moment on Calvin's part. Here is the passage that he quotes (as translated by Arthur Golding):

> And where all other beasts behold the ground with groveling eie,
> He gave to Man a stately looke replete with majestie.
> And willde him to behold the Heaven with countnance cast on hie,
> To marke and understand what things were in the starrie skie.[20]

The passage does indeed extol the human ability to reason, the wondrous capacity to contemplate the wonders of the universe. Calvin uses the quote in a section entitled "God's image and likeness in man" (I: 186).

However there can be almost no doubt, in an era when Ovid was to the verbal and visual arts what Shakespeare is today, that Calvin was ignorant – or expected his audience to be ignorant – of where the passage comes from, and thus the reference is tinged with irony. The lines are from the beginning of *The Metamorphoses*, wedged between Ovid's opening tale of the Creation and a very brief account of the Golden Age, after which things rapidly go downhill. This notion of perfect rational humanity, as opposed to lowly bestiality, is thus undermined by the entire rest of the poem with its tales of transformation – in many cases, of human beings transformed into animals. And it is, of course, the gods themselves who are the agents of radical change, as is pointed out in Ovid's opening invocation:

> Of shapes transformde to bodies straunge, I purpose to entreate,
> Ye gods vouchsafe (for you are they ywrought this wondrous feate)
> To further this mine enterprise.                    (I.1–3)

Ovid's gods – and Calvin's God – are terrifyingly wondrous for their ability to transform. Their world is one of mutability. So while human beings might indeed use their reason to marvel at the wonders of creation, the wonder is not that this creation is static or a monument to stable order. Given the early modern sense of cosmological mutability, and given that Ovid (and Ovid-through-Petrarch) was a predominant literary mode of the sixteenth century, this conjunction of reason and unpredictable transformation would have been both epistemologically and aesthetically familiar to Calvin's audience.

Calvin's reference to Ovid can be seen as both celebratory and debasing. It vaunts the human ability "To marke and understand what things were in the starrie skie." Yet it also suggests how thoroughly human beings are subjected to God's and the gods' universe of Ovidian physics. (Just for fun, we could say that Calvin puts the "ovid" in "providence.") We might be able to understand cosmic order, but that does not enable us to withstand the potential for unexpected transformations at the hand of the divine. The invocation of Ovid also, it would seem, cannot help but color Calvin's image of God. While commentators contend that Calvin's providential God is not whimsical or capricious, the same cannot be said of Ovid's mischievous gods.

Within the *Institutes*, Calvin maintains that the radical acceptance of Providence soothes the soul: "incredible freedom from worry about the future ... necessarily follow[s] upon this knowledge" (I: 219). While this utter renunciation of human agency may be anathema to those of us raised in the wake of liberal humanism, this surrender may have felt wonderfully liberating to those in the sixteenth century. (We should not forget how quickly enthusiasm for Calvin's theology caught on and spread through Europe.) And yet, Calvin himself remained a highly anxious individual, and his anxiety was expressed in his conflicting ideas about the order of the universe. Calvin admires the universe for its order, but is aware of the fragility and contingency of this order. William J. Bouwsma notes in his biography of the reformer that "[Calvin's anxiety] found radical expression in his ambivalence about the order of nature. He clung, at times with frantic tenacity, to the conception of a natural order that had traditionally helped human beings to feel comfortable in the world. But this conception was also antithetical to his deep sense of the incomprehensibility of God and the contingency of the world."[21] This could lead to moments in which "The order of the heavens was, for Calvin, deeply consoling," and in fact, "The natural laws that keep the heavenly bodies harmonious also provided Calvin, in a traditional way, with his model for order in human affairs."[22] And yet, "The rotation of the heavens was for Calvin not proof of the order of nature but 'such a miracle that we should be ravished in astonishment by it.'"[23] It is quite easy to see the profound incompatibility of these perspectives (faith in God rests on the harmonious order of the universe; faith in God rests on the utter acceptance of radical Providence), and to understand how their incompatibility could result in spiritual anxiety.

As I will discuss later in this chapter, Macbeth's anxieties participate in Calvin's. The physical world of *Macbeth* is similarly one of incompatible notions of the universe; this dissonance produces, and is simultaneously produced by, theological incoherence. Calvin exhibits a desire for a set, unalterable universal order even as he seeks to accept the numinous workings of God's providence. In late Elizabethan and Jacobean England, Richard Hooker – who, of course, would prove to be Anglicanism's most prominent theologian – was writing against the grain of Calvin's dominant theology, reasserting a strong sense of a universe ordered by natural law. Hooker, like Calvin, builds his theology from an initial discussion of space. *Macbeth*, as I will show, seemingly dramatizes a spatial environment that is governed by both Calvin's providence and Hooker's law. The fundamental incompatibility of these positions contributes to the play's eerie sense of disorientation.

### 'LAWES' AND NATURE

The decades on either side of 1600 witnessed the dominance of Calvinist theology in England. The two available versions of the Bible (the Geneva Bible and the Bishops' Bible, first published in 1560 and 1568, respectively) contained marginal commentary that was distinctly Calvinist; the thirty-nine quarto editions of the Geneva Bible printed between 1579 and 1615 were bound with a predestinarian catechism.[24] In the 1590s, the archbishops of Canterbury and York (Whitgift and Hutton), along with a string of bishops of London (Aylmer, Fletcher, and Bancroft), endorsed absolute predestination; the Lambeth Articles of 1595 affirmed the church's core Calvinist principles. The Paul's Cross sermons were largely Calvinist, and surviving wills indicate "the successful propagation of Calvinism among the laity."[25] The Thirty-nine Articles, the English confession of faith, had a Calvinist slant (although the Elizabethan Prayer Book did not). If Queen Elizabeth's enthusiasm for Calvinistic doctrine was muted (in no small part due to Knox's treatise arguing against female monarchs), King James actively promoted Calvinist theological orthodoxy (although the structure of Calvin's church was abhorrent to him). It was not until 1615 that Archbishop Laud came out against Calvinism, his subsequent emphasis on the role of the sacraments in itself presenting a refutation of the doctrine of predestination.

The English printing press produced far more editions of Calvin's works than of any other continental reformer, including Luther.[26] Thomas Norton's English translation of the *Institutes* went through nine editions between 1561 and 1634. In England the *Institutes* was also published in Latin (1576) and even Spanish (1597), and between 1549 and 1630 there were eight abridged versions (many of which went into multiple editions) by various editors and translators and in both English and Latin. Calvin's biblical commentaries, sermons, and other tracts were all published in abundance; the sheer number of catechisms indicates the degree to which Calvin was theological mother's milk for generations of English children.[27] In all, sixty-six different editions of Calvin's texts were published in English in the sixteenth century.[28]

While Calvin's own writings were widely published (and, we might thus infer, widely read), by the end of the sixteenth century his thought was morphing into Calvinism, as various authors used his authority but distorted his theology.[29] In England, a central force in the move from Calvin to Calvinism was William Perkins, who was perceived as translating Calvin for the masses, although Perkins seems to conflate the very different theologies of Calvin and the reformer's successor in Geneva, Theodore Beza. Where Calvin discouraged his readers from introspection as a means of determining one's personal state of salvation,[30] Perkins instructed his audience to look inward for signs of election. Looking at the publishing history of Calvin and Perkins, we can see distinctly that in the 1590s Calvin's fortunes wane as Perkins's fortunes wax.[31]

Perkins's interpellation of Calvin would contribute to a distortion of that reformer's theology. Calvin's thought is sometimes characterized as systematic. A. G. Dickens writes that the *Institutes* "was for the most part a systematic exposition of Luther's volcanic utterances," and an influential Anglican theologian has described Calvin's thought as "architectonic."[32] As McGrath notes, however, "The popular conception of Calvin's religious thought is that of a rigorously logical system, centring upon the doctrine of predestination. Influential though this popular icon may be, it bears little relation to reality."[33] Iain M. MacKenzie has discussed how the sixteenth-century Marian exiles brought with them a type of Calvinism that had developed in the Netherlands, known as "Federal Calvinism." He explains, "This had an overwhelming emphasis on double predestination which it hardened into a structure of legalistic proportions, accompanied by an insistence that the elect were observably known by their piety. This is far removed from the Calvinism of Geneva, with its insistence on a predestination in Christ, and such a doctrine used only to safeguard the mystery of the grace of God as over against all human attempts to explain and codify salvation" (p. 3). (Contrary to the assumptions of many today, the doctrine of predestination does not dominate the *Institutes*. The doctrine does not receive sustained attention until Book III, section XXI – or volume II, page 920 of McNeill's standard edition. Even then it is only the direct focus of inquiry for a few chapters.) MacKenzie goes on to explain how Federal Calvinism deviates from Calvin's thought:

The mistake lurking behind [the assertion that Calvin is scholastic and rigidly systematic] is an illusion caused by viewing Calvin through the lens of Federal

Calvinist mechanics, and wrongly perceiving that *soli Deo gloria* must be reduced to predestination. It is perfectly true that Calvin's inspiration is the appreciation that all things are for the glory of God alone, and that predestination is part of this precept. But the God to whose glory all things live and move and have their being is, for Calvin, the God of grace, and not the God of static decrees ... Indeed the very thrust of Calvin's theology attacks any systematization. He criticizes the adamantine edifice of systematized compartments constructed schematically by 'the frigid doctors of the Sorbonne', for he perceived that theology, not only in the last resort but in awareness throughout its process, is dealing with the God who is lord over our thoughts and before whom our thoughts and statements can only dissolve in wonder and awe and worship. The *soli Deo gloria* of Calvin is to be recognized not as the motto of a theological system, but as the very epitaph of all attempts at systematization in theology.

(pp. 4–5)

Not only does Calvin's theological method reject systematization; so too his vision of the universe (which, again, is his vision of God) defies human formularizing.[34] While he invokes familiar structural ways of conceiving of the cosmos (macrocosm-microcosm, astronomical movement[35]), Calvin's universe feels profoundly unstructured, given that it is not only controlled by God but *is* God, a God without a knowable form.

Towards the end of the sixteenth century, then, we find in England a theological climate that is dominated by both Calvin and Calvinism. It is in this moment that Richard Hooker (d. 1600) was writing his massive *Lawes of Ecclesiastical Polity*, a book that would become incredibly influential and eventually be considered a foundational text of Anglicanism.[36]

Hooker would follow in Calvin's footsteps by making his readers self-conscious of their place in a cosmic setting, but he would also lead them into a very different universe. The traditional account of Hooker's magnum opus is that the book charts a *via media* between Catholicism and continental Protestantism. As Kirby notes, however, "[i]n general, the interpretation of the doctrine and institutions of the Elizabethan and Jacobean Church in recent historiography has tended to dismiss the *via media* hypothesis as inappropriate and anachronistic."[37] Instead of creating a middle ground between Rome and continental Protestantism, most historians now agree, Hooker actually sees himself as promoting the English Reformation.[38] Patrick Collison comments that the *Lawes* have a "deep and sustained indebtedness to Calvin's divinity."[39] Kirby contends that Hooker "gives practical expression as it were to Calvin's epistemological motif of the *duplex congnitio dei*," the idea that there is a twofold knowledge of God through Creation and the redemptive incarnation.[40] For both Hooker and Calvin, knowledge of God comes through

Creation; Hooker compares "the virtue of voluntary obedience to the natural law on the part of rational creatures with the external beauty of the hierarchically ordered cosmos."[41]

In contrast with Calvin, this law needs must be rigid, nearly absolute. It does not allow for metamorphosis or a plastic cosmos. In his efforts to establish a working definition of "law," Hooker bases his text on a discussion of the relationship between God and creation that fundamentally constructs his theology.[42] This relationship is one of integration: "the workes and operations of God haue him both for their worker, and for the lawe whereby they are wrought. The being of God is a kinde of lawe to his working: for that perfection which God is, geueth perfection to that he doth ... God therefore is a law both to himselfe, and to all other things besides."[43] God and law here become nearly synonymous. In establishing natural law, God has deliberately restrained his own power in the interest of achieving cosmic harmony: "his wisedome hath stinted th' effects of his power in such sort, that it doth not worke infinitely but correspo[n]dently vnto that end for which it worketh, ... in most decent and comely sort, all things in *measure, number, and waight*" (p. 50, original italics). This is not to say, however, that God has lost his freedom: "Nor is the freedom of the wil of God any whit abated, let or hindered by meanes of this, because the imposition of this law upo[n] himself is his own free & volu[n]tary act. This law therfore we may name eternall, being *that order which God before all ages hath set down with himselfe, for himselfe to do all things by*" (p. 51). Where Calvin argues that those who put their faith in a cosmic system rob God of his will, Hooker maintains that it was the will of God to establish a cosmic system, one which he devised but which he also freely obeys.

Hooker's description of God's law rings true with Calvin's opening depiction of a structuralist God. "That law eternall which God himself hath made to himselfe, and therby worketh all things wherof he is the cause and author, that law is the admirable frame wherof shineth with most perfect bewtie the countenance of that wisedome ... That law which hath bene the patterne to make, and is the Card to guide the world by ... Let no man doubt but that euery thing is well done, because the world is ruled by so good a guide, as transgresseth not his owne law, then which nothing can be more absolute, perfect & iust" (p. 51). In equating law with a "Card" (i.e. a map), Hooker, like Calvin, emphasizes the spatiality of the divine order. But where Calvin's sense of structure becomes complicated and even undermined by providence, Hooker's structuralist sensibility remains firm throughout the *Lawes*. "The law wherby he worketh, is eternall, and therefore can haue no shew or cullor of mutabilitie" (p. 51).

We hear overtones of Aristotle, and indeed, as Kirby writes, in his discussion of law Hooker adopts "Aquinas's neo-Platonic metaphysical logic. Just as the neo-Platonic cosmology accounts for the genesis of the world by means of a downward emanation or procession from the principle of original unity, so also Hooker derives a diverse hierarchy of laws from the eternal law as their 'highest wellspring and fountain.'"[44] Thus, "the authority of human reason consequent upon the revelation of the divine wisdom to the observer of 'the glorious workes of Nature' is a crucial presupposition of his theologico-political system."[45]

God's creation and law, for Hooker, are thus inherently interconnected concepts.[46] In his slide from discussing the nature of law to the laws of nature, Hooker's first book of *The Lawes of Ecclesiastical Politie* echoes Calvin's first book on creation in the *Institutes of the Christian Religion*. Indeed, Hooker writes, "it cannot be, but nature hath some director of infinite knowledge to guide her in all her wayes. Who the guide of nature but only the God of nature? *In him wee liue, moue, and are* [marginal gloss: Acts.17:28]" (p. 54). It is hard to imagine that the erudite Hooker would have been ignorant of the extent to which Book I of Calvin's *Institutes* rested on this biblical verse; given the prominence of those words in Calvin's own text, here Hooker seems to be simultaneously quoting the Bible and Calvin. In fact, just a few sentences later Hooker turns directly to the notion of providence, so crucial in Calvin's theology. "Only thus much is discerned," he writes, "that the naturall generation and processe of all things receyueth order of proceeding from the setled stabilitie of diuine vnderstanding. This appointeth vnto them their kinds of working, the disposition whereof in the puritie of Gods owne knowledge and will is rightly tearmed by the name of *Prouidence*" (p. 54). Hooker's "providence" is clearly not Calvin's. For Calvin, God's providence is unpredictable, illogical, and signals a divine micro-managing of cosmic affairs. For Hooker, providence is about "settled stabilitie" – the redundancy of the phrase emphasizing the orderly, systemic nature of the divine. Hooker's world, both his natural environment and the ecclesiastical polity he is trying to define and create, rests on law. As Peter Lake puts it, "Despite his intermittent hymns to the ultimate inscrutability and majesty of the divine will, Hooker had to insist upon the law-bound nature of God's doings, because the rational intelligibility of God's plan for his creatures stood at the very centre of his case."[47]

Both Hooker and Calvin, then, ground their texts upon a consideration of God's operations in the natural world. Their depictions of these operations, however, are diametrically opposed. Whereas Calvin recognizes system, his emphasis is on the potential for God's will to supersede order and regularity. And while Hooker admits, very briefly and in passing, that there are periodic hiccups in the system of laws (p. 54), his overwhelming emphasis is on the stability of natural law.[48] In one famous passage (an important source of Tillyard's "Elizabethan world picture"[49]), Hooker expounds upon the dire consequences that would result if the world ceased to follow natural laws. I quote the passage at length in order to convey the passion that Hooker brings to the issue of environmental stability:

And as it co[m]meth to passe in a kingdom rightly ordered, that after a law is once published, it presently takes effect far & wide, all states framing the[m] selues thereunto; euen so let vs thinke it fareth in the naturall course of the world: since the time that God did first proclaime the edicts of his law vpon it, heauen & earth haue hearkned vnto his voice, and their labour hath bene to do his wil: He *made a law for the raine.* He gaue his *decree vnto the sea, that the waters should not passe his commandement.* Now if nature should intermit her course, and leaue altogether, though it were but for a while, the obseruation of her own lawes: if those principall & mother eleme[n]ts of the world, wherof all things in this lower world are made, should loose the qualities which now they haue, if the frame of that heauenly arch erected ouer our heads should loosen & dissolue it selfe: if celestiall spheres should forget their wonted motions and by irregular volubilitie, turne themselues any way as it might happen: if the prince of the lightes of heauen which now as a Giant doth runne his vnwearied course, should as it were through a languishing faintness begin to stand & to rest himselfe: if the Moone should wander from her beaten way, the times and seasons of the yeare blend themselues by disordered and confused mixture, the winds breathe out their last gaspe, the cloudes yeeld no rayne, the earth be defeated of heauenly influence, the fruites of the earth pine away as children at the withered breasts of their mother no longer able to yeeld them reliefe, what would become of man himselfe, whom these things now do all serue? See we not plainly that obedience of creatures vnto the lawe of nature is the stay of the whole world?[50]

In opposition to Calvin's interest in the suppressed sea and the variances of celestial motions, Hooker stresses that God is law, and law is order. The breaking of natural laws signifies the end of God – and, Hooker implies, since God is omnipotent, we might rest assured that this environmental chaos, the hypothesized string of "ifs," is merely a nightmarish fantasy.

Cosmic order, and the reliability of that order, is thus, for Hooker, key to the faith. Hooker's position reflects that which MacKenzie attributes to the Laudian divines (a category which, for him, has a chronological scope extending from Elizabethan to Carolinian regimes). The Laudian theology "speaks of the acts of God in correspondence with His Being – an eternal existence of light and truth and love and holiness. The acts of God are acts of His grace, creative acts which correspond in the ordering of creation in the dimension of time and things and the existence of humanity, to His eternal existence" (p. 115). This, indeed, would become the theology of Isaac Newton who, in the final pages of *Principia*, would once again tweak Acts 17:28 ("In him are all things contained and moved; yet neither affects the other: God suffers nothing from the motion of bodies; bodies find no resistance from the omnipresence of God"[51]). God is spatial, omnipresent, and the world is so precisely ordered that it can be measured and observed through the precision of mathematics. For Calvin, the recognition of the material place of the self within God's cosmos, and a true realization that all matter and motion in the universe are utterly dependent upon God's will, ultimately leads to a deeper, more spiritual communion with God. For Hooker, a rational understanding of law and creation as mutually constitutive is the foundation of church and personal faith; the predictability of the cosmic order is proof of a living, orderly, and compassionate God.

### NOR TIME NOR PLACE DO THEN ADHERE

Literary critics have debated whether or not *Macbeth* is a "Calvinist" play. But it is difficult to spot a pure Calvinist in early modern England, where theological taxonomies were hardly crisp.[52] The laity received their theology from a variety of sources: the pulpit, the printing press, conversations with neighbors, their own contemplations, and the notion that this information was clearly marked as "Calvinist" or not is fallacious. The imprecise nature of the term is enhanced by the thinking patterns of the specialists, as the early modern clergy didn't use the label of "Calvinist" for themselves, either. Calvin was considered one great thinker amongst a host of great thinkers, and preachers and theologians borrowed from his writings as they saw fit, not as a mode of restricted self-identification.[53] (By way of analogy, we might consider that today literary scholars use the work of Lacan, Derrida, Marx, Foucault, etc., without declaring themselves part of a particular party – a strict Derridean, say. Even the label of "Marxist," one which has been used as a term of self-identification, has fallen from favor.)

Further clouding the discussion of *Macbeth*'s theology is the propensity of literary scholars to list towards Calvinism rather than towards Calvin. Debates about the play's theological slant have been focused on questions of intention and predestination. The "Calvinism" of literary scholars,

I would contend, is largely the "Calvinism" of Perkins, with the emphasis on determining one's own state of salvation or damnation.[54] While it is not inappropriate to work with Perkins's version of Calvin – indeed, given Perkins's prominence in late sixteenth- and early seventeenth-century England it would be irresponsible to ignore his influence – we need to acknowledge that Perkins presents only one form of processing Calvin's thought.

Even as *Macbeth* defies a convenient theological label, it stages the spatial confusion that results from the irreconcilable presence of different models of the cosmos. The confusion of cosmic structures is manifest, for instance, in the play's temporal irregularities. Numerous critics have noted what Brian Richardson refers to as *Macbeth*'s temporal "deformations" and "violation[s] of chronology,"[55] and Jonathan Gil Harris comments: "*Macbeth* is a play that repeatedly smudges the boundaries dividing the present 'moment' from other times."[56] As Richardson convincingly argues, the frequent and gratuitous references to the hour throughout the play seem to deliberately flag temporal problems.[57] While Macbeth proclaims time to be a constant ("Come what come may,/Time and the hour runs through the roughest day" [1.3.147–8]) and an entity that can be "recorded" (5.5.21), any sense of a regular progression of time is thwarted as the play quickly enters a temporal morass. As Donald Foster writes, "Macbeth is overcome with a temporal vertigo that dizzies his speech."[58] Verb tenses and sentence constructions collapse, as past, present, and future repeatedly collide and compromise each other. Lady Macbeth, for example, claims that Macbeth's "letters have transported [her] beyond/This ignorant present, and I feel now/The future in the instant" (1.5.56–8).

In addition to these abstract temporal expressions, the play also emphasizes the connection of time to celestial movements and therefore cosmic structures. To make an obvious point, while early moderns did not quite share our vocabulary of Einsteinian "space-time," in an age before electricity and the omnipresence of digital clocks (and, for that matter, universal timekeeping) time was viscerally connected to the motion of celestial spheres. Hooker notes the interconnection of motion and time: "God's owne eternitie is the hand which leadeth Angels in the course of their perpetuitie ... the hand that draweth out cælestiall motion, the line of which motion and the thread of time are spun together."[59] In *Macbeth*, however, the connection of time and cosmic motions is used to signal failures in this sense of structure. Ross, for instance, remarks that "by th' clock 'tis day,/And yet dark night strangles the travelling lamp" (2.4.6–7).

With the sun stymied in its progress, the moment brings us back to Calvin's examples of God altering the solar progression. In the Old Testament, though, God stops or reverses time for the good of his people: as a sign to Hezekiah that he will live and the Assyrians will be defeated, as an aid to Joshua in his rout of the Amorites.[60] In *Macbeth*, the alteration of the sun's course has no positive valence, but is only a symptom of a world out of tune. Similarly, the Captain notes, "As whence the sun 'gins his reflection,/Shipwracking storms and direful thunders break,/So from that spring, whence comfort seem'd to come,/Discomfort swells" (1.2.25–8).[61] That which, for Hooker, should serve as a steady reminder of God's order – the constant motion of the sun – here becomes the source of unpredictable danger. As Susan Snyder notes, the sun "refuses to shine on the day following Duncan's murder – and for dramatic purposes darkness continues in Scotland until the usurper's reign comes to its violent end."[62] The sense of temporal chaos within the play extends to lunar as well as solar motion. Fleance observes, "The moon is down; I have not heard the clock" (2.1.2). This is not simply an environment that lacks mechanized chronology; it is a world out of time.[63] The moon is not hidden, but "down" (reminiscent of Hooker's "if the Moone should wander from her beaten way . . .").

*Macbeth* thus becomes acutely aware of its environment, of the presence of space and time and the relationship between the two. This heightened sense of space-time opens questions of human and divine agency. Macbeth seems to long for the world of Hooker (and, we might project, of Newton), a physical world of certainty and order – and yet, as he seems painfully self-aware, he is caught in the volatile physics of Calvin's universe. For Calvin, the surrender to God – the relinquishing of a sense of personal agency in order to accept the mystery of God's operations, the recognition that the self is part of a larger cosmic environment – is (ideally) liberating, part of the process of personal regeneration. For Macbeth, an awareness of his place within the universe leads to a sense of imprisonment. Responding to the news of Fleance's escape from the murderers, Macbeth laments:

> I had else been perfect;
> Whole as the marble, founded as the rock,
> As broad and general as the casing air:
> But now, I am cabin'd, cribb'd, confin'd, bound in
> To saucy doubts and fears.          (3.4.20–4)

Perfection – wholeness – is here associated with the solidity of marble and rock. The sentiment echoes Macbeth's earlier invocation of the "sure and firm-set earth" (2.1.56). But the rest of the play gives the lie to Macbeth's forced or even wistful expressions of spatial certainty. As Lennox reports, "some say, the earth/Was feverous, and did shake" (2.3.59–60). Macbeth indicates that he recognizes his own preoccupation with earthly and temporal surety as a fantasy. While he is concerned that "the frame of things [Arden gloss: "i.e., the universe, both the worlds, celestial and terrestrial"] disjoint, both the worlds suffer" (3.2.16), his description of Duncan's corpse having "gash'd stabs look[ing] like a breach in nature" (2.3.111) reveals the possibility of a cosmic body that can be rent.

Macbeth moves swiftly from the wholeness of marble to the integrity of the air which surrounds him. Just as the marble is smooth and continuous throughout, so too the "broad and general" air, that which encases him (we might say, that in which he lives, moves, and has his being), seems to be of a steady, even consistency. This description of the air (or, more abstractly, of space) appears blatantly inaccurate, however, after the encounter with the witches near the beginning of the play. When the witches disappear, Banquo proclaims, "The earth hath bubbles, as the water has, /And these are of them.–Whither are they vanish'd?" to which Macbeth responds, "Into the air; and what seem'd corporal,/Melted as breath into the wind" (1.3.79–82). The analogy of earth and water creates a sense of the chthonic that is as mobile, fluid, permeable and anomalous as the aquatic. (The idea of "bubbles" is prominent in this play, returning, of course, as refrain in the witches' incantation of "Double, double, toil and trouble:/Fire, burn; and cauldron bubble" [4.1.10–1].) A bubbling earth, like a bubbling sea, is hardly "sure and firm-set." The melting of the corporeal into air enacts another dimension of physics, but what is interesting for my purposes is Macbeth's comment about "breath into the wind" and how quickly he contradicts his own imagery. Breath into the wind signals a type of integration of subject and environment.[64] When Macbeth relates these events to his wife in a letter, however, he creates a much different picture. Lady Macbeth reads how the witches "made themselves air, into which they vanish'd" (1.5.4–5). This line can easily be read as "they made themselves *into* air," but that is not quite what it says: the witches, far from breathing into the wind as participants in a preexisting spatial frame, make their own air. They create new space that they can step into. This idea fractures the notion of a stable spatial structure. It creates a breach in nature.

Calvin urged his readers to become self-conscious of their place as, to borrow an expression from Banquo, "th' inhabitants o'th' earth" (1.3.41). For the inhabitants of *Macbeth*, an environmental self-consciousness could only result in a recognition that there is no stability in this space-time. As Arthur F. Kinney notes, Macbeth's imagination "erodes the normal barriers of time and space."[65] While Kinney's "normal" understanding of time and space is post-Newtonian, Lady Macbeth makes a similar point about the dissolution of absolute space-time. Berating her husband for reversing his plans to kill Duncan, she says:

> . . . Nor time, nor place,
> Did then adhere, and yet you would make both:
> They have made themselves, and that their fitness now
> Does unmake you.                    (1.7.51–4)

A rough paraphrase of these lines would go something like this: When the occasion for killing the king was not right, you would have gone ahead anyway; now that circumstances have lined up in your favor, you can't handle it. But the language of "making" takes us back to the witches making their own air; time and space are *made*, leading to a fantasy of divinity. For Calvin, recognition of cosmic instability leads one to God. For Macbeth, this recognition leads him to play God. Macbeth commands the cosmos: "Stars, hide your fires!" (1.4.50). So, too, his wife proclaims: "O! never/Shall sun that morrow see!" (1.5.60–1). Again, for Calvin, recognition of God's utter omnipotence leads his reader to abandon fantasies of autonomy. For Macbeth, his fantasy of autonomy blinds him from accepting God's omnipotence. At the height of his arrogance, Macbeth scorns the notion that Great Birnam Wood can come to Dunsinane Hill: "Who can impress the forest; bid the tree/Unfix his earth-bound root?" (4.1.95–6) The answer, quite obviously, is an omnipotent God. While Macbeth fails to admit God's power, he has an inflated sense of his own, even setting the terms for the resurrection of the dead: "Rebellious dead, rise never, till the wood/Of Birnam rise; and our high-plac'd Macbeth/Shall live the lease of Nature, pay his breath/To time, and mortal custom" (4.1.97–100). His obvious theological error leads him to think he controls his own place and time, but he can only perceive these through the lens of "mortal custom"; he fails to understand himself as part of a cosmic, divinely driven space and time that is greater than the terms of humanity. Or, as his use of the self-referential third person indicates, he splits himself into God and man, becoming the semblance of a self-contained universe. He fails to recognize himself as part of a greater divine order. He fails to perceive, as the wiser Banquo puts it, "In the great hand of God [he] stand[s]" (2.3.128).

The play ends with a return to rightful divinity. Malcolm promises that "what needful else/That calls upon us, by the grace of Grace,/We will perform in measure, time, and place" (5.9.37–9). By introducing the concept of "measure" here, we seem to be entering the ordered world of Hooker's cosmos. Indeed, the conventional reading of the lines is that chaos is returned to order. But within Calvin's universe, the terms of chaos and order don't even really hold: since there is no steadfast system, there can be no breakdown of that system. While Macbeth's crime might seem to set off the dire chain of Hooker's "what-ifs," such human actions have little effect in a world run completely by divine providence.

Macbeth is a character who exists in a universe whose divine physics he fails to grasp. In trying to manipulate or anticipate the trajectory of his life, in trying to become the agent controlling his actions and direction, he doesn't accept Calvin's notion of predestination, of a radical acceptance in God's will. Even more fundamentally, he resists the very environment he inhabits. He appears to believe – or wants to believe – in Hooker's world of laws, where time and space are reliable constants. This belief clashes with the time and space in which he actually lives. In *Macbeth* we find the dissonant coexistence of two modes of understanding the physical and the divine. We see a character trying to negotiate an environment that is demonstrably operating according to one type of divine physics when his belief structure does not hold with those physics. We see a character trying to process a variable universe through a theology of constants and abso-lutes. In a way, the play stages not just the coexistence of these theologies, but makes them conversant such that each becomes the dark, paranoid fantasy of the other. We find a divine providence that, within the *Institutes*, is generally a sign of God's grace but here is transformed into a world of horrific natural aberrations, a world in which horses eat each other. And, too, Macbeth's adherence to a Hooker-esque reliance on law and structure becomes a travesty in light of the regicide, a gross violation of natural law.

In the end, Macbeth's understanding of the structure of time and space is thus utterly irreconcilable to the cosmic frame he inhabits. We might imagine that Macbeth's predicament was not unfamiliar to some in his Jacobean audience, to those existing in a nexus of contradictory theologies predicated on different understandings of the cosmos.[66] The sense of spatial disorientation with which the play opens is associated with witchcraft, and indeed most of the scholarship on the supernatural in *Macbeth* has focused on the witches. But in some ways the witches are not an end point, rather a symptom of a larger cosmic confusion. Sarah Beckwith writes, "Witchcraft is what happens to a society in flux when it cannot bear or articulate that flux."[67] She draws on sociological/historical studies of early modern witchcraft, but it is striking how prominently spatial metaphors figure in her analysis. The structuring of identity "involved a highly charged awareness of that which simultaneously separates people from each other, and that which connects them – an obsession with borders, margins, edges, or alternatively links, bridges, bonds" (p. 144). Beckwith's spatial modeling provides more than just useful heuristic analogies or metaphors. While changing social structures and transformations in economic systems obviously were very important factors in the early modern obsession with witchcraft, on a more subtle level concern with witches – a concern which entailed questions about human agency in a cosmos of the divine and the demonic – can be viewed as a consequence of the underlying cosmological inconsistency that marked early modern theologies.[68]

The flux in question was not simply one of social relations; it also extended from the order and disorder of the universe, from the very notions of flux and stasis which led not only to a reassessment of demonic physics but to an ambiguous positioning of the self in relation to God. An obsession with cosmic borders, margins, edges – an obsession with the structure of the universe – could complicate or undermine the links, bridges, and bonds existing between people. Inhabiting different theo-cosmologies could make it difficult (then as now) to maintain interpersonal bridges. The theatrical opening of *Macbeth*, with its devilish odor and encompassing auditory chaos, serves to bring an audience together, to unite players and actors in a common spatial field. The contested understandings of witchcraft – the result of contested understandings of cosmic structures, the result of contested notions of the nature of God – could, however, simultaneously create gulfs of theological belief between individuals that could not easily be bridged. Macbeth's progression into isolation – from his society, his environment, and his God – is an extreme case of the cosmological dissonance that many in his audience might have experienced themselves.

FRAMEWORK

I opened this book with a meditation on the architecture of Hamlet's Globe, on the mapping of a supernatural theatrical geography which, while vibrant and present to the original audience, has become flat and largely invisible to us. Here I should like to take another glance at the architectural space of the theater. Now, however, I want to fast-forward to another time and a different space. Upon the restoration of the monarchy in 1660, after a period of brutal civil war and political upheaval, the public theaters reopened. The theater was no longer a wooden O. As Margreta de Grazia succinctly puts it: "The proscenium stage had replaced the platform stage; a perspectival space set off from the audience had supplanted an open stage continuous with the audience."[69] In a brilliant analysis, de Grazia connects this transformed spatial arrangement to Heidegger's essay "The Age of the World Picture":

> Heidegger discusses *representation* as the distinctive feature of the modern period. While he makes no mention of the theater, the proscenium stage seems, like the framed picture, a striking materialization of what he terms 'enframing': a setting up of the world in such a way that it can be perceived and known ... Cartesian or modern knowledge requires, for Heidegger, the enframing or enclosing of what is to be known – a cordoning off of the object from the subject, which both constructs the object as something knowable and defines the subject as the one, apart and against the object, who not only does the knowing but is itself the grounds of knowability. Enframing thus mutually constitutes subject and object; it relates the two by setting them apart and against one another in such a way as to define and differentiate each ... The proscenium stage, like the framed painting, seems a perfect materialization of this modern condition of visibility and knowability. It is self-contained, isolated from the space of the audience by its enclosing walls, just as the painting is separated from viewers by its frame. Not only is the space blocked off from that of the audience; it is artificially defined by its own perspectival and geometrical axes ... What was once a place in which action occurs becomes a *representation* or *picture* of a place in which action occurs.[70]

The move towards historical phenomenology in recent literary studies is, at its core, a recognition of the dominance of this intellectual habit of framing and picturing, our fixation on representation. The new historicist turn towards representation was itself a corrective to early modes of historiography which tended to assume a transparent relation between words (the texts that comprise our historical archive) and history (events which happened in real space-time). Attending to the ideological and social dynamics of "re-presentation" is a means of acknowledging that our access to the past is always already – and forever and ever only can be – mediated. Historical phenomenology, while accepting this premise, explores modes of experience that are not purely representational, which is to say, on some level, modes that are not framed or pictorial. Smith's auditory field and Harris's olfactory surround at the opening of *Macbeth* are attempts to try to break the frame, to imagine ways into the early modern theater that do not enter through the intellectual proscenium arch of the Restoration. The point is not to recover knowledge (enabled and created, in a post-Cartesian moment, by the separation of subject and object), but experience (the sensation of inhabiting a particular moment in space and time). In analyzing *Macbeth*'s dramatic beginning, Smith and Harris do not unpack early modern understandings of witchcraft so much as seek to understand how a theatrical (re)creation of a demonic environment might have felt to actors and audience in that specific space-time.

That said, experience cannot be separated out from knowledge; phenomenology depends on epistemology.[71] De Grazia begins her essay by unpacking the epistemological approach of the "vastly popular" book *The Elizabethan World Picture* by E. M. W. Tillyard. "The notion of an Elizabethan world picture," she writes, "now seems quite odd ... Needless to say, the notion would have seemed odder still to Elizabethans" (pp. 7–8). Not only is the notion of "world picture" an intellectual construct that is being anachronistically imposed upon a culture to which it would be inimical, antithetical, or just plain foreign, but the content of Tillyard's book, the notion that "Elizabethans pictured the world as a divinely ordered cosmos whose various realms (divine, human, animal, vegetable) were held together hierarchically by links, correspondences, and sympathies" (p. 7), also seems here to be questionable. Poststructuralist modes of analysis are deeply suspicious, perhaps even disbelieving, of authoritarian hegemony, and so Tillyard's claim that "this idea of cosmic order was one of the genuine ruling ideas of the age"[72] admittedly sets off alarm bells. It was this distrust of a hegemonic epistemology that made Tillyard anathema to new historicists. But while new historicism focused on isolated photographs (so to speak – we could substitute "anecdotes") in the interest of studying constructions of power (state, gender, race, etc.) and their subversions, it often lacked, as it were, a big picture.

As far as early modern epistemology was concerned, in many ways Tillyard was right. While recognizing the flaws of his frame, and the strangeness of his thinking that he could take a picture in the first place, we should not completely disregard what he saw, or his insights. Tillyard's stated intervention is to reclaim Elizabethan England as a religious period: "People still think of the Age of Elizabeth as a secular period between two outbreaks of Protestantism ... They do not tell us that Queen Elizabeth translated Boethius, that Raleigh was a theologian as well as a discoverer, and that sermons were as much a part of an ordinary Elizabethan's life as bear-baiting." This omission leads to an impartial understanding of the Bard: "Shakespeare's chaos is without meaning apart from the proper background of cosmic order by which to judge it." The outpouring of scholarship of the last decades on early modern religion and culture certainly renders Tillyard's introductory remarks moot in the current intellectual climate. But the fact that most of this scholarship has been concerned more with the local and the terrestrial rather than the cosmic makes his claim about Shakespeare still resonant. Where critics today may easily find fault is with his assertion that "Puritans and the courtiers … had in common a mass of basic assumptions about the world, which they never disputed and whose importance varied inversely with this very meagerness of controversy."[73]

Far from never being disputed, theo-cosmology was fiercely debated. Not only the rarified debates between Aristotelians and new philosophers, or between those following Brahe as opposed to Kepler, but the extensive popular polemical religious literature brought the order of the universe to the forefront of intellectual and spiritual concern. Around the turn of the seventeenth century, debates raged about the relationship of the "visible" and "invisible" churches – that is, the church as it was outwardly manifest on earth and the church as a mystical body of Christ. Such debates held deeply personal ramifications, as individuals and communities struggled to define the relationship of the two – which in turn affected the relationship of the material and the immaterial, of the wicked and the elect, of neighbor and neighbor. Hooker wrote of the church as a "societie supernaturall"[74] even as he was trying to establish a stable divine cosmos through a defined ecclesiastical polity. Meanwhile, "[t]he reformers favored, among other passages, the one which informed that a person's faith, not a church's solemn liturgical occasions or the priests presiding over them, could exorcize demons, even move mountains" (Matthew 17:20).[75] Faith was (among other things) a matter of space and environment, and people were deeply invested in these matters. As Christopher Haigh remarks, early modern men and women "often talked about religion, because they cared about religion and because religion was unavoidable. Life, death, and disaster were explained in religious terms: it was God who brought earthquakes, plagues, and wars, and God who brought sunshine, good harvests, and health."[76] God determined how they lived, moved, and had their being; people in turn tried to fathom God's own existence, movement, and essence.

This cultural conversation was itself framed by notions of cosmic framing. As we have seen, Hooker himself often speaks of frames ("That law eternall which God himself hath made to himselfe, and therby worketh all things wherof he is the cause and author, that law is the admirable frame wherof shineth with most perfect bewtie the countenance of that wisedome"; "the frame of that heauenly arch erected ouer our heads" [pp. 51, 53]). Macbeth, too, is concerned with "the frame of things." Calvin maintains that God "drives the celestial frame" (Battles's translation of "*Orbis machinam*") (I: 197). These are not, however, the frames around a world picture. Rather, they are framework. They structure. These are not the frames that one looks *through*, but the frames that one lives *within*. Or, as Perkins instructed many a child to answer in his catechism, God is to be conceived "[n]ot by framing any image of him in [the] minde ... but ... by his properties and workes."[77] These frames are not devices for separating subject and object, the modern condition of knowledge, but the container for a "divinely ordered cosmos whose various realms (divine, human, animal, vegetable) were held together hierarchically by links, correspondences, and sympathies" (to requote de Grazia's synthesis of Tillyard). They are frames which mark and enable not transcendence – that of God or of the modern knowing subject – but immanence, the participatory interconnectedness of humanity, environment, and divinity.

The problem, as Macbeth puts it, is that "the frame of things disjoint, both the worlds suffer." The fundamentally different theo-cosmologies – frames – put forth by Calvin and Hooker are indeed disjointed, and in *Macbeth* suffering is indeed the consequence of this incompatibility. Snyder observes that "[t]he disintegration and chaos that Macbeth experiences inside this cosmic frame is peculiar to himself, and we understand it as the result of his own action, an action he recognized from the beginning as unambiguously evil ... But this scheme, individual chaos enclosed in a larger moral order, is not the whole story about *Macbeth*. From a different perspective its moral frame appears troublingly unstable."[78] We might modify this statement by noting that the disintegration itself results from the fact that there does not seem to be a single, unified cosmic frame, but a chaotic interplay of frames. And, in a world where the cosmic frame is identified with God himself, the cosmic frame is the moral frame. The troubling instability in the latter is directly connected to the inconsistency of the former. While both Calvin and Hooker understand their work to be for the glory of God, extolling the Creator's magnificence, their spatial epistemologies inevitably clash and negate each other.

To see the world through the proscenium arch is to see the world through a stable frame. While the representation within can be analyzed, studied, appreciated or enjoyed, the frame – or perhaps better yet, the fact that there is a frame in the first place – is assumed. Similarly, to see the world through the absolute space of Newtonian physics (as we largely still do) is to presume a stable cosmic frame. "To see" here is perhaps not quite accurate, as these modes of vision have become so naturalized as to render space invisible. Within the unframed space of the Globe, however, packed with an audience exposed to competing theo-cosmologies, space is neither assumed nor invisible. Just as *Macbeth*'s repeated references to distorted time deliberately flag temporal problems, so too the disordered frame calls attention to spatial instabilities. Within the play – and within the theater – space is not perceived from, to borrow the cartographer's term, the God's eye view, but from multiple points of view, a multiplicity which results in many visions of God. Sixteenth- and seventeenth-century England was not yet a place where people thought globally, but it was a place where people thought Globally, through a plurality of cosmic perspectives.

# CHAPTER 5

# Divine geometry in a geodetic age: Surveying, God, and The Tempest

[I]n the beginning God did square and proportion the heauens for the earth, vsing his rule, leauell, and compasse ...
Godfrey Goodman, *The Fall of Man* (1616), p. 16

At the turn of the seventeenth century, the structure of the universe was in play. As I discussed in the previous chapter, different ways of understanding the cosmos were interrelated with reformist theologies. For John Calvin, the universe was sustained by divine Providence, by the will of God. While God had indeed established a magnificent order of the world, ultimately everything – the spin of planets, the fall of a raindrop, the motion of a human will – was controlled by the hand of the divine. For Richard Hooker, cosmic order rested on natural law, a law that God had established but one to which God also adhered. For the individual, these different strands of Protestant theology entailed not only different possibilities for one's relationship with the divine, but different ways of conceptualizing the world one inhabits.

In this chapter, I move from the theo-spatial epistemologies of cosmology to those of the terrestrial realm. Specifically, I will examine how the cultural prominence of land surveying worked to integrate human beings, space and the divine. The idea that geometry structures the world is an ancient one; in Plato's creation story, the divine being orders the world in his geometric image.[1] What is new in sixteenth- and seventeenth-century England is the degree to which geometric knowledge was disseminated and incorporated into a popular understanding of the environment, both in terms of perceiving the spatial surround and understanding the workings of God. While the practical aspects of surveying – the mechanics of measuring the land, the tools of the trade, and the basic principles of geodetic geometry – might seem to be worlds away from discussions of divinity, I will show how the emergent science of geodesy was grounded in a theological sensibility.

This chapter is divided into four sections that explore different interactions of geometry and divinity. It begins with a wide scope, considering the geometric construction of Kepler's cosmology. The chapter then returns to earth, exploring how early modern English surveying manuals position themselves, and the instruments they describe, within a theological context. From there the scope narrows to examine the triangle, whose interconnected histories as a crucial shape of surveying and as a new symbol of the Trinity led to its merged geometric and religious significance. In all of these early modern discussions, God is described in emphatically trinitarian terms, and therefore a fundamental aspect of trinitarian theology – the idea of perichoresis, that is, the mutually permeable and interconnected relationship of the three persons of a triune godhead – comes to express as well the interrelationship of humanity and environment. In the final section of the chapter, I turn to a discussion of Shakespeare's *The Tempest*. In this play, the relationship of the supernatural, the land, and human beings reflects, if at times distortedly, the environmental understanding described and produced in the period's copious surveying literature.

## A TRINITARIAN COSMOS

To begin, then, I consider the larger European context of theology and geometry. In the early modern period, geometry itself became a language of theology. And as geometry became the language of the cosmos, cosmic inquiry became theological inquiry. In an oft-quoted passage, Galileo describes his vision of the cosmos thus:

Philosophy is written in this grand book – I mean the universe – which stands continually open to our gaze, but it cannot be understood unless one first learns to comprehend the language and interpret the characters in which it is written. It is written in the language of mathematics, and its characters are triangles, circles, and other geometrical figures, without which it is humanly impossible to understand a single word of it; without these, one is wandering about in a dark labyrinth.[2]

The ignorant could see the world around them, but could not read it. Only through mastery of a geometric grammar could one ascend to philosophical, and thus theological, knowledge. The study of geometry was no mere schoolboy's exercise; it was nothing less than the language of God.

Galileo's contemporary, Johannes Kepler, similarly perceived the universe as a divine exercise in geometry. For Kepler, this geometry becomes a means of understanding how human beings inhabit God's space. In his

*Mysterium Cosmographicum* ("The Secret of the Universe"; first edition 1596), Kepler "discovered" the structure of the universe: while adopting a Copernican heliocentric model, Kepler demonstrates that God structured the orbit of the planets so that they fit perfectly inside of the five Platonic solids (cube, pyramid, dodecahedron, octahedron, icosahedron), like internesting Chinese boxes.[3] "What else remains except to say with Plato, 'God is always a geometer'," writes Kepler. "[T]his fitting of the motions to the spheres is very neat, a wonderful piece of handiwork by God the craftsman."[4]

But even in Kepler's own text, God's geometric creation is far more than clever craftsmanship. Just as human astronomy is not merely a mathematical exercise but a means to ascend to God, so too God's geometry is not simply an ingenious display of divine intelligence but a means to provide the perfect habitation for humanity and the perfect setting for human-divine relations. Kepler provides a fascinating account of God's thought process in constructing the universe:

I think that from the love of God for Man a great many of the causes of the features in the universe can be deduced. Certainly at least nobody will deny that in fitting out the dwelling place of the universe God considered its future inhabitants again and again. For the end both of the universe and of the whole creation is Man. Therefore in my opinion it was deemed by God fitting for the Earth, which was to provide and nourish a true image of the Creator, to go round in the midst of the planets in such a way that it would have the same number of them within the embrace of its orbit as outside it. To achieve that, God added the Sun to the other five stars, although it was totally different in kind. And that seems all the more appropriate because, the Sun above being the image of God the Father, we may believe that by this association with the other stars it was bound to provide evidence for the future tenant of the loving kindness and sympathy which God was to practice towards men, even as far as bringing himself down into their intimate friendship. For in the Old Testament he frequently came among their number, and was willing to be known as a friend of Abraham; just as we see the Sun is numbered among the moving stars. However, since the Sun was encircled by the Earth, granted what has been said, that class of bodies which in fact includes the two had necessarily to be contained within the Earth's orbit, that is, in order that those two moving stars along with the unmoving Sun should make up the number of three, which is the number of those outside the Earth. Thus with the Moon as a special case encircling the Earth, the best of Creators placed our domicile in the middle of the seven planets. For if the class of the other three had been added to the Sun, there would have been four stars including the Sun inside the Earth, but only two outside. Since this irregularity of number lacks order, it was dismissed by the Creator.[5]

Considering Kepler's system, we might be tempted to imagine the clock-maker God who would make an appearance half a century later. But in his description of God's rationale for constructing the world in this way, we hardly find a God who detaches himself from human affairs. Kepler's God is deeply engaged with his creation, a part of it, even to the point of entering into the "intimate friendship" of men; the example Kepler provides is from the Old Testament, but it is a short step to the Incarnation. Kepler's assertion that the sun among the stars represents an analogous situation to God among men ("just as we see the Sun is numbered among the moving stars") also hinges between an abstract visual representation and a real cohabitation of God and humanity through creation.

Kepler's geometric universe embodies and enacts the Trinity – not that of the medieval Scholastics, concerned with intra-divine relations (known as *theologia*), but the model of the Trinity concerning God's presence in the world (*oikonomia*). Kepler's insistence that the earth is mid way between two sets of three celestial bodies highlights the importance of the number three, and thus the innately trinitarian structural organization of the cosmos. (While Kepler disregarded the numerology so prevalent in his period, he did retain a belief that the number three was "the perfect number."[6]) More overtly, Kepler – whose ardent, thwarted hope had been to become a Lutheran pastor – proclaims that he was motivated by a desire to locate the Trinity in the cosmic elements. "There were three things in particular about which I persistently sought the reasons why they were such and not otherwise: the number, the size, and the motion of the circles. That I dared so much was due to the splendid harmony of those things which are at rest, the Sun, the fixed stars and the intermediate space, with God the Father, and the Son, and the Holy Spirit."[7] That the Trinity and creation would have an intrinsic unity seems obvious to Kepler: "[I]t is evident that by those laws which God himself in his goodness prescribes for himself, the only thing of which he could adopt the Idea for establishing the universe is his own essence, which can be considered as twofold, inasmuch as it is excellent and divine: first in itself, being one in essence but three in person, and secondly by comparison with created things."[8]

This set of interrelationships – of the trinitarian godhead, and of God's essence and creation – leads Kepler to understand God as a sphere, which becomes a visual model of the Trinity: "[T]he spherical itself, since it is alone and unique in its own kind of quantity, cannot be subject to any other number but three." The sun is an image of God the Father, and "the

Sphere or the Fixed Stars, or the Mosaic waters, at the circumference, [is] the image of the Son, and the heavenly air which fills all parts, or the space and firmament, [is] the image of the Spirit."[9] Elsewhere, he explains that by "Spirit" we are to "understand the immaterial emanation of the Sun, spreading out like light: and you will have here in a few words a summary of my celestial physics."[10]

Imagining the cosmos as a light-filled – and thus God-filled – sphere, Kepler places his reader *inside* of the Trinity. The light in which we live, the very space which we inhabit, is a trinitarian environment; we stand, very literally, inside of the communication of the triune God.[11] Again, Kepler writes in a metaphoric register of images and comparisons ("like light") that quickly slides into a sense of inhabited reality: "Man's dwelling place is the Earth, just as God's, if he has any material dwelling, is certainly the inaccessible light of the Sun."[12] The notion of an abstract model falls away, as we find ourselves basking in God. We can imagine the ecstasy Kepler experienced when he first discovered this geometric structure, the "secret of the universe." (We can also imagine his growing despair when he slowly accepted that the observational data and calculations didn't uphold his theory.[13])

Astronomy here is less a charting of the heavens, a mapping of the spatial relations and movements of heavenly bodies, than it is a means to comprehend the reality of human-divine relations. For Kepler, and perhaps for many of his original readers, understanding the cosmos – and, more particularly, understanding one's place in the cosmic environment, the cosmic surround – is driven by a desire to sense and contemplate one's existence with the trinitarian divine.

MEASURING GOD

The integration of theology and what we would call science in Kepler's writing is to be expected. Theology was the epistemological framework for most early modern intellectual inquiry. While the dividing lines between theology and science (or, more properly, natural philosophy) are by no means clear, the categorical divisions constructed within the period indicate the overwhelming prominence of divinity as an intellectual subject.[14] While we are perhaps not surprised to find speculations about the cosmos infused with the language of divinity, it is a bit startling to realize how much even popular surveying books participate in the spirit of theological investigation. The underlying epistemology of astronomical inquiries – the idea that God works through and inhabits a geometrical cosmos – was shared by those with more pragmatic and earthly concerns.

If men such as Galileo and Kepler were busy geometricizing the heavens, on the face of the earth professional and amateur surveyors were busy translating the land into calculable, geometric terms.[15] From the mid sixteenth to the late seventeenth centuries, the English developed a keen appetite for geometric and geodetic discourse. During this period, as Henry Turner notes, a convergence of social forces led to a "proliferation of practical geometrical manuals,"[16] which resulted in and which was caused by:

[A] specific intellectual formation characteristic of sixteenth-century England, a pre-scientific epistemology that arose out of a convergence between humanist habits of reasoning ... on the one hand, and a growing interest on the part of the educated gentleman in technology and the practical geometrical fields of building, surveying, engineering, and cartography, on the other. Once we recognize this intellectual formation as a distinctive feature of the period, we begin to realize how broadly it extended, across areas of early-modern intellectual and social life that today we are accustomed to regard as quite distinct from one another: from the university college to meadows, workshops, and harbour fortification projects; from textbooks to carpentry and cartography; from military strategy to poetic invention, stylistic experimentation, and techniques of theatrical performance.[17]

Within this cultural moment, geometric knowledge became a feature of the education of the courtly gentleman, and requisite even for the yeoman farmer. Deborah Harkness has also studied this phenomenon, and writes that "[a] steady stream of books relating to mathematics began entering the bookstalls soon after the advent of print in the fifteenth century ... More than 250 books related to mathematics were printed during the reign of Elizabeth, and the slow trickle of accounting manuals and arithmetic texts at the beginning of the reign turned into a flood of books on all sorts of mathematical topics by the end of the sixteenth century."[18] This availability of information was coupled with a concentration of human talent that was able to put it to use. "London could boast the critical mass of expert teachers, skilled technicians, willing pupils, and eager readers that were necessary to transform the aspirations of a few elite mathematicians into a broadly based, vernacular and mathematical way of thinking about the world."[19]

Geometry not only held intellectual and aesthetic appeal, it also became fundamental to understanding the environment and therefore assumed pragmatic import. The sixteenth-century English national project of mapping the land – an effort that ranged from the creation of elaborate county atlases to personal estate maps used for calculating rent and taxes – made a basic knowledge of surveying as important as a basic knowledge of mathematics if one wanted to avoid being cheated and deceived.[20] The emergence of these estate maps, as I have written elsewhere, "fostered a popular fascination with the principles and practices of land surveying. As the lay appetite for geodetic instruction grew, authors vied with one another to capitalize on this widespread desire for written surveying manuals."[21] This was not only the age of the great cartographers such as Ortelius, Mercator, and Saxton – it was the age of do-it-yourself surveying.

Within early modern geodetic discourse, God has created both the celestial and the chthonic according to geometric principles. It is perhaps easier to see the glamour of a geometric God in Kepler's sun-filled spherical Trinity, but sixteenth- and seventeenth-century authors saw God's scheme even in well-manured sheep pastures. Richard Benese writes in *The Boke of Measuryng of Lande as well of Woodland as Plowland, & Pasture in the Feelde* (1563): "For not wythstandynge that God may, and can doe althyng without no[m]bre, measaure, weyght or any poynte of Geometrye, yet when hee gaue the fyrmament the Planettes, and starres, theyr mocions, the earthe, fourme and fashion, the Sea, with other riuers, theyr bankes, hee dyd it by nombre, weyght, and measure. Wherfore I may well extoll this most noble Science" (sig. A5ᵛ). The title page of Thomas Hood's *The Vse of the Two Mathematicall Instruments* (1596) bears an illustration framed by the motto, "Devs imperat astris" ("God commands the heavens") with a presumably divine and imperative finger pointing towards the sun, while the castle and foliage in the foreground depict the earth which is to be measured (see Figure 7).[22]

Constructing a map, while of practical value for assessing taxation, educational value for learning geography, and even entertainment value for the sheer intellectual exercise, is ultimately a way to know God, or at least to engage with God's pattern within the world. Thomas Blundeville's massive geometric *Exercises* (1621) concludes by placing the art of mapping within a biblical, even a soteriological context. The penultimate page (of the final section of the book called "A Briefe Description of Vniversall Maps and Cardes") contains a large map of the earth to be inscribed by the reader. Having spent the previous 798 pages fashioning an educated gentleman, the last word goes to God:

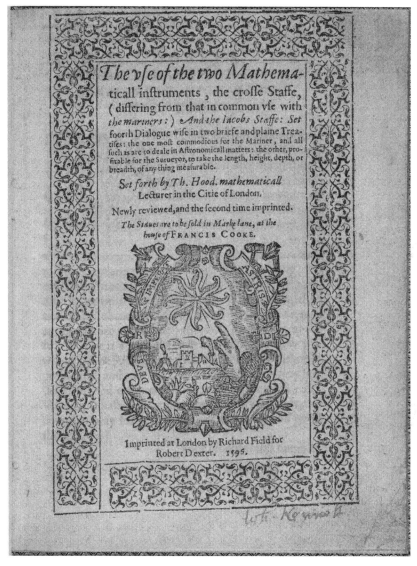

Figure 7 Thomas Hood, *The Vse of the Two Mathematicall Instruments, the Crosse Staffe, (Differing from that in Common Vse with the Mariners) and the Iacobs Staffe.* London, 1596. Title page.

Moreouer you shall find on the right side of this Map, the Peregrinations of the Apostle S. Peter, and right vnder that, the Peregrination of S. Paul, shewing in how many places they preached the Word of God, what Miracles they did, and where. And in the foot of the Map on the right hand is set downe the Peregrination of Iesus Christ, shewing the places where hee preached or did any great Miracles.

. . .

And thus I end, praying you to take my labour herein bestowed, well in worth, which I would not haue done, but that I know this Card to be a necessary Card, and to be made with very good Art, according to the Example of which Card, the sonne of old Mercator hath lately cut forth diuers small Cardes of Europe, traced with lines and circles, like to these his Fathers Card, the vse of which lines and circles, I feare me, that few doe rightly vnderstand, & for that cause I was the more willing here to set downe this plaine description of the Fathers Card. (p. 799)

The useful but misguided card (i.e. map) put forth by the son of Mercator is superseded by the divine "Fathers Card." The map assumes value not only as a means of representing God's creation, but as a mode of remembering and registering the footsteps and miraculous actions of Christ and his apostles.[23] It is thus a means of recognizing God's construction of and participation in the world. It is a means of recording, in other words, both divine transcendence and immanence.

The act of surveying is frequently depicted as an act of participation with the divine. Indeed, the very tools of the trade signal that they serve a theological as well as a geodetic function. The two most prominent surveying instruments both have religious overtones. The Jacob's staff was an instrument used for measuring heights and distance. The first recorded use of this term to signal a geodetic instrument, according to the *Oxford English Dictionary*, was in 1559 (where it was used as a synonym for an "astronomer's staff" [def. 2a]). Another obsolete definition of the term is "A pilgrim's staff" (def. 1), the first use of which appeared about a decade earlier, around 1548. The *OED* informs us that in its use signifying a pilgrim's staff, the word arrives "Sometimes perhaps with a reference to Gen. xxxii. 10" (in which Jacob references crossing the Jordan with only his staff). This comment pairs with the only given etymology: "In sense 1 [i.e. a pilgrim's staff], from St. James (*Jacobus*), whose symbols in religious art are a pilgrim's staff and a scallop shell. In the other senses the name is app. more or less fanciful."

These two meanings of the word – as a tool of measurement, and as a walking stick for a devotional journey – thus appear very close together (1548 and 1559) in the *longue durée* of etymological history. But the separation of theological and geodetic discourses, in the view of the

*OED*, is so absolute that the biblical resonance of the name could only be an instance of playful ("fanciful") wit when applied to the surveying instrument. For an audience being instructed as part of geometric training to plot the peregrinations of Christ and the apostles onto a map, however, the notion of the surveyor as a pilgrim may not have seemed so absurd. Indeed, the connection between the biblical story and the surveying instrument is more than simply suggestive. Hood's text contains "A Dialogue touching the vse of the Iacobs Staffe," in which a scholar seeking instruction on the instrument asks, "Why doe they call it Iacobs Staffe? Was he the first inuentor of the thing[?]" To which the master responds, "I know not that: but they take occasion to call it so, by reason of those wordes which are written *Gen 32.10* where the Patriarch sayth, *That was his Staffe he came ouer Iordane* [sic]: Wherein I thinke, they misconstrue his meaning. Notwithstanding, by whom soeuer it was inuented, the Instrument questionlesse is of singular vse" (sig. Cii <sup>r–v</sup>).[24] Early modern humor is admittedly a bit of an acquired taste, but even to an expert in the field this exchange appears factual rather than "fanciful," as the *OED* would have it. In another devotional text, we read that "*our Conversation must be in Heaven* indeed; but it is not a *Iacobs staffe*, but a *Iacobs ladder* will bring us thither," again indicating a popular association of this surveying tool with the biblical Jacob.[25]

The Jacob's staff was also known as the cross staff.[26] It might initially seem like a bit of a stretch to suggest that the form of the instrument – i.e. a cross – invoked Christological thoughts in its users. But within the greater context of geodetic discourse, it seems probable that the instrument was not immune to Christian iconography. We might consider one image demonstrating its use (Figure 8).[27] Since the instrument works by positioning a moveable cross bar on a longer central shaft, it can have variable shapes. But here the most prominent user of the instrument looks skyward with his staff positioned in such a way as to highlight its visual consonance with Christ's cross; he appears to be charting not simply his environment, but God's heavenly and earthly presence in the world through the perspective of the cross.[28] (We should keep in mind the degree to which Christian iconography saturated early modern sign systems and modes of literacy – as Patricia Crain has discussed, in the sixteenth and seventeenth centuries the first figure of the alphabet was not the letter "A," but the sign of the cross, positioning the very act of learning to read within Christian ideologies.[29]) In another image from George Wither's *A Collection of Emblemes* (1635), we see the hand of God emerging from a cloud and wielding a compass (an image carried over from medieval illustrations), with a cluster

Figure 8 Image demonstrating the use of the Jacob's staff, also known
as the cross staff. Source unknown.

of geographers working to the left (Figure 9). Most prominent amongst
these is the man ecstatically raising a cross staff to the heavens, while a star
above sheds light in a way that is reminiscent of Christ's nativity (and the
building above God's forearm appears to be a church, registering a specifically Christian landscape).

The theological connotations of surveying instruments are even more
obvious in the case of the theodolite. The *OED* exhibits a glaring instance
of tunnel vision in its entry on "theodolite," which contains an unusually
long and complicated note on the etymology of the word:

[*Note.* The name, alike in the Latinized form *theodelitus* and the vernacular
*theodelite* (subseq. *-dolite*), originated in England, and is not known in French
and German until the 19th c. Its first user, and probable inventor, L. or
T. Digges, has left no account of its composition, as to which various futile
conjectures, incompatible with its early history and use, have been offered; such is
the notion that it arose in some way out of *alhidada* or its corruption *athelida*
occurring in Bourne's *Treasure for Travailers* 1578, which an examination of the

Figure 9 George Wither, *A Collection of Emblemes, Ancient and Modern.*
London, 1635, p. 143.

works of Digges and Bourne, where both words occur in their proper senses, shows to be absurd. *Theodelite* has the look of a formation from Greek; can it have been (like many modern names of inventions) an unscholarly formation from θεάομαι "I view" or θεῶ "behold" and δῆλος "visible, clear, manifest", with a meaningless termination?]

"Can it have been ...?" While the *OED* scratches its head trying to think of a possible Greek derivation for "theodolite," let's wander through the word's neighborhood to see the company it keeps: *theo-, Theobroma, theocracy, theocrasia, theocrasy, theocrat, theocratic, theocratical, theocratically, Theocritean, theodicaea, theodicy, theodidact, theodisc, theodolite, Theodosian, Theodotian, theody, theogonal, theogonic, theogonist, theogony, theolatry, theolepsy, theologal, theologant, theologaster, theologate, theologer, theologian, theologic, theological, theologically, theologician, theologico-,*

*theologism, theologist, theologium, theologization, theologize, theologo-, theo-*
*logoumenon, theologue, theology, theolony, theomachy, theomagic, theomancy,*
*theomorphic, theo-mythology, theonomy, theopaschite, theopathetic, theopa-*
*thy, theophagous, theophany, theophilanthropist, theophilanthropy, theopho-*
*bia, Theophrastian, theophylline, theoplasm, theopneust, theopolitics.* Of
these, a few do not have θεός (theos) as a root: "theodisc" is an Old
English word meaning "of or belonging to a nation or people"; "Theodosian" refers to the Roman emperor Theodosius II and "Theodotian" is
a follower of Theodotus of Byzantium (although both of these names are
probably themselves derived from *theos*); "theophylline" is a colorless
alkaloid. The rest of these words, however, all pertain, in one form or
another, to God.[30]

It is possible, as the *OED* suggests, that Leonard Digges chose to name
his new instrument after the Greek θεάομαι "I view" (from whence
comes "theory"). But even the *OED* seems dubious about this. And
certainly θεάομαι was in common circulation much less than θεός
(theos). Therefore it seems much more probable that Digges – a man
living in a period of heightened religiosity, and in a time when the study
of space was directly linked to theology – christened his new invention
"theo-" as a way of signaling that surveying the land, like surveying the
cosmos, was labor in the service of God. As for the rest of the word, which
the *OED* questions as a "meaningless termination," a quick glance at
variants of "dole" are suggestive:

> dole *n.*[4] variant of dool, boundary mark, etc.;
> = dool¹, dole **1**. A boundary or landmark, consisting of a post, a stone,
>   or an unploughed balk or strip of land;
> dole *n*¹ **c**. A portion of a common or undivided field;
> =dale²: **1**. A portion or share of land; *spec.* a share of a common field,
>   or portion of an undivided field indicated by landmarks but not
>   divided off.

Thus, "theodolite": of God and boundaries on the land.

Surveying instruments were even considered in and of themselves
reflections of the divine. In *The Use of both the Globes, Celestiall, and*
*Terrestriall, most plainly delivered in forme of a Dialogue* (1592), Thomas
Hood responds to the question of whether or not heaven is round with
this answer:

> Also this standeth with reason, that the most perfect body should haue the most
> perfect forme, and therefore the heauen being so pure and perfect . . . it requireth
> also the most perfect forme which is Sphericall and rounde, as may appeare by all

the workes of God, where in this roundenesse is especially to bee obserued. 9. Last of all we may take an argument from our Astronomicall instruments which are most fitte being rounde and are deriued from a circle. Thus much for the forme and figure of heauen. (sig. B4ʳ)

The argument that the world is spherical because this is the most perfect shape, and therefore the appropriate abode of God, goes back to Plato's *Timeaus*. The argument that man-made instruments can be used as proof of the shape of the space they were constructed to measure strikes us as oddly tautological, but follows roughly in the same line of reasoning: within the period we find an ontological affinity between the instruments and their objects of measurement.

R[adolph] Agas makes a similar argument in *A Preparative to Platting of Landes and Tenements for Surueigh* (1596), essentially a promotional treatise for the theodolite: "Ther is also the staffe, Astrolabe, Square, Ring, Ruler, Circumferentor, Sector, and halfe protractor, with infinite such other, framed after the fantasie of the Deuisor: all which scarcely perfect parcels and lims of the Sphericall mouer, I do esteeme, and regard for the vses in demonstration accordingly" (p. 3). After a perfunctory nod in the direction of these other instruments, Agas then singles out the theodolite as the most perfect:

Finally, the saide instrument ... carrieth the forme of the first mouer, which commandeth all inferior creatures, and is preferred as most perfect and capeable, by the wisedome and ordinance of the Creator: so in vse and operation (if ye looke skillfully thereinto), this Theodolite commandeth euerie one of her subiects. ... It presently deuideth, such or any other quantity of land into so manye equal, or limited differing parts, as you would desire: & euery one of the[m], into what forme or forms your selfe shal best like of, which is also necessarie for Surueighors, Builders, Imparkers, Gardners, Planters and such like. (pp. 9–10; mislabeled p. 14)

The object itself has the shape of God ("the first mouer," "the Creator"); it is the preferred instrument of God; in its ability to command subjects, the theodolite even assumes God-like qualities. In the hands of laborers, it transforms workaday activities such as surveying, building, and planting into a mode of interacting with and partaking in the divine.

The affinities of the theodolite with God – or, more broadly, with the act of surveying and creation – are graphically manifest in a pair of early seventeenth-century frontispieces: that of Aaron Rathborne's *The Surveyor in Foure Bookes* (1616), and Guillaume de Saluste du Bartas's *His Deuine Weekes & Workes*, translated by Joshuah Sylvester (1605–6). As the ornate

Figure 10 Guillaume de Saluste du Bartas, *Du Bartas His Deuine Weekes & Works.*
London, 1611. Engraved title page.

frontispiece and dedication to the king suggests, Du Bartas's (Protestant)
religious poetry on the Creation was hugely popular; from the 1580s to the
1660s, among English readers Du Bartas "was probably the most admired
of contemporary European writers."[31] It is highly likely that many of those
people able to afford Rathborne's *Surveyor* would have also owned a copy
of Du Bartas's *Deuine Weekes*. The two frontispieces, in any case, are

Figure 11 Aaron Rathborne, *The Surveyor in Foure Books.* London, 1616.
Engraved title page.

conversant (see Figures 10 and 11). The *Deuine Weekes* features two pairs
of columns supporting a couple of spheres, the one astrological, the other
terrestrial. Between these two is a roundel depicting the creation of Eve;
connecting all three images is a triangle surrounding the Tetragrammaton.

Margery Corbett and Ronald Lightbown write: "It may be surmised that the presence of the triangle as a symbol of the Trinity on this title-page is an affirmation of belief in orthodox Christianity against the powerful anti-trinitarian movement ... Possibly with the same thoughts in mind Du Bartas had included lines which sum up the meaning of the Trinity according to the Athanasian Creed."[32] At the bottom of the image, between the two plinths, is a cartouche with an image of the Creation, featuring the sun, moon, lightness, darkness, and earth.

The frontispiece of *The Surveyor* borrows heavily from the image gracing the front of the *Deuine Weekes*. The reproduction of the basic structure of the parallel columns bearing globes is obvious, but what is perhaps more subtle is the similarity of the two celestial spheres. In the celestial sphere on the *Deuine Weekes*, the engraver has combined the lower half of the northern polar region with the upper half of the southern polar region, thus highlighting some constellations (among them the Triangle) while, for lack of space, omitting others.[33] This map of the cosmos is thus highly idiosyncratic, and it is replicated almost exactly on *The Surveyor*.[34] The positioning of the continents on the terrestrial globes is also identical, even if the coastal outlines vary a bit.

Another visual quotation is the ornamental frame on the cartouche; the oval that lies between the plinths on the *Deuine Weekes* is shifted into a circle and moved between the spheres on *The Surveyor*. What is most striking here, however, is not the shift in shape, but the shift in the content of the image. The cartouche which originally encompassed an image of the Creation now houses an image of the surveyor at work. This image also replaces that of the Trinity: the Tetragrammaton is replaced by "Artifex," which translates as both "craftsman" and "originator." The *Deuine Weekes* contains an image of the ark resting on Mount Ararat after the Flood (on the right plinth); *The Surveyor* shifts this image to below the title, replaces the ark with a castle, and shows the surveyor at work mapping the land with a plane table and compass. The God of Creation in the *Diuine Weekes* has now been usurped, so it would seem, by the allegorical, goddess-like figures of Arithmetica and Geometria. The "Artifex" above now stands, pointedly, on the figure of a fool and on Pan, the god of poetry; this is no place for Du Bartas's poetic copia.[35] The book being inscribed is now the surveyor's plat.

It would be easy to read this as part of a teleological narrative about science overwriting religion. The biblical images, even the image signifying a trinitarian God, seem to be superseded by depictions of measurement and calculation. Given the theological bent of so much of the early modern geodetic literature, however, we might consider this image not as a manifestation of writing God out of the picture, but as a different way of writing about God. The theodolite, which is prominently featured where the triangular Trinity once stood, is, as we have seen, an instrument that is associated with divine geometry, even with God. In the place of the trinitarian triangle we find a man measuring land. This act of self-emplacement within a geometric landscape is in and of itself a mode of inhabiting the divine. If the biblical narrative of Creation so prominent in Du Bartas's text is not immediately apparent here, the notion of the Creation is everywhere, since, for many early moderns, God created through geometry. The shift this frontispiece signals is not from religion to science, but from experiencing God through poetry to experiencing God through geometry.

If the frontispiece of *The Surveyor* suggests this visually, the text itself immediately and directly places surveying in the context of divine knowledge. The book opens with a dedicatory letter to Prince Charles. Here is the second sentence of the epistle dedicatory, indeed of the whole book:

Wisedome is defined by CICERO to be *diuinarum atq[ue], humanarum rerum scientia*, of the former part of which definition (being the most absolute) I will leaue to speake vnto those who can better write; yet will thus much auerre, that no man shall obtayne the absolute perfection thereof, being absolutely ignorant of the rules, rudiments and principles of Mathematicall discipline, as the due consideration of that sacred and mysticall *Vnitie* and *Trinitie*, may well approve. (sig. A3$^{r-v}$)

Surveying is thus cast directly as partaking in a trinitarian theology.

The art of surveying, while perhaps motivated by such worldly concerns as taxation, shared in the early modern geometric epistemology which took as a given that God had created the universe according to geometric, mathematical principles, and that discovering those geometric patterns was a means of coming to a better knowledge of, and better relationship with, a triune God. Surveying, while perhaps involving tromping through muck and negotiating sheep, was a form of participating in this divine geometric order. Drawing, perceiving, and sensing a geometric world was a means of divine communication.

Finally, we should note that whereas early modern surveying books were theological, theology texts were often geometric and even geodetic. One of the great texts of late Elizabethan spiritual exercise is, after all, William Perkins's *A Golden Chaine, or The Description of the*

*Theologie, containing the Order of the Causes of Saluation and Damnation* (Cambridge, 1597). Perkins indicates that God, "in perpetuall action, liuing, and moouing in it selfe" (p. 11), is beyond human observation. The inner workings of the soul, however, can perhaps be measured and plotted. The very title of this text, *A Golden Chaine*, perhaps alludes to the surveyor's chain, an instrument of measurement popularized by sixteenth-century surveying manuals. The interpenetration of the geodetic and the theological became even more overt, and more prominent, over the course of the seventeenth century. John Stoughton, for example, writes in *The Heauenly Conuersation and the Naturall Mans Condition* (1640), that "[God's Word] is the *Card and Compasse*, without this, (as there be few men that can draw a straight line, or a circle, without a Rule or compasse) none can leade their life aright, or make straight steps to heaven: with this they may, for as while one line of the Compasse is firmely fastned upon the Card, the other goes steadily the true circuit" (p. 37). God's Word becomes at once map and surveying instrument; the Christian navigating his or her way through this field not only uses this divine compass, but becomes a part of it, physically integrated not only into the landscape but even into the very tools of measurement.

SACRED TRIANGLES

The cultural prominence of surveying in the sixteenth and seventeenth centuries affected not only what people looked at, but how they saw. Elizabeth Spiller has written about the telescope's influence on early modern modes of perception, citing how "Michael Baxandall has suggested that every culture has its own 'period eye': the physical act of seeing is not so much physiologically fixed but is also culturally conditioned in ways that determine cognitive perception. The way one sees determines what one can know ... the telescope clearly shaped the 'period eye' of the early modern age ... Th[e] visual texturing of the world was a product not simply of the telescope but of what the telescope suggests about how we see at all."[36] The same argument can be made for the various surveying instruments – most notably the theodolite and the Jacob's staff – which were popularized in the sixteenth century.[37] Indeed, the number of people trained to see the world through a theodolite vastly overwhelmed the number of the privileged few who peeked through a telescope, let alone worked with one. And with the new geodetic instruments, people saw in triangles.

Today, our immediate spatial environment is dominated by the square: we trade in real estate by the square foot, we measure cargo space in cubic feet, we sketch out plans on graph paper, and the streets of modern cities are laid out in quadratic grids. Given that this is the dominant spatial construction, it is perhaps not surprising to find Rowan Williams, theologian-turned-Archbishop of Canterbury, writing (in the context of a discussion of Wittgenstein) that talk of God "is structurally more like talking about some 'grid' for the understanding of particular objects."[38] The association of God and grid is part and parcel of a naturalized quadratic spatial sensibility. In early modern England, however, the reading public – a population ranging from the university-educated readers of Euclid to the less-trained readers of humbler surveying manuals – learned to conceptualize their space not through squares but through triangles. As we shall now see, the confluence of geodetic measurement and trinitarian symbolism further integrated discussions of God and geometry.

The triangle is the basic unit of land surveying. As Valentine Leigh puts it in *The Moste Profitable and Commendable Science, of Surueying of Landes, Tenementes, and Hereditamentes* (1588), "there is almost no manner of fashioned Land, but it may by diligence be brought, or deuided into Triangles" (sig. O4ʳ), since triangles are "the principallest Rule for measuring of Lande" (sig. P1ʳ).[39] In order to understand the novelty of this assertion, it is important to recognize that as late as the mid sixteenth century most people in England apparently could not name a triangle. The history of the English word gives us a sense of the shape's one-time obscurity. Under the *Oxford English Dictionary*'s first definition for "triangle" ("A figure [usually, a plane rectilineal figure] having three angles and three sides") there are only two pre-1500 examples of the term, both of them somewhat compromised. The first citation of the word is from 1398: "Trevisa *Barth. De P.R.* XVII. cviii. (Tollem. MS.), Some [nuts] ben distinguid in þe cop as it were with þe schap of a triangle [orig. *per formam trianguli*]." The inclusion of the Latin original here suggests that the word is only marginally considered English at this point, or that it hovers between being a foreign word and a domestic one (as in, say, "soirée"). The second citation of the word is from c. 1400: "*Lanfranc's Cirurg.* 258 þe nose is maad of.ij. boones in þe maner of a triangle in þis manner. ΔΔ." What is interesting about this citation is that the author needed to define the shape through a graphic rather than a verbal representation, indicating not only that his audience would be unfamiliar with the Latinate "triangle," but that there was no other English word that could be used to express the concept.

The verbal lacuna that is supplemented by the graphic "Δ" indicates not only the limits of language, but also the field of visual perception. Did medieval people see triangles in their environment? Perhaps; probably. But they apparently weren't noteworthy enough to merit a noun. If I think about it, I can see a difference between rectangles that are nearly equilateral, being very close to squares, and rectangles with a huge discrepancy between length and width, so that they are long and narrow. Art historians, architects, and mathematicians might have different words for these shapes,[40] but this rarefied vocabulary is of no interest or use to the general public since, at present, it is of no use value.

In a way, then, triangles came into being (or came back into being with the popularization of Euclidean geometry) in the sixteenth century. The *OED*'s third historical citation for "triangle" is a straightforward definition: "**1551** RECORDE *Pathw. Knowl.* I. Defin., A triangle is nothinge els to say, but a figure of three corners."[41] Such sixteenth-century examples are abundant, since triangles needed to be defined for the reading public as popular geometric literacy became essential in a newly mathematic and cartographic world.[42] The author of one highly successful surveying manual, for instance, tells his readers, "I would not have you ignorant what peece of Land is called a Triangle, which often shall hereafter be named. It is such a fashioned peece as hath (or is imagined to haue) three sides, and three Angles onely."[43] Geometry books from the period include extensive descriptions of triangles, clearly assuming that such descriptions are required. The public appetite for translations of Euclid indicates that information about triangles and their geometric siblings was not only needed, but hotly desired.[44]

Once the unknown and the unnamed of the geometric world, triangles quickly shot up to be the stars of measurement. Leonard Digges's influential *A Geometrical Practical Treatize Named Pantometria* (1571; quoting here from second edition, 1591) illustrates the pragmatic and imaginative function of the triangle. As is typical of the surveying genre, the book contains an introductory tutorial on different geometric terms, including a definition for "triangle" ("Among Right lined figures, such as haue onely three sides are Triangles, whereof there be sundrie sortes bearing seuerall names, according to the diuersitie of their sides and Angles" [p. 3]). The definition is accompanied by a little illustration of the shape, with "A triangle" inscribed inside of it. The text further emphasizes the theoretical significance of triangles, noting that "all Figures comprehended with streight lines may bee resolued into Triangles: It seemeth most meete, fiist to teach the measuring of Triangles" (p. 57). Triangles are thus the most fundamental shape of surveying; even the most irregular little jut of land can be measured through triangulation.

The mission of early modern surveying books is to train an audience to see the world in triangular terms. Digges's heavily illustrated *Pantometria* demonstrates how, with the assistance of surveying instruments, the height of buildings, the angle of cannon fire, and distance of ships can all be measured by triangular means. In another text called *A Booke Named Tectonicon, Briefly Shewing the Exact Measuring, and Spedie Reckoning All Maner of Land, Squares, Timber, Stone, Steeples, Globes, & c.* (1592), Digges writes that "there is almost no Land, but it may easily be brought by imagination to a Triangle or Triangles, and so most truly measured: therefore, to be short, this order shall be taken. I will first figure and set afore your eyes Triangled Land, and other which by imagination shal be brought into Triangles. Then I will teach the true measuring of them … As these figures are measured, so all triangled land, the other brought into Triangles, of what fashion soever they be, shall be measured" (p. 2$^r$).[45] Triangles, while utterly pragmatic, thus also begin to play an active role in the world of the imagination. The very space in which one exists becomes triangulated – even the unwitting sheep and horses grazing in the pasture are imagined as inhabiting triangles (see Figure 12).

The histories of the triangle as a figure of geodesy and as an emergent symbol of the Trinity are intertwined. Through examining these histories, we can explore the larger interrelation of cartographic land surveying and contemplation of the divine. Indeed, the correspondence of trinitarian symbolism and geodetic technology led not only to abstract thoughts about the nature of God and God's participation in creation, but to an actual physical engagement with the land that was construed as a devotional act. Triangulating the land was portrayed as a means not only of recording God's presence in the world, but of experiencing that presence in an environment understood as deeply, structurally trinitarian.

In the encyclopedic *Symbols: Signs and Their Meaning*, Arnold Whittick offers this commentary for an entry on "Triangle (equilateral) – Christian symbol of the Trinity": "The bare representation of the equilateral triangle … has little to recommend it, as it is an elementary symbol too commonplace to evoke reflection."[46] While mathematicians might wax poetic about the complexities of the triangle (with its "inherent allure"[47]), for most of us the shape does indeed seem "elementary." Learning basic shapes such as triangles, circles and squares is one of the first steps our children take on the path to cultural literacy – indeed, it is one of the first steps towards literacy itself, since shape recognition is a prerequisite for

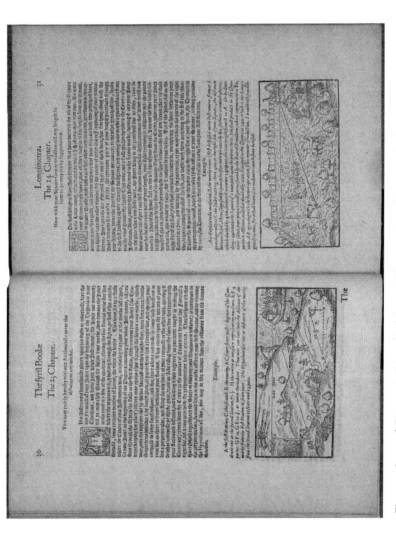

Figure 12 Leonard Digges, *A Geometrical Practical Treatize Named Pantometria*. London, 1591, pp. 30–1.

letter recognition. As inhabitants of the modern world, we have always already known triangles.

The emergence of the triangle as a nameable shape in the mid sixteenth century corresponds with the figure assuming its role as a symbol of the Trinity – in the process of becoming commonplace, triangles did indeed provoke plenty of reflection. While the triangle is frequently presented as an ancient symbol of the Trinity, there does not seem to be extensive evidence that it was a pervasive or even popular symbol.[48] Indeed, the early church does not appear to have developed a coherent trinitarian symbolic language (not surprising in light of the heated debates about the very nature of the Trinity); art historians repeatedly comment on the period's failures of representation in relation to the Trinity.[49] Throughout the medieval period triangular representations were associated with the Trinity, but not the triangle as a simple geometric form: churches began to house stained glass windows with a figure known as the Shield of the Blessed Trinity, which was more properly shield-shaped than a strict triangle, and in the twelfth century paintings signified the identity of God the Father with a triangular halo.[50] We also find examples of animals in triangular arrangements: a sepulcher from Tintern Abbey displays a triangle composed of three fish (another Christian symbol, of course), and a late fifteenth-century stained glass window in Holy Trinity Church, Long Melford, Suffolk shows (rather more mystifyingly) a triangle formed by the ears of three rabbits.[51] Thus while we can follow a chronological trail of triangular representations of the Trinity, in "the Middle Ages it is an extremely rare motif"; it is not until the sixteenth century that the Trinity becomes regularly represented as a triangle proper.[52] As Corbett and Lightbown observe: "[I]t was religious controversy which led to its widespread adoption in the latter part of the [sixteenth] century. At this period the anti-trinitarian movement was well organized and constituted a threat to all the established churches; as a manifesto of the true faith, the triangle, symbol of the Trinity, was placed on title-pages to Bibles and other religious literature and broadsheets in both Catholic and Protestant countries."[53]

As an emergent trinitarian symbol, the triangle participates in a kaleido-scope of sixteenth-century epistemologies. As part of a religious system of signification, the triangle-as-Trinity responds to Reformation discussions about iconoclasm. A number of ecclesiastical historians have addressed what Alexandra Walsham has called "the theological revolution which culminated in the renumbering of the Decalogue," making the prohibition against graven images a self-standing commandment.[54] The iconoclasm debate had direct ramifications on the representation of the Trinity:

From early in the English Reformation it is possible to detect a distinct squeamishness in Protestant circles about representing the three persons of the Trinity in anthropomorphic form [Walsham cites examples from Bucer, Cranmer, Calvin, and the Lambeth articles] ... Dozens of Elizabethan and early Stuart catechisms reiterated the precept that, because God was infinite, immeasurable and "severed from all mortall composition," it was utterly reprehensible and "a most blasphemous debasing of his Majestie" to attempt to create any resemblance of him, an argument which was also applied to the Holy Spirit and to Christ, whose humanity and divinity were declared to be quite indivisible. Hieroglyphic symbols indicative of divine presence, omniscience and power, such as a disembodied eye or the arcane Hebrew letters that comprised the tetragrammaton, might, however, be sanctioned.[55]

One of these hieroglyphs (one often encapsulating the disembodied eye) was, of course, the triangle.

The cultural interest in hieroglyphs was itself part of a widespread intellectual program of creating or inventing perfect language schemes, systems of communication which did not depend on the fallen nature of postlapsarian phonetic linguistics and alphabets. Mathematical languages were in a period of rapid development around the turn of the seventeenth century; the popularity of triangles is a consequence of the same dynamics that led, for instance, to the invention of a symbol for infinity.[56] The fascination with mathematical symbols was not only part of an early modern obsession with perfect language, but was also a consequence of Christian humanism; "[the triangle's] adoption in the fifteenth and sixteenth centuries may have been due to the influence of Platonic and Neo-platonic writings in which the idea of the divinity of numbers and of geometric figures is extensively developed."[57] Triangles also assumed mystical import; they were symbols in alchemical treatises, and they figure prominently in the thought of the highly influential Jacob Boehme.[58] On a more practical level – and probably a more influential one than the rarefied discourse of mathematical languages – triangles assumed cultural prominence because of their centrality in early modern surveying practices, as we have seen. This constellation of intellectual and market forces propelled the triangle into the popular consciousness.

The mathematical and geodetic qualities of triangles may seem to be far afield from the theological implications of the symbol of the Trinity. However, these discourses were deeply intermeshed. The history of the triangle in early modern England brings together a complex interplay of the abstract and the material, the theological and the practical. Amos Funkenstein has said of the sixteenth and seventeenth centuries, "Never before or after were science, philosophy, and theology seen as almost one and the same occupation."[59] The triangle provides us with a point through which we can see this confluence in action. Discussions of surveying – whether mapping the cosmos or the cow pasture – frequently position the act in a theological context, one that is decidedly trinitarian. And discussions of theology frequently position God, and one's relationship with God, in terms of geometry and cartography.[60] These interconnected modes of thought present the individual as existing within a space constructed and discovered through divine geometry. One's very experience of space was construed as geometric, often triangular; the reader/surveyor/soul inhabits a space that is innately trinitarian.

Again, contemporary theological texts frequently incorporate triangles into discussions of God and human-divine relations. William Austin, in *Triangvlvs in Festo Sanctorvm Epiphaniorvm Domini Nostri Iesv Christi* (which appears in his *Devotionis Augustinianae flamma, or, Certaine Devout, Godly, and Learned Meditations* [1637]), describes Epiphany – associated with the baptism of Christ, and thus a deeply trinitarian feast day – thus:

As *Christ* was made knowne, by *three* Manifestations (this *day*): so, is *this Text*, made manifest, by *three words*, in it. And, *they* are, *Videntes, Stella*, and *Gaudium*: which are the *heart* of it: and make a TRIANGLE; to fill *this Day*, in the *three Parts* of it ... Wee will *beginne* (therefore) at the *Epiphany*: the *Manifestation* from *Above*: (at *Stella*) ... It is the *Top* of this *Triangle*, the very *Cone* of this *Pyramis*; whence, it sends downe *Lines*; on *one side*, to *Videntes*, (causing them, to *Come*); and, *on the other*, to *Gaudium*, (causing *that*, to arise): so that, they *both* meete in *it*; and, make a *Triangle* (or, the forme of an *Heart*, turned *upward* ). (p. 57)

The text is accompanied by a marginal illustration of this triangular dynamic.[61]

In his description of the heart as a triangle, Austin uses an early modern commonplace. (We read, for instance, of "The heart, that inward triangle of loue."[62]) The heart was understood as triangular in shape, and was therefore also understood as trinitarian. In a formula that was to become so prevalent as to almost function as an early modern slogan, we read time and again that the heart is the inward expression of the Trinity: if one tries to fulfill it with the world, there will always be empty, aching spaces and corners, since a circle (i.e. the shape of the globe) cannot fill a triangle.[63]

The triangular, trinitarian heart locates the believer within intersecting early modern epistemologies. It establishes an updated form of the microcosm/macrocosm relationship: just as the environment is imprinted with triangles that signify the Trinity, so too the human body is imprinted with a triangle, God's divine signature. The logic of correspondences as a structuring principle of the universe is ancient; the geometric emphasis is distinctly early modern. The triangular heart signals that an individual Christian could fully inhabit a world that was perceived as innately trinitarian; at both a spiritual and a physical level, as both metaphor and geometric practice, the human body reflected and participated in a divine environment.

Thinking of divinity through triangles was not, however, uncontested. The geometric appreciation of God is antithetical to the theology of Saint Augustine, whose writings undergirded those of reformers like Calvin. Augustine, author of one of the most influential treatises on the doctrine of the Trinity, *De Trinitate*, argued elsewhere against representing God through a triangle.[64] (We might speculate that Augustine's opposition to the symbol may be one reason it didn't catch on in the early Church.) For Augustine, the desire to think of God as triangular is a sign of human weakness, of the need to contain and bound a numinous deity in a way that is comprehensible, but thus limited, to the human intellect. The containment of God in a triangle not only presents a false understanding of divine essence, but becomes its own form of idolatry. The triangle separates and distinguishes; it creates boundaries for the three persons of the Trinity; it divides an omnipresent God and establishes distance between heaven and earth. As such, it is antithetical to a triune divinity, the persons of which exist perichoretically, that is, mutually permeating each other. And it expels the human subject from this perichoretic economy, distancing the individual from God's participation in and communion with the world.

What repulses Augustine about imagining God as a triangle is what might have attracted the early modern scientist. Augustine's central critique, it would seem, is that the triangle, as a "construction," works in the interest of an almost taxonomic precision, inviting a perception of "three living masses . . . each bounded by the limits of its own space."[65] Separated into discrete entities, the three persons of the Trinity can be ordered and accurately named. This impulse to divide and label is at the heart of the science that emerged in the seventeenth century, and required a revolution in epistemology and semiotics. Funkenstein writes that "Scientists since the seventeenth century wanted their scientific language to be as unambiguous as possible; therefore, they emptied nature of *intrinsic* meanings ... Things ceased to refer to each other intrinsically, by virtue of their 'participation in' and 'imitation' of each other. Only language was henceforth to refer to things and to constellations of things in a system of artificial, univocal *signs*, such as mathematics. The ultimate prospect of science was a *mathesis universalis* – an unequivocal, universal, coherent, yet artificial language to capture our 'clear and distinct' ideas and their unique combinations."[66] Similarly, James Bono, in an analysis of the passage from Galileo that I cited above, notes that here "[n]ature is not poetic, multilayered, polysemous, mysterious, arcane, and a congeries of resemblances and affinities – the stuff of fictive similes and metaphors. Such falsehoods are 'abhorrent to nature' whose countours are instead defined by the sharp, distinctly etched forms of 'triangles, circles, and other geometric figures.'"[67] Augustine disparages the triangle as a symbol of the Trinity because it makes "clear and distinct" (in Funkenstein's borrowed phrase), or "sharp [and] distinctly etched" (in Bono's phrase), a triune godhead which is instead multi-referential and involves an integration of signifier and signified, of God and creation. For Augustine, the triangle as Trinity is a "phantasm" of human reason; even worse, as one seventeenth-century commentator puts is, it invites people to "make an *Idol* of their Reason."[68]

The ostensible clarity of the triangle is thus fundamentally at odds with what we might call a trinitarian ontology, one in which the *hypostases* (i.e. persons) of the Trinity are separate and yet not separate, distinct and yet united perichoretically. And this trinitarian ontology entailed its own trinitarian epistemology. We might call this a perichoretic semiotics, a privileging of the interconnected and multiple rather than the isolated and unitary. Perichoretic semiotics understands representational systems as having an intrinsic relationship with the world. Signs acquire meaning "by virtue of their 'participation in' and 'imitation' of each other," through being part of an economy of participatory interconnections.

The seventeenth-century triangle was thus caught up not only in divergent epistemologies, but also in emergent semiotic cross-currents. Its non-organic, mathematical qualities appealed to the scientific rationalism that would profoundly alter notions of the universe, and thus notions of the God that created and governed that universe. The triangle can be seen as the perfect symbol – in a symbolic system predicated upon the abstract precision of mathematics – for the God of a mechanical universe. This God does indeed entail a division of *theologia* and *oikonomia*, as it is a notion of the divine that has separated itself from creation.

Indeed, once the perichoretic relationship of creation and divinity begins to fade, the perichoretic relationship of the scholastic *theologia* (the relationship of the three persons of the Trinity to each other) itself becomes superfluous, and the triune God becomes an antique. So too perichoretic semiotics become archaic.[69] But within the context of the seventeenth century, the triangle is still at work within a perichoretic epistemology and a triune God. The triangle would be swept into the signifying systems of the new science, but for much of the sixteenth and seventeenth centuries, having gained cultural prominence through emergent practices of land surveying, the triangle was integrally connected to creation.

THE SPACE OF GOD IN 'THE TEMPEST'

Throughout this book, I have been exploring various ways in which supernatural spatial environments of early modern England integrated elements that, to our eyes, often seem disparate. The determined materiality of a signed demonic contract is located within a larger world that operates according to Ovidian physics. The domestic enclosure of a marital bed is rendered a site of demonic activity by the legacy of the *ars moriendi* tradition. A volcano understood as a locus of purgatory resides in a cartographic, earthly space. An understanding of a cosmic order controlled by divine Providence illogically coexists with an understanding of a cosmic order controlled by divine law.

In trying to give shape to these diverse relationships, I have relied on a variety of metaphors. The nature of early modern religious belief, as I discussed at the end of Chapter 1, is not sedimentary, with subsequent generations and movements neatly depositing a new layer of belief on top of the old, but metamorphic, as these layers are subject to cultural pressures that cause them to warp, swirl, and integrate. The nature of the early modern deathbed I discussed in Chapter 2 was, to use the terminology of Jonathan Gil Harris, that of the palimpsest:[70] the medicalized, humoral account of the deathbed given by William Perkins, for instance, overwrites the *ars moriendi* tradition, but traces of *ars* literature remain visible nonetheless, and the two discursive modes inadvertently interact. The status of Mount Hecla addressed in Chapter 3 can be expressed through Raymond Williams's terms of residual and emergent,[71] with continentally-trained, humanist Icelanders deliberately setting out to recast this volcano not as an earthly portal to the netherworld but as a natural formation on a modern cartographic map. These various ways of casting historical relationships are not, of course, mutually exclusive, and many of the texts I have discussed present more than one type of these interactions.

In analyzing the relationship of geodesy and God, I borrow from the theological language used to describe the Trinity. The idea of perichoresis can be used not only in its original setting of describing the relationship of the three persons of the Trinity, but as an expanded metaphor to consider elements which, while separate, are nonetheless mutually constitutive, integrative, and interpenetrating: at the end of the sixteenth century, a surveying instrument is not just an object with a utilitarian function, and not just an instrument that is used to measure land understood as God's creation, but an object that, through its shape and purpose, *participates* in the divine. This understanding of an object invites us to reconsider some of the post-Cartesian divisions that have come to structure our own understanding of the world: the distinction of the material and the immaterial, the distinction of self and other, and the distinction of self and environment. Kepler's geometrically structured universe is a habitation for both God and humanity; the theodolite in the field unites God, surveyor, and environment; the triangle integrates a triune deity with the mathematical organization of a pasture. Space is construed as geometric; geometry is understood as divine; individuals thus live within a world of this geo-divinity. Like the trinitarian relationship, God, the spatial environment, and human beings exist as distinct unto themselves, and yet are integrally, substantively interconnected with each other.

The larger point of the geodetic God (and the representation of this God through the triangle, which crystallizes the idea of an interconnected deity, humanity, and environment), is that it expresses a unique early modern theological epistemology. An inheritance of patristic and medieval trinitarian theology, with its attendant allegorical understanding of the material world, is woven into the new geometry and new geometric gadgets of the sixteenth and early seventeenth centuries. By the end of the seventeenth century, both the Trinity and allegory were becoming outmoded, and geometry was becoming at once more abstract (in Newtonian physics, for instance) and more popularly naturalized (surveying and its way of seeing the world was no longer an innovation that created a cultural *frisson*, but a matter of economic fact). The years of the Shakespearean theater, however, were the period of the geodetic God.

This epistemology, I will argue, underlies *The Tempest*. Within the play, we find some of the most overt and sustained Christian allegory of the Shakespearean canon.[72] The play's religious dimension, however, has not been the focus of critical inquiry in recent years, as the scholarly conversation has centered instead on the play's colonial politics. As John D. Cox has discussed, over the last half-century analysis of the play has been split between idealist readings and the materialist readings that supplanted them with the advent of the new historicism and cultural materialism of the 1980s and 1990s: "now dominant ['materialist'] ways of interpreting *The Tempest* focus on the social and economic implications of the play rather than its conscious context of ideas and imagination – its 'idealist' context."[73] In a similar vein, Tom McAlindon writes that *The Tempest* has recently been considered "a play whose dominant discourse seeks to euphemize colonialist oppression, yet fails to suppress contradiction";[74] while acknowledging the presence of colonial references in the play, McAlindon persuasively argues that the language of prayer constitutes a more pervasive idiom. In fact, "[t]he discourse of prayer ... is fairly conspicuous in all the romances: it is interinvolved with their providentialist ideology, their special fondness for the numinous, and an idealist mode of characterization that habitually associates noble characters (the heroines especially) with sainthood and divinity."[75] And, in the introduction to his New Cambridge edition of *The Tempest*, David Lindley notes Robert H. West's claim (in *Shakespeare and the Outer Mystery* [1968], p. 84) that the play "does not connect Prospero's magic and spirits overtly with religion ... Shakespeare keeps his dramatic world secular and empirical," and responds: "Superficially this may seem true, but in the play there are more unambiguous references to the Bible and the Prayer Book than to the Virginia tracts, those texts confidently regarded as its sources, and of all the play's recollections it is these which are the most likely to have been picked up by every member of its contemporary audience."[76]

Julia Reinhard Lupton provides a pithy account of the critical motivations and consequences of cultural/materialist approaches: "It is precisely the particularism of culture, set against a universalism presumed bankrupt, that neohistoricist readers of Shakespeare have attempted to salvage, whether in the guise of Othello's blackness, Shylock's Judaism, or Caliban's indigenous claims. In the process, however, the religious foundations of the play's conceptions of these positions are necessarily occluded, reduced, or secularized."[77] My aim here is to reinvigorate a consideration of those religious foundations. I do not seek to resuscitate the idealist mode of the Christian critics of the 1950s and 1960s,[78] but to demonstrate how the dichotomy of idealism and materialism works against the grain of early modern culture, and how the dichotomy of universalism (which includes discussions of the divine) and cultural particularism is a limiting one for scholarship on the period. These dichotomies, given the current dominance of materialism and particularism, elide the numinous. For the study of a culture in which the idea of God was so prominent, this leads to a profoundly lopsided analysis of the period.

I hope to employ the critical practices and materialist modes of analysis that have emerged over the last few decades to better approach an early modern epistemology, and an early modern phenomenology, in which God was central. In short, I aim to historicize God – that is to say, how the divine was understood, experienced, and expressed in sixteenth- and seventeenth-century England. This study of the divinity of surveying practices illustrates one way to historicize God, and to comprehend how, in an era when space was understood in theological terms, the material and the spiritual cannot be segregated (as exemplified even in the triangle). Interrogating the particularities of this confluence allows us not only to better see a distinctive historical epistemology, but to discuss particular cultural expressions of God, rather than perform religious readings of literature predicated on a transhistorical notion of the divine. Let us then begin by considering the particular associations of the play's setting.

The setting of *The Tempest* is arguably the most pertinent of any Shakespearean play, serving not just as a location for the drama or a backdrop of the action, but as a motivating force and rationale for the plot. Within the play, many characters, with their diverse points of view, describe the island's environment. Some of the most extended and visually evocative descriptions come from Iris during the masque sequence:

> Ceres, most bounteous lady, thy rich leas
> Of wheat, rye, barley, vetches, oats, and peas;
> Thy turfy mountains where live nibbling sheep,
> And flat meads thatched with stover them to keep;
> Thy banks with pioned and twilled brims,
> Which spongy April at thy hest betrims
> To make cold nymphs chaste crowns; and thy broomgroves,
> Whose shadow the dismissed bachelor loves,
> Being lass-lorn; thy pole-clipped vineyard,
> And thy sea-marge, sterile and rocky-hard,
> . . .
> You nymphs, called naiads, of the windring brooks,
> With your sedged crowns and ever-harmless looks,
> Leave your crisp channels, and on this green land
> Answer your summons.[79]

The lines obviously emerge from the pastoral tradition, but as McAlidon observes, they are in "a classical idiom complicated with suggestions of an English climate and landscape in a Mediterranean world."[80] While the setting of *The Tempest* can invoke exotic locales (the Bermudas, the Mediterranean, Africa[81]), it is also recognizably English. As such, it participates in some of the theo-spatial understandings familiar to a seventeenth-century audience, especially the period's integration of land and divinity.

That said, the play operates on a subtle level, both in terms of its geographical representations and in its religious idiom. Elsewhere in the Shakespearean corpus, we find direct engagement with the terms and practices of surveying. Shakespeare's plays do, in fact, display a familiarity with surveying that would be expected of a writer living in early modern London, of a shareholder in a theater company concerned with land leases and rebuilding, and of a rising gentleman of the countryside. Some of these surveying references are in passing: a character in *The Merchant of Venice* mentions "Jacob's staff," and another in *Coriolanus* speaks of a cartographic compass.[82] Other references are more sustained.

In *Henry IV, Part 2*, a familiar biblical parable is translated into contemporary terms that would have been legible to an audience comprised of general readers, landowners and builders, and people arrived from an extensively surveyed countryside. In the gospel of Luke, Jesus lays out for a crowd the rather daunting terms of discipleship:

And whosoever doth not bear his cross, and come after me, cannot be my disciple. For which of you, intending to build a tower, sitteth not down first, and counteth the cost, whether he have sufficient to finish it? Lest haply, after he hath laid the foundation, and is not able to finish it, all that behold it begin to mock him, Saying, This man began to build, and was not able to finish. Or what king, going to make war against another king, sitteth not down first, and consulteth whether he be able with ten thousand to meet him that cometh against him with twenty thousand? ... So likewise, whosoever he be of you that forsaketh not all that he hath, he cannot be my disciple. (Luke 14:27–33)

In the play, this building metaphor is exploited by Lord Bardolph in order to put a biblical gloss on the planned rebellion against King Henry. Lord Bardolph's elaboration of the verse adds a trendy, emphatically geodetic vocabulary:

> ... When we mean to build
> We first survey the plot, then draw the model;
> And when we see the figure of the house,

Then must we rate the cost of the erection,
Which if we find outweighs ability,
What do we then but draw anew the model,
In fewer offices, or, at least, desist
To build at all? Much more in this great work –
Which is almost to pluck a kingdom down
And set another up – should we survey
The plot of situation and the model,
Consent upon a sure foundation,
Question surveyors, know our own estate,
How able such a work to undergo,
To weigh against his opposite . . .[83]

This recasting of ancient sacred scripture into the process and mechanics of sixteenth-century land calculation could be read as a crass modern appropriation or as an attempt to make such scripture relevant to its audience. (And the reading one chooses perhaps depends on the degree to which one thinks of Hotspur as Jesus.) Regardless of motive and reception, the passage interweaves geodetic and biblical discourses, a habit that, as we have seen, was popular in the decades around 1600.

In a much later play, *Henry VIII*, the surveyor makes another appearance. The play is also titled *All Is True*, but this is not the case for the surveyor, who was sometimes seen as the early modern version of a used-car salesman, a suspect figure who could gull the ignorant through a false or faulty survey.[84] In this play, the surveyor lives up to his profession's reputation, as he falsely accuses the Duke of Buckingham of treason. When the surveyor makes his slanderous deposition, good Queen Katherine cautions him, "If I know you well,/You were the Duke's surveyor, and lost your office/On the complaint o'th' tenants. Take good heed/You charge not in your spleen a noble person/And spoil your nobler soul" (1.2.172–6). The Duke himself recognizes the surveyor's corruption: "My surveyor is false. The o'er-great Cardinal/Hath showed him gold. My life is spanned already" (1.1.223–4). "Surveyor" here could indicate a more general "overseer of an estate," as the Norton Shakespeare glosses the term (1.1.115). (*OED* def. 1: "One who has the oversight or superintendence of a person or thing; an overseer, supervisor.") But the language of taxation surrounding his appearance, Buckingham's possible pun on "spanned" as measured, and the sixteenth-century popularity of the term to mean "One who had the oversight of the lands and boundaries of an estate and its appurtenances" (*OED*, def. 1e) suggest that "surveyor" here means "surveyor" very much as we understand the word.

These Shakespearean plays are conversant with the process and the stereotypes surrounding the business of land surveying. Indeed, drama of the period more generally was deeply invested in geodesy and its attendant way of seeing and processing the world. As Turner writes,

we find that Renaissance men of letters [including Marlowe, Middleton, Sidney, Shakespeare, Dekker, and Jonson] are beginning to regard poetics, and especially the theater, as a distinctive way of coming to knowledge about metaphysical principles, about society, and about human action, and not simply as a matter of philology, grammar and style. And they arrive at this new epistemological approach to poetics, surprisingly enough, not simply by reading classical authors but by comparing it to practical geometry, early-modern technology, and the mechanical arts that were flourishing around them.[85]

And as Adam Max Cohen has noted, these arts were flourishing right around Shakespeare, who lived and worked in the districts where instrument-makers were concentrated.[86] (In addition to this spatial proximity, the timespan of Shakespeare's career, as Cohen observes, corresponds almost exactly with what Peter Eden has deemed the "golden age of estate cartography," the years 1585–1615.[87])

While *The Tempest* does not contain its own professional surveyor, it does exhibit a geodetic sensibility and epistemology typical of its time. During the storm at the beginning of the play, Gonzalo exclaims, "Now would I give a thousand furlongs of sea for an acre of barren ground – long heath, brown furze, anything" (1.1.65–6). The line, with its little catalogue of foliage, seems odd given the context (that is, a shipwreck in which everyone is seemingly about to perish). Not only does Gonzalo suggest a seemingly disproportionate trade – a thousand furlongs for one acre – but his catalogue of plants is a typical feature of the surveyor's plat, the textual account of the property that included the actual geometrical survey.[88] Frank Kermode, in his Arden edition of the play, compresses a critical history in his gloss on the line: "Many more examples, supplied to Mr Munro by Sir William Craigie, make it fairly certain that Tannenbaum's conjecture is right, and that Gonzalo has here slipped into the familiar language of estate business."[89] The plat-like catalogue is reiterated later in the play, when Ariel recounts of Caliban, Trinculo, and Stephano, "calf-like, they [his] lowing followed, through/Toothed briars, sharp furzes, pricking gorse, and thorns" (4.1.179–80). The island is indeed the acre that Gonzalo bargained for.

It is perhaps to be expected that a nobleman would think of land in terms of "acres," but it is interesting to find a broad range of characters who conceptualize their environment through modes of measurement.

The goddess Ceres speaks of "My bosky acres and my unshrubbed down" (4.1.81). Caliban promises Stephano: "I'll show thee every fertile inch o'th' island" (2.2.145). Sebastian observes that "'twixt [Naples and Tunis]/ There is some space," to which Antonio replies, "A space whose every cubit/Seems to cry out, 'How shall that Claribel/Measure us back to Naples?'" (2.1.258–60).

Ferdinand asserts, "Might I but through my prison once a day/ Behold this maid. All corners else o'th' earth/Let liberty make use of; space enough/Have I in such a prison" (1.2.491–4). The "corners" here do not seem to be so much the proverbial four corners of the flat earth, but the numerous corners of a surveyed space. The sensibility is more quadratic than triangular, and indeed the Shakespearean plays never once include the word "triangle." However, and significantly, *The Tempest* is the only play to employ "angle" in a geometric sense (as opposed to a fishing sense): Ariel leaves Ferdinand "In an odd angle of the isle" (1.2.223).

If *The Tempest* does not lift passages and terminology straight from, say, Rathborne's *The Surveyor*, it does nevertheless portray a geometric way of understanding the lay of the land and the spatial surround. The recurrent references to units of measurement (furlongs, acres, fathom, leagues, cubits, inches[90]) and elements of the survey indicate how naturalized such a vocabulary had become by the early seventeenth century. Gonzalo refers to "contract, succession,/Bourn, bound of land" (2.1.152–3), with "bourn" and "bound of land" being synonymous. Both Gonzalo (3.3.2) and Alonso (5.1.242–4) express a sense of inhabiting a "maze"; again, while not the triangular order of a proper survey, the references to mazes (and their "forthrights and meanders" [3.3.3]) suggest a landscape that has a geometry, even if the characters cannot necessarily perceive the pattern from within.[91] To see how mazes could be associated with surveying, we can look at Francis Quarles's emblem of life as a labyrinth. This image depicts a pilgrim, complete with staff, being guided by a line from an angel on top of a tower; the line forms the hypotenuse of a triangle, and has a striking visual affinity with the geometric conceptualization of space illustrated in surveying manuals such as Digges's *Pantometria* (see Figures 13 and 14). Indeed, with the tower and the ship in the distance, this emblem recreates the recurrent landscapes of the surveying manuals; Quarles's pilgrim appears to have stepped into one of those illustrations.

As the goddess Juno descends during the masque, Iris says she has come to sport "Here on this grass-plot" (4.1.73) – "plot" being a word that drew

Figure 13 Francis Quarles, *Emblemes*. London, 1635, p. 288.

together geographical location, narrative, and surveying practices.[92] There are also repeated references to nautical measurement: Alonso proclaims he will seek his son "deeper than e'er plummet sounded" (3.3.101), Stephano makes the inflated claim that he swam "five and thirty leagues off and on"

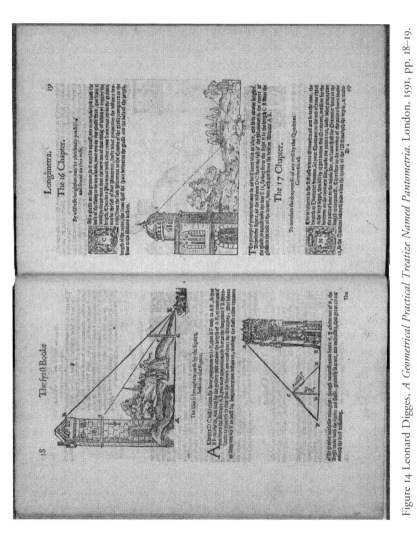

Figure 14 Leonard Digges, *A Geometrical Practical Treatize Named Pantometria.* London, 1591, pp. 18–19.

(3.2.13–14), and Prospero swears "I'll break my staff,/Bury it certain fathoms in the earth,/And deeper than did ever plummet sound/I'll drown my book" (5.1.54–7). Within the geodetic discourse of the period, the measurement of space on land was frequently linked with measuring space at sea, and both emphasized this three-dimensional measurement. If the play does not contain the type of blatant reference to surveying that we find in *Henry IV, Part 2,* it nevertheless illustrates a pervasive mode of conceptualizing the spatial environment through geodetic ways of knowing.

Similarly, while *The Tempest* does not have the dramatic impact of Jupiter dropping from the heavens that we find in *Cymbeline,* the play contains pervasive representations of the divine. Encounters with new, strange, foreign others are repeatedly processed in terms of divinity. Ferdinand assumes that the music he hears must be that of a god: "Where should this music be? I'th' air or th' earth?/It sounds no more, and sure it waits upon/Some god o'th' island" (1.2.388–90). Miranda sees Ferdinand and presumes that he himself is a god: "I might call him/A thing divine, for nothing natural/I ever saw so noble" (1.2.417–19). Ferdinand, in turn, meets Miranda and thinks he has met the goddess: "Most sure the goddess/On whom these airs attend! – Vouchsafe my prayer/May know if you remain upon this island" (1.2.422–4). Caliban understands Stephano to be divine: "These be fine things, an if they be not sprites;/That's a brave god and bears celestial liquor./I will kneel to him" (2.2.114–16); "Hast thou not dropped from heaven?" (2.2.134); "I prithee, be my god" (2.2.146). Alonso sees Miranda and jumps to the same conclusion as Ferdinand: "Is she the goddess that hath severed us/And brought us thus together?" (5.1.187–8).

Perhaps the most dramatically powerful moment of a quasi-divine revelation is this:

GONZALO:     ... Some heavenly power guide us
                    Out of this fearful country.
PROSPERO:                         Behold, sir King,
                    The wronged Duke of Milan, Prospero!     (5.1.105–7)

The revelatory self-identification, with its titles, proper noun, and biblical/liturgical "behold," nearly equates Prospero as the "heavenly power." In a similar if more extenuated instance, at the beginning of the play the Boatswain snaps at Gonzalo, "if you can command these elements to silence and work the peace of the present" (1.1.21–2), suggesting that only a deity can do so; moments later, the lines are echoed in Prospero and Miranda's first appearance: "If by your art, my dearest father, you have/ Put the wild waters in this roar, allay them" (1.2.1–2).

The audience knows that Prospero is not God – indeed, Prospero knows that himself. He came to the island "[b]y providence divine" (1.2.159).[93] There is, throughout the play, a sense of a deity above: "destiny,/That hath to instrument this lower world/And what is in't" (3.3.53–5); "O heaven, O earth" (3.1.68); "Look down, you gods" (5.1.201). Yet at times, the distinction between Prospero and divinity becomes difficult to maintain. On the verge of giving over his power, Prospero makes a soliloquy that tellingly reveals his relationship to super-natural power. While the speech, as is well known, loosely borrows from Medea's invocation in the seventh book of Ovid's *Metamorphoses*,[94] the pattern of second- and first-person pronouns is Prospero's own:

> Ye elves of hills, brooks, standing lakes, and groves,
> And ye that on the sands with printless foot
> Do chase the ebbing Neptune, and do fly him
> When he comes back; you demi-puppets that
> By moonshine do the green sour ringlets make,
> Whereof the ewe not bites; and you whose pastime
> Is to make midnight-mushrooms, that rejoice
> To hear the solemn curfew, by whose aid –
> Weak masters though ye be – I have bedimmed
> The noontide sun, called forth the mutinous winds,
> And 'twixt the green sea and the azured vault
> Set roaring war; to the dread-rattling thunder
> Have I given fire and rifted Jove's stout oak
> With his own bolt; the strong-based promontory
> Have I made shake, and by the spurs plucked up
> The pine and cedar; graves at my command
> Have waked their sleepers, ope'd and let 'em forth
> By my so potent art.                    (5.1.33–50)

The first half is marked by forms of address: "ye elves," "ye that on the sands," "you demi-puppets," "you whose pastime/Is to make ... mush-rooms." Prospero begins to acknowledge the debt he owes ("by whose aid –"), but in the final use of the second person address, suddenly qualifies the elves' power ("Weak masters though ye be"). The recognition of aid is negated by the second half of the soliloquy, in which "ye" and "you" give way to the strong, repeated, declarative "I." It is now Prospero alone who dims the sun, controls the wind, creates war between the heavens and earth, masters the thunder and lightning, shakes the ground, rips up trees and even the dead. It is now Prospero who has become Providence. Over the course of the passage Prospero resembles less a mythical enchanter (like Sycorax) than the Calvinist God (as I discussed in the previous chapter). Gone is aid; now all is attributed to a "so potent art."

Under the terms of the 1606 Act of Abuses, plays could not mention the Christian God on stage. But of all the Shakespearean plays, *The Tempest* comes closest to representing that God. Before the arrival of the shipwrecked voyagers, the island holds the essential persons of Christian theology: the triune deity of Father (Prospero), Son (well, here a daughter, Miranda), and Holy Spirit (Ariel), as well as the devil (or at least the son thereof[95]). The alignment of the characters with the trinitarian hypostases is not completely neat; as Robert L. Reid comments, "while the play's iconic imagery provides a mystery-play drive toward conversion and eschatology, the opacity of that iconography holds the mystery at bay as a continual challenge."[96] But while the play refuses a straightforward reading as religious allegory, the trinitarian associations of the characters seem unmistakable: Prospero as lawgiver, commander, and judge; Miranda as a Christological "advocate" (1.2.478) who suffers with the sinful travelers ("O, I have suffered/With those that I saw suffer" [1.2.5–6]) and offers herself as sacrificial substitute ("Sir, have pity;/I'll be his surety" [1.2.475–6]); Ariel as a spirit working through fire (in the shipwreck, he "flamed amazement" and "burn[ed] in many places" like "Jove's lightening" [1.2.198–9, 201]).[97]

Given this trinitarian presence, we might expect to find the attendant perichoretic relationship of God, humanity, and environment. And indeed, the play abounds with moments when characters and the natural environment become interconnected. For much of the play, however, these moments, many of them cast in strikingly visual terms, do not present a vision of a wholistic communion with a triune deity and Creation. Rather, they appear as contorted, nightmarish versions of union. Prospero describes his brother as the "ivy which had hid [Prospero's] princely trunk/And sucked my verdure out on't" (1.2.86–7). Prospero's tears and the sea become mingled as he "decked the sea with drops full salt" (1.2.155). Ferdinand, who presumes he is about to drown, had, in Ariel's report, "hair up-staring (then like reeds, not hair)" (1.2.213), suggesting an eerie image of an underwater body. This is similar to the morbid depiction of Alonso's purported corpse in Ariel's first song: "Full fathom five thy father lies,/Of his bones are coral made;/Those are pearls that were his eyes" (1.2.397–9). Ariel himself is a spirit who can "dive into

the fire" and "ride/On the curled clouds" (1.2.191–2), "tread the ooze/Of
the salt deep" and "run upon the sharp wind of the north" and do
"business in the veins o'th' earth" (1.2.252–3, 254, 255). In spite of this
ability to penetrate the earth and sea, Ariel's worst punishment is to be
imprisoned within a tree: Ariel was confined by Sycorax "[i]nto a cloven
pine" (1.2.277) for a dozen years, and Prospero threatens to repeat the
sentence, claiming he "will rend an oak/And peg thee in his knotty
entrails" (1.2.294–5). Alonso mourns that "[his] son i'th' ooze is bedded . . .
with him there [he'll] lie mudded" (3.3.100–2), an image that clearly
haunts him, as he repeats it: "I wish/Myself were mudded in that oozy
bed" (5.1.150–1). Indeed, the whole company has been "sea-swallowed"
(2.1.251). These disturbing images – of being intertwined with a parasitic
vine, of a corpse becoming inhabited by creatures of the sea, of being
imprisoned within trees, of a beloved son sunk in the slime of the seafloor,
or being swallowed whole – do in fact present instances of human-
environmental integration, but they are clearly undesirable. The interconnection of men and the natural world is threatening, morbid, and
grotesque.

   Within the play these images are countered, and potentially overcome,
by the presentation of an ideal scenario of human-environmental-divine
integration in the masque. The masque momentarily enacts a theo-spatial
reorganization. Until the masque, the geodetic sensibility is often negative; "bound of land," after all, appears in the catalogue of social evils that
Gonzalo bans in his island Utopia. The masque of Iris, Ceres, and Juno,
by contrast, presents not only a peaceful vision of nature, but one that
recoups a beneficent geodetic God.

   For much of the play, characters have been imagining themselves in a
different space – in Milan, in Tunis, under the sea. The masque, however,
brings about a sense of spatial immediacy: as much as it is a fantastic
vision, it momentarily creates spatial presence. Just before the masque
begins, Prospero asks Ariel to bring the others "here to this place" (4.1.38).
The phrase is redundant: "here" might suffice, "place" is perhaps obvious,
but we have "here," "this," "place." As Juno descends, Iris says that Juno is
coming "Here on this grass-plot, in this very place" (4.1.73). This "here"
could hardly be more insistent: "*Here*, on *this* grass-plot, in *this very place*."
The line not only echoes and intensifies Prospero's directive, it unites the
terrestrial locale of the island and the divine.[98] Prospero's "here" and the
goddess's "here" are one and the same. Ceres's subsequent question of
why she has been summoned "to this short-grass'd green" (83) further
solidifies the connection, as it repeats one of Gonzalo's first reactions to

arriving on the island: "How lush and lusty the grass looks! How green!" (2.1.55). Stephen Orgel comments that "Prospero the illusionist, moving his drama towards reconciliation and a new life, presents in the betrothal masque his own version of Gonzalo's Utopia, a vision of orderly nature and bountiful fruition,"[99] but as well as incarnating Gonzalo's vision the masque also reinforces his actual view of the island landscape.

Juno, Ceres, and Iris here constitute their own Trinity. Juno is "the queen o'th' sky" (4.1.70), Ceres the goddess of the earth, and Iris is the "messenger" (4.1.71, 76) and the rainbow which connects heaven and earth. In contrast to the potentially hostile natural world we have encountered in the play up to this point – including the realistic shipwreck scene at the beginning, which, as Andrew Gurr argues, must have "shocked" the audiences at the original venue of the Blackfriars Theater[100] – we are met with a pacific vision of Juno's messenger interacting with nature, of nurturing water, and the "watery arch" (4.1.71) of Iris's rainbow, biblical symbol of renewed covenant between God and humanity. Ceres says:

> Hail, many-coloured messenger, that ne'er
> Dost disobey the wife of Jupiter;
> Who, with thy saffron wings, upon my flowers
> Diffusest honey-drops, refreshing showers,
> And with each end of thy blue bow dost crown
> My bosky acres and my unshrubbed down,
> Rich scarf to my proud earth.     (4.1.76–82)

The "acres" that earlier were part of the bounds of land that Gonzalo rejects are here recouped into a vision of integration; the types of land description typical of the plat are incorporated into a divine landscape. ("Bosky," *OED a*[1]: "Consisting of or covered with bushes or underwood; full of thickets, bushy.") The geodetic register is further enhanced by Iris's answer to Ceres's query: "A contract of true love to celebrate,/And some donation freely to estate/On the blest lovers" (4.1.84–6). The use of "estate" to signify "bestow" is unusual, and the constellation of plot/ acres/contract/estate infuses the masque with a geodetic register.

The masque is a "most majestic vision" (4.1.118), one which Ferdinand quickly translates from Prospero's "fancies" (4.1.122) into an understanding of the reality around him. "Let me live here ever," he declares, the "here" again seeming to unite the space of the island with the divine space of the masque. "So rare a wondered father and a wise/Makes this place paradise" (4.1.122–4). The spatial environment, perceived as a perichoretic intermingling of the earthly and the divine, has become the idealized one portrayed in the surveying manuals. This perichoresis is then enacted by a dance of agrarian workers – reapers "properly habited" (s.d.) in "rye-straw hats" (4.1.136) – and nymphs. The intermingling reapers and nymphs are one expression of supernatural-human interaction. The harmony and geometric form of the dance itself is another. "God is like a skilful Geometrician," writes Thomas Browne in *Religio Medici*, reiterating a platitude of the period.[101] The dance of the masque traces the patterns of this divine geometry.[102] In another register, so does the act of the surveyor, tracing triangulated land. The masque of *The Tempest*, with its emphatic natural setting, its geodetic discourse, and laborers from the fields, folds these notions of divine geometry together.

*The Tempest*'s masque, "suddenly resplendent and suddenly dissolved, displays Shakespeare's most elaborate stage spectacle," writes Ernest B. Gilman in his fine analysis of the effects – dramatic, narratological, psychological – of the scene's abrupt ending.[103] Prospero halts the masque when he remembers "Caliban and his confederates," and that "the minute of their plot/Is almost come" (4.1.140–2). "Plot displaces plot, but the wrong way round," writes Gilman (216), who argues that here we have anti-masque following masque, contrary to all of the logic and conventions of the genre. For the audience, the impact of this reversal is spatial: "At the moment of its disruption we are dislocated, dislodged from the illusion of the masque. The unexpected antimasque jars us into realizing that we can't live here ever"; "[t]he complete contrary to Ferdinand's rapt wonder is the sense … that the masque is a delusion and a trap for those who would 'live here ever'" (226, 225).

Indeed, the abrupt ending of the masque and the return to the plot of Stephano, Caliban, and Trinculo does seem to take us from the heights into the bogs, undermining the charmingly harmonious scene we have just witnessed with a parallel, but inverted, scenario. The planned treachery undermines the political stability and order that is celebrated in the masque. The trio can be seen as a negative image of the trinity of goddesses (Stephano is now "King Stephano" [4.1.222]; Caliban is the devil incarnate; Trinculo assumes the role of Stephano's servant). Ariel's rudimentary music (he beats his tabor, 4.1.175) is smelled by the threesome, rather than heard (4.1.178). And, what is important for my argument here, the divine spatial environment created by the masque is transformed into something squalid. Ceres's "bosky acres" are countered with "Toothed briars, sharp furzes, pricking gorse, and thorns" (4.1.81; 4.1.180) (the catalogue of flora, again, being a feature of the surveyor's plat). The three conspirators are "dancing up to th' chins," but only in an attempt to avoid "th' filthy-mantled pool" and the "foul lake" (4.1.182–3).

Most powerfully, the divine geometry of the masque is contradicted with a grotesque caricature of measurement. On the cusp of the assassination of Prospero, the three come across his gown. When Caliban urgently tries to return them to their homicidal purpose, he is dismissed as Stephano and Trinculo engage in a moment of banter.

STEPHANO:   Be you quiet, monster. Mistress Line, is not this my jerkin? Now
   is the jerkin under the line! Now jerkin you are like to lose your hair, and
   prove a bald jerkin.
TRINCULO:   Do, do. We steal by line and level, an't like your grace.
STEPHANO:   I thank thee for that jest; here's a garment for't. Wit shall not go
   unrewarded while I am king of this country. "Steal by line and level" is an
   excellent pass of pate. There's another garment for't.

(4.1.236–44)

The humor is opaque. (Not surprisingly, these lines are often cut in performance.[104]) Perhaps the best account of it is in Lindley's edition. "Now ... bald jerkin" is glossed:

Stephano clearly intends a joke. "Under the line" means "at the equator" (whereas we now draw the imaginary line of the equator on the sea, and 'cross' it, in this period the equinoctial line was imagined as drawn in the heavens). A causal relationship is implied between the jerkin being "under the line" and its consequent baldness, which might derive from fevers contracted on long equatorial voyages. Orgel claims a connection "with having one's head shaved in the shipboard horseplay traditionally consequent on crossing the equator". Losing one's hair was, however, associated specifically with sexual disease and its treatment ... The heat of the equator might then be a metaphor for sexual heat, which causes the loss of hair. Levin extended this further by suggesting that "under the line" should be understood anatomically as "below the waist."[105]

The immediate jest, though, the one that gives Stephano such a chuckle that he repeats it and rewards it, is Trinculo's expression "Steal by line and level." Lindley's note on this phrase is a bit more straightforward: "according to the rule, precisely, craftily. The proverbial phrase alludes to a plumb line and a carpenter's level (cf. Tilley, L305)" (196n). But what seems so hilarious to these characters is how the signification of "Mistress Line" is volleyed back in "line and level." The two instances of "line" interact with each other, and therefore the semiotic play is extensive, ranging through the equator, its microcosmic analogue of the waist (and the attendant possibilities for sexual/scatological humor), shaved heads, sexual disease, plumb lines and carpentry.

In this profusion of meaning, the geometric is muddied. The celestial lines of divine geometry, which connect planetary and cosmic order, and the lines of earthly geometry used in practical building, become woven into this joke with its scurrilous possibilities. Additionally, there is a possible allusion to surveying at work. Most editors of the play, like Lindley, cite Tilley,[106] and assert that the reference is to the tools of carpentry. But there is much overlap in the tools of the carpenter's and surveyor's trade. Leonard Digges's *Tectonicon*, a text which instructs readers how to make their own surveying instruments (such as the geometrical square on the side of a ruler, the carpenter's square, and the cross-staff) advertises itself on the title page as a text for surveyors, "land-meters," joiners, carpenters, and masons, indicating the mutual interests and skills of these professions. All used plumb lines and levels.[107] "Lines and levels" were therefore not strictly the domain of carpenters.[108] "To steal by line and level" could easily refer to the practices of deceptive surveyors, who truly could cheat with an inaccurate survey (one created with lines and levels) that resulted in higher rent, or diminished property, or, conversely, increased holdings and thus greater taxes.

The spatial dynamics of this "antimasque," then, do contribute strongly to Gilman's argument that the sudden shift from the dancing nymphs to Caliban and his crew results in a sense of dislocation – in fact, I think that what for Gilman works more as a spatial metaphor is, within the play, presented as actual spatial realities. But while I agree with Gilman's reading of the effect of this immediate moment, I do not think that the ultimate consequence for the audience is to figuratively fall through the trapdoor of the stage, to drop from a scene that descended from the heavens into the hell below. Rather, I think that the masque of the goddesses, and the dance of the nymphs and the reapers, represents a vision of the geodetic God, and an environmental economy of perichoresis. The vision of this idealized state of harmony might be fleeting – and the contrast between divine geometry and its abuse by fallen human beings highlights its elusiveness – but the masque is the spectacular climax of the play, and perhaps its most redemptive moment as well.

Grace Tiffany has argued for the strong presence of Calvinist grace in the Shakespearean romances. The human failings of the tragedies are recycled in these dramas, but "the dominant force in the romances is a providence that thwarts, overcomes, and undoes the crucial errors of the plays' would-be tragic heroes. This force forgives human mistakes, nulli-fying their fatal potential and reducing tragic grandeur to ordinary sin. The word given to this force by the romances themselves is grace."[109] Within *The Tempest*, this divine grace is effected, and given expression, by the environment itself. The rapid juxtaposition of the elaborate staging of the perichoretic vision of divine-human-earth interaction with the fallen antics of Caliban and friends – two scenes which, as we have seen, contain a geodetic sensibility – presents paradisiacal harmonious actions against postlapsarian chaos. Although Prospero has played the role of God in calling up the masque, his creations have in turn acted upon his own human impulse towards sin. The moment of his "project gather[s] to a head" (5.1.1): "the King and's followers" are "[c]onfined together / . . . all prisoners, . . . /In the line grove which weather fends [his] cell./They cannot budge till [his] release" (5.1.7–11). As Ariel was imprisoned in a tree, here all of Prospero's enemies are trapped in a lime grove. They are at Prospero's mercy. And, seemingly against his original intention, he grants it to them.

> Though with their high wrongs I am struck to th' quick,
> Yet with my nobler reason 'gainst my fury
> Do I take part. The rarer action is
> In virtue than in vengeance. They being penitent,
> The sole drift of my purpose doth extend
> Not a frown further.                    (5.1.25–30)

By the grace of Prospero the prisoners will not suffer further retribution, and this proves to be his own redemption also. Prospero breaks his staff, but regains his dukedom.

The play draws to its close with a recasting of imagery. Prospero's prisoners had been trapped in a "circle which Prospero had made" (5.1.57 s.d.); the negative image is replaced with Alsonso's blessing of Ferdinand and Miranda: "Now all the blessings/Of a glad father compass thee about!" (5.1.179–80). The play's recurrent dark imagery of being merged with the natural world is countered with Ariel's joyous plans for his freedom:

> Where the bee sucks, there suck I,
> In a cowslip's bell I lie;
> There I couch when owls do cry.
> On the bat's back I do fly
> After summer merrily.
> Merrily, merrily, shall I live now,
> Under the blossom that hangs on the bough.   (5.1.88–94)

And some of the corrupt associations of lines written upon the earth (Gonzalo's land boundaries, Trinculo's stealing by line and level) are replaced with a depiction of the geodetic God. Gonzalo proclaims, "Look down, you gods,/And on this couple drop a blessed crown,/For it is you that have chalked forth the way/Which brought us hither" (5.1.201–4). The *OED*'s fourth definition of "to chalk" is "a. To mark *out*, as with chalk (*obs.*). b. To delineate, *esp.* by the main features; to outline, sketch out, adumbrate." Interestingly, one of the *OED*'s examples of this usage comes from Arthur Golding's 1571 translation of Calvin's exposition of Psalm 18: "God did but (as it were under a dark shadowe) chalk out the ... kingdome of his sonne." This is the geometer God of Wither's emblem (see Figure 9), the arm from the cloud making and marking the world.

Scholarship on the play that considers its religious orientation frequently concludes that *The Tempest* ends in a form of harmony, often figured in perichoretic terms. McAlindon argues, "instead of legitimizing an intrinsically oppressive hierarchical order, the play, while not dispensing with the hierarchical model of society, advances a leveling, horizontal ethic of interdependence and reciprocity."[110] Grace R. W. Hall contends that "[i]n *The Tempest* Shakespeare integrated atmosphere *and* time *and* characters, creating a unified inclusive vision."[111] Northrop Frye, after observing that Prospero's Epilogue is "in a tone echoing the Lord's Prayer," wistfully concludes, "perhaps our children can ... bring forth again the island that the world has been searching for since the dawn of history, the island that is both nature and human society restored to their original form, where there is no sovereignty and yet where all of us are kings."[112] My own reading is not so sanguine; the weight of the earlier corruption, the treatment of Caliban, and the company's return to the realpolitik of Naples and Milan, suggests the familiar cycle of human fall and redemption.[113] (And, as Orgel notes, "repentance remains, at the play's end, a largely unachieved goal, forgiveness is ambiguous at best, [and] the clear ideal of reconciliation grows cloudy as the play concludes."[114]) Yet the play does present an idealized vision of paradisiacal union (however brief and abruptly aborted this vision might be), and this unity and harmony is understood in environmental terms.

*The Tempest* is thus imbued with a geodetic sensibility and exhibits an early modern faith in geometry, even as it also reveals the limitations of humanity's ability to order the world. In this respect, it is very much like the early modern triangle. On the one hand, the shape stood for the integration of divine order, natural environment, and human intelligence. On the other, the triangle carried the echo of Augustine's disbelief in the ability to capture or comprehend a numinous, expansive God through a geometric shape.

This push-and-pull dynamic of the play is exemplified (and created) by Prospero himself: godlike but utterly dependent on Providence, controlling the environment but at its mercy, beneficent but suspect. In performance, these contradictions might well even be embodied by Prospero. If we take his declaration that he will "break [his] staff" as an indication that he has been carrying a staff on stage, Prospero has visual affinities with both the surveyor and the sorcerer. In fact, the cultural associations of these two sometimes cross-pollinated. Within the period, surveyors were often highly unpopular and suspect figures, as Garrett A. Sullivan, Jr. has discussed in his important book.[115] (The student of early modern English history is comfortably familiar with Saxton's atlas, but we must remember that while making his survey hostilities were such that he required safe passage from town to town.[116]) The widespread popular suspicion of the land surveyor was due in large part to the tensions produced in the transition from feudal to more capitalist notions of land ownership, and the attendant transformations in understandings of social relations.[117] The distrust also stemmed from – or perhaps, was expressed through – popular associations of land surveyors with dark magic.[118] Conversely, magicians could be connected to the surveying arts, as is evident in Henry Peacham's drawing of a magician-scientist wielding a cross-staff and compass (an image included in Orgel's edition of *The Tempest*).[119] The association is powerfully made in another image recognizable to most scholars of the period's drama: the picture of Marlowe's Doctor Faustus on the title page of the play (see Figure 15). The Vaughans include this image in their edition to illustrate the point that "Prospero bears the physical signifiers a Jacobean audience would have associated with power: books, staff and robe."[120] But this list omits the picture's other instruments that would have been familiar to early modern consumers perusing the offerings of the bookstalls around St. Paul's: the prominently featured Jacob's staff and two accompanying surveying instruments.[121]

The discourse of surveying, both in sixteenth- and early seventeenth-century culture and in *The Tempest*, was one of ambiguity, connected to both divine geometry and the dark arts. *The Tempest* stages this contradiction, as well as another, perhaps even more fundamental one. In the first chapter of this book I discussed the concept of Ovidian physics, an early modern understanding of the environment as fluid and plastic. In this last chapter I have considered the counterpart of this notion: a geometric epistemology that posited a world of mathematical order. While this book has been structured along a spectrum from the former to the latter, their relationship is not a linear or consistently antithetical

Figure 15 Christopher Marlowe, *Tragicall Historie of the Life and Death of Doctor Faustus.* London, 1631. Title page.

one. In the image of Doctor Faustus, for instance, we see the convergence of the two: the space is clearly designated as a geometrically conceptualized one, with the floor grid marking out a crude linear perspective and the surveying instruments advertising the ability to mathematically measure space, and yet Faustus is able to conjure devils from the beyond.

*The Tempest* presents a similar dynamic, although Prospero conjures benign spirits instead of demons. Even as Prospero's masque is the visual climax of the play and a powerful theatrical representation of the period's theo-geometry, in its immediate aftermath we encounter an extended account of Ovidian physics. In a famous passage, Prospero explains to a bewildered Ferdinand:

> ... These our actors,
> As I foretold you, were all spirits, and
> Are melted into air, into thin air;
> And – like the baseless fabric of this vision –
> The cloud-capped towers, the gorgeous palaces,
> The solemn temples, the great globe itself,
> Yea, all which it inherit, shall dissolve,
> And, like this insubstantial pageant faded,
> Leave not a rack behind.          (4.1.148–56)

Ferdinand passionately wishes to remain in the "here" – the here of the space of the masque, the here of the space of the stage. But the surety of that space – a space that, like the land, can be measured and represented through geometry – is a partial fantasy. The vision of the masque "melts" and "dissolves" (in the recurrent vocabulary of Ovidian physics[122]). And this dissolution is promised not only for those within the play, but those within "the great globe itself." Even if the play was originally written for the Blackfriars Theater, it is difficult not to hear a metatheatrical resonance here.

I began this book with Hamlet pointing to the world around him, a world that is emphatically "here" (the Globe Theater) and simultaneously the hereafter (the heavens); within that play, this dual dynamic is reiterated as the insistent "here" signifies wooden stage, Danish dirt, and the space of purgatory. I end with Prospero's vision of his own theatrical creation, one which also has an emphatic "here": the space of the stage, Ceres's acres, the fabric of the cosmos. Like that cosmos, the world of *The Tempest* is solid and geometric even as it is labile and metamorphic. It is the paradoxical coexistence of these antithetical epistemologies that marks the supernatural environments of Shakespeare's age.

# Epilogue: Re-enchanting geography

> I have observ'd it in the Modern Writings of this sort of men . . . that they seldom or never finish a Discourse, though it be about Religion, without bringing in of Geometrical terms, especially Angles and Triangles.
>
> John Edwards, *Sermons on Special Occasions and Subjects* (1698), p. 403

In this book, I have sought to bring together the "religious turn" and the "spatial turn" of recent early modern studies. Both the study of religion and the study of space have been enlivened by an outpouring of creative scholarship, but the conversations about these topics have been taking place in different rooms, as it were. I hope to have demonstrated that in sixteenth- and seventeenth-century England, the spatial was inflected by religion, and religion was influenced by notions of space. Maps, for instance, were a way of talking about God, and demons were approached through geography.

The fact that early modern religion and early modern space have been studied more or less separately is the consequence of another metanarrative that organizes the field. In Chapter 1, I discussed how belief in the devil is positioned in a historiographical narrative of secularization. A similar – and, I would argue, related – teleological story is part of cartographic history. Often this trajectory is implicit, although at times it is overtly articulated, such as in D. K. Smith's *The Cartographic Imagination in Early Modern England*:[1]

[M]edieval conceptions of cartography primarily highlighted an emblematic sense of place rather than a mathematic or objective sense of space, and while there was evidence toward the end of the fifteenth century that an incipient awareness of spatial geography was creeping into the popular culture, the fundamentally spiritual and emblematic nature of cartographic representation remained firmly in place. But in the early sixteenth century things began to change. There were breakthroughs in the use of perspective, consistent scale, and the development and dissemination of new surveying techniques. There were improvements in woodcut printing, copperplate engraving, and the widespread proliferation of the detailed maps and views that these techniques allowed. But the key differences between fifteenth- and sixteenth-century cartography, between the medieval and early modern views of the world, were not simply in the way maps looked but in what was expected of them. Maps became more mathematically precise and spatially accurate, more capable of representing the physical world in all its volume and detail, even as a new and wide-ranging cartographic awareness spread throughout England. (pp. 41–2)

The "fundamentally spiritual ... nature of [medieval] cartographic representation" here appears to be a negative, as opposed to the "mathematic or objective sense of space" that was to become the hallmark of early modernity. This progression appears to be tagged as a positive, enlightened one, as is signaled with words such as "breakthroughs," "consistent," "development," "improvements," "precise," "accurate," "more capable," "wide-ranging ... awareness." It is "new." The passage inadvertently echoes the quotation of Jacob Burckhardt I addressed in Chapter 1, with its shift from the medieval "veil of illusion" to an "*objective* treatment and consideration ... of all the things of this world."[2]

It is this teleology that can lead Angus Fletcher to open his recent book *Time, Space, and Motion in the Age of Shakespeare* with the claim, "the Copernican Revolution and the 'New Philosophy,' as John Donne and others frequently called the new science, were so clearly *not religious in character*" (original italics).[3] But as my last chapter demonstrated, the precision of triangles did not push out the omnipresence of God. Rather, the new emphasis on geometry was often itself fundamentally spiritual. Insisting upon the segregation of religion and the spatial sciences is to insist on reading the period through a profound anachronism. As the epigraph of this chapter suggests, by the end of the seventeenth century the interweaving of theology and geometry was so pervasive as to become almost tedious.

An influential book in creating this scholarly division of space and the supernatural has been Henri Lefebvre's *The Production of Space*.[4] Lefebvre studies a process of change between the sixteenth and the nineteenth centuries, and in his account the geometric and the supernatural appear to be utterly mutually exclusive categories. Geometry comes in; the sacred goes out:

During this period the representation of space tended to dominate and subordinate a representational space, of religious origin, which was now reduced to symbolic figures, to images of Heaven and Hell, of the Devil and the angels, and so on. Tuscan painters, architects and theorists developed a representation of space – perspective ... The vanishing line, the vanishing-point and the meeting of parallel lines "at infinity" were the determinants of a representation, at once intellectual and visual, which promoted the primacy of the gaze in a kind of "logic of visualization." (pp. 40–1)

Different notions of space thus enter into a power struggle, with geometric space ultimately proving dominant, and religious space becoming subordinate. This defeated space is allowed to exist only in demarcated "preserves" we can imagine as analogous to the reservations set aside for the defeated Native Americans: "All holy or cursed places, places characterized by the presence or absence of gods ... all such places qualify as special preserves. Hence in absolute space the absolute has no place, for otherwise it would be a 'non-place'; and religio-political space has a rather strange composition, being made up of areas set apart, reserved – and so mysterious" (p. 35). Again, absolute space cannot accommodate the supernatural, so the supernatural can only be corralled, although this socio-political defeat carries its own mystical capital.

The separation of space and the sacred is closely related to another division that underwrites the dominant scholarly understanding of early modern space: the separation of subject and environment. Ricardo Padrón succinctly summarizes part of Lefebvre's argument:

Modernity naturalizes geometric, optical, isotropic space as a fundamental epistemological category and thereby gives undue authority to the abstractions of the mapmaker, the surveyor, the planner, the architect, and the like. Traditional "representational spaces" – spaces as they are perceived – such as the hearth or the geography of the sacred are correspondingly stripped of their authority. In the order of abstraction, everything comes to be understood as either a location or an object within this space, and thereby becomes amenable to systematic understanding, commodification, appropriation, or subordination by a viewing subject.[5]

This development is precisely what D. K. Smith finds in sixteenth-century England. He writes that until the publication of Saxton's county atlases, "to visualize the land, to know its shape and spatial organization, you had to see it, walk through it."[6] By contrast, "to think in terms of maps in early modern England was to reach beyond an immediate, local world of personal experience to a newly concrete understanding of abstract space. Maps became invested with the precision and objectivity of the land itself, and this burgeoning understanding of the measurability and geometrical organization of abstract space brought with it a fundamental change in spatial consciousness ... [A] growing belief in the measureability of mapped space established an epistemology of imaginative control."[7] As "belief" in maps grows (thereby pushing out medieval faith as a mode of spatial organization), so too does a sense of spatial control over the world. This control required, in part, the map to be detached from that which it represents, and the observer to be separate from the observed, as opposed to an antiquated assumption that to know space one needed "to see it, walk through it." This detachment, however, is not easily achieved when the environment in which one lives and the world that is being mapped is trinitarian, one in which God and world are integral.

The distance of subject and map can indeed lead to an "epistemology of imaginative control," and much of the scholarly work on geography to date has been concerned with aspects of social control and power. This approach, however, appears to overlook the geographic discourses that emphasize how the subject has to see the world, to walk through it. Smith takes John Gillies's notion of the "geographic imagination" and adds to it the "cartographic imagination."[8] To this we could add the "geodetic imagination." Much of the geographic literature of the period pertained to surveying, to the act of measuring the land and existing within it. This literature invites a far more phenomenological approach, as the reader is invited, even expected, to walk through the world alert to sensory experience as a means of measuring the land and experiencing the divine.[9] (Bruce Smith has recently written that another term for historical phenomenology, *pace* Timothy Morton, might be "ambient poetics."[10])

I have singled out D. K. Smith's book to use as an exemplum of a scholarly tendency not because it is a bad book, but because it is a good one. It is a fine piece of scholarship that demonstrates the dominant approach to the study of space in the last two decades. But this approach is fundamentally predicated on a working understanding of early modern space as disenchanted; of the geometric and the spiritual as antithetical concepts; and of the separation of subject and environment as a corollary of the rise of the geometric arts. These assumptions, I maintain, can be fallacious: early modern space continued to be understood as supernatural, with regular traffic of angels and demons; geometric space was understood as divine; the subject, in the trinitarian logic of perichoresis, was interconnected with God and environment. I do not mean to contend that all scholarship on early modern space is erroneous, but I do think that the recurrent pattern of telling this history – i.e. in the mid sixteenth century, geometry rapidly ascended and God bowed out – posits a transition that is at best far too abrupt, and at worst historically inaccurate. I think that we should be discussing space in much the same way that Jonathan Gil Harris has written about time. Incorporating the terminology of Michel Serres, Harris considers "the time of Shakespeare" as being polychronic and multitemporal; this time is understood as layered, or pleated, rather than linear and sequential.[11] The space of Shakespeare's time period was similarly folded, similarly polydimensional and multispatial, as the rigors of geometry and the suppleness of the supernatural coexisted in a range of relationships.

In this book, then, I have aimed to begin dismantling what has become a critical commonplace about the relationship of geometric space and the supernatural in late sixteenth- and early seventeenth-century England. More broadly, I hope to open up a discussion of early modern constructions of space that accounts for both the period's flourishing interest in things geometric and its fervent theological questioning. I hope to have shown that the absolutes of an emergent geometric space and the absolutes of the supernatural were not distinct, but intermeshed in a variety of configurations.

We can, therefore, tell a different story, one that does not position geography and cartography – or even more broadly, geometry – within an inevitable process of modern disenchantment. We can see a geometric consciousness that is also a religious one. We can see an understanding of geography that does not tend towards an objective distance between subject and the object of the map, but precisely the opposite: a sense that the subject was integrated into a divinely constructed environment, with the map as a means of interacting with that environment. We can see a geographic sensibility that is not about conferring power, but entirely the reverse: the surveyor within a divine cosmic geometry does not control the environment, but is subject to God. And we can see moments when these various, contradictory modes of consciousness, understanding, and sensibility become entangled and interwoven. This story is perhaps a strange one to tell, but it enables us to re-imagine the sixteenth and seventeenth centuries in ways that are more organic to the period.

# Notes to the text

PROLOGUE: SETTING – AND UNSETTLING – THE STAGE

1 Tom Stoppard, *Rosencrantz and Guildenstern Are Dead* (New York: Grove Press, 1967), p. 17.

2 Ann Thompson and Neil Taylor (eds.), *Hamlet*, by William Shakespeare, The Arden Shakespeare (London: Thomson Learning, 2006). All citations from the play are from this edition.

3 The word appears seven times in *Hamlet*, more than in any other Shakespearean play. Polonius uses it to signify social hierarchy ("they in France of the best rank and station" [1.3.72]); Hamlet uses it to signify decay ("'tis an unweeded garden/That grows to seed, things rank and gross in nature/Possess it merely" [1.2.135–7]); Claudius, in his description of his fratricide/regicide, uses it in a way that seems to merge both of these meanings ("O, my offence is rank: it smells to heaven" [3.3.36]).

4 J. H. Walker (ed.), *King Henry V*, by William Shakespeare, The Arden Shakespeare, Second Series (London and New York: Methuen and Co., Ltd., 1954; Routledge, 1990), Prologue, l. 13. It should be noted that the theater to which the "wooden O" refers is probably the Curtain Theatre and not the Globe, which was still under construction when *Henry V* was performed (see p. 6, n. 13).

5 E. M. W. Tillyard begins his book with this same speech, noting: "This has been taken as one of the great English versions of Renaissance humanism, an assertion of the dignity of man against the asceticisms of medieval misanthropy. Actually it is in the purest medieval tradition: Shakespeare's version of the orthodox encomia of what man, created in God's image, was like in his prelapsarian state and of what ideally he is still capable of being": *The Elizabethan World Picture* (New York: Vintage Books, 1944; [196?]), p. 3.

6 John Gillies, *Shakespeare and the Geography of Difference* (Cambridge University Press, 1994), pp. 87–9.

7 For a discussion of the cartographic implications of "The Globe," see Gillies, *Geography of Difference*, pp. 76–9. For theatrical references, see Russell West, *Spatial Representations and the Jacobean Stage: From Shakespeare to Webster* (Basingstoke and New York: Palgrave, 2002), p. 35.

8 Gillies, *Geography of Difference*, p. 35. Similarly, John Rennie Short states: "Sixteenth-century cosmography marked no sharp epistemological break between the medieval and early modern worldviews. Even the technical gaze of the sixteenth-century cosmographers was not untouched by older conceptions. A geocentric worldview, a belief in astrology and the building blocks of the four elements (earth, air, fire, and water) mingled with new forms of measurement and survey. Cosmographical texts contained both new ways of seeing the universe as well as traditional conceptions of the world": *Making Space: Revisioning the World, 1475–1600* (Syracuse University Press, 2004), p. 35.

9 "Hamlet's utterance actively gestures towards the cosmically figured architecture of the Globe Theatre itself": Gillies, *Geography of Difference*, p. 90, with a footnote to Neville Coghill, *Shakespeare's Professional Skills* (Cambridge University Press, 1964), pp. 8–9.

10 John Gillies's denial of this geography in another essay, for instance, is surprising: "Maps reproduce their own cultural niche at every moment of their cultural dissemination, including within the theater. To appreciate this, one has only to compare the ways maps are used on the Elizabethan stage with the way they are used on the medieval stage. Surviving plats … effectively figure the stage in cartographic terms, with places (Paradise, Heaven, Hell) oriented much as on contemporary *mappa mundi* … Whereas, then, stage and map tend to collapse into each other in the medieval period, they become sharply distinct in the sixteenth century": Editors' Introduction in John Gillies and Virginia Mason Vaughan (eds.), *Playing the Globe: Genre and Geography in English Renaissance Drama* (Madison: Fairleigh Dickinson University Press; London: Associated University Presses, 1998), p. 24. The representation of heaven and hell in the Globe theater might have become vertical (i.e. heaven is up and hell is down) as opposed to horizontal, and perhaps their forms are more subtle and less visible, but this carry-over from medieval staging seems obvious to me. Another example of not taking references to the "heavens" as pertaining to heaven can be found in Siobhan Keenan and Peter Davidson, "The Iconography of the Globe" in J. R. Mulryne and M. Shewring (eds.), *Shakespeare's Globe Rebuilt* (Cambridge University Press, in association with Mulryne and Shewring, 1997), p. 149. As evidence that the heavens were painted, the authors cite from *Julius Caesar* ("the skies are painted with unnumb'red sparks") and the line from *Hamlet* about "fretted with golden fire.": "In both cases, the terminology employed by Shakespeare is that of the artificer and points towards the construction of the artificial 'heavens'." Certainly this is true, but it does not mean that the lines do not *also* refer to the skies or to heaven, that they could not carry a wider range of signification.

11 William J. Lawrence, *The Physical Conditions of the Elizabethan Public Playhouse* (1927; reprint, New York: Cooper Square Publishers, Inc., 1968), pp. 109–22. See also Keenan and Davidson, "Iconography," pp. 149–50.

12 Quoted in Lawrence, *Physical Conditions*, p. 110.

13 Andrew Gurr, *The Shakespearean Stage 1574–1642*, 3rd edn. (Cambridge University Press, 1992), p. 182. Lawrence contends that: "Before 1600 only two traps were employed, one of no particular intricacy; but less than a score of years later no fewer than five were in regular use" (*Physical Conditions*, p. 10); the novelty of the theatrical technology might have made it even more visible to an early modern audience, and characters such as Lucifer in T. M.'s *The Black Book* (1604) make a point of referencing the fact that they have just popped up from below (cited in Lawrence, *Physical Conditions*, p. 7).

14 "Eschatology," according to the *OED*'s definition, is: "The department of theological science concerned with 'the four last things: death, judgement, heaven, and hell'." In conversations with scholars over the years, I have come to realize that for many the term is associated primarily with the end of days and the last judgment. While this is one facet of its meaning, I am using the word throughout this book to apply to discussions of heaven and hell more generally, not in a specifically apocalyptic way.

15 John Lear (ed.), *Kepler's Dream* [*Somnium, sive Astronomia Lunaris*], trans. Patricia Frueh Kirkwood (Berkeley and Los Angeles: University of California Press, 1965), p. 7.

16 As Margreta de Grazia has recently noted: "At several points, the dialogue, perhaps accompanied by gesture, activates the stage's eschatological layout": *Hamlet without Hamlet* (Cambridge University Press, 2007), p. 42. One such instance is when Hamlet says: "I'll speak to it, though hell itself should gape/And bid me hold my peace" (1.2.243–4), a reference to the hellmouth, a stage convention of medieval drama that continued into the sixteenth century. See Robert Lima, "The Mouth of Hell: The Iconography of Damnation on the Stage of the Middle Ages" in György E. Szőnyi (ed.), *European Iconography East and West: Selected Papers of the Szeged International Conference June 9–12, 1993* (Leiden, New York, and Cologne: E. J. Brill, 1996), pp. 35–48; and Gary D. Schmidt, *The Iconography of the Mouth of Hell: Eighth-Century Britain to the Fifteenth Century* (Selinsgrove: Susquehanna University Press; London: Associated University Presses, 1995), Ch. 6.

INTRODUCTION: THE SPACE OF THE SUPERNATURAL

1 Bruno Latour, *We Have Never Been Modern*, trans. Catherine Porter (Cambridge, Mass.: Harvard University Press, 1993), p. 3.

2 Saint Augustine, *Confessions*, trans. Garry Wills (New York: Penguin Books, 2006), p. 4.

3 *The Holy Bible*, Authorized King James Version (New York: Oxford University Press, n.d.).

4 Plato, *Timaeus and Critias*, trans. Desmond Lee (London and New York: Penguin Books, 1965; 1977), p. 45. Similarly, Aristotle declares that space is "like a vessel or container"; Aristotle, *Physics*, trans. Robin Waterfield, Oxford World's Classics (Oxford University Press, 1996), p. 88.

5 See the conclusion of Brian Greene's *The Elegant Universe: Superstrings, Hidden Dimensions, and the Quest for the Ultimate Theory* (New York: Vintage Books, 1999), p. 387.

6 Isaac Newton, *Principia*, ed. Stephen Hawking (Philadelphia and London: Running Press, 2002), p. 6.

7 Neil Smith and Cindi Katz, "Grounding Metaphor: Towards a Spatialized Politics" in Michael Katz and Steve Pile (eds.), *Place and the Politics of Identity* (London: Routledge, 1993), p. 75.

8 Henry Turner, *The English Renaissance Stage: Geometry, Poetics, and the Practical Spatial Arts 1580–1630* (Oxford University Press, 2006), p. 12.

9 Stuart Clark, *Thinking with Demons: The Idea of Witchcraft in Early Modern Europe* (Oxford University Press, 1997), pp. 151–60.

10 I do not want to suggest too strongly that the newly white-washed walls of Protestant churches instantly converted parishioners to an understanding of absolute space, an understanding which in turn precluded belief in supernatural interactions. As Peter Marshall and Alexandra Walsham remind us, while "[w]e cannot of course ignore the fact that the rise of Newtonian and Cartesian models of physics and philosophy posed grave challenges for established angelology ... [t]here was ... no inevitability that angels would vanish in the new dawn of 'rational' thought and find themselves sidelined by the 'birth of modern science'": "Migrations of Angels in the Early Modern World" in P. Marshall and A. Walsham (eds.), *Angels in the Early Modern World* (Cambridge University Press, 2006), p. 35.

11 Peter Harrison, *The Bible, Protestantism, and the Rise of Natural Science* (Cambridge University Press, 1998), p. 116; citing M. Rubin, *Corpus Christi: The Eucharist in Late Medieval Culture* (Cambridge University Press, 1991), p. 1.

12 Harrison, *The Bible*, pp. 114, 131.

13 Joseph R. Roach, *The Player's Passion: Studies in the Science of Acting* (Newark: University of Delaware Press; London and Toronto: Associated University Presses, 1985), p. 39.

14 Norbert Elias, *The Civilizing Process: The History of Manners and State Formation and Civilization*, trans. Edmund Jephcott (Oxford and Cambridge, Mass.: Blackwell, 1994), p. 211.

15 See Jonathan Sawday, *The Body Emblazoned: Dissection and the Human Body in Renaissance Culture* (London and New York: Routledge, 1995).

16 John Sutton, *Philosophy and Memory Traces: Descartes to Connectionism* (Cambridge University Press, 1998), p. 41.

17 Michael C. Schoenfeldt, *Bodies and Selves in Early Modern England: Physiology and Inwardness in Spenser, Shakespeare, Herbert, and Milton* (Cambridge University Press, 1999), pp. 3, 38.

18 Editors' Introduction in Mary Floyd-Wilson and Garrett A. Sullivan, Jr. (eds.), *Environment and Embodiment in Early Modern England* (Basingstoke and New York: Palgrave Macmillan, 2007), p. 2. Floyd-Wilson and Sullivan should be credited with fostering this line of inquiry through the wonderful

conference "Inhabiting the Body/Inhabiting the World" they organized at the University of North Carolina, Chapel Hill in 2004. This volume for Palgrave grew out of that conference, as did a special issue of *Renaissance Drama*, n.s. 35 (2006) that they also co-edited. A slightly different model of positioning the humoral body in a larger economy – that is, moving away from inwardness – is provided in Jonathan Gil Harris's *Sick Economies: Drama, Mercantilism, and Disease in Shakespeare's England* (Philadelphia: University of Pennsylvania Press, 2004). For example: "The humoral model does not cut the body off from the world. If anything, it stresses the impossibility of separating the body from the external elements on which it depends – air, food, drink, even astrological influences" (p. 14).

19 For an excellent summary of this idea in ancient and medieval thought, see Harrison, *The Bible*, pp. 44–56. The quote from Ambrose is from the *Hexameron*, and is cited in Harrison at p. 48.

20 Leonard Barkan, *Nature's Work of Art: The Human Body as Image of the World* (New Haven and London: Yale University Press, 1975), p. 14.

21 Additionally, we should note how prominently the microcosm-macrocosm homology figured in political discourse, as was emphasized long ago by E. M. W. Tillyard; see *The Elizabethan World Picture* (New York: Vintage Books, 1944; [196?]), pp. 88–91, 94–9.

22 I turn again to the description of Joseph Roach: "Each humour corresponds to both a characteristic passion and an element of nature: choler, like fire, dry and hot, fuels anger; melancholy, like earth, dry and cold, embodies grief; the sanguinary humour, like air, is moist and hot, and leads to amatory passions; the phlegmatic, like water, is wet and cold, and if not inert, shows itself as fear or astonishment. The basis for this system resided in the common-sense idea that the body is made up of the same substances found elsewhere in nature, and that order, as in the world at large, is achieved through equilibrium, balance, and proper mixture (*eukrasia*)" (*Player's Passion*, p. 39).

23 Mary Floyd-Wilson, "English Mettle" in Gail Kern Paster, Katherine Rowe, and Mary Floyd-Wilson (eds.), *Reading the Early Modern Passions: Essays in the Cultural History of Emotion* (Philadelphia: University of Pennsylvania Press, 2004), p. 134.

24 John Gillies, *Shakespeare and the Geography of Difference* (Cambridge University Press, 1994), p. 35.

25 Barkan, *Nature's Work of Art*, p. 21.

26 Barkan has a typographic error for "Helkiah," writing "Helkanah" (*Nature's Work of Art*, p. 25). For a more subtle reading of how Crooke is rhetorically positioning his work, see Katherine Rowe, *Dead Hands: Fictions of Agency, Renaissance to Modern* (Stanford University Press, 1999), p. 36.

27 For one textual example of this, see Bernhard Klein's reading of Peter Apian's *Cosmographia* (1524), which illustrates "[t]he degree to which the traditional equation between body and space – the conceptual centre of the micro/macrocosm analogy – began to collide with the contemporary perception of global space": *Maps and the Writing of Space in Early Modern England and Ireland* (Basingstoke: Palgrave, 2001), p. 26.

28 John Calvin, *Institutes of the Christian Religion*, 2 vols., ed. John T. McNeill, trans. Ford Lewis Battles (Philadelphia: The Westminster Press, 1960), I: 35, 37.

29 See Gail Kern Paster, *The Body Embarrassed: Drama and the Disciplines of Shame in Early Modern England* (Ithaca: Cornell University Press, 1993) and *Humoring the Body: Emotions and the Shakespearean Stage* (Chicago and London: The University of Chicago Press, 2004); Schoenfeldt, *Bodies and Selves*; Mary Floyd-Wilson, *English Ethnicity and Race in Early Modern Drama* (Cambridge University Press, 2003); Bruce R. Smith, *The Acoustic World of Early Modern England: Attending to the O-Factor* (Chicago and London: The University of Chicago Press, 1999).

30 Bruce R. Smith, "Premodern Sexualities," *Publication of the Modern Language Association*, 115 (2000), 325–6.

31 Smith, *Acoustic World*, p. 10.

32 In his most recent book, *The Key of Green: Passion and Perception in Renaissance Culture* (Chicago and London: The University of Chicago Press, 2009), Bruce R. Smith ends his opening paragraph with what appears to be a winking acknowledgment of the biblical verse: "'Green' invites us to consider that subjects, especially *thinking* subjects, don't exist apart from the objects amid which they live, move, and think" (p. 1). On p. 8, Smith provides another sharp synopsis of what he means by "historical phenomenology."

33 For an extended meditation on how poetry can be used in the field of philosophy of religion, see Mark R. Wynn, *Faith and Place: An Essay in Embodied Religious Epistemology* (Oxford University Press, 2009). See also his *Emotional Experience and Religious Understanding: Integrating Perception, Conception and Feeling* (Cambridge University Press, 2005), Ch. 6.

34 It should be noted that the period's pamphlet literature was also interested in the supernatural; see John Twyning's *London Dispossessed: Literature and Social Space in the Early Modern City* (Basingstoke: Macmillan Press, Ltd.; New York: St. Martin's Press, Inc., 1998), Ch. 4.

35 "Hymne to God my God, in my sicknesse" (ll. 13–15) in C. A. Patrides (ed.), *John Donne: The Complete English Poems*, Everyman Library (London and Rutland, Vt.: J. M. Dent, 1994), p. 386.

36 Galileo Galilei, *Dialogue Concerning the Two Chief World Systems: Ptolemaic and Copernican*, trans. Stillman Drake (1953; reprint, New York: The Modern Library, 2001), p. 294.

37 As the seventeenth century progressed, differing notions of space-time were taken to an extreme by religious radicals. My favorite is still the Quakers' – they went naked in an attempt to re-recreate the conditions of Eden, and conceptualized themselves as moving in a bubble of an alternate eschatological space-time continuum from their neighbors. See my *Radical Religion from Shakespeare to Milton: Figures of Nonconformity in Early Modern England* (Cambridge University Press, 2000), Ch. 6.

38 Wendy Wall, *Staging Domesticity: Household Work and English Identity in Early Modern Drama* (Cambridge University Press, 2002), p. 15.
39 Cynthia Marshall, *The Shattering of the Self: Violence, Subjectivity, and Early Modern Texts* (Baltimore and London: The Johns Hopkins University Press, 2002), pp. 2–3.
40 For a discussion of the success of catechisms, see Christopher Haigh, *The Plain Man's Pathways to Heaven: Kinds of Christianity in Post-Reformation England, 1570–1640* (Oxford University Press, 2007), pp. 27, 30.
41 Greene, *Elegant Universe*, p. 129.
42 *Ibid.*, p. 127; he attributes the coinage of the term to John Wheeler.
43 D. J. Hopkins, *City/Stage/Globe: Performance and Space in Shakespeare's London* (New York and London: Routledge, 2008), p. 52.
44 Turner, *English Renaissance Stage*, p. 159, original italics.
45 See Martin Brückner and Kristen Poole, "The Plot Thickens: Surveying Manuals, Drama, and the Materiality of Narrative Form in Early Modern England," *English Literary History*, 69 (2002), 617–48.
46 David Hillman, "*Homo Clausus* at the Theatre" in Bryan Reynolds and William N. West (eds.), *Rematerializing Shakespeare: Authority and Representation on the Early Modern English Stage* (Basingstoke and New York: Palgrave Macmillan, 2005), p. 174.
47 The reference is to Jonas Barish, *The Antitheatrical Prejudice* (Berkeley: University of California Press, 1981), pp. 80–131. For a fascinating discussion of "[t]he particularly Aristotelian physics of the shapeshifting actor," see William N. West, "What's the Matter with Shakespeare? Physics, Identity, Playing" in Carla Mazzio (ed.), *Shakespeare and Science, South Central Review*, 26 (2009), 103–26 (see 116 in particular).

I    THE DEVIL'S IN THE ARCHIVE: OVIDIAN
PHYSICS AND 'DOCTOR FAUSTUS'

1 I am, perhaps, presumptuous in my assumption of disbelief. I may well have readers who do believe in the devil. Statistically, the odds are high, at least in the United States. Most Americans (64 percent) believe in hell; in 1997, nearly half of the people who said they believe in hell agreed with the statement: "Hell is a real place where people suffer eternal fiery torments" (and is thus, I presume, a place that requires the devil and his minions); see Jeffery L. Sheler, "Hell Hath No Fury," *U.S. News & World Report*, 31 (January 2000), 45, 47. But since I do not anticipate that all Americans will be reading this chapter, and since I assume that within the rarified readership of academia the percentage of people who believe in the devil is much lower than the national average, I will work with the premise that most of my readers don't believe in the devil, at least not in the same way as, say, Cotton Mather would have.
    Throughout this essay, I refer to "the devil" in the singular, although I recognize that the devil has a long history of being both singular and plural. On the myriad names for the devil, see Jeffrey Burton Russell, *Lucifer: The*

*Devil in the Middle Ages* (Ithaca and London: Cornell University Press, 1984), pp. 248–9.

2 Keith Thomas, *Religion and the Decline of Magic* (New York: Charles Scribner's Sons, 1971), p. 471. Thomas's source for the quote is Edward Rogers, *Some Account of the Life and Opinions of a Fifth-Monarchy Man* (London: Longmans, Green, Reader and Dyer, 1867), p. 13.

3 For an extensive discussion of this tradition, see Don LePan, *The Cognitive Revolution in Western Culture*, vol. I, *The Birth of Expectation* (Basingstoke and London: Macmillan, 1989), Chs 1–3. LePan is a forerunner in calling for a recognition of historically variant cognitive processing, even as he repeatedly affirms that medieval and early modern thought was childish (see e.g. pp. 66–8).

4 Jacob Burckhardt, *The Civilization of the Renaissance in Italy*, trans. Benjamin Nelson (New York: Harper Colophon Books, 1958), vol. I, p. 143. The emphases are originally Burckhardt's; see *Die Cultur der Renaissance in Italien* (Leipzig: E. U. Seemann, 1869), p. 104.

5 For a discussion of the developmental teleology in Elias's *The Civilizing Process*, Weber's *The Protestant Ethic and the Spirit of Capitalism*, and Taylor's *Sources of the Self*, see Lyndal Roper, *Oedipus and the Devil: Witchcraft, Sexuality and Religion in Early Modern Europe* (London and New York: Routledge, 1994), pp. 4–7. As much as Roper moves away from the traditional Burckhardt-Weber-Elias model of human development, her own psychoanalytical approach and the title's emphasis on the Oedipal continue to locate the supernatural within a discourse of childhood development.

6 For a discussion of the politics of the term, see Margreta de Grazia, "World Pictures, Modern Periods, and the Early Stage" in John D. Cox and David Scott Kastan (eds.), *A New History of Early English Drama* (New York: Columbia University Press, 1997), esp. pp. 9–13. See also de Grazia, "The Modern Divide: From Either Side," *Journal of Medieval and Early Modern Studies*, 37 (2007), 453–67; Douglas Bruster, "Shakespeare and the End of History: Period as Brand Name" in Hugh Grady (ed.), *Shakespeare and Modernity: Early Modern to Millennium* (London and New York: Routledge, 2000), pp. 176–85.

7 This tendency to patronize, or to find risible, earlier understandings of the demonic finds its origins in early modern writing itself. See Aron Gurevich, trans. János M. Bak and Paul A. Hollingsworth, *Medieval Popular Culture: Problems of Belief and Perception* (Cambridge University Press; Paris: Editions de la Maison des Science de l'Homme, 1988), p. 184.

8 Max Weber, *The Sociology of Religion*, 4th edn., trans. Ephraim Fischoff (Boston: Beacon Press, 1922; 1993), p. 1.

9 Thomas's work is punctuated by references to Africa or "primitive" beliefs, such as his comment early in the book: "The line between magic and religion is one which it is impossible to draw in many primitive societies; it is equally difficult to recognise in medieval England" (p. 50).

10 A central essay in this regard is Greenblatt's "Shakespeare and the Exorcists" in *Shakespearean Negotiations: The Circulation of Social Energy in Renaissance*

*England* (Berkeley and Los Angeles: University of California Press, 1988), pp. 94–128. For a critique of this approach, see Jean-Christophe Mayer, *Shakespeare's Hybrid Faith: History, Religion and the Stage* (New York: Palgrave Macmillan, 2006), pp. 9–11.

11 For a thoughtful survey of recent work on religion, see Ken Jackson and Arthur F. Marotti, "The Turn to Religion in Early Modern English Studies," *Criticism*, 46 (2004), 167–90; they offer a succinct account of the state of the "secularization thesis" in current scholarship at 172–4.

12 Jackson and Marotti, "Turn to Religion," 167.

13 I admittedly put my first book in this category; see *Radical Religion from Shakespeare to Milton: Figures of Nonconformity in Early Modern England* (Cambridge University Press, 2000).

14 See Debora Kuller Shuger, *Political Theologies in Shakespeare's England: the Sacred and the State in* Measure for Measure (Basingstoke and New York: Palgrave, 2001); Julia Reinhard Lupton, *Citizen-Saints: Shakespeare and Political Theology* (The University of Chicago Press, 2005).

15 Philip Lorenz, "Introduction," *English Language Notes*, 44 (2008), 142. The comment comes in a summary of Kenneth S. Jackson's essay "'More Other than You Desire' in *The Merchant of Venice*," *English Language Notes*, 44 (2006), 151–6. See also Lorenz, "Notes on the 'Religious Turn': Mystery, Metaphor, Medium," *English Language Notes*, 44 (2006), 163–74, esp. 164.

16 Katharine Eisaman Maus, "Sorcery and Subjectivity in Early Modern Discourses of Witchcraft" in Carla Mazzio and Douglas Trevor (eds.), *Historicism, Psychoanalysis, and Early Modern Culture* (New York and London: Routledge, 2000), p. 326. For an example of an analysis that appears sympathetic to Scot, see Stephen Greenblatt, "Shakespeare Bewitched" in Jeffrey N. Cox and Larry J. Reynolds (eds.), *New Historical Literary Study: Essays on Reproducing Texts, Representing History* (Princeton University Press, 1993), pp. 114–18.

17 Stuart Clark, *Thinking with Demons: The Idea of Witchcraft in Early Modern Europe* (Oxford University Press, 1997), p. 182.

18 Thomas McAlindon, *Doctor Faustus: Divine in Show* (New York: Twayne Publishers, 1994), p. 33.

19 John D. Cox, *The Devil and the Sacred in English Drama, 1350–1642* (Cambridge University Press, 2000), p. 1.

20 See John Parker's review in *Christianity and Literature*, 52 (2003), 262–5.

21 E. K. Chambers, *The Elizabethan Stage* (Oxford: Clarendon Press, 1923).

22 Chambers, *The Elizabethan Stage*, vol. III, p. 423.

23 Chambers cites three historical documents of this event (vol. III, pp. 423–4); Cox notes that there was an additional document and cites an article by Eric Rasmussen (*The Devil and the Sacred*, p. 233, n. 35), but Rasmussen actually argues that the reference to on-stage devils in *The Black Book* was most likely *not* to a production of *Faustus*; see Rasmussen, "*The Black Book* and the Date of *Doctor Faustus*," *Notes and Queries*, 235 (n.s. 37), 170.

24 See, for instance, John Russell Brown, "Marlowe and the Actors," *Tulane Drama Review*, 8.4 (1964), 157; and Michael Goldman, "Marlowe and the

Histrionics of Ravishment" in Alvin Kernan (ed.), *Two Renaissance Myth-makers: Christopher Marlowe and Ben Jonson. Selected Papers from the English Institute, 1975–76* (Baltimore and London: The Johns Hopkins University Press, 1977), p. 40.

25 The body of work on European and American witchcraft is extensive, and I will just cite some representative titles here. See, for example, Paul Boyer and Stephen Nissenbaum, *Salem Possessed: The Social Origins of Witchcraft* (Cambridge, Mass.: Harvard University Press, 1974); John Putnam Demos, *Entertaining Satan: Witchcraft and the Culture of Early New England* (Oxford University Press, 1982); Alan Macfarlane, *Witchcraft in Tudor and Stuart England* (New York and Evanston: Harper and Row, 1970); H. R. Trevor-Roper, *The European Witch-Craze of the Sixteenth and Seventeenth Centuries and Other Essays* (New York: Harper Torchbooks, 1956; 1969); Richard Weisman, *Witchcraft, Magic, and Religion in 17th-Century Massachusetts* (Amherst: University of Massachusetts Press, 1984).

26 Again, I offer a sampling of representative titles: Anne Llewellyn Barstow, *Witchcraze: A New History of the European Witch Hunts* (San Francisco: HarperSanFrancisco, 1994); Carol F. Karlsen, *The Devil in the Shape of a Woman: Witchcraft in Colonial New England* (New York: Vintage Books, 1989); Elizabeth Reis, *Damned Women: Sinners and Witches in Puritan New England* (Ithaca and London: Cornell University Press, 1997); Lyndal Roper, *Oedipus and the Devil*, cited at n. 5 above.

27 See Luke Wilson, *Theaters of Intention: Drama and the Law in Early Modern England* (Stanford University Press, 2000), Ch. 5.

28 Sigmund Freud, "A Seventeenth-Century Demonological Neurosis" in James Strachey (ed.), *The Standard Edition of the Complete Psychological Works of Sigmund Freud* (London: The Hogarth Press; Toronto: Clarke, Irwin and Co., 1981; 1961), vol. XIX, p. 72.

29 Freud, "Demonological Neurosis," p. 72.

30 Freud thanks Dr. Payer-Thurn of the Fideikommissbibliothek for his help in studying the manuscript, and points out that Payer-Thurn was drawn to the document for its parallels with the story of Faust (p. 73).

31 Peter Gay, *A Godless Jew: Freud, Atheism, and the Making of Psychoanalysis* (New Haven and London: Yale University Press; Cincinnati: Hebrew Union College Press, 1987), pp. 11–12.

32 Bruce R. Smith, "Premodern Sexualities," *Publication of the Modern Language Association*, 115 (2000), 325–6.

33 This and all citations from David Bevington and Eric Rasmussen (eds.), *Doctor Faustus*, by Christopher Marlowe, Oxford Drama Library (Oxford: Clarendon Press, 1995). I will be using the B-text, although virtually all of the passages cited are identical in A and B. Here, 2.1.30–75.

34 The B-text in the Bevington and Rasmussen edition has "old wives' tables," although the A-text has "tales." Since other editions are consistent in "tales," and since Bevington and Ramussen do not gloss "tables," I am assuming that "tables" is a typographic error.

35 The historian's tendency to present demonic evidence in terms of fiction or
narrative is illustrated in a quick study of Roper's and Thomas's texts. Roper
does not take any of the witches' testimonies as evidence of a "real" encounter
with the devil: "[I]t is hard to know how to interpret documents which we do
not believe to be factual. But witchcraft confessions and accusations are not
products of realism, and they cannot be analysed with the methods of
historical realism" (*Oedipus and the Devil*, p. 202). Instead, her entire
approach assumes these particular historical documents to be a form of
narrative. She states that we must "attend to [their] imaginative themes"
and "investigate two sides of the story" (*Oedipus and the Devil*, p. 202).
Throughout, Roper speaks of the women's accounts as "fantasy" (p. 227),
invokes similes such as "[l]ike the fairies of fairytale who are not invited to the
baptism" (p. 209), and draws analogies with "the tendency in folktale to
populate a story with evil stepmothers" (p. 217). She invokes the theatrical as
well, referring to "a certain kind of psychic dramatic script" (p. 215), arguing
that "[i]nterrogation for witchcraft ... offered the accused a theatrical opportunity to recount and restage ... conflicts" and asking, "But what are the
themes of these dramas?" (p. 232). Roper periodically stops to ponder the
reality factor, commenting that "[t]here is no mileage ... in the usual
historical strategy of teasing out the 'real' from the fantastic elements in this
account. We cannot isolate the point at which events which we know to be
'real' ... end, and where the fantastic begins" (p. 233). This difficulty arises
from "another salient feature of difference in seventeenth-century witch
narratives: the role of the Devil. To us, the fantasies which surround him
seem clearly part of the realm of the imaginary, more definitively unreal than
the material I have been describing. But to them he was part of the real
world" (p. 233). This admission of reality, however, is almost immediately
undermined by the subsequent claim that "[b]ecoming a witch meant
engaging in an intimate relationship, usually sexual, with the Devil *as a
character*, and consequently, its discovery entailed the analysis of the well-
springs of the witch's own personality, motives, and emotions" (p. 234, my
emphasis). The witch's testimony is thus quickly converted back into fictional, narrative terms, offering up a text rich with psychoanalytic potential.

   Although Roper and Thomas present wildly disparate modes of historiography, they share this propensity to fictionalize historical documents
pertaining to the demonic. In his discussion of the devil, Thomas is clear,
even emphatic, about the narrative qualities of these sources: "Medieval
preachers enlivened their sermons with terrifying *stories* of the Devil's
repeated appearances" (p. 470); "Influential preachers [of the Reformation]
filled the ears of their hearers with *tales* of diabolic intervention in daily
life" (p. 471); "*Stories* of Satan's personal appearance" was cited by many
(p. 472); "Most of these *anecdotes*" pertained to those who invoked the
Devil in conversation (p. 472); "Such Faustian *legends* were in common
circulation ... They made excellent cautionary *tales*" (p. 473); the diarist
Oliver Heywood "recorded the *story* of the boy who, having read the *story* of
Faustus, decided to invoke the Devil" (p. 473); "The *stories* told about his

intervention in daily affairs showed him punishing perjurers" (p. 476) (all emphases mine). The devil thus moves freely through a variety of narrative genres: legend, drama, morality tales, gossip. How do we reconcile this fictional, even literary quality of the devil's appearance with what Thomas discerns as a literal early modern truth? "For most men the literal reality of demons seemed a fundamental article of faith" (p. 475). Literary scholars might gripe that their historian counterparts often fail to see the fiction in the archives (to borrow the title from Natalie Zemon Davis's book), that they fail to attend to the vicissitudes of representation in their textual harvesting of facts. In Thomas (as in Roper), we find the opposite proclivity, as he positions texts originally perceived as fact – "the literal reality" – in terms of fiction.

36 Stephen Greenblatt, *Hamlet in Purgatory* (Princeton and Oxford: Princeton University Press, 2001), p. 35.

37 Greenblatt, *Hamlet in Purgatory*, p. 47.

38 Bruce R. Smith, "Introduction," *Shakespeare Studies*, 29 (2001), 22. Smith is developing the idea from Michael C. Schoenfeldt, *Bodies and Selves in Early Modern England: Physiology and Inwardness in Spenser, Shakespeare, Herbert, and Milton* (Cambridge University Press, 1999), p. 8. Gail Kern Paster also argues that language which is "bodily or emotional figuration for us ... was the literal stuff of physiological theory for early modern scriptors of the body": "Nervous Tension," in David Hillman and Carla Mazzio (eds.), *The Body in Parts: Fantasies of Corporeality in Early Modern Europe* (London and New York: Routledge, 1997), p. iii. It should be pointed out that this distinction of metaphor and the materially "real" was being discussed within the early modern period as well. In *A Discourse of the Subtill Practises of Deuilles by VVitches and Sorcerers* (1587), George Gifford answers objections "that the Deuill is called a Serpent by an Allegorie, and therefore what necessity to take it there of a beast?" with the response: "I answere that the Deuil indeed is by a metaphor called a serpent in many places of holy scripture. But doth it therefore follow that in this place [i.e. the Garden of Eden] was none but he?" (sig. F3ʳ).

39 Jonathan Bate, *Shakespeare and Ovid* (Oxford: Clarendon Press; New York: Oxford University Press, 1993), p. 28; Lynn Enterline, *The Rhetoric of the Body from Ovid to Shakespeare* (Cambridge University Press, 2000), p. 23.

40 The reference is to a song, "Carmen de Pulice," "popularly attributed to Ovid, although it is probably medieval in origin"; Roma Gill (ed.), *The Complete Works of Christopher Marlowe*, vol. II, *Doctor Faustus* (Oxford: Clarendon Press, 1990), p. 76.

41 See John Frederick Nims (ed.), *Ovid's Metamorphoses: The Arthur Golding Translation 1567* (Philadelphia: Paul Dry Books, 2000), VIII.264 *passim*, V.605 *passim*.

42 See William Godwin, *Lives of the Necromancers* (London: Frederick J. Mason, 1834), p. 84. For the incident with the dog, see Alister Cameron, *The Pythagorean Background of the Theory of Recollection* (Menasha, Wisc.: George Banta Publishing Co., 1938), p. 12.

43 Sig. A5ᵛ. Quoted in Paul H. Kocher, *Science and Religion in Elizabethan England* (San Marino: The Huntington Library, 1953), p. 151.

44 We are, in fundamental, cognitive ways, still within a Cartesian and Newtonian world; we trade in real estate, for example, conceptualized in terms of square and cubic footage, and we understand physics as the workings of formulae. It might be said that modernity has tempered, qualified, or dismissed the Cartesian self and the Newtonian universe: Freud brings mind and body into dialogue, Einstein shifts the universe from absolutism to relativity. But Freud's seminal essay on the unconscious, "The Uncanny," opens by defining ego development as a process of the self "mark[ing] itself off sharply from the external world," and Einstein's famous formula of $E=mc^2$ has become an iconic reminder that the universe is understood through mathematical certitude. Sigmund Freud, "The Uncanny" in James Strachey (ed.), *The Standard Edition of the Complete Psychological Works of Sigmund Freud* (London: The Hogarth Press, 1955; 1981), vol. XVII, p. 236. In a different version of this essay, I explore this idea more fully; see my "Physics Divined: The Science of Calvin, Hooker, and *Macbeth*," in *Shakespeare and Science*, Carla Mazzio (ed.), *South Central Review*, 26.1–2 (2009), 127–52. It might also be said that quantum mechanics and the advent of string theory are restructuring how we understand physics and space, but to date I would argue that these concepts remain, for most, abstract rather than experiential. See also my related article, "Psychologizing Physics," *Shakespeare Studies*, 33 (2005), 95–100.

45 See the essays in Gail Kern Paster, Katherine Rowe, and Mary Floyd-Wilson (eds.), *Reading the Early Modern Passions: Essays in the Cultural History of Emotion* (Philadelphia: University of Pennsylvania Press, 2004).

46 Again, this issue is addressed in many of the essays in Mary Floyd-Wilson and Garrett A. Sullivan, Jr. (eds.), *Environment and Embodiment in Early Modern England* (Basingstoke and New York: Palgrave Macmillan, 2007).

47 This is the larger argument of Mary Floyd-Wilson's *English Ethnicity and Race in Early Modern Drama* (Cambridge University Press, 2003).

48 See Reginald Scot, *The Discoverie of Witchcraft* (New York: Dover Publications, Inc., 1930; 1972), p. 6; Johann Weyer, [*De praestigiis daemonum*, 1583], George Mora *et al.* (eds.), *Witches, Devils, and Doctors in the Renaissance* (Binghamton, New York: Medieval & Renaissance Texts & Studies, 1991), p. 165.

49 Stevie Simkin, *A Preface to Marlowe* (Harlow, UK: Longman, 2000), p. 99.

50 Clark, *Thinking with Demons*, p. 168.

51 Clark, *ibid.*, p. 156.

52 See Clark, *ibid.*, Part Two.

53 Clark, *ibid.*, p. 191; Charles Webster, *From Paracelsus to Newton: Magic and the Making of Modern Science* (Cambridge University Press, 1982), p. 82.

54 Clark, *ibid.*, pp. 191–2.

55 John Cotta, *The Triall of Witch-craft, Shewing the Trve and Right Methode of the Discouery*, facsimile reprint (Amsterdam: Theatrum Orbis Terrarum Ltd.; New York: Da Capo Press, 1968).

56 Clark, *Thinking with Demons*, p. 192. The preceding explanations of meta-morphosis are also found on this page, and attributed to their various sources.

57 Clark, *Thinking with Demons*, p. 167.

58 Maus, "Sorcery and Subjectivity," p. 330.

59 For an explanation of the function of animal transformations, see Wayne Shumaker, *The Occult Sciences in the Renaissance: A Study in Intellectual Patterns* (Berkeley: University of California Press, 1972), p. 93.

60 Such accounts are not only found in fiction; in *De praestigiis daemonum* (1583), Weyer, a skeptic voice within the period, relates matter-of-factly an instance of a monk's ill-considered contract being retrieved from hell (p. 505).

61 Brian Easlea, *Witch-hunting, Magic and the New Philosophy: An Introduction to the Debates of the Scientific Revolution 1450–1750* (Brighton: The Harvester Press and Atlantic Highlands: Humanities Press, 1980), p. 111.

62 Cynthia Marshall, *The Shattering of the Self: Violence, Subjectivity, and Early Modern Texts* (Baltimore and London: The Johns Hopkins University Press, 2002), p. 2; Jonathan Sawday, *The Body Emblazoned: Dissection and the Human Body in Renaissance Culture* (London and New York: Routledge, 1995), p. ix.

63 Smith, "Premodern Sexualities," 326.

64 The fullest exploration of the reciprocity of environment and humoralism is Floyd-Wilson's *English Ethnicity*, cited at n. 47 above.

65 Leonard Barkan, *The Gods Made Flesh: Metamorphosis and the Pursuit of Paganism* (New Haven and London: Yale University Press, 1986), p. 30.

66 Gail Kern Paster, "Melancholy Cats, Lugged Bears, and Early Modern Cosmology: Reading Shakespeare's Psychological Materialism across the Species Barrier" in Paster, Rowe, and Floyd-Wilson (eds.), *Reading the Early Modern Passions*, p. 116.

67 Here are a few Shakespearean examples of Ovidian physics. Antony: "Let Rome in Tiber melt, and the wide arch/Of the ranged empire fall. Here is my space./Kingdoms are clay" (*Antony and Cleopatra*, 1.1.35–7). King Henry IV: "Make mountains level, and the continent,/Weary of solid firmness, melt itself/Into the sea" (*Henry IV, Part II*, 3.1.46–8). Montano: "If it ha' ruffianed so upon the sea,/What ribs of oak, when mountains melt on them,/Can hold the mortise?" (*Othello*, 2.1.7–9). Lucrece: "For stones dissolved to water do convert./O, if no harder than a stone thou art,/Melt at my tears, and be compassionate" (*Rape of Lucrece*, 592–4). Venus: "My flesh is soft and plump, my marrow burning./My smooth moist hand, were it with thy hand felt,/Would in thy palm dissolve, or seem to melt" (*Venus and Adonis*, 142–4).

68 Rogers, *Some Account*, p. 14.

69 Lorraine Daston, "Marvelous Facts and Miraculous Evidence in Early Modern Europe" in James Chandler, Arnold I. Davidson, and Harry Har-ootunian (eds.), *Questions of Evidence: Proof, Practice, and Persuasion across the Disciplines* (Chicago and London: The University of Chicago Press, 1994), p. 272.

70 Thomas Sprat, *History of the Royal Society*, ed. Jackson I. Cope and Harold Whitmore Jones (Saint Louis: Washinton University Studies, 1958), pp. 61–2.

## 2 SCENE AT THE DEATHBED: 'ARS MORIENDI,' 'OTHELLO,' AND ENVISIONING THE SUPERNATURAL

1 Bernard Spivack, *Shakespeare and the Allegory of Evil: The History of a Metaphor in Relation to His Major Villains* (New York: Columbia University Press, 1958), p. 452.

2 See Samuel Y. Edgerton, Jr., *The Renaissance Discovery of Linear Perspective* (New York: Basic Books, 1975; Harper and Row, 1976).

3 Edgerton, *Renaissance Discovery*, p. 164.

4 Julie Stone Peters, *Theatre of the Book 1480–1880: Print, Text, and Performance in Europe* (Oxford University Press, 2000), p. 191. See, more broadly, pp. 191–4.

5 See Stephen Orgel and Roy Strong, *Inigo Jones: The Theatre of the Stuart Court* (London: Sotheby Parke Bernet; Berkeley and Los Angeles: University of California Press, 1973), and Lauren Shohet, *Reading Masques: The English Masque and Public Culture in the Seventeenth Century* (Oxford University Press, 2010).

6 Edgerton, *Renaissance Discovery*, p. 164. See also Peters, *Theatre of the Book*, p. 191.

7 Stephen Greenblatt, *Shakespearean Negotiations: The Circulation of Social Energy in Renaissance England* (Berkeley and Los Angeles: University of California Press, 1988), pp. 110–11.

8 Edgerton, *Renaissance Discovery*, p. 7.

9 See e.g. Lyle Massey, *Picturing Space, Displacing Bodies: Anamorphosis in Early Modern Theories of Perspective* (University Park, Penn.: The Pennsylvania State University Press, 2007).

10 The phrase is Yeats's, from "Sailing to Byzantium."

11 For the connection between the Vice and devils, see John D. Cox, *The Devil and the Sacred in English Drama, 1350–1642* (Cambridge University Press, 2000), pp. 76–81, and Leah Scragg, "Iago – Vice or Devil?," *Shakespeare Survey*, 21 (1968), 53–65.

12 D. J. Hopkins, *City/Stage/Globe: Performance and Space in Shakespeare's London* (New York and London: Routledge, 2008), p. 23. See my longer discussion of Hopkins's work in the Introduction, pp. 21–2.

13 All citations of the play are from E. A. J. Honigmann (ed.), *Othello*, The Arden Shakespeare, Third Series (London: Thomson, 1999; 2002).

14 Bettie Anne Doebler, "Othello's Angels: The *Ars Moriendi*," *English Literary History*, 34 (1967), 165.

15 For histories of the *ars moriendi* tradition, see Mary Catharine O'Connor, *The Art of Dying Well: The Development of the* Ars Moriendi (New York: Columbia University Press, 1942); Nancy Lee Beaty, *The Craft of Dying:*

*A Study in the Literary Tradition of the* Ars Moriendi *in England* (New Haven and London: Yale University Press, 1970); David William Atkinson, *The English* ars moriendi, Renaissance and Baroque Studies and Texts, vol. V, Eckhard Bernstein (ed.) (New York: Peter Lang, 1992), Introduction; Donald F. Duclow, "*Everyman* and the *Ars moriendi*: Fifteenth-Century Ceremonies of Dying," in *Fifteenth-Century Studies*, vol. VI, Guy R. Mermier and Edelgard E. DuBruck (eds.) (n.p.: Michigan Consortium for Medieval and Early Modern Studies, 1983), 93–113. For the *ars moriendi* in their medieval context, see Paul Binski, *Medieval Death: Ritual and Representation* (London: British Museum Press, 1996), esp. pp. 40–3.

16 See Eamon Duffy, *The Stripping of the Altars: Traditional Religion in England c. 1400–c. 1580* (New Haven and London: Yale University Press, 1992), p. 316. Ralph Houlbrooke notes that these temptations persist in Richard Baxter's "Directions to the Sick" in his *Christian Directory* (1673): *Death, Religion and the Family in England 1480–1750* (Oxford: Clarendon Press, 1998), p. 175.

17 For a discussion of women and the *ars moriendi*, see Patricia Phillippy, *Women, Death and Literature in Post-Reformation England* (Cambridge University Press, 2002), Ch. 7; Mary Ellen Lamb, "The Countess of Pembroke and the Art of Dying" in Mary Beth Rose (ed.), *Women in the Middle Ages and the Renaissance* (Syracuse University Press, 1986), pp. 207–26; and Houlbrooke, *Death, Religion and the Family*, p. 185.

18 In addition to the images reproduced here, see as a sampling Duffy, *Stripping of the Altars*, plates 115–19; Lionel Cust, *The Master E. S. and the "Ars Moriendi": A Chapter in the History of Engraving during the XVth Century* (Oxford: Clarendon Press, 1898), pp. 25, 27, 29, 31, 33, 35, 40, 42, 44, 46, 48, 50, 52, 54, 56, 58, 60. See also *The Complaynt of the Soule* (1532), STC 5610.

19 The overwhelming majority of sixteenth-century *ars moriendi* texts emphasize the devil's reality. That the demons in Pynson's *The Art and Crafte to Knowe Well to Dye* (1495) are assumed to be an actual presence becomes clear when it is recommended that *Moriens* say the crede, "To the ende ... that the deuylles which haue horroure to here it be put aback and dryuene awaye" (sig. a2ʳ); or when holy water is recommended "to the ende that the deuylles be putt a backe fro[m] them" (sig. b2ᵛ); or when at the end of the text Satan flees back "into that stynkyng prison of derkenesse eternall" (sig. b6ʳ). So too *The Maner to Dye Well* (1578) emphasizes the devil's role at the deathbed: "The diuel doth with al his engines and snares seeke to intrap mans Soule at the very howre of death" (sig. E2ᵛ). The devil's physicality is manifest in the fact that the demons arrive bearing books, an external, physical log of *Moriens*'s iniquities: "A number of Deuilles bringing with them great bookes, in which are written the offences of man, and they claime those whose sinnes are

written therein, and they will violentlie draw with them both their soules and bodies to hel" (sig. A2ᵛ). Peter of Lucca, in *A Dialogue of Dying Wel* (translated by the recusant Richard Verstegan in 1603), gives a face to these demons, describing how the soul "[sees] the divels appeare before her with moste foule and vglie shapes, like [fierce] lyons watching to deuour her" (sig. C7ʳ).

20 William Weston, *An Autobiography from the Jesuit Underground*, trans. Philip Caraman (New York: Farrar, Straus and Cudahy, 1955), pp. 142–3.

21 Aron Gurevich, *Medieval Popular Culture: Problems of Belief and Perception*, trans. János M. Bak and Paul A. Hollingsworth (Cambridge University Press; Paris: Editions de la Maison des Sciences de l'Homme, 1988), pp. 186–7. After "only to the artist," Gurevich footnotes A. Teneti, *La vie et la mort à travers l'art du XVe siècle* (Paris, 1952) (no page).

22 Houlbrooke, *Death, Religion and the Family*, p. 151.

23 Erasmus repeatedly portrays the demonic encounter in physical terms. He describes how Biblical sayings can help *Moriens* fend off despair, "thoughe the hole route of euyls with al the diuels in hel shuld inuade him" (sig. A8ᵛ); he warns how the devil will "layith about him with all his engins and falsities" (sig. C5ᵛ); he notes that in death "we must fight hande to hande, nor there is no skypping away" (sig. D6ᵛ). Erasmus advises the dying man to gaze steadfastly on the crucifix so that "the venomous bytynges of the sleynge spirites shal not noye hym" (sig. Fʳ), and so that he can focus his attention and block his ears when "[t]he dyuel barketh ayenst vs such thinges as wold brynge man downe to desperation" (sig. Fᵛ), "howe moche so euer that our enemy the dyuell leapeth aboute, how moch so euer he inuadeth vs" (sig. F3ᵛ). Citations are from Desiderius Erasmus, *Preparation to Deathe* (1538), facsimile reprint (Amsterdam: Theatrum Orbis Terrarum, Ltd.; Norwood, N.J.: Walter J. Johnson, Inc., 1975).

24 We find the inverse of Katherine's dialogue with the devil in John More's *A Liuely Anatomie of Death* (1596). Here, it is the devil's lines which we hear while *Moriens's* responses are merely supplied as general directives: "First therefore in this our preparation, let vs arme our selues against these temptations, with which both diuell, world, and flesh, will mightily assaile vs. What man (saith the deuill) wilt thou dye? why then, beholde the company of thy sinnes, the wrath of God, the graue, and hell are ready to deuoure thee: the Law is thy Iudge which doth condemne thee. To these temptations of the deuill we must oppose Christes righteousnesse, satisfactions, and merits, in which God holdeth himselfe fullye appeased. The world it setteth abroche his baites. What, wilt thou dy (O man) why see thy goodly buildings, thy bags of golde, thy landes and liuings, thy rents and reuenues, thy pastime and thy pleasures, thy Iewels, and thy treasures, thy delights, and all that thy heart desireth" (sig. E1ᵛ-E2ʳ). Another dialogue with the devil appears in *A Brief Discovrse of the Christian Life and Death, of Mistris Katherin Brettergh* (1612), pp. 13–15, analyzed by Nathan Johnstone in *The Devil and Demonism in Early Modern England*

(Cambridge University Press, 2006), p. 130. In Johnstone's rationalist reading, the demonic dialogue "might also be a source of strength for the tempted and those who watched over them. For it could dispel the tyranny intrusive thoughts exercised over the conscience by identifying lines of defence and counter-argument" (p. 130). Although I am focusing here on devils, angels were also presumed to be present, an idea that from the 1550s to the 1650s "persists as a tremulous subtext of Protestant writing on the art of dying": Peter Marshall, "Angels Around the Deathbed: Variations on a Theme in the English Art of Dying" in Peter Marshall and Alexandra Walsham (eds.), *Angels in the Early Modern World* (Cambridge University Press, 2006), p. 95.

25 Houlbrooke, *Death, Religion and the Family*, p. 148.

26 Marshall, "Angels Around the Deathbed," p. 84.

27 Marshall, "Angels Around the Deathbed," p. 91. He continues: "In mature Protestant soteriology, the grace of God was simply irresistible: the 'elect' could not fall away at the last moment, and did not require a panoply of ritual support to help them seize an offer of salvation which it lay in their power to refuse. In the course of the Tudor Reformations, therefore, the elaborate 'last rites' of the medieval Catholic Church were radically curtailed, and the process of dying was reconceived as an opportunity for giving expression to the effectual faith of a life well lived."

28 Houlbrooke, *Death, Religion and the Family*, p. 157.

29 I am citing throughout from Atkinson's edition of the original 1561 text in *The English* ars moriendi; here, p. 103.

30 Houlbrooke, *Death, Religion and the Family*, p. 165. For a textual example, see Samuel Ward, *The Life of Faith in Death. Exemplified in the Liuing Speeches of Dying Christians* (1622).

31 As Phoebe S. Spinrad has discussed, the need for long declarations of faith was a result of the Reformation and a proliferation of creeds. Whereas the medieval *Moriens* would simply be asked basic questions to which he could respond "ye" or "nay," by the middle of the sixteenth century lengthy, detailed credos were being represented as de rigueur: *The Summons of Death on the Medieval and Renaissance Stage* (Columbus: Ohio State University Press, 1987), pp. 40–1.

32 Johnstone, *The Devil and Demonism*, p. 137.

33 Philippe Ariès, *The Hour of Our Death: The Classic History of Western Attitudes toward Death over the Last One Thousand Years*, trans. Helen Weaver (New York: Barnes and Noble, 1977; 2000), p. 107 – see also p. 108; Duffy, *Stripping of the Altars*, p. 317; Houlbrooke, *Death, Religion and the Family*, pp. 161, 158, 188; Duclow, "*Everyman* and the *Ars moriendi*," p. 103.

34 Houlbrooke, *Death, Religion and the Family*, pp. 194–5. See also Ariès, *Hour of Death*, pp. 18–19.

35 David Cressy, *Birth, Marriage and Death: Ritual, Religion, and the Life-Cycle in Tudor and Stuart England* (Oxford University Press, 1997), p. 391. See also Houlbrooke, *Death, Religion and the Family*, p. 156.

36 The proliferation of *ars moriendi* texts in early modern England must be considered not simply as the renovation of a medieval genre, but as participating in the emerging literature of self-fashioning. We might mentally shelve the *ars moriendi* texts with those early modern books designed for the autodidactic genteel reader. As they morphed from a medieval genre to a Renaissance one, the Art of Dying texts participated in the same cultural dialogue with books such as Leonard Cox's *The Arte of Rhethoryke* (1524), Thomas Campion's *Observations in the Art of English Poesie* (1602), Edward Davies's *The Art of War* (1619), John Artley's *The Art of Riding* (1584), and Thomas Blundeville's *The Art of Logike* (1599), to list just a few. This vogue for didactic manuals helps explain why, as David Cressy notes, "Far from fading with the Reformation, the medieval *ars moriendi* ... enjoyed a lively revival under Elizabeth and the early Stuarts" (*Birth, Marriage and Death*, p. 389). Like riding or rhetoric, death could seemingly be mastered with practice and earnest application. As Robert Hill observed in the early seventeenth century, "it is the art of all arts, and science of all sciences, to learn to die" (cited in Cressy, *Birth, Marriage and Death*, p. 389).

37 Houlbrooke briefly discusses the account recorded by William Weston, which I quoted above, and his parenthetical explanation typifies a response to the sighting of demons which medicalizes the phenomenon: "(Their presence could have been terrifyingly real for a fever-stricken man familiar with the woodcuts of the *Ars Moriendi*.)"; *Death, Religion and the Family*, p. 157; see also p. 201.

38 Dennis Kezar, "Samson's Death by Theater and Milton's Art of Dying," *English Literary History*, 66 (1999), 296.

39 This skepticism is part of a larger early modern discourse of doubt in the context of demonology, and efforts to provide rational, often medical (humoral), accounts of demonic action. See Stuart Clark, *Thinking with Demons: The Idea of Witchcraft in Early Modern Europe* (Oxford University Press, 1997), pp. 198, 265, 272.

40 I am citing from the 1616 edition.

41 For example, Henry Montagu, in *Contemplatio Mortis et Immortalitatis* (1631), writes, "They take their marke amisse who iudge a man by his outward behauiour in his death. If you know the goodnesse of a mans life, iudge him not by the strangenesse of his death. When a man comes to bee iudged, his life, and not the manner of his death, shall giue the euidence with him, or against him. Many that liue wickedly, would seeme to die holily, more for feare to be damned, then for any loue to goodnesse" (pp. 115–16); cited in Spinrad, *The Summons of Death*, p. 43.

42 Houlbrooke, *Death, Religion and the Family*, p. 167. Taylor also moves away from emphasizing the demonic. For instance, while his text reaches back to the traditional *ars moriendi* tradition of including the temptation of impatience, his account does not involve the demonic. In fact, Taylor reverses the *ars moriendi* tradition that ran through the sixteenth century of counseling the dying person to patiently bear the pangs of death, arguing that it is

natural for *Moriens* to cry out, and that this should be encouraged. See Jeremy Taylor, *Holy Living and Holy Dying*, vol. II, P. G. Stanwood (ed.) (Oxford: Clarendon Press, 1989), pp. 71–2.

43 Perkins writes, "When thou art tempted of Satan and [see] no way to escape, euen plainly close vp thine eyes, and answer nothing, but commend thy cause to God. This is a principall point of Christian wisdome which we must follow in the houre of death. If thy flesh tremble, and feare to enter into an other life, and doubt of saluation; if thou yeild to these things, thou hurtest thy self: therefore close thine eyes as before, & say with S. Stephen, *Lord Iesus into thy hands I commend my spirit*, and then certenly Christ will come vnto thee with all his Angels and be the guides of thy way. *Luther.*" (*A Salue for a Sicke Man*, p. 111).

44 Doebler, "Othello's Angels," 165.

45 Gabriel Egan, "Hearing or Seeing a Play? Evidence of Early Modern Theatrical Terminology," *The Ben Jonson Journal*, 8 (2001), 327–47. He finds that for the period 1550–1650, "the preponderance of visual over aural phrasing is more than twelve to one" (332).

46 Marguerite A. Tassi, *The Scandal of Images: Iconoclasm, Eroticism, and Painting in Early Modern English Drama* (Selinsgrove: Susquehanna University Press, 2005), p. 16.

47 Michael Neill, "Unproper Beds: Race, Adultery, and the Hideous in *Othello*," *Shakespeare Quarterly*, 40 (1989), 412.

48 Critics have posited different accounts of how the bed might have been used in performance. Neill provides a summary of the debate: "It is not clear whether the bed is merely to be displayed inside the discovery space or to be thrust forward onto the main stage. Economy of design favors the former alternative, theatrical effectiveness the latter" ("Unproper Beds," 402n). See also Richard Hosley, "The Staging of Desdemona's Bed," *Shakespeare Quarterly*, 14 (1963), 57–65. For the use of beds on stage, see also Andrew Gurr, *The Shakespearean Stage 1574–1642*, 3rd edn. (Cambridge University Press, 1992), p. 188, and T. J. King, "Staging of Plays at the Phoenix in Drury Lane, 1617–42," *Theater Notebook*, 19 (1965), 162.

49 Hosley, "Staging," 60.

50 *Ibid.*

51 According to the online concordance Shakespeare Searched, "bed" and "beds" appear a combined 22 times in *Othello*, 20 in *Romeo and Juliet*. The only other plays which contain more than 10 instances of the word are *Cymbeline* (15), *Hamlet* (12), *A Midsummer Night's Dream* (12), and *The Taming of the Shrew* (12): www.opensourceshakespeare.com/concordance/o/?i=763826. Dec. 8, 2008.

52 The implication that the wedding sheets will become the winding sheets is in keeping with the practice of using household linens in burial, and the common link between weddings and funerals; see Clare Gittings, *Death, Burial and the Individual in Early Modern England* (London and Sydney: Croom Helm, 1984), pp. 110–12.

53 Doebler, "Othello's Angels," 165.

54 *Ibid.*, 157.
55 Lois Potter, *Othello*, Shakespeare in Performance series, ed. J. R. Mulryne and J. C. Bulman (Manchester and New York: Manchester University Press, 2002), p. 6.
56 Neill, "Unproper Beds," 385; Virginia Mason Vaughan, *Othello: A Contextual History* (Cambridge University Press, 1994), p. 59; Emily C. Bartels, *Speaking of the Moor: From* Alcazar *to* Othello (Philadelphia: University of Pennsylvania Press, 2008), p. 173.
57 The word "heaven" and its cognates (exclusive of "heavens" as signifying the sky) appear 67 times, far more than in any other Shakespearean text. Most of the plays use these less than 20 times, with a handful (*Henry VIII, Hamlet, King John*) containing 40–50 instances: www.opensourceshakespeare.com/concordance/o/?i=764029. Dec. 8, 2008. Many of these references come in the form of ejaculations or idiomatic expressions. To wit: Brabantio: "O heaven, how got she out?" (1.1.167); Montano: "Pray heavens he be" (2.1.34); Cassio: "let the heavens/Give him defence against the elements" (2.1.44–5); Emilia: "what he will do with it/Heaven knows, not I" (3.3.301–2); Desdemona: "Heaven bless us!" (3.4.83); Othello: "By heaven" (4.1.19); Iago: "I would to heaven he were!" (4.1.272); etc. It would be an obvious stretch to claim that in each of these instances the speaker is presumed to be thinking of the afterlife or the domain of the divine. However, with the extensive repetition of "heaven" the word continuously rings from the stage, imbuing the play with a sense of eschatological geography.
58 Martin Elliott, *Shakespeare's Invention of Othello: A Study in Early Modern English* (Basingstoke and London: The Macmillan Press, 1988), pp. 81–2. The citation here is to Helen Gardner, "The Noble Moor," *Proceedings of the British Academy*, XLI (1955), 189–205.
59 Iago is particularly fond of devil references. Cannons are "like the devil" (3.4.137), as are women, who become "devils being offended" (2.1.111). In a rare moment of the Spanish language on the Shakespearean stage, Iago offers up the colorful exclamation, "Diablo, ho!" (2.3.157). Cassio (whom Iago calls "a devilish knave" [2.1.242]), clearly knows his own demon: "O thou invisible spirit of wine, if thou hast no name to be known by, let us call thee devil!" (2.3.277–9); "It hath pleased the devil drunkenness to give place to the devil wrath" (2.3.291–2); "Every inordinate cup is unblest, and the ingredience is a devil" (2.3.302–3). Cassio and Bianca's tiff is marked by hurled insults involving the devil: Cassio to Bianca: "Throw your vile guesses in the devil's teeth" (3.4.184); Bianca to Cassio: "Let the devil and his dam haunt you!" (4.1.147).
60 Anthony Gerard Barthelemy, *Black Face Maligned Race: The Representation of Blacks in English Drama from Shakespeare to Southerne* (Baton Rouge and London: Louisiana State University Press, 1987), p. 156.
61 Bartels, *Speaking of the Moor*, p. 160. In Bartels's discussion, Othello is figured as "the open-ended cultural exchange he embodies and propels" (p. 188); his association with the demonic is never discussed. A reference to

the "oil of hell" appears in Thomas Dekker's *Lust's Dominion; or, The Lascivious Queen* (1600): "put the Moors habits on,/And paint your face with the oil of hell" (5.2.167–72); cited in Barthelemy, *Black Face Maligned Race*, p. 107. See also Eldred Jones, *Othello's Countrymen: The African in English Renaissance Drama* (London: Oxford University Press, 1965), p. 122.

62 Vaughan, *Othello*, p. 51.

63 *Ibid.*, p. 9.

64 Strangely, in spite of her book's subtitle ("a contextual history"), Vaughan makes no reference to the *ars moriendi* tradition in her otherwise fine survey. Her chapter on race (Ch. 3) only speaks of the associations of blackness and the Satanic in passing (*Othello*, pp. 60, 61, 67).

65 See, for example, Jack D'Amico, *The Moor in English Renaissance Drama* (Tampa: University of South Florida Press, 1991), pp. 39, 51, 61, 108, 110, 121, 166.

66 Barthelemy, *Black Face Maligned Race*, p. 72. He argues that the emergence of the Vice figure in the morality plays caused Satan and lesser demons to disappear (p. 72): "once the vice becomes recognizable by his methods, manners, and goals, distinguishing physical features prove redundant or unnecessary. Satan and his black face become a hindrance to the dramatic action, blackface obsolete in the characterization of evil" (p. 74). But if the Vice seemed to be pushing out the black devil, the prevalence of Moors on the early modern stage brought back the visual figure of the devil.

67 Elliot H. Tokson, *The Popular Image of the Black Man in English Drama, 1550–1688* (Boston: G. K. Hall and Co., 1982), p. 54. Tokson, too, suggests that the image emerges from the mode of portraying the devil in medieval morality plays (p. 55).

68 Tokson, *Popular Image*, p. 67 (see also p. 63); Jones, *Othello's Countrymen*, p. 129.

69 Roberto Bellarmino, *The Art of Dying Well*, trans. Edward Coffin (St. Omer: English College Press, 1622), pp. 274–5; cited in Phillippy, *Women, Death and Literature*, p. 217.

70 Erasmus, *Preparation*, sig. B5$^r$. Othello has also been associated with Death from *Everyman*: M. D. Faber, "The Summoning of Desdemona: *Othello*, V. ii.1–82," *American Notes and Queries*, 9 (1970), 37n, referencing Francis Douce (ed.), *The Dance of Death* (London, 1833), p. 230.

71 See William E. Engel, *Mapping Mortality: The Persistence of Memory and Melancholy in Early Modern England* (Amherst: University of Massachusetts Press, 1995), p. 72.

72 The legacy of this dual portrayal of the devil, as both an actual devil and as more metaphoric, has entered into literary criticism, with skepticism taking the day. Edward Pechter summarizes Empson's argument about Iago's relationship to the devil thus: "The only way 'to justify calling Iago' the devil is to psychologize and socialize the concept": *Othello and Interpretive Traditions* (Iowa City: University of Iowa Press, 1999), p. 60. The resistance to

confronting Iago's demonic identity might result from a sense that this is
something of an analytical dead end, providing too pat an explanation for his
identity. Robert B. Heilman writes, "Although reading *Othello* as if it were
explicitly a dramatization of a Christian world view can be very enlightening,
the Christian materials are so much in the foreground and are so numerous
and distinct that they hardly offer a structural problem or provide a final way
into the problems of verbal and actional drama. If we start by simply calling
Iago a 'devil,' we risk using the myth of evil as a substitute for the analysis of
the individual ...": *Magic in the Web: Action and Language in* Othello
(Westport, Ct.: Greenwood Press, 1956), p. 42.

73 Paul Yachnin, "Magical Properties: Vision, Possession, and Wonder in
   *Othello*," *Theatre Journal*, 48 (1996), 205; Spivack, *Shakespeare and the Allegory
   of Evil*, pp. 19, 33; Vaughan, *Othello*, p. 73; Potter, *Othello*, p. 131; D'Amico,
   *The Moor*, p. 177; Honigmann, *Othello*, p. 111.

74 Greenblatt, *Shakespearean Negotiations*, pp. 119, 123.

75 Clark, *Thinking with Demons*, p. 166; see also pp. 163, 192.

76 See, for instance, Bartels, *Speaking of the Moor*, Ch. 7, esp. pp. 168–80.

77 Pechter, Othello *and Interpretive Traditions*, p. 89. He is writing specifically
   about 4.2.58–68, although the comment easily applies to the play more
   generally.

3   WHEN HELL FREEZES OVER: THE FABULOUS
     MOUNT HECLA AND 'HAMLET'S' INFERNAL GEOGRAPHY

1 Cited in Dion Boucicault, "Shakspere's Influence on the Drama," *The North
   American Review*, 147.385 (1888), 681.

2 To repeat a definition from my Prologue, I am using "eschatology" to refer
   generally to matters of the afterlife. Eschatology, according to the *Oxford
   English Dictionary*'s definition, is "the department of theological science
   concerned with 'the four last things: death, judgment, heaven, and hell'."

3 Scholars have debated whether the religious orientation of *Hamlet* is Prot-
   estant or Catholic. Those arguing for the Protestant slant include Alan
   Sinfield, "Hamlet's Special Providence," *Shakespeare Survey*, 33 (1980),
   89–97; Chris Hassel, Jr., "Hamlet's 'Too, Too Solid Flesh'," *Sixteenth
   Century Journal*, 25 (1994), 609–22 and "The Accent and Gait of Christians:
   Hamlet's Puritan Style" in Dennis Taylor and David Beauregard (eds.),
   *Shakespeare and the Culture of Christianity in Early Modern England* (New
   York: Fordham University Press, 2003), pp. 287–310; Mark Matheson,
   "*Hamlet* and 'A Matter Tender and Dangerous'," *Shakespeare Quarterly*,
   46 (1995), 383–97. Those positioning *Hamlet* as a Catholic play include
   David N. Beauregard, *Catholic Theology in Shakespeare's Plays* (Newark:
   University of Delaware Press, 2008), Ch. 5; John E. Curran, Jr., Hamlet,
   *Protestantism, and the Mourning of Contingency* (Aldershot, UK and Bur-
   lington, Vt.: Ashgate, 2006). Older studies include Roy Battenhouse, "The
   Ghost in *Hamlet*: A Catholic Lynchpin?," *Studies in Philology*, 68 (1951),
   161–92; Miriam Joseph, "Discerning the Ghost in *Hamlet*," *PMLA*, 76

(1961), 493–502 and *"Hamlet*, a Christian Tragedy," *Studies in Philology*, 59
(1962), 119–40. My own sense is that, as in many of Shakespeare's engage-
ments with religion, the play stages the interaction of theological positions
without advocating one. Greenblatt's theological positioning of the play, in
which "a young man from Wittenberg, with a distinctly Protestant tem-
perament, is haunted by a distinctly Catholic ghost" (*Hamlet in Purgatory*,
p. 240), seems appropriate to me.

4 Purgatory has been a favorite topic of recent English historiography, but
perhaps a postcard-sized account would still be helpful for some readers.
(One of the best books on the subject is Peter Marshall, *Beliefs and the Dead
in Reformation England* [Oxford University Press, 2002].) For centuries, it
was believed that upon death nearly everyone underwent a period of
cleansing, or purging, of the soul's sins, since only the pure could enter
heaven. The English imagined purgatory with a creative, sadistic zeal that
outstripped even the continent's colorful, Dantean visions; see Eamon Duffy,
*The Stripping of the Altars: Traditional Religion in England c. 1400–c. 1580*
(New Haven and London: Yale University Press, 1992), p. 344; see, more
generally, Ch. 10. For an example, see the account of the extensive tortures of
Margaret, a nun whose sins were loving her pet dog and liking her food:
Marta Powell Harley, *A Revelation of Purgatory by an Unknown, Fifteenth-
Century Woman Visionary: Introduction, Critical Text, and Translation*, Stud-
ies in Women and Religion, vol. XVIII (Lewiston and Queenston: The
Edwin Mellen Press, 1985). See also Robert Easting, "'Send thine heart into
purgatory': Visionaries of the Other World" in Helen Cooper and Sally
Mapstone (eds.), *The Long Fifteenth Century: Essays for Douglas Gray* (Oxford:
Clarendon Press, 1997), pp. 185–203.

Fortunately, there were ways to accelerate the purgatorial process. Individuals had some degree of control over their afterlife while still living on earth,
since the positive effects of good works could help to counterbalance the
negative impact of sin on the great cosmic scorecard. This belief resulted in a
culture of charitable donation; such gifts were a form of after-life insurance,
since those in the endowed hospital, monastery or almshouse were commissioned to pray for the donor's soul; prayers offered in abundance could speed
the process of purgation and ascension to heaven. The less wealthy formed
prayer guilds to pray for past members (on the assumption that future
members would do the same for them). If the downside of the purgatorial
system was near-universal post-mortem torture, the upside of the system was
its almost bookkeeping logic. The debts of the dead could be paid by the
living; purgatory functioned by a system of compensation and redemption by
proxy. (The most notorious consequence of this was the sale of papal indul-
gences.) This belief in the agency of the living to mitigate the torment of the
dead created an intergenerational chain of dependence.

A combination of politics and religious reformation led to purgatory being
officially disavowed by the established church in the sixteenth century,
although as many have discussed (both then and now), belief in purgatory,

which had structured centuries of social and familial relations, was not instantly snuffed out. Whatever Protestant divines might decree, and however willing the laity might have been to cast off other vestiges of popish superstition, the populace tenaciously clung to traditional practices connected to a purgatorial understanding of the afterlife, especially those rituals surrounding death (see e.g. Duffy, *Stripping of the Altars*, p. 577). Still, belief in purgatory seems to have dropped off quite quickly at the end of the sixteenth century. The emotional effect of the intergenerational difference in belief is not only studied in *Hamlet,* but in current historiography of the Reformation; see e.g. Peter Cunich, "The Dissolution of the Chantries" in Patrick Collinson and John Craig (eds.), *The Reformation in English Towns, 1500–1640* (Basingstoke and London: Macmillan Press Ltd.; New York: St. Martin's Press, Inc., 1998), pp. 167, 170, 173; and D. P. Walker, *The Decline of Hell: Seventeenth-Century Discussions of Eternal Torment* (The University of Chicago Press; London: Routledge and Kegan Paul Ltd.; The University of Toronto Press, 1964), p. 59. While the seventeenth-century terms of the debate over purgatory shifted from Biblical exegesis to philosophical debates about materialism, questions about the spatial configuration of the afterlife persisted; see Philip C. Almond, *Heaven and Hell in Enlightenment England* (Cambridge University Press, 1994), pp. 33–5. Indeed, in the mid seventeenth century we even see the resurgence of what Almond calls a "Protestant purgatory" (see p. 79; and more broadly, pp. 77–80).

5 This chapter has been influenced by Peter Marshall's essay "'The map of God's word': Geographies of the Afterlife in Tudor and Early Stuart England" in Bruce Gordon and Peter Marshall (eds.), *The Place of the Dead: Death and Remembrance in Late Medieval and Early Modern Europe* (Cambridge University Press, 2000), pp. 110–30.

6 Joseph Glanvill, *A Blow at Modern Sadducism in some Philosophical Considerations about Witchcraft* (1668), p. 115. Cited in Almond, *Heaven and Hell,* p. 35.

7 Robert Burton, *The Anatomy of Melancholy* (New York: Empire State Book Co., 1924), pp. 318–19. Similarly, see William Fulke: "If any punishment remayne, it must needes ryse by proportion, weyght, continuaunce, number and quantity, which if it be not all discharged in this lyfe, then it is to be aunswered in the lyfe to come. By proportion *Maister Allen?* What proportion? *Arithmaticall* or *Geometricall?* If it be by *arithmaticall* proportion, then so many thousandes of sinnes, whereof euery one deserueth one death, must be punished by so many thousand deathes. If by *geometricall* proportion, then so many offences committed against that infinite maiesty, can not be aunswered, but by infinite and eternal punishment, and which way so euer you take it, by weight, number, time or measure, it is euident, that while you seeke for purgatory, you haue founde out hell." *Two Treatises written against the Papistes* (1577), p. 46.

8 Almond, *Heaven and Hell,* p. 73; for a synopsis of Swinden's argument, see pp. 125–6. For a broader discussion about how the new astronomy affected religious beliefs, see John Hedley Brooke, *Science and Religion: Some Historical Perspectives* (Cambridge University Press, 1991), pp. 83–9.

9 Margreta de Grazia, Hamlet *without Hamlet* (Cambridge University Press, 2007).

10 Stephen Greenblatt, *Hamlet in Purgatory* (Princeton and Oxford: Princeton University Press, 2001). Greenblatt's touchstone for the label of "a poet's fable" (p. 35) is a quote from William Tyndale's *An Answer to Sir Thomas More's Dialogue* (Cambridge: Parker Society, 1850), p. 143. Calvin's position is pertinent here: "But the structure of purgatory has just as much solidity as any thing can have which is, in regard to things unknown, fabricated by the brain of man, without the word of God": *Articles Agreed Upon by the Faculty of Sacred Theology of Paris ... with The Antidote* (1542), in John Calvin, *Tracts and Treatises on the Reformation of the Church*, vol. I, trans. Henry Beveridge (Grand Rapids, Mich.: Wm. B. Eerdmans Publishing Co., 1958), p. 100.

11 Greenblatt, *Hamlet in Purgatory*, p. 35.

12 Kirsten Hastrup, *Nature and Policy in Iceland 1400–1800: An Anthropological Analysis of History and Mentality* (Oxford: Clarendon Press, 1990), p. 273.

13 Samuel Purchas, *Purchas His Pilgrimage, or Relations of the VVorld and the Religions Obserued in al Ages and Places Discouered* (1617), p. 924. "Hecla" is here spelled "Heela," but this must be a typesetter's error; elsewhere in the text "Hecla" is used. "Hekla" is a variant, and the form most commonly used today. I am using "Hecla" as it was the more common early modern form.

14 John Frith, *A Disputation of Purgatorye* (1531), sig. b5$^v$.

15 Thomas White, *The Middle State of Souls. From the hour of death to the Day of Judgment* (1659), p. 3; cited in Almond, *Heaven and Hell*, p. 72.

16 Marshall, "'The map of God's word'," p. 116. For another example of a discussion of the whereabouts of purgatory, see Thomas Becon, *The Reliques of Rome* (1563), sig. Ee4$^r$. An early Reformation church tract, *The Institvtion of a Christen Man* (1534), under "the article of purgatorie," encourages prayer for the dead but includes this qualification: "But for asmoche as the place, where they be, the name therof, and kynde of peynes there also, be to vs vncertayne by scripture" (sig. P7$^v$). Lewys Evans, in the Protestant book *The Castle of Christianitie* (1568), writes: "This [Purgatory] is a place (as they appoint it) wherein only small offences be remitted in the next life. If you ask them where this place is, they can not agree, you appose them, so that *quod non inuenit vsquem, esse putate nusquam*. They haue sought heauen, they have sought hell, *itum est in viscera terrae*, they haue sought euen the verie bowels of the earth, and yet can not feyned Purgatorie be founde, there is none before the time of darknesse, that euer heard of such an Inne. But is there trowe ye, and such place at al?" (sig. F2$^v$; see also F4$^v$).

17 Marshall, "'The map of God's word'," p. 113–14.

18 See Marshall, *ibid.*, p. 124.

19 This and all subsequent references to the text are from Ann Thompson and Neil Taylor (eds.), *Hamlet*, The Arden Shakespeare, Third Series (London: Thomson Learning, 2006).

20 For a quick summary of pre-new historicist explanations of the ghost, see Harry Morris, *Last Things in Shakespeare* (Tallahassee: Florida State University Press, 1985), p. 19n.

21 Here I strongly disagree with the gloss of Thompson and Taylor: "It seems curious that the men, in all three texts, seem to recover from the shock of seeing the Ghost and move so quickly to the indirectly related topic of Denmark's preparations for war, though this preoccupation makes the Ghost's reappearance more effective" (*Hamlet*, p. 155n). Old Hamlet, after all, "was and is the question of these wars" (1.1.110).

22 John Gillies, *Shakespeare and the Geography of Difference* (Cambridge University Press, 1994), p. 87. See, more broadly, pp. 87–91.

23 In *Historia Mundi: or Mercator's Atlas. Containing his Cosmographicall Description of the Fabricke and Figure of the World* (1635), we read that "Here is so great plenty of fish, that they lay them in great heapes out of doores, and so sell them, the heapes being higher than the tops of their houses" (p. 37).

24 Gunnar Karlsson, *Iceland's 1100 Years: The History of a Marginal Society* (London: Hurst and Company, 2000), p. 127.

25 For a thumbnail sketch of the political transformations, see Hastrup, *Nature and Policy in Iceland 1400–1800*, pp. 31–2, 116–17.

26 *Ibid*, p. 137.

27 William Cuningham, *The Cosmographical Glasse Conteinyng the Pleasant Priniciples of Cosmographie, Geographie, Hydrographie, or Nauigation* (1559), p. 176.

28 Karlsson attributes the phrase to the Icelandic historian Björn Þorsteinsson's dissertation from 1970 (*Iceland's 1100 Years*, p. 118).

29 Karlsson, *Iceland's 1100 Years*, p. 119.

30 Hastrup, *Nature and Policy in Iceland 1400–1800*, p. 123.

31 In a single raid in 1627, pirates (arriving in four ships from Morocco and Algeria) abducted 410 Icelanders, or about 0.75 percent of the total population. The prisoners were taken to Algeria, where they were enslaved awaiting ransom from Denmark and other European nations. Ten years later, 27 of the captives managed to return to Iceland (Karlsson, *Iceland's 1100 Years*, pp. 143–5, 147).

32 I have used the Latin edition for the images, as it is most readily available to me as an original archival text. The English translations are from Gerhard Mercator, *Atlas or a Geographicke Description of the Regions, Countries and Kingdomes of the World* (Amsterdam, 1636); here, p. 46.

33 Here I disagree with Marshall, who writes, "With the expansion and mapping of the known world, the idea that Hell and Paradise could be situated in this world, under exotic volcanoes or on distant islands, was looking increasingly anachronistic, surviving only as self-consciously literary and philosophical conceits" ("'The map of God's word'," p. 126).

34 Hastrup, *Nature and Policy in Iceland 1400–1800*, p. 266, with a reproduction of the map.

35 *Ibid*, p. 133.

36 Arngrímur subsequently wrote a history of Iceland in Latin entitled *Crymogæa* (Greek for "ice-land") (Hamburg, 1609); "*Crymogæa* is the manifesto of Icelandic patriotism" (Karlsson, *Iceland's 1100 Years*, p. 157).

37 Hastrup, *Nature and Policy in Iceland 1400–1800*, p. 215.

38 *Ibid.*

39 "And we do also hold, yt the Islanders are no whit nearer vnto this extreame & darke prison, in regard of the situation of place, then the Germans, Danes, Frenchmen, Italians, or any other nation whatsoeuer. Neither is it any thing to the purpose, at all to dispute of the place or situation of this dungeon. It is sufficient for vs, that (by the grace and assistance of our Lord Iesus Christ, with whose precious blood we are redeemed) we shall neuer see that vtter darknesse, nor feele the rest of the torments that be there. Now let vs shut vp the disputation concerning the hell of Island" (Hakluyt, *The Principal Nauigations*, p. 563).

40 Elisha Coles, *An English Dictionary Explaining the Difficult Terms that are Used in Divinity, Husbandry, Physic, Philosophy, Law, Navigation, Mathematicks, and Other Arts and Sciences* (1677), sig. Q4$^r$.

41 The text that accompanies Mercator's map of Iceland, for instance, describes Iceland's mountains "the tops whereof are always white with snow, the nether parts burne with fire: the first is called *Hecla*" (p. 46); Mercator's *Historia Mundi* quotes: "In *Iseland* (saith *Georgius Agricola*) there are three very high Mountaines, whose tops are alwayes white with continuall Snow, the bottomes doe burne with continuall Fire" (p. 34); Cuningham writes, "the toppes of which are co[n]tinually couered with snow" (*Cosmographical Glasse,* p. 175); Patrick Gordon notes, "*Hecla* a terrible *Volcano*, which (though always covered with Snow up to the very Top) doth frequently Vomit forth Fire and Sulphurous matter": *Geography Anatomiz'd* (1699), p. 221.

42 John Lear, *Kepler's Dream* [*Somnium, sive Astronomia Lunaris*], trans. Patricia Frueh Kirkwood (Berkeley and Los Angeles: University of California Press, 1965), pp. 87–9.

43 The name "Duracotus" is picked because "the sound of this word came to me from a recollection of names of a similar sound in the history of Scotland, a land that looks out over the Icelandic ocean" (Lear, *Kepler's Dream*, p. 87n); "Iceland is situated near the polar circle. This I heard also from Tycho Brahe, who made this calculation on the basis of an account of a Bishop of Iceland" (p. 92); and within the story, Duracotus is sold by his mother (who gathers herbs on Mount Hecla) to a sea captain who sets out for Bergen, Norway, but gets blown off course and ends up going between England and Norway to Denmark.

44 "That S. Patriks purgatorie in *Ireland*, lies fast by the sea side, neare vnto a mountaine called *Hecla*, where our mother the holie Church of Rome doeth beleeue, that the sillie soules are as ill punished in yse, as in fire": Philips van Marnix van St. Aldegonde, *The Bee Hiue of the Romishe Church*, trans. George Gilpin (1579), sig. 146$^v$.

45 See Kepler's notes in his *Somnium,* numbers 13, 16, 19, 20 (in Lear, *Kepler's Dream*, pp. 92–3). One wonders if Brahe's own northern island observatory contributed to the scientific fantasies about northern islands.

46 Burton, *Anatomy*, p. 319.

47 *Ibid.*, p. 317.

48 Karlsson writes that "[g]eographical literature was popular in 16th-century Europe, and Iceland, with its extraordinary natural features, of course became one of its favoured subjects" (*Iceland's 1100 Years*, p. 157). Sebastian Munster's *Cosmographie Universalis* (Basle, 1550), for instance, contains a depiction of Mount Hecla in eruption; this text went through multiple editions from 1550 to 1614 and appeared in Latin, German, French, and Italian. See Henry Phillips, Jr., "An Account of an Old Work on Cosmography," *Proceedings of the American Philosophical Society*, 18.105 (1880), 444, 448. Another text discussing Mount Hecla is Dithmar Blefkens, *Islandia, sive populorum & mirabilium quae in ea insula reperiuntur accuratior descriptio* (Leiden, 1607), cited in Rienk Vermij, "Subterranean Fire: Changing Theories of the Earth during the Renaissance," *Early Science and Medicine*, 3 (1998), 326n. This article contains fascinating information about how volcanic activity was primarily of interest to medical circles trying to understand terrestrial heat in light of Aristotle's categorization of the earth as cold.

49 Deborah E. Harkness, *The Jewel House: Elizabethan London and the Scientific Revolution* (New Haven and London: Yale University Press, 2007).

50 For the theological issues surrounding the relationship of the place of burial to the afterlife of the soul, see Marshall, "'The map of God's word'," 116–123. See also David Cressy, *Birth, Marriage, and Death: Ritual, Religion, and the Life-Cycle in Tudor and Stuart England* (Oxford University Press, 1997), Ch. 18.

51 Harold Jenkins (ed.), *Hamlet*, The Arden Shakespeare, Second Series (London and New York: Methuen & Co., 1982; Routledge, 1989), p. 223n.

52 To borrow again from Jenkins's gloss: "To seek a particular source for this belief is to ignore the very great fame of St. Patrick's Purgatory, in an Irish cave, much visited by pilgrims. The story was that all who spent a day and night there would both be purged of their sins and have visions of the damned and the blest" (*Hamlet, ibid.*, p. 224n). For an extended discussion of St. Patrick's Purgatory, see Greenblatt, *Hamlet in Purgatory*, pp. 75–101. Significantly, as Greenblatt notes, this is the only time that St. Patrick is invoked in the Shakespearean corpus (p. 233).

53 Greenblatt, *Hamlet in Purgatory*, p. 99. For a contemporary account of the rise and fall of the place, see Henry Jones, *Saint Patricks Purgatory: Containing the Description, Originall, Progresse, and Demolition of that Superstitious Place* (1647).

54 Greenblatt's extended discussion of the implications of Hamlet's "*Hic et ubique*" (1.5.156) also seems to capture this sense of spatial ambiguity. He writes, "The words obviously refer to restless movement, a certain placelessness" (*Hamlet in Purgatory*, p. 234), and yet, "In the context of the Ghost's claim that he is being purged, and in the context, too, of Hamlet's invocation of Saint Patrick, the words *hic et ubique*, addressed to the spirit who seems to be moving beneath the earth, seem to be an acknowledgment of the place where his father's spirit is imprisoned" (p. 235). The words, then, are both about place and placelessness.

55 John Florio, *A vvorlde of words* (1598), p. 455.
56 http://en.wikipedia.org/wiki/Mount_Hekla; June 18, 2009. The page cites *Thorarinsson, Sigurdur Hekla, A Notorious Volcano*, trans. Jóhann Hannesson and Pétur Karlsson (Reykjavík: Almenna bókafélagið, 1970), p. 17.
57 Robert Boyle, *New Experiments and Observations touching Cold* (1665), p. 394.
58 Many authors yoke Mounts Hecla and Aetna. Cuningham writes, "Hecla, which co[n]tinually (like to the mountaine Aetna) doeth burne" (*Cosmographical Glasse*, p. 175). Arngrímur, as translated in Hakluyt, finds the idea that Hecla is the site of purgatory "no lesse reprochfull then false, and more vaine & detestable then Sicilian scoffes" (*Principall Voyages*, p. 561); similarly, he quotes "Cardane" as saying: "There is Hecla a mountaine in Island, which burneth like vnto Aetna" (p. 562). Peter Heylyn writes in *Mikrokosmos* (1625): "In this Iland is the hill of *Heckleso* [sic], vomiting flames of fire like *Ætna* of *Sicily*: of which also the blind Papists haue the same superstitious opinion, namely, that vnder them is *Purgatory*" (p. 528). Edmund Bohun, in *A Geographical Dictionary* (1693), defines Hecla as "a burning Mountain in *Island* . . . The Natives call it, *one of the mouths of Hell*. It vomits Floods and Rivers of Fire like *Ætna* and *Vesuvius*, notwithstanding its nearness to the *Polar* Circle" (p. 186). Gabriel Richardson states in *Of the State of Europe* (1627) that the three Icelandic volcanoes are "Aethna-like flaming with fires" (p. 39).
59 An early modern gloss of "Thule" as "Iceland" is provided in Mercator's *Historia Mundi: or Mercator's Atlas* and its description of "Iseland": "The most does suppose this bee that *Thule* mentioned by the Ancients, which also *Ptolemie* doeth call *Thule*; the middle whereof he placeth in the 30. Degree of Latitutde, and 63. of Longitude . . . An Island the most famous of all other with Poets, when by this, as being the farthest part of the World, they would intimate any thing farre distant" (p. 33).
60 Ruth Padel, www.ruthpadel.com/pages/HowStrangelyFogoBurns.htm; June 3, 2009. The lyrics for "Thule" are on this website. This essay by the poet Padel offers an interesting close reading of the lyrics to "Thule" as both a written and sung text. She notes that "Weelkes's Dedication to the book containing 'Thule', makes one of the earliest contemporary Shakespearian allusions: to *Henry VI, Part 2* and its philistine character Jack Cade," and suggests that the "wondrous I" of the second part of the madrigal points towards *Hamlet*. She also outlines intriguing connections between this text and that of Kepler's *Somnium*, and Kepler's association with two of Tycho Brahe's cousins, Rosenkrantz and Gyldensterne.
61 Mary Floyd-Wilson, *English Ethnicity and Race in Early Modern Drama* (Cambridge University Press, 2003), p. 4. See also Daryl W. Palmer, "*Hamlet's* Northern Lineage: Masculinity, Climate, and the Mechanician in Early Modern Britain," *Renaissance Drama*, n.s. 35 (2006), 3–25.
62 Greenblatt reads the fact that "the Ghost on the battlements returns not in the semblance of the poisoned man whose flesh has hideously crusted over but in the complete armor of the powerful warrior-king" (*Hamlet in*

*Purgatory,* p. 214) in terms of the psychology of memory, but within the play characters comment on his garb in terms of its association with a frigid battle (one which involved sleds and ice). It is interesting to recognize the challenges that this armor has posed in modern performances; as Ann Rosalind Jones and Peter Stallybrass note (after quoting the actor John Gielgud), audiences have laughed at a clanking, armored ghost. "Ridicule, rather than fear, has been the usual lot of Hamlet's Ghost": *Renaissance Clothing and the Materials of Memory* (Cambridge University Press, 2000), p. 246. The comical effect is evidence of a modern epistemological rift between the material and the supernatural, a division that would not have been part of early modern understandings.

63  Lewes Lauaterus, trans. R. H., *Of Ghostes and Spirites walking by Nyght* (1572), p. 103. See also Easting, "Send thine heart," p. 187.

64  The text goes on to state that "But because no man that is well in his wits, will thinke that Hell is in this Mountayne, yet it may be demanded, whence the Hill hath this matter, whereby it should bring forth so many yeeres flames, so many ashes, and such abundance of Pumis stones?" (Purchas, *Purchas His Pilgrimage,* p. 648), and answers the question in geological terms. The rapid movement from asserting the reality of the spirits, while denying Hecla's status as a portal to Hell, demonstrates again how early modern notions of reason do not align with our own.

65  See the very different glosses of the line in Jenkins, *Hamlet,* p. 258n; Thompson and Taylor, *Hamlet,* p. 261n; Philip Edwards (ed.), *Hamlet, Prince of Denmark,* The New Cambridge Shakespeare (Cambridge University Press, 1985, 2003), p. 146n; G. R. Hibbard (ed.), *Hamlet,* The Oxford Shakespeare (Oxford: Clarendon Press, 1987), p. 223n.

66  A few examples: "Sulphur is there so ple[n]tifull that you may for the 4. Part of a ducate, haue a thousande weight" (Cuningham, *Cosmographical Glasse,* p. 175); "The *Vulgar* believe the Mountain *Hecla* to be the Prison of *damned Souls.* Mines of *Sulphur* are found in it, with which the Merchants drive a Traffick" (Bohun, *Geographical Dictionary,* p. 208); "From this cold and barren Island, are yearly exported Fish, Whale-Oyl, Tallow, Hides, Brimstone, and White Foxes Skins" (P. Gordon, *Geography Anatomiz'd,* p. 221); "Hecla *brimstone* is digged in great abundance, sent into forraine parts" (Richardson, *Of the State of Europe,* p. 39); "[S]eeing Brimstone is digged out of the Earth throughout the whole Land ..." (Purchas, *Purchas His Pilgrimage,* p. 648); "Not far from *Hecla* are Pits of brimstone," and "*Brimstone* is dug up in *Islandia* by the Mountain *Hecla,* and that without fire": Jo[h]annes Jonstonus, *An History of the Wonderful Things of Nature set forth in Ten Severall Classes* (1657), pp. 37, 101.

67  Cuningham, *Cosmographical Glasse,* p. 175; P. Gordon, *Geography Anatomiz'd,* p. 221.

68  Thompson and Taylor, *Hamlet,* p. 466.

69  Here is the line: "No jocund health that Denmark drinks today/But the great cannon to the clouds shall tell,/And the King's rouse the heaven shall bruit again,/Re-speaking earthly thunder" (1.2.125–8) For a discussion of

contemporary English-Danish relations (which at the turn of the seventeenth century were very active, in part because of James's marriage to Queen Anne of Denmark) and the excessive drinking habits of King Christian IV, see Michael Srigley, "'Heavy-headed revel east and west': Hamlet and Christian IV of Denmark" in Gunnar Sorelius (ed.), *Shakespeare and Scandinavia: A Collection of Nordic Studies* (Newark: University of Delaware Press; London: Associated University Presses, 2002).

70 For Shakespeare's knowledge of Hakluyt, François Laroque cites Numa Broc, *La Géographie de la Renaissance, 1420–1620* (Paris: Editions du C.T. H.S., 1986), p. 225; Laroque, "Shakespeare's Imaginary Geography" in Andrew Hadfield and Paul Hammond (eds.), *Shakespeare and Renaissance Europe*, Arden Critical Companions (London: Thomson Learning, 2005), p. 196.

71 Thompson and Taylor's gloss on "canonized" (1.4.47) is interesting: "Pursuing the cannon/canon pun noted at 1.2.132, Booth (49–50) points out that we have recently heard the cannon [see 6 SD and n.] and that the bones themselves seem to become projectiles here, bursting out of the grave. The repetition of *burst* (46, 48) is slightly awkward, an effect exaggerated in Q1, where it occurs three times in five lines" (206n). ("Booth" is Stephen Booth, "Close Reading Without Readings" in Russ McDonald (ed.), *Shakespeare Reread: The Texts in New Contexts* [Ithaca, NY: Cornell University Press, 1994], pp. 42–55).

72 See Jenkins, *Hamlet*, p. 391n; Thompson and Taylor (p. 428n), whose edition has a stage direction for Laertes to leap out of the grave before grappling with Hamlet (5.1.247); and S. P. Zitner, "Four Feet in the Grave," *TEXT* 2 (1985), 139–48.

73 De Grazia, Hamlet *without Hamlet*, p. 146; see also p. 35, and her entire chapter, "Doomsday and domain."

74 Hakluyt, *Principall Voyages*, p. 562.

75 The only Shakespeare play that mentions Iceland is *Henry V*, when Pistol says, "Pish for thee, Iceland dog! thou prick-eared cur of Iceland!" (2.1.43–7).

76 Anthony Low, "*Hamlet* and the Ghost of Purgatory: Intimations of Killing the Father," *English Literary Renaissance*, 29 (1999), 459–60. Low cites several examples: "Hamlet says that he is 'Prompted to my revenge by heaven and hell' (2.2.580), as if he is repressing the real source of his prompting. Similarly, when he refrains from killing Claudius at his prayer ... he vows ... to 'trip him that his heels may kick at heaven/And that his soul may be as damn'd and black/As hell, whereto it goes' (3.3.93–5). Hamlet takes no thought of Purgatory; he conceives of two states or places, with nothing in between. Nor does he consider the third place when he answers Claudius's question, 'Where is Polonius?' Hamlet mockingly replies: 'In heaven, send thither to see. If your messenger find him not there, seek him i'th'other place yourself' (4.3.32–5). There is no doubt where that 'other place' is, or that he thinks Claudius properly belongs there" (459–60).

77 See *Tarltons Newes out of Purgatorie* (1590) for a comic pamphlet addressing purgatory (one that also engages with the theological debates on the subject, including Calvin's position; see sig. B2$^r$); Jane Owen's *An Antidote Against Purgatory* (1634) argues for the reality of purgatory, stressing the importance of good works and alms ("Epistle Dedicatory").

78 Gail Kern Paster, *Humoring the Body: Emotions and the Shakespearean Stage* (Chicago and London: The University of Chicago Press, 2004), p. 37.

79 Russell West, *Spatial Representations and the Jacobean Stage: From Shakespeare to Webster* (Basingstoke and New York: Palgrave, 2002), p. 3.

80 Laroque, *Shakespeare's Geography*, pp. 197, 218–19.

#### 4 METAMORPHIC COSMOLOGIES: THE WORLD ACCORDING TO CALVIN, HOOKER, AND MACBETH

1 John Calvin, *Institutes of the Christian Religion*, 2 vols., ed. John T. McNeill, trans. Ford Lewis Battles (Philadelphia: The Westminster Press, 1960), I: 59. Citations to the *Institutes* will be included parenthetically with volume and page numbers.

2 All quotations are from Kenneth Muir (ed.), *Macbeth*, The Arden Shakespeare, Second Series (London: Thomson Learning, 1951; 2006); here, 1.1.1–12. The date of composition for the play is unclear; Muir posits sometime between 1603 and 1606 (p. xx).

3 Bruce R. Smith, *The Acoustic World of Early Modern England: Attending to the O-Factor* (Chicago and London: The University of Chicago Press, 1999), p. 276.

4 Jonathan Gil Harris, "The Smell of Macbeth," *Shakespeare Quarterly*, 58 (2007), 486. This article was reworked into Chapter 4 of Harris's subsequent book, *Untimely Matter in the Time of Shakespeare* (Philadelphia: University of Pennsylvania Press, 2009). This quote appears in a slightly modified form on p. 138 of that book ("moments" and "fields" appear in quotation marks). I will be quoting from both versions of this essay, since in some cases the earlier article economically condenses arguments that would become dispersed throughout the book.

5 Harris, *Untimely Matter*, p. 120.

6 Philip Benedict, *Christ's Churches Purely Reformed: A Social History of Calvinism* (New Haven and London: Yale University Press, 2002), p. 231.

7 The difference between Calvin and Hooker reflects larger trends in theological positions. For sixteenth-century reformers, "general providence," or God's sustaining of natural order, and "special providence," God's concern with individual cosmic events, were all part of God's radical sovereignty. By stark contrast, for seventeenth-century mechanists, "although God was sovereign over a world that He created and, in principle, could suspend or change natural laws to accomplish a special purpose, in practice He did not tamper with the laws of nature. He was a God of general providence and only rarely, in the case of miracles, a God of special providence": Gary B. Deason, "Reformation Theology and the Mechanistic Conception of Nature" in

David C. Lindberg and Ronald L. Numbers (eds.), *God and Nature: Historical Essays on the Encounter between Christianity and Science* (Berkeley: University of California Press, 1986), p. 187.

8 John Stachniewski, "Calvinist Psychology in *Macbeth*," *Shakespeare Studies*, 20 (1988), 169.

9 Richard Allestree, *The Whole Duty of Mourning and the Great Concern of Preparing Our Selves for Death, Practically Considered* ([London], [1695]), pp. 89–90.

10 Calvin's move away from an Aristotelian cosmos is in keeping with sixteenth-century natural philosophy, as described by Amos Funkenstein, *Theology and the Scientific Imagination from the Middle Ages to the Seventeenth Century* (Princeton University Press, 1986), p. 67.

11 Alister E. McGrath, *A Life of John Calvin: A Study in the Shaping of Western Culture* (Oxford: Basil Blackwell, 1990), p. xiv.

12 *Ibid.*

13 As Deason explains, this understanding of water comes from Aristotelian physics – earth is heavy and therefore falls towards the center, whereas water is lighter ("Reformation Theology," p. 177). This notion of the artificial sea level is one to which Calvin returns in his other writings as well. William J. Bouwsma writes: "The possibility of death by water seemed to him, indeed, implicit in the arrangement assigned in traditional physics to the elements; because water is lighter, it ought totally to cover the earth. Only the power of God – though, he reminded himself, this could be depended on – restrains water from submerging the whole earth. The survival of the human race from moment to moment thus depends on God's keeping the seas under an *unnatural* control": *John Calvin: A Sixteenth-Century Portrait* (New York and Oxford: Oxford University Press, 1988), p. 33.

14 Francis Oakley, "Christian Theology and the Newtonian Science: The Rise of the Concept of the Laws of Nature," *Church History*, 30 (1961), 437.

15 Oakley, "Christian Theology," 443, 448–9.

16 Charles Trinkaus, "Renaissance Problems in Calvin's Theology," *Studies in the Renaissance*, 1 (1954), 68.

17 See Calvin, *Institutes*, I: 35, 54, 62 (actually a reference to Acts 17:27, but with implications of the subsequent verse), 191, 198, 203.

18 It should be noted that the phenomenological modes that were required for Book I, entitled "The Knowledge of God the Creator," are disparaged when we arrive at Book II, "The Knowledge of God the Redeemer." Having arrived at a particular understanding of God through the senses, the reader is now required to shed physical perception in favor of spiritual perception; see e.g. I: 280.

19 W. J. Torrance Kirby, *Richard Hooker, Reformer and Platonist* (Aldershot, UK and Burlington, Vt: Ashgate, 2005), p. 71.

20 John Frederick Nims (ed.), *Ovid's Metamorphoses: The Arthur Golding Translation 1567* (Philadelphia: Paul Dry Books, 2000), I.97–100.

21 Bouwsma, *John Calvin*, p. 33.

22 *Ibid.*, p. 73, see also p. 81.

23 *Ibid.*, p. 166.

24 The details in this paragraph are drawn from Nicholas Tyacke, *Anti-Calvinists: The Rise of English Arminianism c. 1590–1640* (Oxford: Clarendon Press, 1987), pp. 1–30. See also John T. McNeill, *The History and Character of Calvinism* (New York: Oxford University Press, 1954), p. 314, and Ch. 19 more broadly. For a succinct history of Calvinism in sixteenth-century England, see Benedict, *Christ's Churches*, Ch. 8.

25 Tyacke, *Anti-Calvinists*, p. 3.

26 David Harry Stam, *England's Calvin: A Study of the Publication of John Calvin's Works in Tudor England* (unpublished Ph.D. thesis, Northwestern University, 1978), p. 8.

27 "Catechising was particularly widespread in the English church. Many ministers seemed convinced that using catechisms had led to a noticeable improvement in the understanding shown by congregations about their religion. Vast numbers of a wide variety of official and unofficial catechisms were published in England, with estimates suggesting that by the early seventeenth century over 750 000 catechisms were in circulation in a country of only around four million people": Graeme Murdock, *Beyond Calvin: The Intellectual, Political, and Cultural World of Europe's Reformed Churches, c. 1540–1620* (Basingstoke and New York: Palgrave Macmillan, 2004), p. 105, citing I. Green, *The Christian's ABC: Catechisms and Catechizing in England, c. 1530–1740* (Oxford: Clarendon Press, 1996) and I. Green, "'For Children in yeeres and children in understanding': The Emergence of the English Catechism under Elizabeth and the Early Stuarts," *Journal of Ecclesiastical History*, 37 (1986), 397–425.

28 The figure is from a table from Rodolphe Peter and Jean-Pierre Gilmont, *Bibliotheca Calviniana* (Geneva, 1991–2000), reprinted in Benedict, *Christ's Churches*, p. 92. R. T. Kendall counts ninety editions, although he includes reissues: *Calvin and English Calvinism to 1649* (Oxford University Press, 1979), p. 52n. This number far outweighs publication in any other continental language other than Latin and French. Benedict notes that "no other author would be as frequently printed in England over the course of the second half of the century as Calvin. The peak years for Calvin editions came between 1578 and 1581, when six to eight of his books appeared each year. By the last decades of the century, his works had eclipsed those of all other theologians in the library inventories of Oxford and Cambridge students" (*Christ's Churches*, p. 245).

29 "Calvinist" is now considered a misleading term by many historians (who prefer "reformed"), since the term unduly associates a single individual with a tradition that combined the influence of many theologians: Nigel Voak, *Richard Hooker and Reformed Theology: A Study of Reason, Will, and Grace* (Oxford University Press, 2003), p. xvii.

30 See *Institutes*, II: 968–9. Calvin scholars tend to emphasize that Calvin discouraged the type of personal scrutiny endorsed by early seventeenth-century "Calvinist" reformers like Perkins; see Hall, "Calvin Against the

Calvinists," 29. David Foxgrover, however, argues that introspection is in fact a part of Calvin's theology; the sources he cites for this are primarily from Calvin's biblical commentaries, not the *Institutes*: "Self-Examination in John Calvin and William Ames" in W. Fred Graham (ed.), *Later Calvinism: International Perspectives*, Sixteenth Century Essays and Studies, vol. XXII (Kirksville, Mo.: Sixteenth Century Journal Publishers, Inc., 1994), pp. 451–69.

31 From the time he published his first major work in 1589, Perkins became a publishing sensation; he quickly became "one of the most widely read English writers" (Tyacke, *Anti-Calvinists*, p. 29). Before his death in 1602 (at age forty-four), he had seen seventy-six editions (including repeated issues) into print; of these, seventy-one were published after 1590 (Kendall, *Calvin and English Calvinism*, p. 53n). If we compare the English publishing histories of Perkins and Calvin, it looks as if Perkins supplanted Calvin as the preferred theologian. The publishing of Calvin's own words drops off precipitously after 1590. From 1590 to 1600, there were only six editions of Calvin's texts; twelve English editions of the *Institutes* appeared between 1574 and 1587, while only three more were published before 1600 (Kendall, *Calvin and English Calvinism*, p. 52). Eventually, Perkins's Calvinism would be reimported to the continent, as his work was translated into Hungarian, Czech, Dutch, French, German, and Spanish. See Patrick Collinson, "England and International Calvinism 1558–1640" in Menna Prestwich (ed.), *International Calvinism 1541–1715* (Oxford: Clarendon Press, 1985), p. 223; and I. Breward, "The Significance of William Perkins," *Journal of Religious History*, 4 (1966), 113.

32 A. G. Dickens, *The English Reformation*, 2nd edn. (The Pennsylvania State University Press, 1964, 1989), p. 14; H. R. McAdoo, *The Spirit of Anglicanism* (London: A. & C. Black, 1965), p. 25, cited in Iain M. MacKenzie, *God's Order and Natural Law: The Works of the Laudian Divines* (Aldershot and Burlington, Vt.: Ashgate, 2002), p. 5. Similarly, see the comments of H. C. Minton, *Calvin Memorial Addresses* (Savannah, 1909), p. 37, cited in Henry R. Van Til, *The Calvinistic Concept of Culture* (Grand Rapids, Mich.: Baker Book House, 1959), p. 49. Deason writes that "In his discussion of Providence in the *Institutes*, Calvin formulated a systematic view of God's relation to the natural world" ("Reformation Theology," p. 176), but shortly thereafter contends that "Depending on his purpose, God may command natural things such as water, wind, or trees to behave according to their natures or against them. In both cases their action and end depend on Him … Here again Calvin saw the complete subjugation of the elements to the Word of God" (p. 177).

33 McGrath, *A Life of John Calvin*, p. 147. See pp. 147–50 for a discussion of Calvin's idea in relation to "system" and systematic theology. See also Collinson, "England and International Calvinism," p. 217.

34 Basil Hall writes, "It would be unjust to understand [Calvin's] theology as a system in the old scholastic sense, for Calvin would have regarded

system-making as an all too human intellectual arrogance": "Calvin Against the Calvinists" in G. E. Duffield (ed.), *John Calvin*, Courtney Studies in Reformation Theology (Grand Rapids, Mich.: William B. Eerdmans Publishing Co., 1966), pp. 20–1.

35 Calvin's "works dating from the 1550s are often peppered with discussion of Aristotelian cosmology": McGrath, *A Life of John Calvin*, p. 35, citing C. B. Kaiser, "Calvin's Understanding of Aristotelian Natural Philosophy" in R. V. Schnucker (ed.), *Calviniana: Ideas and Influences of Jean Calvin*, Sixteenth Century Essays and Studies 10 (Kirksville, Mo.: Sixteenth Century Journal Publishers, 1988), pp. 77–92. For Calvin's reference to microcosm/macrocosm, see *Institutes*, I: 54.

36 Since the *Lawes* was published in increments over many decades, it is misleading to give one publication date. The preface and the first four books, which are the sections that I am discussing here, were published in one volume in 1593. For a tight account of the publishing history, see Kirby, *Richard Hooker*, pp. 1–2. Patrick Collinson writes that "Hooker must have been writing all through those five years [1588–93], especially if, as appears possible, all eight books existed at least in draft by early 1593": "Hooker and the Elizabethan Establishment" in Arthur Stephen McGrade (ed.), *Richard Hooker and the Construction of Christian Community* (Tempe, Ariz.: Medieval and Renaissance Texts and Studies, 1997), p. 153.

37 Kirby, *Richard Hooker*, p. 58. See also Debora Shuger, "'Societie Supernaturall': The Imagined Community of Hooker's *Lawes*" in Arthur Stephen McGrade (ed.), *Richard Hooker and the Construction of Christian Community* (Tempe, Ariz.: Medieval and Renaissance Texts and Studies, 1997), pp. 307–9.

38 See the survey and summary of recent historiography on Hooker in Voak, *Richard Hooker*, pp. 1–19.

39 Collinson, "Hooker and the Elizabethan Establishment," p. 155. Some scholars have commented on what they perceive as Hooker's odd failure to engage with Calvin's thought. Hooker hardly ever addresses questions of predestination, for instance. "In the context of his time," writes Brian Cummings, "the sheer reticence of the million words of *Ecclesiastical Polity* on this subject is incredible": *The Literary Culture of the Reformation: Grammar and Grace* (Oxford University Press, 2002), p. 318; see pp. 314–19 for a discussion of Hooker's engagement with Calvin – or lack thereof. See also the extended discussion of "Hooker and Calvinist Orthodoxy" in Peter Lake, *Anglicans and Puritans? Presbyterianism and English Conformist Thought from Whitgift to Hooker* (London: Unwin Hyman, 1988), pp. 182–97. This section also suggests both that Hooker's ideas were being disseminated in public discourse (an anonymous pamphlet of 1600 attacked his ideas [p. 187]) and that his theology, potentially challenging to the Calvinist orthodoxy, caused his ideas to be less widely circulated (p. 186).

40 Kirby, *Richard Hooker*, p. 74.

41 W. J. Torrance Kirby, "Richard Hooker's Theory of Natural Law in the Context of Reformation Theology," *Sixteenth Century Journal*, 30 (1999), 691

42 A. S. McGrade provides a concise synopsis of the role of Book I in setting up Hooker's theological and social framework in Richard Hooker, *Of the Laws of Ecclesiastical Polity* (abridged edn.), ed. A. S. McGrade and B. Vickers (London: Sidgwick and Jackson, 1975), pp. 22–3.

43 Citations are from Richard Hooker, *Of the Lawes of Ecclesiasticall Politie* (London, 1594; facsimile reprint, Amsterdam: Theatrvm Orbis Terrarvm Ltd.; New York: Da Capo Press, 1971). Here, pp. 49–50.

44 Kirby, *Richard Hooker*, pp. 3–4.

45 *Ibid.*, p. 8.

46 See Rowan Williams, *Anglican Identities* (Cambridge, Mass.: Cowley Publications, 2003), pp. 42–3. For a discussion of how natural law and providence were perceived in the seventeenth century, see Reid Barbour, *Literature and Religious Culture in Seventeenth-Century England* (Cambridge University Press, 2002), Ch. 7, "Nature (II): Church and Cosmos," esp. the discussion (pp. 218–31) of George Hakewill's *An Apologie or Declaration of the Power and Providence of God in the Government of the World* (Oxford, 1635).

47 Lake, *Anglicans and Puritans?*, p. 148.

48 In this, Hooker is in keeping with the scientific developments of his day. See Deason, "Reformation Theology," and Christopher Hill, *The Intellectual Origins of the English Revolution Revisited* (Oxford: Clarendon Press, 1997), p. 62.

49 See E. M. W. Tillyard, *The Elizabethan World Picture* (New York: Vintage Books, 1944; [196?]), p. 16. Tillyard writes: "If the Elizabethans believed in an ideal order animating earthly order, they were terrified lest it should be upset, and appalled by the visible tokens of disorder that suggested its upsetting. They were obsessed by the fear of chaos and the fact of mutability; and the obsession was powerful in proportion as their faith in the cosmic order was strong. To us *chaos* means hardly more than confusion on a large scale; to an Elizabethan it meant the cosmic anarchy before creation and the wholesale dissolution that would result if the pressure of Providence relaxed and allowed the law of nature to cease functioning" (p. 16). The passage from Hooker is used to exemplify this sentiment. Significantly, Tillyard doesn't address Calvin's influence in his seminal work of scholarship.

50 Hooker, *Lawes*, pp. 52–3. See the reading of this passage by Brian Vickers (McGrade and Vickers, *Laws*, pp. 56–8).

51 Isaac Newton, *Principia*, ed. Stephen Hawking (Philadelphia and London: Running Press, 2002), p. 427.

52 For an intelligent discussion of the "hybrid" nature of religious identity in the period (and Shakespeare's in particular), see Jean-Christophe Mayer, *Shakespeare's Hybrid Faith: History, Religion and the Stage* (New York: Palgrave Macmillan, 2006), pp. 1–9.

53 MacKenzie, for instance, notes that even William Laud and Lancelot Andrewes appeal to Calvin (*God's Order*, pp. 8, 120).

54 See especially Stachniewski, "Calvinist Psychology," and Graham Parry, "A Theological Reading of *Macbeth*," *Caliban*, 21 (1984), 133–140. Parry writes of

*Macbeth*: "We are in a Calvinist world where men are consigned to damnation or salvation by an inexorable God" (140). Stachniewski, in particular, seems to be working with the ideas of Federal Calvinism and its emphasis on double predestination (171). This understanding of Calvin leads Stachniewski to a vocabulary that is unabashedly harsh and judgmental. He writes of "the bleak Calvinist view" and "Calvin's grim view of human nature" (173), and "the gloating Calvinist fascination with the mental processes of the reprobate" (183, followed by a quote from the *Institutes*). Part of his explication of *Macbeth* as a "Calvinist" play depends upon tracing how the play reflects "a Table [prefixed to the *Works* of William Perkins] displaying the phases of experience through which the elect and the reprobate would pass" (175). This table, though, probably would have been anathema to Calvin. Another example of scholarly conflating of Calvin(ism) and Perkins can be found in K. Tetzeli von Rosador's intriguing essay, "'Supernatural Soliciting': Temptation and Imagination in *Doctor Faustus* and *Macbeth*" in E. A. J. Honigmann (ed.), *Shakespeare and His Contemporaries: Essays in Comparison* (Manchester University Press, 1986), p. 45. One edition of Perkins's work opens with the claim that "William Perkins was the most famous and influential spokesman for Calvinism of his day"; Thomas F. Merrill (ed., and intro.), *William Perkins 1558–1602: English Puritanist* (Nieuwkoop, The Netherlands: B. De Graaf, 1966), p. ix.

55 Brian Richardson, "'Hours Dreadful and Things Strange': Inversions of Chronology and Causality in *Macbeth*," *Philological Quarterly*, 68 (1989), 283, 287.

56 Harris, *Untimely Matter*, p. 123.

57 Richardson, "Hours Dreadful," 287.

58 Donald Foster, "*Macbeth's* War on Time," *English Literary Renaissance*, 16 (1986), 327.

59 Hooker, *Lawes*, Book V, pp. 190–1.

60 This text figured prominently in early modern debates about astronomy, and factored into Galileo's trial; see Peter Harrison, *The Bible, Protestantism, and the Rise of Natural Science* (Cambridge University Press, 1998), p. 112.

61 Muir glosses "reflection" as "turning back at the vernal equinox" (*Macbeth*, p. 7n).

62 Susan Snyder, "Theology as Tragedy in *Macbeth*," *Christianity and Literature*, 43 (1994), 290.

63 Throughout *Macbeth*, we encounter formulations that bring together time and space, or, more broadly, materiality, as time becomes an object in space. Macbeth speaks of "this bank and shoal of time" (1.7.6), and, in proclaiming to the murderers his enmity towards Banquo he says, "in such bloody distance,/That every minute of his being thrusts/Against my near'st of life" (3.1.115–17), uniting the language of space ("distance") with measures of time ("minute"). Malcolm subtly materializes time when he comments, "We shall not spend a large expense of time" (5.9.26). More obliquely, Macduff speaks of "wholesome days" (4.3.105). And even more distant, but still, I think, within the same orbit, Macbeth describes dawn,

the changing of time, with the incredible expression, "Light thickens" (3.2.49).

64 See Gail Kern Paster, "Becoming the Landscape: The Ecology of the Passions in the Legend of Temperance" in Mary Floyd-Wilson and Garrett A. Sullivan, Jr. (eds.), *Environment and Embodiment in Early Modern England* (Basingstoke and New York: Palgrave Macmillan, 2007), pp. 137–40.

65 Arthur F. Kinney, "Imagination and Ideology in Shakespeare: The Case of *Macbeth*" in Robert P. Merrix and Nicholas Ranson (eds.), *Ideological Approaches to Shakespeare: The Practice of Theory* (Lewiston: The Edwin Mellen Press, 1992), p. 59.

66 Jacqueline E. Lawson argues that within *Macbeth* there are in fact multiple frames of space-time. Although her attempt to map the geography of *Macbeth* onto Dante's *Inferno* seems to me overly schematic, she traces three orders of Duncan, Macbeth, and Malcolm, "each of these orders ... self-contained, each occupying its unique place in nature, time, and space": "The Infernal Macbeth," *The Aligarh Critical Miscellany*, 1 (1988), 35. Lawson contends that for Duncan, "nature is stable" (35), as it is for Malcolm. For Macbeth, by contrast, "time and space" will not be "redeemed" until "order is once more restored to the state" (37).

67 Sarah Beckwith, "The Power of Devils and the Hearts of Men: Notes Towards a Drama of Witchcraft" in Lesley Aers and Nigel Wheale (eds.), *Shakespeare in the Changing Curriculum* (London and New York: Routledge, 1991), p. 154.

68 Intriguingly, the peak period of English interest in demonology coincided with the period in which the English church was most dominated by Calvinist theology. The labile physics of Calvin's cosmos seem to allow for the types of physical aberrations typical of witchcraft.

69 Margreta de Grazia, "World Pictures, Modern Periods, and the Early Stage" in John D. Cox and David Scott Kastan (eds.), *A New History of Early English Drama* (New York: Columbia University Press, 1997), p. 18.

70 De Grazia, "World Pictures," p. 19.

71 My thinking throughout this chapter has been shaped by Paul Rodaway's *Sensuous Geographies: Body, Sense and Place* (London and New York: Routledge, 1994), esp. the intro. and Ch. 2, "Perception Theory and the Senses."

72 Tillyard, *Elizabethan World Picture*, p. vii.

73 *Ibid.*, pp. 3, 17, 4.

74 See Shuger, "Societie Supernaturall," esp. pp. 320–1.

75 Peter Iver Kaufman, *Prayer, Despair, and Drama: Elizabethan Introspection* (Urbana and Chicago: University of Illinois Press, 1996), p. 15.

76 Christopher Haigh, *The Plain Man's Pathways to Heaven: Kinds of Christianity in Post-Reformation England, 1570–1640* (Oxford University Press, 2007), p. 5.

77 William Perkins, *The Fovndation of Christian Religion* (1597), p. 6.

78 Snyder, "Theology as Tragedy," 290.

5 DIVINE GEOMETRY IN A GEODETIC AGE: SURVEYING,
GOD, AND 'THE TEMPEST'

1 Plato, *Timaeus and Critias*, trans. Desmond Lee (London and New York: Penguin Books, 1965; 1977), p. 45.

2 Galileo, *The Assayer* (1623); quoted in Stillman Drake and C. D. O'Malley, trans., *The Controversy on the Comets of 1618: Galileo Galilei, Horatio Grassi, Mario Guiducci, Johann Kepler* (Philadelphia: University of Pennsylvania Press, 1960), pp. 183–4.

3 Due to space limitations, I am not able to include an image of this model here, but it is easily searchable on Google; see e.g. http://galileo.phys. virginia.edu/classes/109N/1995/lectures/kepler.html (with an interesting lecture). July 19, 2010. See also the frontispiece of Johannes Kepler, *Mysterium Cosmographicum* [The Secret of the Universe], trans. A. M. Duncan (New York: Abaris Books, 1981). *Mysterium* was originally published in 1596, and revised in 1621.

4 Kepler, *Mysterium Cosmographicum*, pp. 97, 209.

5 *Ibid.*, p. 107.

6 *Ibid.*, p. 105.

7 *Ibid.*, p. 63.

8 *Ibid.*, p. 93.

9 *Ibid.*, p. 95.

10 This is from Kepler's own gloss of his writing: *Mysterium Cosmographicum*, p. 219.

11 Kepler reiterates this structural idea of the Trinity in his later work, *Harmonice mundi* (1619); Johannes Kepler, *The Harmony of the World*, trans. and ed. E. J. Aiton, A. M. Duncan, and J. V. Field (Philadelphia: American Philosophical Society, 1997), 304–5. Footnote 27 (pp. 304–5n) lists all of the places in which Kepler associates the Trinity with a sphere.

12 Kepler, *Mysterium Cosmographicum*, p. 167.

13 Amos Funkenstein, *Theology and the Scientific Imagination from the Middle Ages to the Seventeenth Century* (Princeton University Press, 1986), p. 30; see also p. 314.

14 In the catalogue compiled by the London bookseller Andrew Maunsell in 1595, the titles he listed under "matters of Diuinitie" outnumber those he categorized as "Sciences" by a ratio of 8:1: Elizabeth Spiller, *Science, Reading, and Renaissance Literature: The Art of Making Knowledge, 1580–1670* (Cambridge University Press, 2004), p. 11. We should not, however, undervalue the number of texts of science; according to Christopher Hill, "Over ten per cent of the books listed in the *Short Title Catalogue* between 1475 and 1640 deal with the natural sciences. Nine out of every ten of these books were in English. With the doubtful exception of Italy, no country has anything like so high a proportion of vernacular scientific books at this date": *The Intellectual Origins of the English Revolution Revisited* (Oxford: Clarendon Press, 1997), p. 17.

15 While Kepler's writings were certainly known in England during the seventeenth century, his audience was a rarified one. Kepler had various points of

contact with English culture. He was a correspondent of Thomas Hariot, and Kepler's *Somnium* (1634, although circulating in pirated editions before then), about a voyage to the moon, influenced other English writers; see John Lear, *Kepler's Dream* [*Somnium, sive Astronomia Lunaris*], trans. Patricia Frueh Kirkwood (Berkeley and Los Angeles: University of California Press, 1965), pp. 15n, 19.

16 Henry S. Turner, *The English Renaissance Stage: Geometry, Poetics, and the Practical Spatial Arts 1580–1630* (Oxford University Press, 2006), p. 33.

17 Turner, *English Renaissance Stage*, p. 14. The importance of mathematical (and thus geometrical) knowledge is illustrated by the founding of London's Gresham College in 1597, established "with the express purpose of making practical mathematical knowledge available to a population of urban merchants, tradesmen, seamen, and gentlemen. The college was surrounded by an elaborate network of lecturers, private tutors, booksellers, instrument-makers, and courtiers, all of whom made London a centre for applied mathematical activity" (Turner, *English Renaissance Stage*, p. 78). In 1619, Oxford established Chairs in astronomy and geometry; see Allan Chapman, "The Mid-Seventeenth Century" in John Fauvel, Raymond Flood, and Robin Wilson (eds.), *Oxford Figures: 800 Years of the Mathematical Sciences* (Oxford University Press, 2000), p. 79.

18 Deborah E. Harkness, *The Jewel House: Elizabethan London and the Scientific Revolution* (New Haven and London: Yale University Press, 2007), p. 104. See, more broadly, Ch. 3.

19 Harkness, *Jewel House*, p. 103.

20 See Martin Brückner and Kristen Poole, "The Plot Thickens: Surveying Manuals, Drama, and the Materiality of Narrative Form in Early Modern England," *English Literary History*, 69 (2002), 641–2. John Rennie Short notes that "The dissolution of the monasteries had created a large pool of commodified land, as the vast estates of the religious orders became part of the commercial land market. The enclosure of land, a process of privatization of public lands into private hands – especially the hands of the already wealthy – was also creating a more capitalistic land market that needed to be mapped and surveyed": *Making Space: Revisioning the World, 1475–1600* (Syracuse University Press, 2004), p. 87. For a good account of the social ramifications of surveying, see Bernhard Klein, *Maps and the Writing of Space in Early Modern England and Ireland* (Basingstoke, UK: Palgrave, 2001), Ch. 2. See also D. K. Smith, *The Cartographic Imagination in Early Modern England: Re-writing the World in Marlowe, Spenser, Raleigh and Marvell* (Aldershot, UK; Burlington, Vt.: Ashgate, 2008), pp. 43–52.

21 Brückner and Poole, "The Plot Thickens," 619; see, more generally, 619–24.

22 Hood's text was first published in 1590. The ornate title page of Edmund Gunter's *The Description and Vse of the Sector, the Crosse-staffe and Other Instruments* (1623) also pictures someone aiming a cross-staff at the sun, suggestive of a theological context.

23 In this, Blundeville's map carries over a medieval practice of indicating important events in the history of Christianity on maps; see Evelyn Edson, *Mapping Time and Space: How Medieval Mapmakers Viewed Their World*, The British Library Studies in Map History, vol. I (London: The British Library, 1997), p. 163. What is distinctly new in Blundeville's text is the do-it-yourself approach to this kind of religious mapping.

24 The real "first inventor of the thing" is alleged to have been Levi ben Gerson, a fourteenth-century mathematician: A. W. Richeson, *English Land Measuring to 1800: Instruments and Practices* (Cambridge, Mass. and London: The Society for the History of Technology and the MIT Press, 1966), p. 84.

25 John Stoughton, *The Heauenly Conuersation and the Naturall Mans Condition* (1640), p. 58. The title of another sermon, John Wing's *Iacobs Staffe to Beare Vp, the Faithfull. And to Beate Downe, the Profane* (Flushing, Zealand, 1621), delivered to the Merchant Adventurers of England, seems to be punning on the instrument.

26 Richeson, *English Land Measuring*, p. 84. For a pithy history of the cross-staff, see John Roche, "The Cross-Staff as a Surveying Instrument in England 1500–1640" in Sarah Tyacke (ed.), *English Map-Making 1500–1650* (London: The British Library, 1983), pp. 107–11. Roche speculates that "[t]he upsurge in the number of texts on the instrument between 1578 and 1624 surely reflects an increased use of it" (p. 109).

27 I have not been able to find the original source of this image. It is reproduced in an undated book publisher's catalogue from Adam Matthew Publications for their list in the history of science and technology. I would like to thank Richard Kuhta, Eric J. Weinmann Librarian (now retired), and Georgianna Ziegler, Louis B. Thalheimer Head of Reference, at the Folger Shakespeare Library for their zealous assistance in trying to hunt down the image. Thanks, too, to Martin Brückner for his search efforts. The image is almost certainly sixteenth-century, although the landscape does not appear to be English.

28 This is in keeping with the devotional discourse of the period, in which Christ's cross is presented as its own point of geometric orientation; see Thomas Playfere's sermon in *The Whole Sermons of that Eloquent Diuine, of Famous Memory* (1623), pp. 170–1.

29 Patricia Crain, *The Story of A: The Alphabetization of America from* The New England Primer *to* The Scarlet Letter (Stanford University Press, 2000), pp. 19–26.

30 In a remarkable passage, Bernhard Klein reiterates the *OED*'s puzzlement about the word's etymology, even as he immediately quotes a passage connecting the instrument to God: "In Digges' *Pantometria*, a far more advanced measuring instrument makes its first appearance: the theodolite, a term of uncertain etymology, coined by Digges as a lasting contribution to the English language. For an arcane sixteenth-century expression the theodolite has had an impressive career, linguistically and technically, perhaps owing to the vague intellectual authority of its Greek sounding syllables. Radolph Agas praised it in the highest terms: 'it carrieth the forme of the first mouer, which commandeth all inferior creatures, and is preferred as

most perfect and capeable, by the wisedome and ordinance of the Creator: so in vse and operation ... this Theodolite commandeth euerie one of her subiects' [9–10]" (*Maps*, pp. 50–1). Richeson also has a long footnote on the origin of the name, and cites that W. W. Skeat and Ernest Weekley, in their *Etymological Dictionaries of the English Language*, suggest a derivation from the Old French, but that "Skeat ... is more inclined to believe that it is a reference to a mathematician named Theodulus. A search does not indicate any Greek mathematician of importance by this name" (*English Land Measuring*, pp. 58–9).

31 Anne Lake Prescott, "The Reception of Du Bartas in England," *Studies in the Renaissance*, 15 (1968), 144.

32 Margery Corbett and Ronald Lightbown, *The Comely Frontispiece: The Emblematic Title-Page in England 1550–1660* (London, Henley and Boston: Routledge & Kegan Paul, 1979), p. 101.

33 Corbett and Lightbown, *Comely Frontispiece*, p. 102.

34 In an interesting genealogy, the image may itself have been taken from an engraving originally intended for Thomas Hood's *The Use of the Celestial Globe*. A. M. Hind, *Engraving in England in the 16th and 17th Centuries: A Descriptive Catalogue*, Part I, *The Tudor Period* (1952), p. 141, cited in Corbett and Lightbown, *Comely Frontispiece*, p. 102.

35 Klein reads this image (*Maps*, pp. 46–9) and reiterates Crystal Bartolovich's point that "the image, in short, champions the cool rationality of geometrical surveying which is actively engaged in suppressing the carnivalistic elements of a symbolic space inhabited by fool and faun – that is, allegorical representations of unreason and nature" (p. 48); citing Crystal Lynn Bartolovich, "'Spatial Stories': *The Surveyor* and the Politics of Transition" in Alvin Vos (ed.), *Place and Displacement in the Renaissance* (Binghamton, NY: Center for Medieval and Early Renaissance Studies, 1995), p. 273.

36 Spiller, *Science, Reading, Literature*, p. 103, citing Michael Baxandall, *Painting and Experience in Fifteenth-Century Italy: A Primer in the Social History of Pictorial Style*, 2nd edn. (Oxford University Press, 1991), pp. 29–108.

37 See Short, *Making Space*, p. 151.

38 Rowan Williams, "'Religious Realism': On Not Quite Agreeing with Don Cupitt," *Modern Theology*, 1 (1984), 15.

39 First edition of this text is from 1577, with additional printings and editions in 1578, 1588, 1592, and 1596. For a brief contextual history of many of the surveying manuals cited in this chapter, see Short, *Making Space*, pp. 132–41.

40 A highly unscientific survey of people I know in these fields, however, reveals that even these specialists do not have a common name for this shape. Sixteenth-century surveying manuals do not always distinguish between what we call a rectangle and a square – an elongated rectangle in Valentine Leigh's *The Moste Profitable and Commendable Science, of Surueying of Lands, Tenementes, and Hereditamentes* (1588) is labeled as a square,

defined as a shape having "equall of breadth at bothe endes, and equall of length at both sides" (sig. O3ᵛ); it is not requisite that all sides be equidistant. Thomas Blundeville, in *M. Blundeville His Exercises* (1594), labels what we today would call a rectangle a "long square" (p. 129).

41 The text from which this example comes is Robert Recorde, *The Pathway to Knowledge, Containing the First Principles of Geometrie, as they may moste aptly be Applied vnto Practice, bothe for Vse of Instruments Geometricall, and Astronomicall and also for Proiection of Plattes in Euerye Kinde, and therefore much Necessary for all Sortes of Men* (1551), sig. B2ᵛ. The subsequent pages illustrate varieties of triangles, which include three-sided figures with curved lines as well as straight ones. Recorde's text was more of a textbook than a scholarly edition; the first full translation of Euclid's *Elements* was by Henry Billingsley in 1570 (with a preface by John Dee); see John Fauvel and Robert Goulding, "Renaissance Oxford" in Fauvel, Flood, and Wilson (eds.), *Oxford Figures*, pp. 48–50.

42 For an account of the ascendancy of mathematics, see G. J. Whitrow, "Why did Mathematics Begin to Take Off in the Sixteenth Century?" in Cynthia Hay (ed.), *Mathematics from Manuscript to Print, 1300–1600* (Oxford: Clarendon Press, 1988), pp. 264–9.

43 Leonard Digges, *Tectonicon* (1556), p. 1ᵛ. This text was republished in 1592, 1605, 1614, 1625, 1630, 1634, and 1637, an indication of the popularity of the genre.

44 Thomas Blundeville, for example, opens a section of *M. Blundeville His Exercises* (1597) with an expectation of his audience's ignorance: "Minding to treate of the principles of Cosmographie . . . I think it good first to expound vnto you certaine termes of Geometry, without the which the vnlearned shall hardly vnderstand the Contents of this Treatise" (p. 127); he then proceeds to introduce terms like point, line, and angles before defining various shapes.

45 It should be recognized that Leonard Digges's *Pantometria* was in fact published posthumously by his son Thomas, a skilled mathematician in his own right. *Tectonicon* proved enduringly popular, going through at least twenty editions between 1556 and 1692; here I am citing from the 1592 edition.

46 Arnold Whittick, *Symbols: Signs and Their Meaning* (London: Leonard Hill Limited, 1960), p. 281.

47 Cornelius Lanczos, *Space Through the Ages: The Evolution of Geometrical Ideas from Pythagoras to Hilbert and Einstein* (London and New York: Academic Press, 1970), p. 49.

48 I have not been able to locate an extensive study on this symbol in the early church – perhaps because it was not widely used. F. R. Webber writes that "It seems that the earliest Christians hesitated to express so profound a mystery as that of the Trinity in the form of symbols. With the coming of fierce controversies in the early Church, where it was necessary to defend the doctrine of the Trinity against false teachers both within the Church and outside of it, certain definitive symbols were developed. What Christians

had always believed was now expressed in graphic form ... The equilateral triangle ... is one of the oldest of the Trinity emblems": *Church Symbolism: An Explanation of the More Important Symbols of the Old and New Testament, the Primitive, the Mediaeval and the Modern Church*, 2nd edn. (Cleveland: J. H. Jansen, 1938; facsimile reprint, Detroit: Gale Research Company, 1971), p. 40. Webber does not provide any specific instances of the use of this symbol, although Engelbert Kirschbaum *et al.* note that it appears on early Christian graves in Africa ("Auf frühchr. Grabsteinen Afrikas wird das Christusmonogramm durch das D. umgeben od[er] bekrönt"): *Lexikon der Christlichen Ikonographie*, vol. I (Rome, Freiburg, Basel, Vienna: Herder, 1968), p. 525. It is also worth noting that this was already an available symbol; Xenocrates (d. 324 BC) stated that the triangle symbolized God; see Carl G. Liungman, *Dictionary of Symbols* (Santa Barbara, Cal.; Denver, Col.; Oxford, UK: ABC-CLIO, 1991), p. 306.

A much more expansive account of trinitarian images used in late antiquity is provided by André Grabar, *Christian Iconography: A Study of Its Origins*, trans. Terry Grabar, Bollingen Series 35.10 (Princeton University Press, 1968), pp. 12–16. It is striking that in his detailed account of trinitarian images of this period, Grabar does not discuss the triangle as a trinitarian symbol; instead, we find groupings of three human forms. This contradicts the assertion by Peter and Linda Murray that "The earliest representation of God the Father as a man does not appear to be before the late 13th century": *The Oxford Companion to Christian Art and Architecture* (Oxford and New York: Oxford University Press, 1996), p. 544. Similarly, F. Edward Hulme writes that "Representations of the Trinity do not appear till somewhat late in the history of art. Figures or symbols of the Saviour may be met with at a very early period, as also the dove and other symbolic forms of the Holy Spirit; but for centuries no sculptor or painter ventured on any symbol of similitude of the first Person of the Trinity" (*The History, Principles and Practice of Symbolism in Christian Art* [London: Swan Sonnenschein and Co.; New York: The Macmillan Co., 1909], p. 30).

49 Louis Réau observes, "Rien de plus difficile à concevoir et par suite à traduire plastiquement qu'un Dieu à la fois *triple et un (Deus trinus et unus)*, la Trinité dans l'Unité *(Trinitas in unitate)*. Sujet ingrat entre tous: car l'esprit se heurte à une contradiction, au moins apparente, qui devait laisser les artistes perplexes. Les théologiens eux-mêmes n'y voyaient pas plus clair" (as Réau exemplifies with a story of Augustine): *Iconographie de l'art Chrétien*, vol. 2.1 (Paris: Presses Universitaires de France, 1956), p. 17. Grabar writes, in respect of the Trinity, that "the image-makers of late antiquity failed here" and that "[t]he most ancient images of the Trinity can, then, be summed up in this way: they are rare and imperfect, especially in view of the great importance of discussions of trinitarian problems during all the centuries of late antiquity" (*Christian Iconography*, pp. 112, 116).

50 For the Shield, see Webber, *Church Symbolism*, p. 44; for the nimbus see Whittick, *Symbols*, pp. 223. Kirschbaum *et al.* also note that the triangular

nimbus appears in the late Middle Ages ("Seit dem SpätMA bezeichnet ein Nimbus in D[reieck]form Gottvater bisw. als Vertreter der Trinität") (*Lexikon*, p. 525). For a sense of the larger medieval context of geometry and theology, see Paul M. J. E. Tummers, "Geometry and Theology in the XIIIth Century: An Example of Their Interrelation as Found in the Ms Admont 442. The Influence of William of Auxerre?," *Vivarium*, 18 (1980), 112–41 and Megan M. Hitchens, "Building on Belief: The Use of Sacred Geometry and Number Theory in the Book of Kells, f. 33r," *Parergon*, n.s. 13.2 (1996), 121–36. See also Robert Styer, "Lines, Triangles, and the Trinity," presented at the "Experience of God in the Disciplines" conference, Villanova University, November 2001. I am very grateful to Professor Styer, from the Department of Mathematical Sciences, Villanova University, for sharing his research with me.

51 For the fish, see Whittick, *Symbols*, p. 184. I am grateful to Barbara Newman of Northwestern University for bringing this window to my attention.

52 The claim that the triangle is rare in the Middle Ages is made by Corbett and Lightbown, *Comely Frontispiece*, p. 100, citing G. Stuhlfauth, *Das Dreieck. Die Geschichte eines religiösen Symbols*, 1937. I am piecing this chronology together from a variety of sources. Réau places the emergence of the triangle proper as a trinitarian symbol in the seventeenth century: "cet emblème devenu courant dans l'architecture religieuse est innconnu au Moyen âge et même à la Renaissance: il n'apparaît qu'au XVII^e siècle" (*Iconographie*, p. 18). Whittick's examples seem to reinforce this: "Austria provides numerous examples of its use in Renaissance architecture. As symbolical of God [the eye] is usually shown in the centre of an equilateral triangle, symbolical of the Trinity" (*Symbols*, p. 181). This sentence is followed by a catalogue of examples beginning with one from 1626; it is not entirely clear if this is used as an example of "Renaissance" (a notoriously capacious and ambiguous temporal category) or if it is considered post-Renaissance. A similarly vague date is provided by George Ferguson in *Signs and Symbols in Christian Art* (New York: Oxford University Press, 1954), who writes that "[i]n the later period of Renaissance painting, the Eye of God surrounded by a triangle is used to symbolize the Holy Trinity" (p. 64). (Ferguson also identifies the triangular nimbus, as a sign of the Trinity, to be an indicator of God the Father in Renaissance art [pp. 158, 268]; he concurs with the consensus that "[t]he equilateral triangle is the symbol of the Trinity" [p. 276].) An earlier example of the Trinity being displayed as a triangle is given in Murray and Murray, *Oxford Companion to Christian Art*, p. 542, where under the entry for "Triangle" (the entry is entirely about the triangle as a symbol of the Trinity), an example is cited: "Pontormo: *Supper at Emmaus* (1525: Uffizi) is unusual in having the triangle with the Eye of God over the head of Christ." This example, even if it is "unusual," would seem to give credence to Clara Erskine Clement's statement that "Since the sixteenth century the Father has been symbolized by the triangle ... the triangle became extremely popular on account of the ideas or teaching which

it embodied": Katherine E. Conway (ed.), *A Handbook of Christian Symbols and Stories of the Saints* (Boston: Ticknor and Company, 1886; reprint, Detroit: Gale Research Company, 1971), pp. 10–11. Kirschbaum *et al.* identify this development as a northern European phenomenon, also beginning in the sixteenth century: "In der nordniederl. Kunst des späten 16. bis 18. Jh. begegnet man öfters dem D[reieck] m[it] dem in hebr. Schr. eingeschriebenen Namen Gottes" (*Lexikon*, p. 525); they include an image of the Shield of the Blessed Trinity from 1524 which has now assumed a form close to that of an equilateral triangle (*Lexikon*, p. 526). A French image (c. 1500) in the collections of the Free Library of Philadelphia (shelfmark Lewis E M 66:21) depicts God the Father, Christ, and Christ holding a dove as the Holy Spirit jointly holding on to a triangle. I am grateful to Laura Cochrane for bringing this image to my attention, as well as the article by Ursula Rowlatt, "Popular Representations of the Trinity in England, 990–1300," *Folklore*, 112 (2001), 201–10.

53 Corbett and Lightbown, *Comely Frontispiece*, p. 40.

54 Alexandra Walsham, "Angels and Idols in England's Long Reformation" in Peter Marshall and Alexandra Walsham (eds.), *Angels in the Early Modern World* (Cambridge University Press, 2006), p. 141.

55 Walsham, "Angels," pp. 142–3. The embedded quotations are from Alexander Nowell, *Catechisme or First Instruction and Learning of Christian Religion* (1570), p. 8; John Dod and Robert Cleaver, *A Plaine and Familiar Exposition of the Ten Commandments* (1610), pp. 66–7.

56 This symbol was first used by John Wallis in *De sectionibus conicis* (1655). I am grateful to Jim Beaver for bringing this to my attention.

57 Corbett and Lightbown, *Comely Frontispiece*, p. 100.

58 For an explanation of how the triangle is used in alchemy to represent different elements, see J. C. Cooper, *An Illustrated Encyclopedia of Traditional Symbols* (London: Thames and Hudson, 1978), p. 180. Boehme wrote extensively on the Trinity, and triangles figure repeatedly in texts such as his *Signatura rerum* (1651), *The Fifth Book of the Author . . . Of the Becoming Man or Incarnation of Jesus Christ* (1659), *Jacob Behmen's Theosophick Philosophy* (1691), and *Mysterium magnum* (1656).

59 Amos Funkenstein, *Theology and the Scientific Imagination*, p. 3.

60 See, for example, the extract from John Stoughton's *The Heauenly Conuersation and the Naturall Mans Condition* (1640) on p. 186.

61 Similarly, see the complex triangular theology of Robert Fludd in *Mosaicall Philosophy Grounded upon the Essentiall Truth* (1659), with a graphic illustration (p. 152).

62 W. B. and E. P., *A Helpe to Discourse. Or, A Miscellany of Merriment. Consisting of Wittie, Philosophical and Astronomicall Questions and Answers* (1619), p. 22.

63 I have found dozens of examples of this image. Here are just a few: Thomas Playfere, *Hearts Delight. A Sermon Preached at Pauls Crosse in London in Easter Terme. 1593* (1603), sig. D1$^{r-v}$; Thomas Adams, *The White Deuil, or The Hypocrite Vncased in a Sermon Preached at Pauls Crosse, March 7.1612*

(1613), p. 54; *Mystical Bedlam, or the VVorld of Mad-men* (1615), p. 10; W.B. and E.P., *A Helpe to Discourse*, pp. 67–8.

64 Augustine, Letter 120, in *Letters 100–155*, vol. II/2, ed. Boniface Ramsey, trans. Roland Teske (Hyde Park, N.Y.: New City Press, 2003), p. 133.

65 *Ibid.*

66 Funkenstein, *Theology and the Scientific Imagination*, pp. 28–9.

67 James J. Bono, *The Word of God and the Languages of Man: Interpreting Nature in Early Modern Science and Medicine*, vol. I (Madison: The University of Wisconsin Press, 1995), pp. 196–7.

68 John Cockburn, *Jacob's Vow, or, Man's Felicity and Duty in Two Parts* (Edinburgh, 1696), p. 194.

69 See Funkenstein, *Theology and the Scientific Imagination*, p. 49. See also Peter Harrison, *The Bible, Protestantism, and the Rise of Natural Science* (Cambridge University Press, 1998), pp. 3–4.

70 Jonathan Gil Harris, *Untimely Matter in the Time of Shakespeare* (Philadelphia: University of Pennsylvania Press, 2009), pp. 13–19.

71 See Raymond Williams, *Marxism and Literature* (Oxford University Press, 1977), pp. 121–8.

72 See Robert L. Reid, "Sacerdotal Vestiges in *The Tempest*," *Comparative Drama*, 41 (2007), 497–9 and his endnote 23 (511).

73 John D. Cox, "Recovering Something Christian about *The Tempest*," *Christianity and Literature*, 50 (2000), 32. See his endnote 5 (47) and bibliography for a representative catalogue of materialist scholarship on the play. See also the list in the second endnote of Tom McAlindon, "The Discourse of Prayer in *The Tempest*," *Studies in English Literature, 1500–1900*, 41 (2001), 351. The materialist/postcolonial readings of the play depend heavily upon an understanding of its geographic location in the Americas. As Goran Stanivukovic notes, "[s]cholars have already detached *The Tempest* from its firm place in postcolonial criticism by reading it as a Mediterranean play"; this geographic relocation of the setting allows him to "displace the postcolonial approach to *The Tempest* criticism with a revisioning of this play as allegorizing humanism's positive and negative characteristics": "*The Tempest* and the Discontents of Humanism," *Philological Quarterly*, 85 (2006), 91. See his second endnote (115n) for a quick bibliography of the colonial approach, and the fifth note (115n) for a list of sources that relocate the play in the Mediterranean. Many of these appear in Peter Hulme and William H. Sherman (eds.), The Tempest *and Its Travels* (Philadelphia: University of Pennsylvania Press, 2000). One of the first scholars to call for a reconsideration of the play's location was David Scott Kastan, *Shakespeare after Theory* (London: Routledge, 1999), p. 185.

74 McAlindon, "The Discourse of Prayer," 335.

75 *Ibid.*, 336.

76 David Lindley (ed.), *The Tempest*, by William Shakespeare, The New Cambridge Shakespeare (Cambridge University Press, 2002), p. 50.

77 Julia Reinhard Lupton, "Creature Caliban," *Shakespeare Quarterly*, 51 (2000), 20. We might take as an illustration of Lupton's point Stephen Orgel's eighty-seven-page introduction to the play, which contains virtually no reference to religion; see Stephen Orgel (ed.), *The Tempest*, by William Shakespeare, The Oxford Shakespeare, ed. Stanley Wells (Oxford: Clarendon Press, 1987). For a more extended account of the universal and the particular, see Julia Reinhard Lupton, "The Religious Turn (to Theory) in Shakespeare Studies," *English Language Notes*, 44 (2006), 146–8.

78 For a few typical examples, see J. A. Bryant, *Hippolyta's View: Some Christian Aspects of Shakespeare's Plays* (Lexington: University of Kentucky Press, 1961); Roland Mushat Frye, *Shakespeare and Christian Doctrine* (Princeton University Press, 1963); Robert H. West, "The Christianness of Othello," *Shakespeare Quarterly*, 15 (1964), 333–43; Edward Hubler, "The Damnation of Othello: Some Limitations on the Christian View of the Play," *Shakespeare Quarterly*, 9 (1958), 295–300. Hubler (who is himself writing as a Christian critic) summarizes the movement thus: "This criticism is most often concerned with imagery and symbolism, which are somehow deified, much as some Victorians deified character" (295).

79 This and all citations from the text are from Virginia Mason Vaughan and Alden T. Vaughan (eds.), *The Tempest*, by William Shakespeare, The Arden Shakespeare, Third Series (Walton-on-Thames: Thomas Nelson and Sons Ltd., 1999). Here, 4.1.60–9, 128–31.

80 McAlindon, "Discourse of Prayer," 347.

81 For a discussion of the play's location, and especially the long critical tradition of associating it with the Americas, see Vaughan and Vaughan, *Tempest*, pp. 39–54, 98–108.

82 In *The Merchant of Venice*, Shylock swears "By Jacob's staff" (2.5.35) – not specifically in a geodetic context, but it is likely that many in the audience would have known of a Jacob's staff, and thus perhaps this was comical. In *Coriolanus*, a citizen says, "and truly I think if all our wits were to issue out of one skull, they would fly east, west, north, south, and their consent of one direct way should be at once to all the points o'th'compass" (2.3.18–21).

83 Stephen Greenblatt *et al.*, *The Norton Shakespeare*, based on the Oxford edition (New York and London: W. W. Norton and Co., 1997), 1.3.41–55. This passage is also discussed by Turner, *English Renaissance Stage* (p. 239), who does not address the biblical source, and Adam Max Cohen, *Shakespeare and Technology: Dramatizing Early Modern Technological Revolutions* (New York and Basingstoke: Palgrave Macmillan, 2006), who does (p. 175).

84 See Brückner and Poole, "The Plot Thickens," 641–2, 644.

85 Turner, *English Renaissance Stage*, p. 11.

86 Cohen, *Shakespeare and Technology*, pp. 2, 31. See Ch. 1 for an overview of the technological milieu of early modern England.

87 Cohen, *Shakespeare and Technology*, pp. 171–2, citing Peter Eden, "Three Elizabethan Estate Surveyors: Peter Kempe, Thomas Clerke, and Thomas

Langdon" in Sarah Tyacke (ed.), *English Map-Making 1500–1650* (London: British Library, 1983), p. 76.

88 See Brückner and Poole, "The Plot Thickens," 621.

89 Frank Kermode (ed.), *The Tempest*, by William Shakespeare, The Arden Shakespeare, Second Series (London and New York: Routledge, 1954; 1990), pp. 8–9n.

90 Throughout their edition, the Vaughans are particularly good at glossing these values and converting them to modern units of measurement.

91 For mazes and mapping, see J. B. Harley, "Meaning and Ambiguity in Tudor Cartogprahy," in Tyacke (ed.), *English Map-Making*, pp. 34–5.

92 See Brückner and Poole, "The Plot Thickens." See also Turner, *English Renaissance Stage*, pp. 21–5, and, more broadly, Ch. 2. Turner's footnotes for that chapter record other scholars who have touched on the topic.

93 Additionally, Prospero is obviously associated with figures of Renaissance magic: see Barbara A. Mowat, "Prospero, Agrippa, and Hocus Pocus," *English Literary Renaissance*, 11 (1981), 281–303. For a quick survey of scholarship on *The Tempest* and magic, see Lindley, *Tempest*, pp. 45–53.

94 See John Frederick Nims (ed.), *Ovid's Metamorphoses: The Arthur Golding Translation 1567* (Philadelphia: Paul Dry Books, 2000), VII.265–81. Prospero's "Ye elves of hills, brooks, standing lakes, and groves" is clearly borrowing from "ye Elves of Hilles, of Brookes, of Woods alone,/Of standing Lakes" (VII.265–6), although the connection to the rest of the passage is much less direct.

95 A contemporary audience probably would have read Caliban more seriously as a demonic figure. Prospero calls him a "demi-devil" (5.1.272) and a "thing of darkness" (5.1.275), both labels of the demonic. Even his exclamation of "O ho, O ho!" (1.2.350) might have been a verbal marker of a demonic identity. Lindley glosses the line: "This exclamation appears in earlier drama as a characterization of a villain or mischief-maker, and especially of Satan himself," with examples (p. 119n). Alden T. Vaughan and Virginia Mason Vaughan contend that Caliban's name could come from the gypsy word for black, *cauliban* or *kaliban*; *Shakespeare's Caliban: A Cultural History* (Cambridge University Press, 1991), pp. 33–4.

96 Reid, "Sacerdotal Vestiges," 499.

97 Ariel's fire has repeatedly been associated with St. Elmo's fire (see Orgel's gloss, p. 112n), but the Holy Spirit is also identified with the fire of Pentecost.

98 The insistent spatial immediacy also pertains to time. See Judith E. Tonning, "'Like This Insubstantial Pageant, Faded': Eschatology and Theatricality in *The Tempest*," *Literature and Theology*, 18 (2004), 375.

99 Orgel, *The Tempest*, p. 47. Orgel provides a tight account of how the masque of *The Tempest* reflects Jacobean masque culture (pp. 43–50), although he begins the introduction to his edition by addressing what he considers exaggerated critical claims about the play's reliance on masque (pp. 1–3).

100 Andrew Gurr, "*The Tempest's* Tempest at Blackfriars," *Shakespeare Survey*, 41 (1989); reprinted in Peter Hulme and William H. Sherman (eds.), *The Tempest*, by William Shakespeare (New York and London: W. W. Norton

and Co., 2004), p. 265; Gurr asserts: "*The Tempest* was the first play Shakespeare unquestionably wrote for the Blackfriars rather than the Globe" (p. 251).

101 Thomas Browne, *The Religio Medici and Other Writings* (London: J. M. Dent and Sons, Ltd.; New York: E. P. Dutton and Co., Inc., 1906; 1947), p. 18. "Few Elizabethan writers on mathematics failed to bring in somewhere this idea of God the geometer," writes Paul H. Kocher in *Science and Religion in Elizabethan England* (San Marino: The Huntington Library, 1953), p. 151.

102 The masque often traces out a complex geometric pattern, one with neo-Platonic and metaphysical significance; these patterns could be connected to the movement of the planets or rivers. See Thomas M. Greene, "Labyrinth Dances in the French and English Renaissance," *Renaissance Quarterly*, 54 (2001), 1403–66, for Jonson's masques, 1448–56. Jonson's *Masque of Beauty* (1608), for instance, contains a maze dance and imagines the path of the Thames through Kent and Essex in cartographic terms (1452). In addition to the Neo-Platonic content of many Jacobean masques, the rivalry between Jonson and Inigo Jones in the first decade of the seventeenth century contributed to masques making many more references to geometry and mathematics (Turner, *English Renaissance Stage*, p. 248).

103 Ernest B. Gilman, "'All Eyes': Prospero's Inverted Masque," *Renaissance Quarterly*, 33 (1980), 214.

104 Christine Dymkowski (ed.), *The Tempest*, by William Shakespeare, Shakespeare in Production Series, eds. J. S. Bratton and Julie Hankey (Cambridge University Press, 2000), pp. 294–5.

105 Lindley, *Tempest*, p. 196n. The Levin reference is to "Anatomical Geography in *The Tempest*, IV.i.235–8," *Notes & Queries*, 11 (1964), 142–6. See also Orgel's gloss for the line and "the conventional association of the equator with steamy sex" (*The Tempest*, p. 185n).

106 M. P. Tilley, *A Dictionary of the Proverbs in England in the Sixteenth and Seventeenth Centuries* (Ann Arbor: University of Michigan Press, 1950).

107 Richeson, *English Land Measuring*, pp. 135–9, 53–5.

108 They could be associated, more broadly, with geometrical measurement; Ben Jonson, in his annotations of Vitruvius, makes note of "the rule and compass" and "straight line, & levels"; cited in Turner, *English Renaissance Stage*, p. 257.

109 Grace Tiffany, "Calvinist Grace in Shakespeare's Romances: Upending Tragedy," *Christianity and Literature*, 49 (2000), 421.

110 McAlindon, "Discourse of Prayer," 336.

111 Grace R. W. Hall, The Tempest *as Mystery Play: Uncovering Religious Sources of Shakespeare's Most Spiritual Work* (Jefferson, NC; London: McFarland & Company, Inc., 1999), p. 9.

112 Northrop Frye, *Northrop Frye on Shakespeare*, ed. Robert Sandler (New Haven and London: Yale University Press, 1986), p. 186.

113 And, as B. J. Sokol observes of Shakespeare's early plays, "[d]eclarations of post-lapsarian human perfectibility are enunciated ... only to be mocked soon after": *A Brave New World of Knowledge: Shakespeare's* The Tempest

*and Early Modern Epistemology* (Madison: Fairleigh Dickinson University Press; London: Associated University Presses, 2003), p. 147.

114 Orgel, *The Tempest*, p. 13.

115 Garrett A. Sullivan, Jr., *The Drama of Landscape: Land, Property, and Social Relations on the Early Modern Stage* (Stanford University Press, 1998), esp. pp. 41, 65, 68.

116 Sullivan, *The Drama of Landscape*, pp. 70–1.

117 Sullivan, *The Drama of Landscape*, esp. Chs. 1 and 2.

118 E. G. R. Taylor, "The Surveyor," *The Economic History Review*, 17 (1947), 121–33.

119 Orgel, *The Tempest*, p. 22; the image is captioned as "Henry Peacham, 'Inopportuna Studia', emblem of a royal magician-scientist, from ΒΑΣΙΛΙΚΟΝ ΔΩΡΟΝ, a manuscript emblem book based on the treatise by James I. (Ms. Roy. 12.A fol. 30ʳ, emblem xxxv.)." In this image, the magician/scientist is clearly holding up a cross-staff in one hand (in the position familiar from surveying books) and a compass in the other. (Orgel does not comment on the surveying element of the image.) The interested reader will want to compare this image to my Figure 8.

120 Vaughan and Vaughan, *Tempest*, p. 64.

121 Given the crudeness of the image, it is difficult precisely to identify the instrument immediately above the Jacob's staff. It could be an astrolabe or a rudimentary theodolite. (See the image from *Pantometria* reproduced in Richeson, *English Land Measuring*, p. 61.) The object on the left of the image is probably a terrestrial sphere, possibly *in plano*. Thanks to Martin Brückner for identifying these objects. For another image that demonstrates a public interest in picturing surveying instruments, see the ornamental frontispiece of Edmund Gunter, *The Description and Vse of the Sector, the Crosse-staffe and Other Instruments* (1624).

122 See Ch. 1, n. 67.

## EPILOGUE: RE-ENCHANTING GEOGRAPHY

1 D. K. Smith, *The Cartographic Imagination in Early Modern England: Re-writing the World in Marlowe, Spenser, Raleigh and Marvell* (Aldershot, UK; Burlington, Vt.: Ashgate, 2008).

2 Jacob Burckhardt, *The Civilization of the Renaissance in Italy*, vol. I, trans. Benjamin Nelson (New York: Harper Colophon Books, 1958), p. 143. See my Ch. 1, pp. 26–8.

3 Angus Fletcher, *Time, Space, and Motion in the Age of Shakespeare* (Cambridge, Mass.; London: Harvard University Press, 2007), p. 2.

4 Henri Lefebvre, *The Production of Space*, trans. Donald Nicholson-Smith (Oxford and Cambridge, Mass.: Blackwell Publishers, 1974; 1991).

5 Ricardo Padrón, *The Spacious Word: Cartography, Literature, and Empire in Early Modern Spain* (Chicago; London: The University of Chicago Press, 2004), p. 39.

6 Smith, *Cartographic Imagination*, p. 65.

7 *Ibid.*, p. 42.

8 *Ibid.*, p. 10. Smith cites John Gillies, *Shakespeare and the Geography of Difference* (Cambridge University Press, 1994) and "Marlowe, the Timur Myth, and the Motives of Geography" in John Gillies and Virginia Mason Vaughan (eds.), *Playing the Globe: Genre and Geography in English Renaissance Drama* (Madison: Fairleigh Dickinson University Press, 1998), pp. 203–29.

9 See Martin Brückner and Kristen Poole, "The Plot Thickens: Surveying Manuals, Drama, and the Materiality of Narrative Form in Early Modern England," *English Literary History*, 69 (2002), 621–3, for an account of how surveying manuals instructed their readers to walk through the land they are surveying. Note 14 (646n) of this article references a manual in the collections of the Folger Shakespeare Library with marginalia indicating that a reader did indeed take the book into the field, making the genre an ambient one.

10 Bruce R. Smith, *The Key of Green: Passion and Perception in Renaissance Culture* (Chicago; London: The University of Chicago Press, 2009), pp. 7–8. Smith cites Timothy Morton, *Ecology Without Nature: Rethinking Environmental Aesthetics* (Cambridge, Mass.: Harvard University Press, 2007), p. 34. For a theoretical account of the ambient sensation of space, see Paul Rodaway, *Sensuous Geographies: Body, Sense and Place* (London; New York: Routledge, 1994), esp. Ch. 2.

11 Jonathan Gil Harris, *Untimely Matter in the Time of Shakespeare* (Philadelphia: University of Pennsylvania Press, 2009), pp. 3–4.

# Index

*Note:* page references in italics indicate illustrations and diagrams.

278

Made in the USA
Coppell, TX
12 December 2020